ENERGY FOLLIES

Conversations about energy law and policy are paramount, undergoing new scrutiny and characterizations. *Energy Follies: Missteps, Fiascos, and Successes of America's Energy Policy* explores how a century of energy policies, rather than solving our energy problems, often made them worse and how Congress and other federal agencies grappled with remedying seemingly myopic past decisions. Sam Kalen and Robert R. Nordhaus investigate how misguided or naive energy policy decisions caused or contributed to past energy crises and how it took years to unwind their effects. This work recounts the decades-long struggles to move to market supply and pricing policies for oil and natural gas in order to make competition work in the electric power industry and to tame emissions from the coal fleet left to us by the 1970s coal policies. These historic policies continue to present struggles, and this book reflects on how we ought to learn from our past mistakes in addressing future challenges.

Robert R. Nordhaus was the Federal Energy Regulatory Commission's (FERC) first General Counsel and later served as General Counsel for the Department of Energy during the Clinton administration. From 1963 to 1974, he was Assistant Counsel in the Legislative Counsel's Office of the US House of Representatives, where he assisted in drafting many of the nation's prominent legislative programs, including the 1970 Clean Air Act. He was also an adjunct faculty member at George Washington Law School and Georgetown University Law Center.

Sam Kalen is the Centennial Distinguished Professor of Law at the University of Wyoming College of Law, as well as the founder and co-director of the Center for Law and Energy Resources in the Rockies at the University of Wyoming. He is the author of numerous law review articles and coauthor of *Basic Practice Series: ESA (Endangered Species Act)* (2012) and *Natural Resources Law and Policy* (2016).

Energy Follies

MISSTEPS, FIASCOS, AND SUCCESSES OF AMERICA'S ENERGY POLICY

ROBERT R. NORDHAUS

Van Ness Feldman, LLP

SAM KALEN

University of Wyoming

CAMBRIDGE
UNIVERSITY PRESS

University Printing House, Cambridge CB2 8BS, United Kingdom

One Liberty Plaza, 20th Floor, New York, NY 10006, USA

477 Williamstown Road, Port Melbourne, VIC 3207, Australia

314–321, 3rd Floor, Plot 3, Splendor Forum, Jasola District Centre,
New Delhi – 110025, India

79 Anson Road, #06–04/06, Singapore 079906

Cambridge University Press is part of the University of Cambridge.

It furthers the University's mission by disseminating knowledge in the pursuit of
education, learning, and research at the highest international levels of excellence.

www.cambridge.org
Information on this title: www.cambridge.org/9781108423977
DOI: 10.1017/9781108539388

© Robert R. Nordhaus and Sam Kalen 2018

First published 2018

Printed in the United States of America by Sheridan Books, Inc.

A catalogue record for this publication is available from the British Library.

ISBN 978-1-108-42397-7 Hardback
ISBN 978-1-108-43920-6 Paperback

Contents

Figures

Preface

When, in 1986, Robert Nordhaus offered me a job, I could not have anticipated how much Bob would influence my career. Energy law at the time was witnessing a transition with dramatic changes, and its allure for lawyers was on the cusp of an incline. Bob had been at the fulcrum of many of those and earlier changes. Early in his career, he served with the House Legislative Counsel and as Counsel to the House Commerce Committee, where he helped draft several of the nation's important regulatory programs, including the 1970 Clean Air Act and federal energy programs following the 1973 oil embargo. He then served, under President Jimmy Carter, as a member of the Energy Policy and Planning Office and as Assistant Administrator of the Federal Energy Administration. When Congress changed the Federal Power Commission to the Federal Energy Regulatory Commission, Bob served as its first General Counsel. Later, President Clinton, in 1993, appointed Bob as General Counsel to the Department of Energy, a position he occupied until 1997. This history of and commitment to public service, along with his tenure in private practice, informed how Bob approached challenges confronting energy and environmental policy, with a keen appreciation for the need to protect our environment and approach energy policy pragmatically. When, therefore, I began my introduction to energy and environmental law with Bob as one of my mentors, I could not have been luckier. Bob taught those who worked with him to pay meticulous attention to details, and with a comprehensive knowledge of many fields, he constantly challenged his colleagues. And when, a few years ago, we agreed to combine our efforts and write this book, I could not have been more humbled.

When, tragically, Bob passed away on December 24, 2016, I lost more than just a coauthor; I said goodbye to a mentor, a friend, and a colleague. Finishing *Energy Follies* presented a unique challenge as well. I had to do my best to ensure that the chapters that follow reflect Bob's insights and perspective, and as such, I had to avoid making alterations that modified what Bob and I discussed. I can only hope I was successful, and to the extent that I may have made mistakes, I wish to apologize to

Bob, my teacher and friend. Specifically, Bob never had the opportunity to review the last chapter in the book, although we talked seemingly innumerable times about the substance of the chapter. If, unfortunately, in translating those conversations into words I erred in conveying my coauthor's insights, I once again take full responsibility and hope that Bob would forgive my failure as one of his many students.

Acknowledgments

As with any endeavor building off years of experience and conversations, acknowledging all those who assisted is impracticable. Yet both Bob and I benefited greatly from our colleagues over the years at Van Ness Feldman, a Washington, DC, law firm specializing in energy, environment, and natural resource issues. While the material discussed in this book does not reflect the views of that firm or its clients, it benefited enormously from the years of support and assistance of attorneys and other professionals as well as assistants in the firm. Bob, I am sure, would have wanted to thank individually his assistant, Penny Storms, and to have acknowledged the support from his wife, Jean, and his two children, Ted and Hannah. This book could not have been written without their generosity and assistance.

I would like to thank the Wyoming College of Law for its generous support, as well as those who offered insightful comments on the book's material, including Steven Weissman and James E. Hickey. Finally, I want to express my appreciation to my son, Joshua, who worked as a research assistant for me one summer, and to my father, Albert, who spent time before he passed away sending me information that he thought useful. My wife, Karen Ventura-Kalen, of course supported me in countless ways, including spending a semester in Washington while I worked with Bob.

1

Introduction

Energy-laden discourses over the last four plus decades often tout external events animating energy law and policy – embargos, natural gas shortages, blackouts, unhealthy air, rising carbon dioxide (CO_2) levels – and they occasionally focus on players presumably responsible for those events – vindictive Arab sheiks, greedy energy producers, scheming commodity traders, and recalcitrant utilities refusing to clean up their coal-fired power plants. When conversations instead shift toward specific energy policies themselves, those policies often are faulted for intruding into markets, not controlling markets enough, or poorly controlling markets, such as for oil, coal, natural gas, or renewables. Reflecting on his time in the Senate, Senator Bennett Johnston of Louisiana opines how "[i]f the first lesson of energy history is expect the unexpected, the second and a related lesson is the difficulty of anticipating market forces and regulating price and supply." Each time decision makers thought that they knew best and intruded into markets, Senator Johnston posits, they often made the wrong choice – "largely because these are political judgments, ideologically driven and ponderously arrived at without proper appreciation of the facts – or after the facts have changed."[1] And then all too often today energy policy remains cloaked behind sound bites: the war on coal, "drill-baby-drill," or an all-of-the-above strategy. Each sound bite comes infused with an ideological or political bent, illustrated most recently with the 2017 mantra of "energy dominance." Indeed, two scholars posit that "[e]nergy policy in the United States is shaped by ideological conflicts between the political parties and power interests with large assets at stake."[2]

Less insidious factors may affect energy policy decisions as well. Energy producers, for instance, may lack sufficient incentives to explore new technologies. Inflation and economic conditions may retard investment – particularly if energy consumption continues declining on a per capita basis. Conversely, as we are currently witnessing with wind and solar power, both technologies have been around for some time, yet the

---

[1] Bennet Johnston, *In Energy, Expect the Unexpected: And Let the Market Show the Way*, ENERGY DAILY, Sept. 26, 2013, at 9.
[2] David E. Adelman, *David B. Spence, Ideology vs. Interest Group Politics in U.S. Energy Policy*, 95 N.C. L. REV. 339 (2017).

recent tax incentives and state policies provided enough of an impetus for not only promoting those technologies but also, in part, reducing the costs through research and development (R&D) programs. Consumers, too, may rebel against investments if they consider the costs too high. This occurred during the 1970s' energy crisis, when consumers fought against certain proposed policies.

Yet something more fundamental permeates the struggle of the United States to craft an ever-changing energy policy. In a fascinating account of aspects of energy policy's past, Peter Grossman explains how energy "legislation has produced mostly waste and confusion." He suggests that energy policy during the past four decades "has been a pursuit not of policies that failed but rather of conceptually failed policies." This is because, he aptly posits, much of our modern rhetoric, translated into policy, presumes that energy policy proceeds from two now misguided narratives, first that "[t]he United States has a dangerous dependence on foreign oil" and, second, that energy markets do not work efficiently. Where this takes him, though, is to the conclusion that "the only issue that should be addressed by energy policy is energy" and that intervention in the market should occur only following an "explicit identification of market failure." This even leads him to question all energy subsidies, including for renewables – which he suggests would be a "niche" market without the subsidies. Of course, under the guise of promoting the need for "institutional changes," Grossman does advocate legal changes to address, for instance, changing the electric grid to a smart grid.[3]

But Grossman's affinity for minimal governmental intrusion into markets ought to be tempered somewhat. Our capacity for technological achievements often follows governmental commands. This occurred when the US automobile industry complained how it could not install catalytic converters quickly enough, and it did. It occurred later with the debate surrounding the installation of technological systems for controlling emissions from power plants. When the automobile industry claimed during its fight with California that it could not effectively sell enough hybrid vehicles in the California market and that Honda and Toyota were effectively "dumping" (selling at below cost) their cars, the US industry not too long after began selling their hybrids in the US market. And when, for example, Grossman questions the efficacy of claims for electric cars or electric power from renewables, history suggests otherwise, as we may be on the cusp of an electric vehicle transition. To be sure, when Samuel Insull promoted the electric vehicle in the early twentieth century, the idea faded because little incentive – other than Insull's desire to ˙ase sales of electric energy – existed for its production or consumption.

'herefore examine aspects of energy law and policy's history from a different ive: energy law and regulation enjoy an iterative relationship with discrete lather than being the product of discrete events, energy-related decisions,

ER GROSSMAN, U.S. ENERGY POLICY AND THE PURSUIT OF FAILURE 324, 332–37 (Cambridge Univ. .ess 2013).

whether by Congress, courts, or executive agencies, are at least in part the cause of them. The chapters that follow chronicle how decisions by the Supreme Court, Congress, and federal agencies have shaped the energy industry and, on many occasions, have led to unintended and sometimes disastrous results, prompting Congress and federal agencies to attempt to correct these missteps. But much remains to be done if we are committed to modernizing our energy systems to meet twenty-first-century environmental and consumer protection goals.

What we learn from examining critical junctures in our country's struggle to develop an energy policy that integrates and effectively responds to environmental and economic policies is that our hubris often triggers problems, which then leads to further hubris as policymakers attempt to solve those problems. It is nothing short of folly to assume that policymakers have the capacity to anticipate how their decisions will unfold and notably where they will go awry. A folly has two definitions. The first is a "foolish act, idea or practice." The second is a "lavishly produced theatrical review." Energy policy decisions over the last century by Congress, the Supreme Court, and federal agencies combine both kinds of follies – well-intentioned but misguided decisions on energy and environment enlivened by political theater in Congress. These decisions admittedly include successes – albeit, though, some that merely remedy earlier mistakes. *Energy Follies* recounts the follies and occasional successes of US energy policy in terms of their impact on energy supply, economic costs, and the environment, and it suggests some lessons for addressing how legal and institutional changes could modernize our energy systems.   ⇐ Thesis

The book's next eight chapters focus on specific critical junctures or events over the last century that have shaped our modern energy systems. To set the stage, Chapter 2 begins by chronicling how modern federal energy law first emerged with the passage of the Federal Water Power Act in 1920. While this became the country's first principal foray into crafting a federal law focusing on electric energy, Congress and the president debated for years the narrow quest of how best to harness the power potential of the nation's waters. And, for our purposes, it reflected early-twentieth-century issues that dissipated within several subsequent decades. Chapter 3 then portrays the events precipitating the need for further federal regulation of interstate electric and natural gas systems. As both electric and natural gas systems sprawled across state lines, resolving who would or could regulate these burgeoning industries became elemental. The Supreme Court weighed in with its 1927 decision in *Public Utilities Commission* v. *Attleboro*, pushing the electric industry into two jurisdictional spheres – with intrastate retail rates regulated by the states and wholesale interstate rates left unregulated until Congress passed the 1935 Federal Power Act (FPA). Though the *Attleboro* opinion was dubious even when released, the Court solidified the jurisdictional divide a few decades later, locking in a jurisdictional bright line that neither the Federal Energy Regulatory Commission (FERC) nor the states can change. As use of the grid has changed with distributed generation, demand response, and the need for a rapid shift to low-carbon resources, jurisdictional disputes arising from the bright line hover over challenges to modernize the electric grid. Chapter 4, consequently, continues with how *Attleboro* continues to infect modern dialogues and why Congress' response in the FPA of closing the *Attleboro* regulatory gap has since triggered an animated dialogue over the act's crude structure for addressing today's challenges.

We show how the California energy crisis in 2000–1 resulted from design flaws in the state's newly "deregulated" power markets. To begin with, FERC failed to adequately control electric generators' market power in California's new wholesale power markets. At the same time, the state required its utilities to purchase most of their wholesale power through these inadequately regulated wholesale markets. The state also froze retail rates, leaving virtually no elasticity of demand. This flawed market design allowed generators and traders – such as Enron – to withhold generation from the market and drive up wholesale power prices, triggering rolling blackouts, utility insolvencies, large increases in retail rates, and ultimately the recall of Governor Gray Davis.

The next four chapters portray how the electric grid suffered from siloed consideration of events confronting the interstate flow of natural gas, oil production and imports, and coal use by the power sector. Chapter 5 reviews how the Supreme Court and Federal Power Commission decisions in the 1950s, 1960s, and 1970s regulating natural gas producers selling gas interstate resulted in the 1970s' natural gas shortages in the gas-consuming markets, as producers sold into more lucrative intrastate markets rather than the price-controlled interstate market. While this dynamic was well understood by the mid-1970s, it took Congress until roughly the end of the 1980s to remove all such wellhead price controls. We then describe, in Chapter 6, how the Arab oil embargo petroleum shortages and gasoline lines in the mid-1970s were exacerbated by uncoordinated federal regulatory policies. With the embargo, however, the consequences of the compartmentalized federal regulatory regime became painfully evident. US oil import dependence, and vulnerability to interruption of these imports, resulted in no small part from the interstate natural gas shortages that impelled utilities and industry to switch from gas to oil, from utility conversions from coal to oil (an inexpensive compliance option when faced with the newly enacted Clean Air Act), and from Nixon's price controls on oil that fostered increased petroleum consumption but decreased domestic production.

Chapters 7 and 8 follow by examining the history surrounding coal's rise to prominence in the energy sector as US oil and gas supplies became constricted. And it would be construction of new coal-fired power plants from the middle to late 1970s and onward that would dramatically change the composition of the electric grid, leading to increased health risks, acid rain, and escalating greenhouse gas emissions. Coal producers and utilities stubbornly resisting modern pollution controls on their coal power plants generally shoulder most of the blame for coal's resulting public health impacts. The reality, however, is slightly more complicated. Power plants that once burned coal and had switched to lower-sulfur oil were urged to convert back to coal. The 1978 Fuel Use Act, part of President Carter's National

Energy Plan, prohibited using oil and gas in most new power plants. The boom in coal-fired power and its public health consequences consequently followed from Carter administration decisions elevating coal to the principal fuel for electric generation. But, notably, this occurred with an appreciation for the health and environmental risks and yet without adequate assurance under the Clean Air Act that emissions from these plants would be controlled, leading to most likely thousands of premature deaths over a thirty-year period.

The first comprehensive energy statute, the 1975 Energy Policy and Conservation Act (EPCA), was enacted in response to the embargo. The act extended Nixon's oil price controls, arguably exacerbating our oil import vulnerability by decreasing petroleum production. But, more significantly, in the long term EPCA also established several major programs, including the strategic petroleum reserve and the corporate average fuel economy (CAFE) standards for automobiles and appliance efficiency standards – all with the objective of reducing energy use and the nation's vulnerability to future disruptions of oil supply. Carter's 1978 National Energy Act significantly advanced these objectives, and Chapter 9 examines how EPCA's CAFE standards for cars and light trucks (including SUVs) successfully increased new vehicle fuel economy and decreased petroleum use during CAFE's first decade. But, because of structural defects in the statute (the statutory limit of 27.5 miles per gallon on the standards for cars and the inability to deal with changes in the car-to-truck product mix) and low oil prices, the chapter adds how CAFE did little to increase fuel economy or decrease fuel consumption for the next twenty-five years.

Meddlesome decisions by courts, Congress, and federal agencies exemplify critical junctures where hubris produced follies. The following chapters, therefore, describe how they occurred, how policymakers struggled to deal with them over the years, and the extent to which they have been corrected. And many have in fact been successfully corrected. Others have become less pressing because of technological and market developments, such as the shale oil and gas revolution. After forty years, dysfunctional producer price controls on natural gas were finally eliminated. Oil price controls expired in 1981, after a decade of attempted regulation of the oil industry. The United States now enjoys sufficient oil in storage to tide it over a five-month total interruption in oil imports. And while Carter's coal policies were reversed in the 1980s, the Environmental Protection Agency (EPA) is still struggling to clean up the coal-fired power plants built during that era.

Yet, while many past energy follies have been corrected, considerable work remains. Whether or how the Trump administration will address climate change is an unfolding story – but all reports highlight the urgency for all nations, including the United States, to act swiftly and sufficiently if the earth's average rising temperature is to be capped at 2°C. To be sure, market forces here in the United States are driving utilities to shutter coal-fired power plants, and building any new plants (absent the commercialization of technology for capturing and storing carbon) is highly unlikely. Still, by 2075, 10 million Americans could be "substantially affected" by climate change, according to a November 2017 Congressional Budget Office projection. The 2017 National Climate Assessment similarly warned how "[g]lobally annually averaged surface air temperature has increased by about 1.8°F (1.0°C) over the last 115 years (1901–2016). This period is now the warmest in the history of modern civilization," with "[t]he last few years ... [seeing] record-breaking, climate-related weather extremes, and the last three years ... the warmest years on record for the globe." Other 2017 reports caution that unless global use of coal for energy is eliminated by 2050, sea level rise will be dramatic – threatening coastal communities.

Our modern energy systems here and across the globe must evolve to meet this challenge. The internal combustion engine and the electric grid can no longer operate as they have in the past. Whether the path toward modernization will be retarded here in the United States by old relics from the 1920s and 1930s remains unclear. Chapter 10 therefore posits how the current legal and institutional framework for the energy industry must be modernized to deal with climate, volatile world oil markets, and a potentially decentralized energy delivery system. It summarizes some lessons gleaned from the last eleven decades of formulating energy law, regulation, and policy by Congress, courts, and federal agencies. The lessons, as they unfold in the following chapters, suggest

- **Avoiding Overly Prescriptive Statutes.** The long-term public health, climate, and acid rain consequences of the Carter coal program were in large measure attributable to the inflexibility of the Fuel Use Act and the grandfathering policy embedded in the Clean Air Act. In other examples, the inability of the CAFE program to increase fuel economy after 1985 was in part a result of a statutory limit on the relevant agency's ability to increase the passenger car standard to above 27.5 miles per gallon (MPG). The agency's unwillingness to aggressively increase the standards for pickups and SUVs also contributed to the post-1985 stall-out. And gasoline lines and oil import dependency were exacerbated by rigid price control and allocation requirements in the 1970s, including with the Emergency Petroleum Allocation Act. All these problems were attributable to prescriptive statutory provisions that denied agencies flexibility to correct mistakes and respond to changes in market conditions. For the next generation of energy and environmental policies to work, they must build in this necessary flexibility.
- **Giving Agencies Latitude to Do Their Jobs.** Courts, notwithstanding their protestations to the contrary, make important policy choices when deciding cases. It occurred when the Supreme Court held that Rhode Island could not establish a rate for the sale of electricity outside its borders. It occurred again with the gas producer regulation under the *Phillips* case. These choices sometimes substantially constrain agencies in carrying out their statutory responsibilities – leaving the agency with an unworkable program. Modern administrative law purports to give

a measure of deference to agencies in interpreting statutes they administer, but they occasionally are constrained because of Congress's lack of foresight. Courts ought to tread carefully in determining whether agencies must regulate (as in *Phillips*) or when they enjoy the power to regulate.

- **Responding Quickly to Flawed Regulations.** The California energy crisis of 2000–1 is an example of agency paralysis inflicting massive damage on the public. FERC's failure to promptly correct California market design flaws and rein in market manipulation led to blackouts, large rate increases, and utility insolvencies that prompt action could have avoided. Agencies must have the tools to make prompt course corrections in their regulatory programs and be willing to use those tools.
- **Coordinating Regulatory Programs.** One of the lessons of the Arab oil embargo's disruptions is that the cumulative impact of different agencies' regulatory programs requires careful attention and, ultimately, coordination within the executive branch. The California energy crisis provides similar instruction – failure of FERC and the state of California to work together exacerbated the effects of the crisis. FERC waited for the state to lift its retail rate freeze, and the state insisted that FERC reduce wholesale prices. Agency coordination is essential to successful energy policy outcomes.
- **Making Statutory Changes as Necessary.** As energy technology and markets develop and environmental needs and public health imperatives change, the statutory framework for energy and environmental law must change as well. Congress will need, in the vernacular, to get off its duff and legislate with clarity of purpose and yet without hubris of prescription, particularly on addressing climate change.

These lessons imbue the pages of the historic struggle of the United States to craft a national energy policy; they jump from the story of the follies along the way committed by Congress, courts, and the executive branch. With each new energy-related challenge, policymakers confront critical junctures that define a path forward – a path often then embedded in our economic fabric that later stimulates subsequent challenges. This, unfortunately, is our past. It has not necessarily served us well, and yet we seem to have learned little. Take, for instance, Department of Energy Secretary Perry's foray into energy policy when, as one of his first principal policy actions, the administration sought to prod FERC effectively into promoting coal and nuclear power plants under the guise of protecting the reliability of the electric grid. The reaction was swift – his initiative ignored the operation of the modern electric grid. It is imperative, therefore, that the lessons from each of the following chapters chronicling the evolution of federal energy policy are not lost on those who might naively or otherwise make similar mistakes, similar follies.

2

Federal Energy Regulation Begins Flowing

Federal involvement in what would become the *energy space* evolved as engineers displayed how water could be harnessed to produce electric energy. Early on, pre–Civil War factory machinery, particularly in the Northeast, tapped available water resources. After the Civil War, Congress passed individual statutes authorizing private development along navigable waters. By the late 1800s, such legislation began sanctioning and encouraging hydroelectric power. This, of course, paralleled the nation's policy of making western public lands available for disposition to state or private actors willing to profit from using that land. In 1879, for example, Congress "authorized and empowered" the Secretary of War "to lease the water power" to the Moline Water Power Company. Five years later, Congress awarded the Saint Cloud Water Power & Mill Company the right to develop waterpower from the Mississippi River. Congress also began delegating authority to the Secretary of War to grant development rights, and by 1896, it more generously allowed sales of electric power from rights of way on public lands.

Three years earlier, though, when President Cleveland ceremoniously closed the circuit, electrifying the great "White City" in May 1893, the nation's policy toward energy law began its journey toward a collision course with the future. Chicago's great fair of the nineteenth century, named the "White City," perhaps best captures how energy resources would become the foundation for American progress. Celebrating the 400th anniversary of Christopher Columbus, the World's Columbian Exposition of 1893 exhibited how planning, urban life, and electricity combined to illustrate democracy's progress. "The buildings would be lit with 7,000 arc and 120,000 incandescent lamps, which would be among the most striking technologies on display, demonstrating the newfangled wonders of electricity."[1] One aptly dubbed structure tucked within this diminutive city was the "Electricity"

---

[1] WILLIAM CRONON, NATURE'S METROPOLIS: CHICAGO AND THE GREAT WEST 341–42 (W.W. Norton & Co. 1991). Westinghouse provided the electricity, while Thomas Edison, who lost that contract, secured the ability to light "the fairgrounds with tens of thousands of his incandescent bulbs." W.H. BRANDS, AMERICAN COLOSSUS: THE TRIUMPH OF CAPITALISM, 1865–1900, at 511 (Anchor Books 2010).

building.[2] Phillip Schewe observes that "[w]hen cultural historians look back at the fair ... what they see ... was the glittering arrival of electricity."[3] Engineers, conversely, focus instead on how nascent technology capable of converting alternating current (AC) to direct current (DC) could power cities, allowing a large generating station to produce high-voltage energy that could then be used for powering the fair's attractions. They observe how, while Thomas Edison may have furnished the incandescent bulbs for the fair, it was Edison's rival, George Westinghouse, who supplied the electricity and eventually elevated deploying longer AC power lines over Edison's favored DC current – a significant development allowing electricity to be transmitted farther than with DC current.[4]

At the cusp of the progressive era, Chicago and its fair exemplified how technology and demographics became symbiotic with the new economy and its capital concentration, wage laborers, interstate markets, and, commensurately, the vertically integrated and centralized electric grid. After all, 1893 was the year when Emile Durkheim wrote how "science can help us adjust ourselves, determining the ideal toward which we are heading confusedly."[5] The ability to transport products across the nation's railways, to communicate over telegraph wires and through the mail, and to travel with the automobile made it such that "[c]ity and country were growing closer together."[6] When Frederick Jackson Turner delivered his famous remarks at the fair about the frontier thesis and the closing of the American West, the cities, with their rising populations, factories, and burgeoning electric trolleys, stood to benefit if they could be energized with electricity.

Concentrating ownership and control over that generation and what would soon become the electric grid seemed almost preordained. Henry Demarest Lloyd, a writer for the *Chicago Tribune*, years earlier published an *Atlantic Monthly* article indicting the concentration of power in the railroad and oil industries, followed by his 1894 *Wealth Against Commonwealth*. His *Atlantic* article explored how Americans suffered economically from Standard Oil Company's monopolization of petroleum, fixing its prices in US cities (excluding New York) and controlling all the pipelines and transportation networks.[7]

---

[2] *See* NORMAN BOLOTIN & CHRISTINE LAING, THE WORLD'S COLUMBIA EXPOSITION: THE CHICAGO WORLD'S FAIR OF 1893 78–80 (Univ. of Illinois Press 1992).

[3] PHILLIP F. SCHEWE, THE GRID: A JOURNEY THROUGH THE HEART OF OUR ELECTRIFIED WORLD 53 (Joseph Henry Press 2007).

[4] Richard D. Cudahy & William D. Henderson, *From Insull to Enron: Corporate (Re)Regulation after the Rise and Fall of Two Energy Icons*, 26 ENERGY LAW J. 35, 45 (2005). Several books identified in the Bibliographic Note, such as HAROLD L. PLATT, THE ELECTRIC CITY: ENERGY AND THE GROWTH OF THE CHICAGO AREA, 1880–1830 (Univ. of Chicago Press 1991), explore the birth of the modern electric grid and the contributions by Samuel Insull and Thomas Edison.

[5] EMILE DURKHEIM, THE DIVISION OF LABOR IN SOCIETY 34 (G. Simpson trans., 1933).

[6] CRONON, *supra* note 1, at 332–33. *See also* HAROLD U. FAULKNER, POLITICS, REFORM AND EXPANSION 1890–1900 49 (Harper 1959).

[7] Henry Demarest Lloyd, *The Story of a Great Monopoly*, ATLANTIC MONTHLY (March 1881); HENRY DEMAREST LLOYD, WEALTH AGAINST COMMONWEALTH (1894).

That the electric grid would follow suit seemed natural, particularly once Samuel Insull illustrated how his burgeoning empire could efficiently deliver low-cost power to Chicago consumers. Low-cost power would increase demand, and by controlling the market, all with little risk. Insull "ingeniously developed the business model to affordably bring electricity into homes, stores, offices, and industry" and was the "father of the modern electricity industry."[8] He promised affordable electricity to the masses by capitalizing on the economies of scale associated with large, centralized generating stations that would service large areas rather than smaller stations serving highly localized areas. This model, however, required sufficient demand for electricity, or what is called *load*. The utilities consequently championed electric trolleys and new electric appliances and abandoning of on-site generation. Insull further recognized that by adding load, the marginal cost of generation became cheaper. By further spreading load across the entire day, a generation plant could run more often and, with more sales even at a lower price, pay off the capital costs of construction.

Insull encouraged utilities to accept state public utility supervision of energy rates (i.e., cost of service with a rate of return) in return for a franchise guaranteeing the exclusive right to serve a territory.[9] For him, regulatory rate supervision posed little risk because he favored selling energy at as low a price as possible, even unreasonably low, to ensure that electricity would become a necessity. This began part of the regulatory bargain, with utilities acceding to rate supervision and receiving in return the assurance of a customer base (and an obligation to then provide service to that customer base). Of course, while the nation's population then still mostly lived in rural communities, urban centers were fast becoming the loci of interest, control, and power. It is not surprising, therefore, that cities were the drivers of development of large-scale energy capacity to feed the needs of mass production, lighting, electric trolleys, and consumers. In some cities, for instance, such as New York, electric trolleys consumed about half of all electricity.[10] A lecturer in London in 1893 observed how a central station worked well for large towns due to

> the great inconvenience of generating power in the small quantity and at the irregular times at which it is wanted for many purposes. For good or for ill, population gathers into huge communities, in which there is a complex development of social and

---

[8] ROBERT L. BRADLEY, JR., EDISON TO ENRON: ENERGY MARKETS AND POLITICAL STRATEGIES 19 (Wiley 2011). Judge Cudahy and Professor Henderson provide a useful portrait of the history surrounding Insull and Edison. Cudahy & Henderson, *supra* note 4, at 39–72. *See also* FOREST MCDONALD, INSULL: THE RISE AND FALL OF A BILLIONAIRE UTILITY TYCOON (Univ. of Chicago Press 2004).

[9] DAVID E. NYE, ELECTRIFYING AMERICA: SOCIAL MEANINGS OF NEW TECHNOLOGY 180–81 (MIT Press 1990). Insull "crusade[d] to convince the industry to accept rate regulation in return for franchise protection." BRADLEY, *supra* note 8, at 172; *see also ibid.* at 86–88, 123–26; SCHEWE, *supra* note 3, at 69 (referring to a "Faustian Bargain"). *See generally* Forest McDonald, *Samuel Insull and the Movement for State Utility Regulatory Commissions*, 32 BUS. HIST. REV. 241 (1958).

[10] W.S. MURRAY ET AL., U.S. GEOLOGICAL SURVEY, A SUPERPOWER SYSTEM FOR THE REGION BETWEEN BOSTON AND WASHINGTON 33 (1921) (half of New York's energy was consumed by its trolleys).

industrial life. In such communities there is a constantly increasing need of mechanical power. In addition to manufacturing operations, demands for power arise for transit, for handling goods, for passenger lifts, for water supply, and for sanitation.[11]

And by owning, controlling, or influencing all facets from the fuel source to production and distribution – in short, by becoming vertically integrated – Insull could build his empire. "Insull's empire," therefore, included "manufactured (coal) gas distribution, natural gas transmission, and urban transportation (a major user of power)."[12] And between the early 1900s and the 1920s, the delivery of electricity shifted from a primarily municipal (street lighting) and industrial base to an economy-wide customer base.[13] Phillip Schewe observes how, by the 1920s, more capital was being invested in electricity than in "any other single decade of spending during the railroad boom of the previous century."[14]

The emergence of the electric grid converged with several salient developments following the turn of the century to propel hydroelectric power generation onto the national stage. To begin with, although wood and hydroelectric generation fueled our increasing manufacturing economy prior to the Civil War, steam generation became a favored energy source following the demographic and economic changes in the post–Civil War period.[15] People and manufacturing moved toward the cities, and both steam and electric railways made these centers of the new consumer economy more accessible. The original concept of a central station suffered from limiting technology and the cost associated with transporting power more than a few miles.[16] Cities often were far removed from where a hydroelectric power plant could be located, and early transmission lines could only run less than a few hundred miles. The consulting engineering firm Stone & Webster, which would later build one of the largest early projects at Keokuk Dam in Iowa in 1913, proudly designed in 1890 a mile-long DC transmission system from the Saccrappa Dam along the Presumpscot River in Maine to a nearby mill.[17] Only eight years earlier the first hydroelectric power project opened in Appleton, Wisconsin.

[11] WILLIAM C. UNWIN, HOWARD LECTURES: ON THE DISTRIBUTION AND TRANSMISSION OF POWER FROM CENTRAL STATIONS 5 (Longmans, Green, & Co. 1894).
[12] BRADLEY, *supra* note 8, at 19, 97.
[13] NYE, *supra* note 9, at 56, 261. "Nationally, as late as 1905 less than 10 percent of all motive power was electrical; by 1930 the figure had jumped to 80 percent." *Ibid.* at 13. And "[t]he electrification of the domestic market began in earnest only after 1918." *Ibid.* at 265. The growth of central generation stations grew after 1910, and overall electric consumption "more than doubled" in the 1920s. RONALD E. SEAVOY, AN ECONOMIC HISTORY OF THE UNITED STATES: FROM 1607 TO THE PRESENT 268 (Routledge 2006).
[14] SCHEWE, *supra* note 3, at 109.
[15] LOUIS C. HUNTER, A HISTORY OF INDUSTRIAL POWER IN THE UNITED STATES, 1780–1930 485–541 (Univ. of Virginia Press 1979).
[16] THOMAS P. HUGHES, NETWORKS OF POWER: ELECTRIFICATION IN WESTERN SOCIETY 83 (Johns Hopkins Univ. Press 1993).
[17] SAM BASS WARNER, JR., PROVINCE OF REASON 55 (Harvard Univ. Press 1984).

Plants a little further from cities became more feasible once George Westinghouse pushed the industry toward using AC transmission lines, which could cover longer distances than DC lines. In 1891, a project in Frankfurt, Germany, demonstrated "the potential of using distant water-power sites to supply electricity to heavily populated industrial areas."[18] Serious efforts to explore tapping Niagara Falls began around late 1889, and the success in Germany comforted the US engineers looking to supply power into Buffalo, New York. Before the end of the century, the Willamette Falls Electric Company remarkably transmitted 3,000 volts roughly fourteen miles from Oregon City to Portland.[19] Not until much later, however, could transmission lines carry power beyond 300 miles.[20]

Even with transportation a limiting factor, a national dialogue over hydroelectric power generation germinated throughout the first decade of the twentieth century. To begin with, Congress passed the oddly named "revocable permit law" in 1901 authorizing the Interior Secretary to issue rights of way across public lands and other reservations for, among other things, facilities related to electric power.[21] Of course, by this time, many power sites already had passed into private ownership. The following year, Congress enacted the 1902 Reclamation Act promoting western water resource development, and it continued enacting targeted statutes authorizing specific electric power generation projects.[22] A few years later it passed the 1906 General Dam Act, requiring individual congressional assent for each project and establishing conditions for their development.[23] This effectively gave Congress control over future hydroelectric power project proposals. One example of this piecemeal and cumbersome statutory process was Congress's 1906 authorization of the Secretary of War's ability to allow waterpower diversions from the Niagara River.[24] Then, allowing such use of the nation's water resources intensified when an opinion by Teddy Roosevelt's Attorney General, George Woodward Wickersham, interpreted the Act as precluding the United States from charging

[18]   HUGHES, *supra* note 16, at 137, 139.
[19]   F.A.T. Furfari, *Westinghouse and the AC System: 1884–1895*, 8 IEEE INDUS. APPLICATIONS MAG. 8, 10 (2002).
[20]   A.E. PARKINS & J.R. WHITAKER, OUR NATURAL RESOURCES AND THEIR CONSERVATION 314 (1936). In 1918, for instance, a Westinghouse Electric official testified that transmission then could carry energy up to 200 miles. Water Power: Hearings Before the H. Comm. on Water Power., 65th Cong., 2nd Sess. 171 (March 1918) [hereinafter 1918 Hearing].
[21]   Act of February 15, 1901, ch. 371, 31 Stat. 790. In 1905, Congress transferred certain authorities to the Department of Agriculture. *See* Act of February 1, 1905, ch. 288, 33 Stat. 628; *see also* Act of March 4, 1911, ch. 238, 36 Stat. 1253 (agricultural lands). Secretary of Interior Frank Lane and others considered this legislation ineffective and warranting repeal – but only if replacement legislation were secured. Water-Power Development and Use of Public Lands, 64th Cong., 1st Sess., H.R. Rep. No. 64–16, at 10 (January 4, 1916) [hereinafter H.R. Rep. No. 16].
[22]   JEROME G. KERWIN, FEDERAL WATER-POWER LEGISLATION 81, 85–89, 10511, 129–30 (Columbia Univ. Press 1926); *see also* MICHAEL C. ROBINSON, WATER FOR THE WEST: THE BUREAU OF RECLAMATION 1902–1977 918 (Pub. Works Hist. Soc'y 1979).
[23]   Act of June 21, 1906, ch. 3508, 34 Stat. 386.   [24]   Act of June 29, 1906, ch. 3619, 34 Stat. 626.

waterpower developers a fee for using these resources, prompting Congress to amend the law in 1910.[25]

President Roosevelt objected to this ad hoc approach to private water resource development. He unleashed his dissatisfaction by issuing several vetoes of congressional measures. One measure would have allowed the Muscle Shoals Power Company to continue to pursue its power project, and the president noted how the United States should be compensated for the use of its natural and public resources.[26] Gifford Pinchot later characterized this veto as the "first sign of change" in allowing private interests to use our water resources.[27] According to Milton Conover, "[t]hese vetoes constituted a rallying-point in the water-power situation," and they prompted Congress's 1910 amendment to the 1906 General Dam Act.[28] While this was occurring, the conservation movement began voicing concerns about the adverse consequences of power projects to our nation's river systems. Indeed, the battle over Hetch Hetchy and San Francisco's thirst for water and hydroelectric power surfaced as a prominent project precipitating widespread interest and controversy.[29]

Notably, national conversations about the use of our water resources would become a progressive tenet. Even Teddy Roosevelt's New Nationalism favored national control.[30] Progressives not only firmly believed in the capacity of experts to plan our society but also further assumed that they could do so with the facility of ensuring that we both use and conserve our natural resources for future generations. President Roosevelt lamented how "the failure to use our own [rivers] is astonishing,

[25] Charles K. McFarland, *The Federal Government and Water Power, 1901–1913: A Legislative Study in the Nascence of Regulation*, 42 LAND ECON. 441, 449 (1966). For the history of these and other early efforts, *see* MILTON CONOVER, THE FEDERAL POWER COMMISSION: ITS HISTORY, ACTIVITIES, AND ORGANIZATION (Johns Hopkins Univ. Press 1923); Frank R. McNinch, *The Evolution of Federal Control of Electric Power*, 12 J. OF LAND & PUB. UTIL. ECON. 111 (1936). For a discussion of the Forest Service's approach to charging for the use of water resources within forest reserves, *see* GIFFORD PINCHOT, BREAKING NEW GROUND 336–38 (Island Press 1974).

[26] 36 Cong. Rec. 3071 (1903); *see also* 42 Cong. Rec. 4698 (1908) (Rainy River veto); 43 Cong. Rec. 9788o (1909) (James River veto). *See generally* CONOVER, *supra* note 25, at 48 51, 53 (discussing the Rainy River veto and Taft's veto of the Coosa River project); *see also* McNinch, *supra* note 25, at 112–13 (discussing vetoes and their importance).

[27] PINCHOT, *supra* note 25, at 327.

[28] CONOVER, *supra* note 25, at 33, at 53. See Act of June 23, 1910, ch. 359, 36 Stat. 593. Between 1910 and 1916, Congress approved just thirteen projects. CONOVER, *supra* note 25, at 53. In 1912, Congress provided the Secretary of War with general authority to augment any otherwise authorized dam with improvements "as may be considered desirable for the future development of its water power." Act of July 25, 1912, ch. 253, 37 Stat. 201, 233. A year earlier, Congress granted the Secretary of Agriculture generic authority to regulate and approve rights of way across forest system lands, including rights of way for "electrical poles and lines for the transmission and distribution of electrical power." Act of March 4, 1911, ch. 238, 36 Stat. 1235, 1253.

[29] NORRIS HUNDLEY, JR., THE GREAT THIRST: CALIFORNIANS AND WATER, 1770S–1990S 169–90 (Univ. of California Press 1992); ROBERT W. RIGHTER, THE BATTLE OVER HETCH HETCHY: AMERICA'S MOST CONTROVERSIAL DAM AND THE BIRTH OF MODERN ENVIRONMENTALISM 117 (Oxford Univ. Press 2005).

[30] THEODORE ROOSEVELT, *President of the United States, The New Nationalism* (August 31, 1910), *in* AMERICAN PROGRESSIVISM: A READER 211–23 (Ronald J. Pestritto & William J. Atto eds., 2008).

and no thoughtful man can believe that it will last," adding how we ought to deploy our river systems to their "utmost" for irrigation, power, and water supply.[31] The president believed that coal supplies were dwindling and that waterpower could fill the void. Tapping water resources correctly, though, would require expert planners, and Roosevelt urged assembling just such a team. He charged the Inland Waterways Commission, a team of experts, with developing a comprehensive water resource plan and deemed the Commission "a recognized authority on water power."[32] This emphasis on water resources expanded the "conservation" agenda beyond national forests and helped precipitate the symbolic birth of the "conserva-tion" movement.[33] By 1908, the progressive "conservation" community began exam-ining how best to use the nation's water resources without allowing private, monopolistic control. Wisconsin University President, Charles Hise, echoed the prevailing optimistic sentiment by suggesting how waterpower might furnish the nation's entire power requirements – albeit limited only by the technical barriers inhibiting long-distance transmission lines.[34]

Yet several policies first needed resolution before any significant water resource development could occur. Should states or the federal government regulate the potential concentration of ownership of waterpower resources? Should states or the federal government decide whether to own or regulate waterpower use? Or, perhaps, should water resources be developed by private entities or, alternatively, by govern-mental entities such as municipalities, states, or the federal government? If the former, should private developers be regulated – or, instead, should they just be sold the resource at some appropriate price? And if private development would be allowed, would developers enjoy a perpetual "right" to the resource, or could the United States or a state later recapture the resource for the public's benefit?

The fear of industry consolidation and monopolization of water resources natu-rally captured most attention – after all, the issue dominated many national dialo-gues (perhaps the most prominent fear of consolidation was with the oil industry). Indeed, in 1910, thirteen companies reportedly owned one-third of the nation's waterpower resources. In 1916, the House Committee on Public Lands noted that "more than 90 percent of the water power in the public-land States is owned by 28 private corporations and their subsidiaries, and that 6 of these control together over

---

[31]   Preliminary Report of the Inland Waterways Commission, S. Doc. No. 60–325, at iii–v (1st Sess. February 26, 1908) [hereinafter Preliminary Report].

[32]   Theodore Roosevelt, *The Inland Waters Commission*, Sci. 996–97 (June 26, 1908).

[33]   *See* Judson King, The Conservation Fight: From Theodore Roosevelt to the Tennessee Valley Authority 13 (Public Affairs Press 1959); Preliminary Report, *supra* note 31, at iii–iv. The commission's effort prompted a White House commission on conservation and a resulting national conference. The National Conservation Commission, thereafter, published a comprehensive report that, unfortunately, Congress would ignore. *See* Charles Richard Van Hise, The Conservation of Natural Resources in the United States 5–12 (Macmillan Co. 1910); W.J. McGee, The Conservation of Natural Resources, *reprinted in* Proceedings of the Mississippi Valley Historical Association for the Year 1909–1910 361, 374–75 (1910).

[34]   Van Hise, *supra* note 33, at 119–22, 136.

56 per cent of the developed power." And seventeen of those twenty-eight companies had some form of relationship with General Electric Company.[35] In his 1908 message accompanying the interim report of the Inland Waterways Commission, President Roosevelt emphasized the evils of the "consolidation of companies controlling water power."[36] He feared that private monopolies would own and control too many waterpower sites and "ordered the withdrawal from entry of large areas along streams in the Rocky Mountain and Pacific States, on recommendation of the Reclamation Service."[37] A report by the Commissioner of Corporations addressed the issue of industry concentration, recommending governmental supervision over development of waterpower facilities but not over the electric rates from that development.[38] States echoed a similar refrain, such as in a 1915 North Carolina Supreme Court opinion where the court feared the consequences of industry concentration when considering a company's ability to condemn property in the narrows along the Green River. It wrote how

> [p]robably the most feared combination to be guarded against is the acquisition of the water powers of the country by one or more great aggregations of capital, which in view of the certainty of the exhaustion of our coal measures at no distant date will give such monopolies the full control of light, heating and power, and with them domination over the very means of existence of the public.[39]

That same year, Senate Resolution No. 544 charged the Agriculture Secretary with "furnish[ing] the Senate with all information in his possession as to the ownership and control of the water-power sites in the United States," along with "any facts bearing upon the question as to the existence of a monopoly in the ownership and control of hydroelectric power in the United States." The resulting report warned of an "increasing tendency toward concentration in the control of the development, distribution, and sale of electric power," with the potential ability to influence other industries, such as banking, through interlocking directorates and other similar devices. This structure hampered any individual state's ability to oversee utility projects within its borders.[40]

Along with industry concentration, conversations often targeted the efficacy of allowing private control rather than federal, state, or municipal development. Municipal ownership for water supply, for example, already had become robust. And as of 1902, roughly 22 percent of the electric power generation facilities were

[35] NYE, *supra* note 9, at 288. *See also* H.R. Rep. No. 16, *supra* note 16, at 10–11.

[36] Preliminary Report, *supra* note 16, at v. The Preliminary Inland Waterways Report emphasized the need for active federal and state regulation of the monopolization in the power sector. KING, *supra* note 33, at 14.

[37] BENJAMIN HORACE HIBBARD, A HISTORY OF THE PUBLIC LAND POLICES 508 (Univ. of Wisconsin Press 1965).

[38] Frederick P. Royce, *A Consideration of the Report of Commissioner of Corporations on Water Power Development of the United States*, 10 STONE & WEBSTER 335 (1912); KERWIN, *supra* note 22, at 156.

[39] Blue Ridge Interurban Ry. Co. v. Hendersonville Light & Power Co., 86 S.E. 296, 296–97 (N.C. 1915).

[40] *See* Sec'y of Agric., Electric Power Dev. in the U.S. S. Doc. No. 64–316, pt. I, at 3 (1st Sess. 1916).

municipally owned and operated, jumping to 27 percent five years later, and rising to 30 percent by 1912. Yet these publicly owned facilities were small plants, producing only about 5 percent of the total generating capacity. At the federal level, conversely, the United States in 1907 had constructed the Laguna Dam in Imperial Valley, California and a federal dam and canal system along the Snake River in Idaho, all opposed by the trade association for the emerging electric utility industry.[41] Progressives generally accepted that waterpower ought to be controlled rather than owned by the public. But who would control was an open question. Several governors believed that if states could not own the resource, they at least ought to be the ones controlling the resource. In 1915, the Western States Water Power Conference proclaimed its desire that states ought to control the resources within their domain.[42] Nebraska, though, echoed a seemingly dominant view that some governmental supervision was necessary and possibly coordinated federal and state agencies to offset the growing control by private industry.[43]

In 1911, former President Roosevelt championed alternatively for federal supervision, in lieu of allowing state-chartered monopolies. That year an editorial in the magazine *Conservation* discussed waterpower's importance and why the matter of governmental control had entered a "critical stage."[44] And the concept of placing responsibility in a federal commission for supervising the development of waterpower was gaining currency. In 1913, the National Conservation Congress, at Gifford Pinchot's urging, passed a resolution favoring federal supervision. When the nation elected Woodrow Wilson, "[w]aterpower development" had become "a matter of great concern to the whole country; it was before the public as it never had been."[45] In the few years prior to 1920, the necessity of coordinating with some counterpart federal commission heightened for newly formed state commissions as well. Maine, for instance, created its commission in 1918.[46]

But so, too, forces advocating for public ownership of water resources carried significant resonance. Water resources, after all, had become a public resource –

---

[41]   See Evans Clark, Municipal Ownership in the United States (1916); Nye, *supra* note 9, at 300.
[42]   E.g., Western States Water Power Conference, Call, Resolutions and Official Proceedings (C.C. Chapman Pub. Portland, Oregon, September 21–23, 1915). *See also* Benjamin Parke De Witt, The Progressive Movement: A Non-Partisan, Comprehensive Discussion of Current Tendencies in American Politics 352 (1915).
[43]   *See Governors Uphold Rights of States*, N.Y. Times 3 (January 20, 1910).
[44]   *Editorial*, 1 Am. Conserv. 193, 195 (July 1911).
[45]   Kerwin, *supra* note 22, at 171. *See* Commissioner of Corporations, Water-Power Development in the United States XV (1912). Samuel Hayes chronicles how conservation captivated the progressive movement in what has since become seminal history of the conservation philosophy during the progressive era. Samuel P. Hayes, Conservation and the Gospel of Efficiency: The Progressive Conservation Movement, 1890–1920 (Harvard Univ. Press 1959, Antheneum ed., 1972). For a key participant's view of this effort, *see* Gifford Pinchot, *The Long Struggle for Effective Federal Water Power Legislation*, 14 Geo. Wash. L. Rev. 9 (1945).
[46]   Kerwin, *supra* note 22, at 204. Morton Keller, Regulating A New Economy: Public Policy and Economic Change in America, 1900–1933 162 (Harvard Univ. Press 1990); Conover, *supra* note 25, at 15–16.

considered by courts as matters for state superintendence. Forces favoring public ownership paralleled the conversation surrounding President Wilson's program for federally developing waterpower (and other potentials) at the Tennessee Muscle Shoals site.[47] The question of who should benefit from hydroelectric energy generation, after all, surfaced during San Francisco's fight surrounding Hetch Hetchy.[48] With waterpower development impeded, a several-year national conversation ensued over whether water resources should be privately tapped or owned and controlled by the federal government. Indeed, as one writer puts it, the "public-versus-private-power conflicts dominated the world of electricity for a half a century."[49]

Utilities naturally favored federal regulation, undoubtedly to avoid difficulties attendant with an ad hoc process for securing specific individual authorization from Congress or being subjected to varying state programs. With that said, over 400 projects were authorized through some other means prior to the passage of the 1920 Federal Water Power Act (FWPA).[50] Of course, not surprisingly, the significant number of hydroelectric power applications with the Federal Power Commission (FPC) demonstrated industry's favorable attitude toward the federal legislation (once Congress passed its waterpower act). Utilities began submitting preliminary permits after passage of the FWPA, and by the close of 1920, the FPC received 137 applications. Electric power generation from waterpower (federal and state) rose from 8.9 million horsepower in 1921 to over 12 million by 1928. In fact, by 1928, hydroelectric power generation reportedly accounted for roughly 40 percent of the energy generated by the private electric utilities. A 1929 drought then reduced hydroelectric power generation, potentially signaling the need for other, more stable resources.

The lack of federal legislation may have impeded waterpower's growth, although other factors were at play as well, such as transmission constraints. Testifying in 1918 and comparing coal with hydroelectric energy, a Westinghouse Electric official noted that "[i]t has been frequently pointed out that, as the nation's coal supply is depleted, the cost of coal must rise, thus increasing the cost of steam-electric power as a competitor and raising the market value of hydroelectric power accordingly." But he added how hydroelectric energy was potentially less desirable than steam energy because of seasonal variation in water flow affecting generation potential. This led him to conclude that hydroelectric energy could not effectively compete

[47] NORTH CALLAHAN, TVA: BRIDGE OVER TROUBLED WATERS (1980); PRESTON J. HUBBARD, ORIGINS OF TVA: THE MUSCLE SHOALS CONTROVERSY 1920–1932 (1961); C. HERMAN PRITCHETT, THE TENNESSEE VALLEY AUTHORITY: A STUDY IN PUBLIC ADMINISTRATION 3–30 (UN Press 1943); RICHARD LOWITT, GEORGE W. NORRIS: THE PERSISTENCE OF A PROGRESSIVE (1971); THOMAS K. MCCRAW, TVA AND THE POWER FIGHT 1933–1939 (1971).
[48] RIGHTER, *supra* note 29, at 167–90; HUNDLEY, JR., *supra* note 29, at 187–90.
[49] RIGHTER, *supra* note 29, at 167. In 1920, the United States Geological Survey even floated the possibility of a nationally owned and operated electric grid, an idea unsurprisingly rejected by private developers. BRADLEY, *supra* note 8, at 175.
[50] 1927 FPC SEVENTH ANN. REP. 18.

with steam generation. Indeed, a Pacific Gas & Electric official testified that transmitting hydroelectric energy over 200 miles cost roughly four to five times as much as an equivalent coal-fired steam plant (if coal was available).[51] But still, as of 1920, however, waterpower development lagged when compared with that of coal.

Although Congress began meaningfully debating waterpower legislation in 1916, another four years would pass before it could resolve the principal policy issues and adopt the 1920 FWPA.[52] The Secretary of Agriculture, in particular, championed federal legislation, particularly because Forest System lands contained "approximately one-half of the water-power of the West."[53] And in 1917, Agriculture Secretary David F. Houston urged adopting a commission model, with the three principal departments "vitally concerned in water-power legislation" at the helm.[54]

By this time, federal commissions following the mold of the Interstate Commerce Commission had become accepted. Congress, after all, had passed the Pure Food and Drug Act in 1906, as well as the Federal Trade Commission Act in 1914. After a few years of active consideration, Congress eventually acted in 1920. The 1936 Chairman of the FPC would later herald how "[t]he 15-year battle of the conservationists to safeguard the Nation's water power came to a successful climax in 1920 when, under the courageous leadership of Woodrow Wilson, the Federal Water Power Act became law."[55] The FPC would be slightly different than prior commissions, this one consisting of high-ranking officials – the Secretary of the Interior, the Secretary of War, and the Secretary of Agriculture.

Congress charged these cabinet-level officials with regulating hydroelectric power projects along interstate navigable waters, water bodies across national boundaries, and federal public lands and reservations.[56] It gave the FPC authority over intrastate rates affecting interstate rates, although it contemplated a new form of federalism by allowing state public utility commissions the authority to regulate rates for sales in either intra- or interstate as well. Section 19 of the FWPA conditioned the issuance of a license on the licensee's abiding by "reasonable regulation" of "any duly constituted agency of the State in which the service is rendered or the rate is charged." Section 20 further provided "[t]hat when said power or any part thereof shall enter into interstate . . . commerce the rates charged and the service rendered . . . shall be reasonable, nondiscriminatory, and just to the customer." Section 20 also intimated acquiescence to federal authority by adding how the FPC would have jurisdiction if no state agency exists for any state "directly concerned" to enforce the act's proscriptions. According to the 1916 House Public Lands Committee,

> [w]here the business of a hydroelectric concern is wholly intrastate and the State has a utility board, rate fixing and regulation is left entirely with the State and is not molested by the Federal Government in any way. On the other hand, if the business

---

[51]   1918 Hearing, *supra* note 20, at 172–5, 216, 220–21, 702.
[52]   The Federal Water Power Act, ch. 285, 41 Stat. 1063 (1920).   [53]   Conover, *supra* note 25, at 45.
[54]   *Ibid.* at 46, 69 (quoting 1917 Dep't of Agric. Ann. Rep. at 37).   [55]   McNinch, *supra* note 25, at 114.
[56]   Federal Water Power Act, ch. 285, §§ 19, 20, 41 Stat. 1063, 1073–74, 16 U.S.C. §§ 791–828c (1920).

is interstate, or even intrastate business, when the State has provided no utility board, then and in that event regulation is fixed by the Secretary of the Interior until such time as Congress may confer it upon the Interstate Commerce Commission, a water-power commission, or such other body as Congress may elect to confer it upon.[57]

It was well known that some of these waterpower projects were engaged in interstate commerce: a primary proponent of the legislation, and later the first executive officer for the new FPC, O. C. Merrill, noted in 1918 that waterpower companies already operated in multiple states simultaneously. He posited how it would not necessarily create a problem to allow states the ability to regulate rates for electricity moving across state boundaries because states could regulate sales within their own borders, and if someone objected, then, quite possibly, it could be regulated by the new federal commission. Indeed, Merrill testified that

where a transmission line runs across a State line, and the same company serves customers in two or more States, that so long as the power of regulation of rates and of service is and can be exercised by the local authorities it had better be left with the local authorities. If any cases should arise where there is a disagreement between the authorities of two or more States over questions of rate or service regulations, and it could not be settled between those authorities, then it is intended that the matter may come before the commission for settlement.

When asked whether the legislation's drafters considered simply giving the FPC authority to regulate "interstate business," Merrill responded they had, but believed "that matters of rates and services which are local in their character should be handled by the local authorities, if possible." He explained how several projects in the Pacific Northwest and California crossed state boundaries, and "if the only criterion of jurisdiction is whether the lines cross State boundaries," then all such projects would be under "exclusive control of the commission."[58] Notably, through these provisions, the act established one of the early regimes for what today we call

57 H.R. Rep. No. 16, *supra* note 21, at 13. Soon after Congress passed the FWPA, the FPC alluded to its ability, if necessary, to regulate rates for interstate sales but saw "at the present time little probability that occasion for such action will arise." 1921 FPC FIRST ANN. REP. 62–63 (Gov't Printing Off. 1921). The FPC infrequently invoked its ability to regulate intrastate rates in the absence of a state utility commission; it barely regulated interstate rates by 1940. ROBERT D. BAUM, THE FEDERAL POWER COMMISSION AND STATE UTILITY REGULATION 177–79, 182 (American Council on Pub. Aff. 1942). In 1929, the Commission concluded that states could only regulate interstate waterpower rates if Congress specifically approved an interstate compact – that is, the FWPA Section 20 did not itself serve "as Congressional authorization of interstate agreements." *Ibid.* at 181. In 1941, the Third Circuit rejected this interpretation. Safe Harbor Water Power Corp. v. F.P.C., 124 F.2d 800, 808 (3d Cir. 1941), *cert. denied,* 316 U.S. 663 (1942).
58 1918 Hearing, *supra* note 20, at 67–68, 99–100. A later witness also discussed how local state commissions (such as Nevada), overseeing sales to in-state residents, could regulate sales of energy from out of state. *Ibid.* at 414, 416–17 (Statement of Mr. Hall). Testifying later in the hearings, however, Agriculture Secretary Houston chose his words carefully by alluding only to state commissions' authority over intrastate business. *Ibid.* at 660.

cooperative federalism. Indeed, the Supreme Court would later observe how Congress resolved its concern with "divided authority" by careful "integration of the respective jurisdictions."[59] The act, therefore, purportedly furnished a framework for cooperative federal and state efforts rather than usurping all state authority. An early illustration of how this could occur was the Conowingo hydro-electric project along the Susquehanna River. The project would sell power across state lines, and its transactions involved multiple jurisdictions. It sought the approval from utility commissions in Maryland and Pennsylvania and from the FPC. The three Commissions held joint hearings to examine the project, with the FPC concluding that the proceeding "furnished an excellent test of the regulatory features of the act and has demonstrated that with such cordial cooperation as existed in this case there need be no conflict in matters of regulatory jurisdiction between the Federal commission and the commissions of the several States."[60] Of course, this did not obviate subsequent state efforts questioning whether Congress had impermissibly intruded into their constitutional domain.[61]

Next, by creating the FPC, the act resolved the duel between those who favored private capital investment (the winners) and those who believed that hydroelectric power generation ought to be federally owned and managed (the losers). Responding to President Theodore Roosevelt's 1908 plea that Congress must provide the United States or individual states with the ability to recapture the resource if necessary, Congress included several important provisions. First, it protected against a perpetual monopolization of resources by private entities by imposing a fifty-year maximum on FPC-issued licenses to hydroelectric power projects along the nation's navigable waters. Second, it afforded state and municipal entities a preference toward purchasing electricity if they too sought to develop the resource and compete against a private entity for the right to develop a project. This idea of affording a preference had become well established for federal programs and would continue after the FWPA's passage. Third, on the expiration of any license, the United States could "take over and thereafter [] maintain and operate any project" and associated property "upon the condition that before taking possession it shall pay the [licen-see's] net investment." Many considered this one of the most important components of the new legislation.[62] And fourth, the act required that licensees pay the United

[59] First Iowa Hydro-Elec. Coop. v. Fed. Power Comm'n, 328 U.S. 152, 174 (1946).

[60] 1926 FPC Sixth Ann. Rep. 6–9 (Gov't Printing Off.).

[61] New Jersey v. Sargent, 269 U.S. 328 (1926) (dismissed state claim for what today would be lack of standing); *see also* United States v. West Virginia, 295 U.S. 463 (1935) (similar result with suit by United States). Other challenges to the Act also were dismissed. E.g., Appalachian Elec. Power Co. v. Smith, 67 F.2d 451 (4th Cir. 1933), *cert. denied* 291 U.S. 674 (1934); Ala. Power Co. v. Gulf Power Co., 283 F. 606 (M.D. Ala. 1922).

[62] *See* H.R. Rep. No. 99–507, at 12. Later, in 1936, FPC Chairman McNinch described the recapture provision as "[o]ne of the most important provisions of the Act of 1920." McNinch, *supra* note 25, at 115.

States for the use of federal lands "or other property," as well as for the costs of administering the act.

Finally, the act reflected the Progressive and New Deal embrace of scientific management or planning. After all, scientific management accepted our capacity for managing resources to maximize productivity and use. This was the mantra of Gifford Pinchot for both forest and water resources. It permeated discussions about the role of government in regulating private industry; it infused the business world and the followers of Frederick W. Taylor; and it, not surprisingly, justified the growth of modern zoning regulation.[63] Congress, consequently, provided in Section 10 of the FWPA that the FPC could issue a license on the condition that "[t]he project adopted . . . shall be such as in the judgment of the commission will be best adapted to a comprehensive scheme of improvement and utilization for the purposes of navigation, of water-power development, and of other beneficial uses."[64]

The FPC's early years were anything but stellar. In his review of the history, Donald Swain describes the agency as "ineffective," marred by a lack of money, staff, and, even, interest among the commissioners.[65] At first, the FPC could not even hire a complete staff and instead tapped employees from each commissioner's own agency. By 1927, the FPC warned that it could not enforce the act until Congress supplied money and personnel.[66] Congress finally appropriated funds once the agency refused to issue any new licenses. Between, for instance, 1920 and 1929, "the FPC convened only ninety-nine times, with the usual meeting lasting less than thirty minutes."[67] Also, in lieu of acting like a modern regulatory agency – the objective of Executive Secretary O. C. Merrill – the FPC instead heeded the wishes of the emerging electric utility industry, and regulation arguably existed in "name only." Swain would later report how "[t]he ineffectiveness of the commission became so apparent that Congress instituted a full investigation in early 1930."[68]

In late 1929, President Herbert Hoover addressed one problem with the FPC by calling for the establishment of a "full-time commission."[69] Congress responded in 1930, establishing the FPC as an independent agency with commissioners, in lieu of being run by an otherwise distracted cabinet-level body. Unfortunately, the new legislation did not immediately cure the agency's woes.[70]

---

[63] SAMUEL HABER, EFFICIENCY AND UPLIFT: SCIENTIFIC MANAGEMENT IN THE PROGRESSIVE ERA 1890–1920 (Univ. of Chicago Press 1964); SAMUEL P. HAYES, CONSERVATION AND THE GOSPEL OF EFFICIENCY: THE PROGRESSIVE CONSERVATION MOVEMENT, 1890–1920 (Univ. of Pittsburgh Press 1959); THOMAS K. MCCRAW, PROPHETS OF REGULATION: CHARLES FRANCIS ADAMS, LOUIS D. BRANDIES, ALFRED E. KAHN (Belknap Press 1984).

[64] Section 10(a), 41 Stat. at 1068.

[65] DONALD C. SWAIN, FEDERAL CONSERVATION POLICY 1921–1933 113–114, University of California Publications in History, Vol. 76 (Univ. of California Press 1963).

[66] 1927 FPC SEVENTH ANN. REP. 2 (Gov't. Printing Off.); *see also* BAUM, *supra* note 57, at 23–26.

[67] SWAIN, *supra* note 65, at 115.   [68] *Ibid.* at 114–115.   [69] BAUM, *supra* note 57, at 27.

[70] SWAIN, *supra* note 65, at 115; *see also* Pub. L. No. 71–412, 46 Stat. 797 (1930). Earlier amendments occurred as well, such as in 1921 when Congress prohibited licensing any project or project works

HYDROELECTRIC POWER'S POSTSCRIPT

To be sure, after World War II, hydroelectric power became a symbol for how federal programs could energize our economy, and policymakers correspondingly perceived hydroelectric resources as immune from both the challenges confronting the supply/demand balance for coal and the resource constraints of oil and gas. After all, Congress had established the Tennessee Valley Authority in 1933, the Hoover Dam was built in 1936, and the Bonneville Power Administration was established in 1937. By 1940, hydroelectric power generation supplied roughly 40 percent of the nation's electricity, having more than tripled its total national capacity in just two decades. In 1948, for instance, then Secretary Krug informed President Truman that "[w]e should be doing much more in determining our energy reserves, in producing and using our fuels less wastefully, and in developing power from inexhaustible hydroelectric power sources instead of exhaustible coal, oil and gas."[71]

This, of course, would all change by the 1960s, with the advent of an emerging environmental consensus typified by the now-famous story surrounding Consolidated Edison's (Con-Ed) ill-fated attempt to develop a pumped storage project at Storm King Mountain (formerly Butter Hill).[72] That the FPC, at the time tagged with being a poorly managed agency, would become a focal point for environmental protection seems today quite natural – after all, the proposed damming of the Colorado River along the Grand Canyon in the 1960s, as well as the fight to protect Dinosaur National Park, illustrated how dams had become an environmental target.[73] By the early 1960s, Con-Ed sought additional generating capacity, necessary, as the 1960s would strikingly demonstrate, to bolster not only an otherwise unreliable electric grid but also one lacking sufficient generating capacity.[74] The company's fossil fuel–fired generation plants in New York had produced the nation's worst sulfur dioxide (SO_2)

"within the limits of as now constituted of any national park or national monument" unless expressly allowed by Congress. Act of March 3, 1921, 41 Stat. 1353 (1921).

[71] Craufurd D. Goodwin, *The Truman Administration: Toward a National Energy Policy*, in Energy Policy in Perspective: Today's Problems, Yesterday's Solutions 1, 37 (Craufurd D. Goodwin et al. eds. Brookings Inst. 1981).

[72] Robert H. Boyle, The Hudson River: A Natural and Unnatural History (W.W. Norton & Co. 1969); Robert D. Lifset, Power on the Hudson: Storm King Mountain and the Emergence of Modern American Environmentalism (Univ. of Pittsburgh Press 2014); Allan R. Talbot, Power Along the Hudson: The Storm King Case and the Birth of Environmentalism (E.P. Dutton & Co. 1972).

[73] *See generally* Jon M. Cosco, Echo Park: Struggle for Preservation (Johnson Books 1995); Russell Martin, A Story that Stands Like a Dam: Glen Canyon and the Struggle for the Soul of the West (Henry Holt & Co. 1st edn, 1990). Historian Patricia Limerick writes how, with the Echo Park controversy, "the well-established expectation that large dams would continue to be built went sailing off a cliff and landed in a heap." Patricia Nelson Limerick & Jason L. Hanson, A Ditch in Time: The City, the West, and Water 166 (Fulcrum Pub. 2012).

[74] Lifset, *supra* note 72, at 87.

problems, and it would be years before the company could secure additional nuclear energy from soon-to-be-proposed additional generating capacity at Indian Point.[75] As the largest proposed pumped storage project in the world, the Cornwall Project would avoid increasing SO_2 emissions by providing peaking power potentially capable of averting blackouts or planned brownouts.

But the Cornwall Project (including its accompanying transmission line) threatened the scenic beauty for the surrounding communities. If completed, it would destroy the historic charm of this part of the Hudson River Valley, and moreover, it would produce a colossal ecological disruption. When concerned citizens first saw a proposed illustration for how the project would effectively shave off a considerable portion of the mountain, they became energized and, in doing so, precipitated the modern paradigm for environmental citizen engagement.[76] Before the FPC, though, the citizens had little reason for optimism. The Commission's acceptance of Con-Ed's need for power overcame any meaningful interest in exploring alternative energy resources or the likely ecological or other adverse effects of the project. The FPC even rejected an entreaty by the New York State Legislative Committee requesting that the Commission reopen its proceedings to address the ecological and scenic effects of the project. As one of the lawyers involved in the lawsuit recently observed, "no FPC license for a hydroelectric power plant had been successfully challenged on the merits, and there was little reason to be optimistic about a case where the central issue was a complaint that the Project would damage scenic beauty."[77] When, in March 1965, the FPC granted Con-Ed's license application, the citizen group successfully sought a friendlier forum at the Second Circuit.

In a now-classic opinion issued within two months of the dramatic 1965 blackout in New York, the Second Circuit strongly rebuked the FPC. Judge Hayes began by noting how the case had attracted wide attention. He then opined that the FPC had not adequately compiled a sufficient administrative record to support its judgment, had not considered all the relevant issues, and had not examined other possible alternatives. Of considerable importance, the Federal Power Act (FPA) charged the Commission with balancing the relevant factors for deciding whether to license a project – the list of factors included the area's recreational and scenic value. That charge, according to Judge Hayes, affirmatively obligated the FPC to explore "and consider all relevant facts." And in one of administrative law's most memorable statements, he observed:

> In this case, as in many others, the Commission has claimed to be the representative of the public interest. This role does not permit it to act as an umpire, blandly

---

[75] The company operated the largest oil-fired generation facility in the country, known as the Big Allis (1,000 MW), at Ravenswood. TALBOT, *supra* note 72, at 70–71.

[76] Albert K. Butzel, *Storm King Revisited: A View from the Mountaintop*, 31 PACE ENVTL. L. REV. 370, 374 (2014).

[77] *Ibid.* at 372.

calling balls and strikes for adversaries appearing before it; the right of the public must receive active and affirmative protection at the hands of the Commission.[78]

Perhaps seemingly focused too much on the need for power rather than the environment, Con-Ed responded to the decision by suggesting that it would pursue securing a license from the FPC on remand from the Second Circuit – although the project's fate seemed sealed nonetheless. After further litigation, Co-Ed shuttered its project following the Hudson River Peace Treaty (involving the company's nuclear plants).

Entering the 1970s, hydroelectric power generation confronted the dialectic of those who believed that no new resource sites remained and those intent on removing already existing projects. In the searing report by Ralph Nader's group, *Vanishing Air*, the authors dismissed hydroelectric power as constrained by the lack of available water bodies.[79] But it was the impact of hydroelectric power in cases such as *Storm King* that undoubtedly chilled interest in new development. After all, President Carter had his federal hit list for federal dams, and *Storm King* signaled a similar fate for any new federally licensed dams. The era of new large hydroelectric power projects was now over – at least for now – and most current conversations focus on small or low-impact hydroelectric power generation.

To be sure, hydroelectric energy promoted economic development in several regions of the country, and its benefits over other fossil fuel generation resources is undoubtedly worthwhile toward transitioning to a low-carbon or carbon-free economy. But the conflicts surrounding these projects, from *Storm King* and since, suggest a somewhat flawed statutory program. The original act focused on planned water resource development – with perhaps insufficient appreciation for actual comprehensive river planning or ecological consequences. Though amended in the 1980s and subsequently adjusted in minor respects since, the FPA has not proved adept at adapting to modern challenges confronting the industry – with today many relicensings ending in settlements with interested stakeholders. Most larger projects that have been operating for over fifty years now take over a decade (and sometimes two) to navigate the relicensing process – an almost debilitating process driven more by environmental considerations, such as through the FPA's assignment of conditioning authority to land-managing agencies (if federal or Native American reservation lands are involved), the Act's amendments, including addressing fish passage concerns, or the requirements of the Clean Water Act and the Endangered Species Act than by any energy-specific or planning requirements of the FPA. Perhaps the folly of it all is that the basic structure of the Act, although tweaked since the 1920s, generally remains in place during an era that is far removed from what Congress confronted during the first decades of the twentieth century.

[78] Scenic Hudson Pres. Conf. v. F.P.C., 354 F.2d 608 (2d Cir. 1965).
[79] JOHN C. ESPOSITO, VANISHING AIR: RALPH NADER'S STUDY GROUP REPORT ON AIR POLLUTION 94 (Grossman Pub. 1970).

3

The Supreme Court Creates a Gap

The Federal Water Power Act's (FWPA's) development chronicled in Chapter 2 occurred as regulatory oversight of electric generation and transmission pushed the boundaries of federal and state power. Initially, governmental supervision of the industry surfaced in the form of conditions to municipal franchises. A state or municipality would grant a gas or electric utility the authority to operate within their locale. What followed next was the emergence of state public utility commissions, capable of regulating individual vertically integrated utilities systems in urban areas that gradually became interconnected with each other during the nascent years of the twentieth century. But, along the way, two developments impaired the ability of state commissions to regulate privately owned utilities in their states. The multistate electric utility holding company was the first development. Holding companies, because of their size, multistate nature, and complexity, defied effective regulation by the states. And, because of their financial abuses, they threatened the viability of their controlled local utility operating companies.

The second development, though, was a choice by the US Supreme Court to establish limits on state authority to regulate natural gas and electric industries. In 1927, the Supreme Court decided *Public Utilities Commission* v. *Attleboro Steam & Electric Co*. The Court held that the United States Constitution's dormant Commerce Clause barred states from regulating interstate wholesale sales of electric power. This clause is implied by the Constitution's grant to Congress of the power to regulate interstate commerce and, so the argument goes, correspondingly limits the states' ability to engage in certain forms of regulation. They may regulate retail sales and intrastate sales, but – unless Congress acted and provided otherwise – no agency could regulate interstate wholesale electricity sales. States that by then had developed a rudimentary form of cost-based rate regulation were unable to ensure that the utilities they regulated would purchase power at cost-based rates. The Court's decision created a regulatory gap: states could not regulate interstate transmission and sales, and no federal agency could either because the FWPA only regulated hydroelectric power generation. The opinion, consequently, prompted passage of the Federal Power Act (FPA) eight years later, and yet, unfortunately, the 1927 ghost of *Attleboro* still haunts us today.

This chapter explores how the illusion surrounding *Attleboro* surfaced and generated today's *Attleboro* ghost that still influences modern efforts to transition to a green economy.

CITIES, PROGRESSIVISM, AND ELECTRICITY MARKETS

The expanding electric grid occurred while Progressivism favored governmental supervision over our nation's energy resources. A tenet for many early-twentieth-century Progressives was scientific planning and an enhanced role for the government vis-à-vis the regulation of social and economic relations. Active federal involvement began during the second half of the nineteenth century, and a cascade of federal legislation occurred shortly thereafter. But federal supervision over electric and natural gas infrastructure lagged many other sectors of the economy. For these two industries, attention generally gravitated toward state public utility commissions – establishing and avoiding confiscatory rates, as well as defining the role of the judiciary and developing workable legal rules for contracts, torts, and property law as they affect the energy industry. Various reforms at the state commission level converged with an apparent interest in both utility commissions and the industry to explore uniform approaches to the industry. Indeed, as one observer commented: "innumerable national, professional and trade organizations have unified the United States to much the same degree that the individual state was unified three decades ago."[1]

Interest in electric energy at the national level centered principally on waterpower development and associated industry consolidation, as discussed in Chapter 2. But Congress's 1920 FWPA deftly avoided establishing jurisdictional lines for the sale and transmission of electric energy. For instance, it allowed state public utility commissions the ability to regulate rates for sales of electricity in either intra- or interstate transactions. Soon after Congress passed the FWPA, the Federal Power Commission (FPC) alluded to its ability, if necessary, to regulate rates for interstate sales but saw "at the present time little probability that occasion for such action will arise."[2]

The dialogue over waterpower already had raised the specter of monopolizing resources, and the electric industry was rapidly consolidating – coinciding with the national conversation over corporate capitalism and what Justice Louis Brandeis referred to as "bigness." To be sure, consolidation and creation of holding companies helped secure capital investment and ensure sufficient electric power generation capacity and a corresponding load. Arrangements with the electric or interurban trolley system (as Insull achieved with Chicago Edison), for instance, guaranteed a ready market and a favorable load curve that ensured a consistent generation need.

---

[1]   Clarence M. Updegraff, *The Extension of Federal Regulation of Public Utilities*, 13 Iowa L. Rev. 369, 370–71 (1928).
[2]   1921 Fed. Power Comm'n First Ann. Rep. 62–63.

Consolidating ownership of facilities allowed companies to generate sufficient capital for the large investments necessary to expand their systems and diversify their load for different patterns of use.[3] But public outcry questioned whether the electric transportation network and accompanying electric generation system should be in public or private ownership – or controlled by a select few.[4] The financial arrangements of these massive holding companies was highly precarious and often beyond the reach of state regulation. The public tenor generally against holding companies carried into the utility arena, and eventually, the Federal Trade Commission (FTC) examined industry concentration. That inquiry gained even more currency once it became more well know that utilities had engaged in vibrant misleading public relations campaigns and may even have bought votes to sway policies.[5]

As natural monopolies, however, holding companies could capitalize on the economies of scale, attract private capital, and correspondingly expand the electric grid. Governmentally owned electric systems (public power) began waning by the 1920s and "[b]y 1932 ... produced only about 5 percent of the nation's electricity."[6] As of 1922, there were reportedly 3,774 privately owned electric power systems and 2,581 municipally owned systems.[7] Between 1900 and 1934, the country's energy production rose from 2 billion kWh to 90 billion kWh.[8] Privately owned utilities promoted Insull's view of minimal state regulatory oversight through public utility commissions. However, as they grew in organizational structure and infrastructure, achieving even greater economies of scale, these utilities naturally pushed the boundaries of effective state oversight. Although the numbers may not be precise, one author suggests that by the time of *Attleboro*, roughly "10.07 percent of the power produced for public consumption moved interstate."[9] And it was well understood at the time that the industry's growth, which would roughly double just between 1922 and 1930, was tied to an interconnected interstate grid.[10]

[3] RONALD SEAVOY, AN ECONOMIC HISTORY OF THE UNITED STATES FROM 1607 TO THE PRESENT 270–72 (Routledge 2006); JEROME G. KERWIN, FEDERAL WATER-POWER LEGISLATION 45–46, 56 (Columbia Univ. Press 1926); *see also* REPORT OF THE COMMISSIONER OF CORPORATIONS ON WATER-POWER DEVELOPMENT IN THE UNITED STATES, at 9, 95–118.
[4] SAMUEL P. HAYS, THE RESPONSE TO INDUSTRIALISM 1885–1914 109 (Univ. of Chicago Press 1957).
[5] ROBERT L. BRADLEY, JR., EDISON TO ENRON: ENERGY MARKETS AND POLITICAL STRATEGIES 176 (Wiley 2011); RICHARD HIRSCH, POWER LOSS: THE ORIGINS OF DEREGULATION AND RESTRUCTURING IN AMERICAN ELECTRIC UTILITY SYSTEM 40 (MIT Press 1999).
[6] DAVID E. NYE, ELECTRIFYING AMERICA: SOCIAL MEANINGS OF A NEW TECHNOLOGY 140, 179–80 (MIT Press 1990).
[7] NAT'L ELEC. LIGHT ASS'N, POLITICAL OWNERSHIP AND THE ELECTRIC LIGHT AND POWER INDUSTRY 5 (1925).
[8] Dozier A. DeVane, *Highlights of Legislative History of the Federal Power Act of 1935 and the Natural Gas Act of 1938*, 14 GEO. WASH. L. REV. 30 (1945).
[9] *Ibid.* at 31.
[10] William C. Scott, *State and Federal Control of Power Transmission As Affected by the Interstate Commerce Clause*, 14 PROC. ACAD. POL. SCI. 135 (1930); Richard D. Cudahy & William D. Henderson, *From Insull to Enron: Corporate (Re)Regulation after the Rise and Fall of Two Energy Icons*, 26 ENERGY LAW J. 35, 55 (2005).

CONSTITUTIONAL NARRATIVE FOR EMERGING ENERGY MARKETS

The US Supreme Court would need a constitutional narrative under the Commerce Clause for reviewing whether states or the federal government could regulate this sprawling network of lines and interstate sales. A narrative had surfaced for the railroad industry: two markets emerged, the short-haul in-state service market and the interstate long-haul transport market, and state commissions promoted harmful economic rate discrimination favoring the former over the latter. The solution for that industry was to have Congress step in and regulate the industry, but not necessarily telling the states that they were prohibited from establishing intrastate rates that affected the interstate traffic even before Congress acted. The fact that Congress could or perhaps should act – a theme imbued throughout the Progressive era, did not resolve how far state jurisdiction would extend or whether both the states and Congress could share potential jurisdiction subject to Congress's preemptive authority.

The Supreme Court generally disallowed both state and federal jurisdiction over an activity, called *concurrent jurisdiction*, if it deemed that activity as involving interstate commerce. The Court's analysis expanding the scope of federal power began to limit how far a state could go in regulating certain activities. If, therefore, an activity was treated as involving interstate commerce, the Court might preclude states from regulating that conduct unless Congress otherwise allowed it. This occurred because the Court generally treated matters involving interstate commerce as exclusively within Congress's domain. The Court gleaned from the Constitution's Commerce Clause, which gave Congress the authority to regulate "interstate commerce," an implied or "dormant" prohibition that limited states from regulating "interstate commerce." In 1925, conservative Justice Van Devanter echoed the prevailing doctrine when he observed how states could "incidentally and remotely" affect interstate commerce for *permissible* reasons, but regardless of a state's motivation, it could not "directly interfere [] with or burden [] such commerce."[11] That would amount to an impermissible attempt by the state to regulate "interstate commerce."

In the transportation realm, for instance, the Supreme Court wrestled with the somewhat porous federal-state dividing line, allowing some state authority when the Court perceived of it as a valid exercise of the police power but otherwise limiting the state's ability to regulate the interstate activity itself. In one instance, Justice Brandeis invalidated a Washington state law requiring a certificate before a motor vehicle company could use the highways to transport passengers for hire.[12] Washington denied Buck's certificate request because the route was otherwise adequately served by other transportation means. Buck claimed that Washington denied him his rights under the Fourteenth Amendment, which protects against states denying a person equal protection under the law or due process, and that Washington's program violated the dormant Commerce Clause. The Supreme

[11] Shafter v. Farmers' Grain Co., 268 U.S. 189, 199 (1925).
[12] Buck v. Kuykendall, 267 U.S. 307 (1925).

Court accepted how certain state measures would be permissible, if they were reasonably related to a legitimate state interest and avoided directly regulating interstate commerce. After all, the Court had allowed states to impose safety-related measures for interstate railroads.[13] But Washington's program addressed neither safety nor some other legitimate state interest; rather, it focused on competition in interstate travel – not just burdening but obstructing it contrary to the Commerce Clause. By contrast, a state could enforce traditional common-law common carrier obligations on interstate carriers.[14] For the exploding automobile industry, the Court allowed states to require that vehicle owners (even if they will travel in interstate commerce) register and license their vehicles in the state, and states could exercise their power to impose reasonable limitations on vehicle weight, even when those vehicles traveled in interstate commerce.[15]

In the somewhat analogous context of regulating interstate transmission of telegraph messages, Justice Holmes held that states were barred from regulating it.[16] The state commission ordered that the telegraph companies (which provided the ticker services) refrain from engaging in discriminatory behavior when sending price quotations from the New York Stock Exchange (NYSE). The telegraph companies had contracts with the NYSE, limiting ticker services to brokers approved by the NYSE. The NYSE denied approval for ticker services to a Boston stockbroker, who had previously been served and sought approval from the NYSE to renew his service. Nothing suggested that the broker had done anything to warrant the NYSE's decision.[17] And prior cases already confronted the unique nature of the contracts between the NYSE and the telegraph companies.[18] Justice Holmes "reasoned" that because the transmission was in interstate commerce, it was "withdrawn from state control."[19] To Holmes, interstate commerce continues until the article of commerce reaches its endpoint. Just where that endpoint occurred, though, would confound the Court for decades. Of course, when the case was before the Massachusetts Supreme Court, that court avoided any meaningful discussion by concluding that the transmissions were neither part of interstate commerce nor governed by the act of June 18, 1910 regarding interstate telegraph transmissions.[20]

Additional wrinkles surfaced, however, when the Supreme Court confronted the distinction between permissible police power measures and impermissible

[13] Atl. Coast Line R.R. Co. v. Georgia, 234 U.S. 280 (1914) (headlights); Vandalia R.R. Co. v. Pub. Serv. Comm'n, 242 U.S. 255 (1916) (headlights on trains); Smith v. Alabama, 124 U.S. 465 (1888) (fitness of railroad engineer). *Cf.* S. Ry. Co. v. King, 217 U.S. 524, 539 (1910) (Holmes, J., dissenting).

[14] Mo. Pac. R.R. Co. v. Larabee Flour Mills Co., 211 U.S. 612 (1909); Cleveland, Cincinnati, Chi. & St. Louis Ry. Co. v. Illinois, 177 U.S. 514, 516 (1900).

[15] Morris v. Duby, 274 U.S. 135 (1927); Kane v. New Jersey, 242 U.S. 160 (1916); Hendrick v. Maryland, 235 U.S. 610 (1915).

[16] W. Union Tel. Co. v. Foster (*Foster II*), 247 U.S. 105 (1918).

[17] W. Union Tel. Co. v. Foster (*Foster I*), 113 N.E. 192 (Mass. 1916).

[18] Tucker v. W. Union Tel. Co., 158 N.Y.S. 959 (Sup. Ct. 1915).   [19] *Foster II*, 247 U.S. at 114.

[20] *Foster I*, 113 N.E. at 198. In Hopkins v. United States, 171 U.S. 578, 597–601 (1898), the court held that stockyard exchange transactions were not part of interstate commerce.

restraints on interstate commerce involving state regulation of natural resources. "[I]t is difficult to define [the police power] with sharp precision. It is generally said to extend to making regulations promotive of domestic order, morals, health, and safety."[21] Contemporary scholars, for instance, debated whether a state enjoys an unfettered propriety interest in its natural resources within its borders – and perhaps an obligation to protect those resources for its citizens (some state constitutions contain natural resource clauses), as well as whether the Commerce Clause imposes any restraint on the exercise of that power, assuming some proprietary interest.[22] After all, capacious state control over water resources posed problematic issues. One of the nation's early western water planners, Elwood Mead, commented in 1903 that "[i]t would seem that some sort of interstate regulation is required."[23] Justice Holmes was a bit more solicitous of state regulation, however.[24]

General game laws along with oil and gas resource programs posed similar issues. States often sought to regulate hunting, fishing, or subsequent shipment of illegally obtained game or fish.[25] Professor Ernst Freund explained how history supported state control, but he doubted that it would justify allowing greater freedom for preventing the export of game out of a state.[26] And this seemed implicit in what has since become a seminal opinion, *Greer v. Connecticut*, where the Supreme Court upheld Connecticut's ability to prohibit the interstate shipment of lawfully obtained game.[27] For oil and natural gas, states could protect such common resources against waste, and even regulate their production as a matter of local concern.[28]

---

[21] Hannibal & St. Joseph R.R. Co. v. Husen, 95 U.S. 465, 470–71 (1877).

[22] Dwight Williams, *The Power of the State to Control the Use of Its Natural Resources*, 11 MINN. L. REV. 129 (1926–27). Courts generally embraced a theory that a state as a sovereign could protect such common resources in trust for its citizens. E.g., State v. Rodman, 59 N.W. 1098 (Minn. 1894).

[23] ELWOOD MEAD, IRRIGATION INSTITUTIONS: A DISCUSSION OF THE ECONOMIC AND LEGAL QUESTIONS CREATED BY THE GROWTH OF IRRIGATED AGRICULTURE IN THE WEST 337 (Macmillan & Co. 1903).

[24] Hudson Cty. Water Co. v. McCarter, 209 U.S. 349, 356 (1908).

[25] *In re* Phoedovious, 170 P. 412 (Cal. 1918); Hornbeke v. White, 76 P. 926 (Colo. App. 1904); State v. Snowman, 46 A. 815 (Me. 1900); Stevens v. State, 43 A. 929 (Md. App. 1899); State v. Whitten, 37 A. 331 (Me. 1897); State v. Rodman, 59 N.W. 1098 (Minn. 1894); *In re* Maier, 37 P. 402 (Cal. 1894); Roth v. State, 37 N.E. 259 (Ohio 1894); Phelps v. Racey, 60 N.Y. 10 (1875); *cf.* Allen v. Wyckoff, 2 A. 659 (N.J. 1886); Moulton v. Libbey, 37 Me. 472 (1854).

[26] ERNST FREUND, THE POLICE POWER: PUBLIC POLICY AND CONSTITUTIONAL RIGHTS 445–46 (Univ. of Chicago Press 1904). E.g., Manchester v. Massachusetts, 139 U.S. 240, 265–66 (1891); Foster-Fountain Packing Co. v. Haydel, 278 U.S. 1 (1928). A program exuding some illegitimate state motive might fail, however. E.g., Leonard v. Earle, 279 U.S. 392 (1929).

[27] 161 U.S. 519 (1896), *overruled by* Hughes v. Oklahoma, 441 U.S. 322 (1979).

[28] Ohio Oil Co. v. Indiana, 177 U.S. 190 (1900). Earlier, the court accepted as part of "common experience or knowledge" the unique "ownership" nature of oil and gas resources. Brown v. Spilman, 155 U.S. 665, 670 (1895); *see also* Ohio Oil Co. v. Indiana, 177 U.S. 190 (1900); *cf.* Lindsley v. Nat. Carbonic Gas Co., 220 U.S. 61 (1911) (statute protecting against waste of mineral waters and carbonic acid constitutional).

But, notably, the Court wielded the Commerce Clause to prevent states from monopolizing oil and gas resources within their borders. Absent some check on state action, the emerging use of liquid fuels and accompanying transportation network could have been severely affected – at precisely the time when such fuels were competing with coal and becoming the basis for the nascent automobile industry. In *West v. Kansas Natural Gas Co.*, for instance, the Court rebuffed Oklahoma's attempt to prohibit the interstate transportation of natural gas produced in the state.[29] While the Court accepted some similarities with other resources such as wildlife, it held that a state could not deny all right to develop the resource, and here Oklahoma's purpose of creating a limited (in-state) market was unacceptable. The Court reflected its concern by adding how any other holding might allow hoarding of resources by resource-abundant regions.[30]

The Court nevertheless tolerated less intrusive rate regulation for petroleum and natural gas. States, for instance, enjoyed oversight authority for natural gas delivered by distributors to retail customers in the state, even if that gas arrived through interstate channels. In *Public Utilities Commission v. Landon*, the Court applied Chief Justice Marshall's *original package doctrine* – the ending point for when an article traveling in commerce ceased being treated as in interstate commerce.[31] The Chief Justice initially developed the doctrine for goods being imported from another country. But it was merely a legal fiction permitting a state's exercise of its police power once a product had come to rest in a state and had been removed from its original package.

Yet, applying the original package doctrine could be troubling. In *Pennsylvania Gas Co. v. Public Service Commission*, the Court upheld state regulation of natural gas sales delivered directly to local consumers when the gas moved in interstate commerce.[32] The Court considered the service to local consumers a matter of local concern, not requiring any uniform federal standard. Conversely, Justice Holmes rejected allowing a state the ability to tax petroleum produced in two different states and gathered together and shipped through an interstate pipeline.[33] Holmes reasoned that because no party had title to any specific oil and its destination (in state or out of state) is unknown, it was beyond the state's power. According to Holmes, the "transmission of this stream of oil was interstate commerce from the beginning of the flow," and, consequently, the tax was invalid. Holmes' somewhat cryptic opinion

---

[29] 221 U.S. 229 (1911). The statute purportedly was designed to arrest the large waste of gas occurring at the time; subsequent statutes made gas pipelines common carriers. *See* J. STANLEY CLARK, THE OIL CENTURY 160–61 (Univ. of Okla. Press 1958).

[30] Kan. Nat. Gas Co., 221 U.S. at 255. *See also* Kan. Nat. Gas Co. v. Haskell, 172 F. 545, 572 (E.D. Okla. 1909).

[31] Pub. Utils. Comm'n Kan. v. Landon, 249 U.S. 236, 240, *vacated*, 249 U.S. 590 (1919). *See also* W. Oil Ref. Co. v. Lipscomb, 244 U.S. 346 (1917) (with shipment of oil not intended for state, mere stoppage did not break interstate character).

[32] 252 U.S. 23, 31 (1920).

[33] Eureka Pipe Line Co. v. Hallanan, 257 U.S. 265, 272 (1921); U.S. Fuel Gas Co. v. Hallanan, 257 U.S. 277, 281 (1921).

and conception of the market ultimately would become problematic if applied to electric energy. It also would become problematic for Holmes, who was willing to afford considerable leeway to states when protecting resources for in-state residents.

This became evident two years later when the Supreme Court resolved a challenge by Pennsylvania and Ohio against West Virginia.[34] West Virginia, at the time, was the largest producer of natural gas and initially allowed foreign and domestic corporations to operate (and even exercise eminent-domain authority) within its borders and ship gas through pipelines to markets in Pennsylvania and Ohio. As those markets developed, consumers grew dependent on West Virginia's gas. Indeed, the Court emphasized gas's importance for domestic consumption for schools and other users; the "health, comfort, and welfare" of the citizens seemed to be at risk. But, as demand began exceeding supply, not all states could enjoy the resource. In 1919, West Virginia addressed the risk by passing a statute requiring "retention within the state of whatever gas may be required to meet the local needs for all purposes" – affording West Virginia citizens a preferential right to the perceived dwindling gas supply. The neighboring states sued immediately, and while the Court accepted the case and recognized its national importance, it observed that precedent favored Ohio and Pennsylvania. Natural gas was an article of commerce, and West Virginia "serious[ly] interfere[d]" with its transmission in interstate commerce. The Court's earlier decisions in *West v. Kansas Natural Gas* and *Landon* made this clear.

Oddly, Justice Holmes, joined by Justice Brandeis, would have upheld the statute. They reasoned that the act applied before the gas began moving in interstate commerce. Holmes, in short, saw "nothing in the commerce clause to prevent a State from giving a preference to its inhabitants in the enjoyment of its natural advantages."[35] The case was closely divided and possibly quickly decided to avoid losing Justice Day's vote (Day was about to retire).[36] According to Brandeis, it also was poorly argued and garnered little interest from the bar – even though it was of national significance.[37] Justice Van Devanter, moreover, authored the majority opinion, and as one of the Court's more conservative justices, he wrote few opinions and seemingly ought to have favored state authority. That Justice Day joined his opinion effectively affirming the need for federal involvement is even more interesting, considering that Justice Day wrote for a majority of the Court in *Hammer* v. *Dagenhart*, where the Court held that Congress could not prohibit articles manufactured with the aid of child labor and destined for an interstate market. According to Day, "the mere fact that they were intended for interstate commerce transportation does not make their production subject to federal control under the commerce clause."[38]

---

[34] Pennsylvania v. West Virginia, 262 U.S. 553 (1923).   [35] *Ibid.* at 600–2.

[36] Alpheus T. Mason, William Howard Taft: Chief Justice 224 (Oldbourne 1964).

[37] *Letter from Louis Brandeis to Felix Frankfurter* (Nov. 20, 1923), *in* 5 Letters of Louis D. Brandeis 104–5 (State Univ. of New York Press, Melvin I. Urofsky & David W. Levy eds., 1978).

[38] 247 U.S. 251, 271–72 (1918). And while Day did not object to Congress's authority to regulate wages for interstate railway employees, he objected to its regulation as a violation of due process. *See* Wilson v. New, 243 U.S. 332, 365–66 (1917) (Day, J., dissenting).

But Holmes' dissent aside, by the mid-1920s the law seemed clear – even if somewhat confusingly and inappropriately constructed: states could not interfere with the interstate shipment of natural gas; rather, they could only regulate local sales. In *Missouri ex rel. Barrett* v. *Kansas Natural Gas Co.*, therefore, the Court explained how retail sales to consumers were local – as if the interstate article had come to rest in the state and could be regulated, but until then the wholesale transactions in interstate commerce were of a national character.[39] For the emerging interstate gas market, while this made state regulation difficult, it was seemingly workable because the Court tolerated the authority of a state commission to force a company to continue servicing a local community from gas produced in the state even though the gas was comingled with gas transported from another state in interstate pipelines and sold both to local consumers and to a local distribution company.[40] But, as the Supreme Court recently observed, these cases precluded a host exporting state from regulating the sale of gas to an out-of-state local distributor for resale, eventually prompting the passage of the Natural Gas Act in 1938.[41]

THE INTERSTATE GRID AND A RATE INCREASE?

A notorious northeastern electric utility precipitously forced the Supreme Court to apply this unsettled constitutional narrative to state electric utility regulation. When the Court decided *Attleboro*, electricity had become the foundation for the new consumer economy. By the early 1920s, the FPC reported how there already were over "102 central-station corporations or public agencies generating in excess of a hundred million kilowatt hours each of electric energy."[42] This electricity transformed cities through the formation of city-dominated factories, lighting, and electric trolleys, among other things. It also generally helped lift the country out of its pre–World War I depression.[43] The electric utility industry, though, particularly in the Northeast, grappled with how to interconnect transmission systems, whether and how states could control their own natural water resources for waterpower development, and whether state public utility commissions could effectively regulate an expanding grid. The FPC commented on the need for a "settled public policy of uniform application" for the industry, not just with hydroelectric power generation, and that such a policy should embrace "harmonious action between the Nation and the States and between State and State."[44] This translated into preventing states from erecting barriers to the "interchange of electricity." And that the FPC favored new legislation became evident when it added how "[l]egislation which interferes with

---

[39]   265 U.S. 298, 309 (1924).   [40]   People's Nat. Gas Co. v. Pub. Serv. Comm'n, 270 U.S. 550 (1926).
[41]   Oneok, Inc. v. Learjet, Inc., 135 S. Ct. 1591 (2015).
[42]   1924 FED. POWER COMM'N FOURTH ANN. REP. 14.
[43]   JEFFRY A. FRIEDEN, GLOBAL CAPITALISM: ITS FALL AND RISE IN THE TWENTIETH CENTURY 143–47, 157–59 (W.W. Norton & Co. 2006). *See also* NYE, *supra* note 6, at 157–85.
[44]   1923 FED. POWER COMM'N THIRD ANN. REP. 8 (1923).

the programs should be repealed or modified; necessary affirmative legislation should be had."[45]

The need for an interconnected system seemed particularly acute in the Northeast, generating talks about developing a *superpower*. When World War I ended, railroad bottlenecks, coal strikes, capital markets, and the 1920 FWPA and other influences prompted electric utilities to explore new arrangements for interconnecting grids – or regional systems.[46] One prominent idea was to establish a supergrid in the Northeast.[47] The region between New England and the nation's capital explored developing a "superpower" utility – an interconnected "regional power system with which to generate, transmit and distribute electrical energy to the railroads and industries within" its territory.[48] Utilities at the time appreciated the need to cooperate in interconnecting and delivering energy in an efficient manner.[49] With congressional money, William S. Murray completed an analysis in 1920 about the merits of a new superpower system. Christopher Jones describes how, along with Murray's report, Gifford Pinchot touted "Giant Power's" attributes – a focus on providing electric energy to displace difficult human labor.[50]

Herbert Hoover weighed in, too, delivering a speech to the National Electric Light Convention in April 1922 urging the merits of a coordinated approach toward power supply – but the idea languished because the governors of New York and Pennsylvania were more concerned about public rather than private ownership of power generation. Hoover, as a participant in the development of the Colorado River Company, a chairman of the Superpower Committee, and having overseen 10 public utility commissions, again encouraged, in 1923, that utilities cooperatively develop "uniform principles and policies for 'coordinated State regulation.'"[51] He

---

[45] *Ibid.* at 9–10.   [46] SEAVOY, *supra* note 3, at 268, 274.

[47] KENDRICK A. CLEMENTS, THE LIFE OF HERBERT HOOVER: IMPERFECT VISIONARY, 1918–1928 257 (Palgrave 2010).

[48] W.S. Murray, *Superpower Investigation between Boston and Washington*, 77 ELECTRICAL WORLD 27 (Jan. 1, 1921); W.S. MURRAY ET AL., A SUPERPOWER SYSTEM FOR THE REGION BETWEEN BOSTON AND WASHINGTON (U.S. Geological Survey 1921) [hereinafter MURRAY ET AL.]. Murray supervised the Department of the Interior's report on the superpower system. *See* Felix Frankfurter & James M. Landis, *The Compact Clause of the Constitution: A Study in Interstate Adjustments*, 34 YALE L. J. 685, 709 n.98 (1925).

[49] "In these days of team play among public utilities the subject of interconnection rises to large importance ... as a policy to be followed whenever feasible." *Effective Interconnection Requires Team Play*, 77 ELECTRICAL WORLD 186 (Jan. 15, 1921); *see also* A.T. Throop, *Improvement of Interconnection by Liberal Co-operation*, 77 ELECTRICAL WORLD 202 (Jan. 15, 1921). Engineering, however, was not considered a barrier for a superpower but rather – along with financial considerations – it was the need to overcome some state corporation laws by establishing a federally chartered company that would be supervised by state utility commissions. *See Second General and Executive Session: Samuel Insull and James A. Perry Make Notable Addresses – Superpower Survey Discussed – Reports of Rate Research and Lamp Committees*, 77 ELECTRICAL WORLD 1287 (June 4, 1921).

[50] CHRISTOPHER F. JONES, ROUTES OF POWER: ENERGY AND MODERN AMERICA 206–09 (Harvard Univ. Press 2014).

[51] CLEMENTS, *supra* note 47, at 257; JUDSON KING, THE CONSERVATION FIGHT: FROM THEODORE ROOSEVELT TO THE TENNESSEE VALLEY AUTHORITY 142, 167 (Public Aff. Press 1959).

repeated this again a few years later, adding that states enjoyed sufficient regulatory ability to oversee the industry.[52]

Such coordinated, interconnected efforts became technologically more feasible with the advent of high-power 220-kV transmission lines.[53] The FPC that same year noted how "[t]here has been much discussion in recent years of the subject of 'superpower.'" The FPC defined a superpower as "existing generating stations ... electrically interconnected to a greater degree than now prevails and that, whether as additions to existing facilities or as substitutes for what has become obsolete or inadequate, new stations when built shall be of large size and high efficiency."[54] Indeed, the FPC observed how a considerable portion of the Pacific already had been interconnected with the exception of a 25-mile gap, that the Southeast too had been interconnected, and that the features of the Northeast to Mid-Atlantic regions were appropriate for a similar endeavor. Proponents, however, acknowledged unresolved legal issues, such as whether state-created charters or a federal charter would be necessary.[55]

The superpower concept garnered sufficient attention that a prominent 1925 article by soon to be Justice Felix Frankfurter and James Landis included a lengthy discussion about the role of compacts for future energy development.[56] The article explored the superpower dialogue and encouraged putting the electric utility industry under some federal control analogous to the Interstate Commerce Commission. The initial question posed was not whether states could act (or enter interstate compacts), but rather whether states enjoyed exclusive authority to regulate the industry. While rejecting any suggestion that Congress could not act, they instead proposed an "interstate arrangement" and eloquently added how the Commerce Clause had become problematic.[57]

UTILITY COMMISSION CHANGES A CONTRACTUAL RATE

The failure to develop a uniform system or superpower permitted one of the largest loads in the Northeast, served by the Narragansett Electric Light Company (Narragansett) and aided by the Rhode Island Public Utility Commission (RI PUC), to test how far a state utility commission might favor local residents over out-of-state electric needs. At the time, Providence was the second largest load center in New England, with about 58 percent of the load of Boston, and Narragansett was one of the largest utilities, chartered by Rhode Island in 1884 and originally engaging in

---

[52]   JOHN F. WASIK, THE MERCHANT OF POWER: SAM INSULL, THOMAS EDISON, AND THE CREATION OF THE MODERN METROPOLIS 149–50 (Palgrave 2006).
[53]   *Power Transmission at 220,000 Volts*, 77 ELECTRIC WORLD 74 (Jan. 8, 1921); *see also* Clinton Jones, *Building First 220,000-Volt Transformers*, 77 ELECTRICAL WORLD 301 (Feb. 5, 1921).
[54]   1923 FED. POWER COMM'N THIRD ANN. REP. 5–6.
[55]   *Murray Declares Superpower System Must Have Adequate Return*, 77 ELECTRICAL WORLD 220 (Jan. 22, 1921).
[56]   Frankfurter & Landis, *supra* note 48, at 708–18.   [57]   *Ibid.* at 714–19.

business solely within the state.[58] With Marsden Perry at its helm, Narragansett grew as a multifaceted company controlling a large portion of the state's electric lighting, gas lighting, water service, and electric streetcar service. With political assistance, it secured the necessary long-term exclusive (monopoly) franchise to provide service. The streetcar service secured a "'perpetual' franchise . . . to replace the old-twenty-to-twenty-five year franchises," and with power being supplied from the electric company, it seemingly had an assured market.[59] By controlling all these entities, Perry became "the state's utility king."[60] Although Perry was long gone, the company by the 1920s was undoubtedly well known and remained mercurial as it considered whether to join the New England power system.[61] After all, it was under Perry's leadership that, in 1902, the nation witnessed one of its more prominent strikes – with Perry refusing to abide by the newly passed 10-hour work law.[62] And it was under Perry and others (including Rhode Island's powerful Senator Nelson W. Aldrich) that muckraker Lincoln Steffens focused national attention on the holding company's control over the state's utility system: writing for _McClure's Magazine_ in 1905, Steffens exposed how the electric utility and street railway curried political favoritism and insulation.[63]

Thus it is not surprising that the RI PUC obliged when Narragansett sought a rate increase affecting its only out-of-state customer. It is quite exceptional, however, that prevailing constitutional dogma on the Commerce Clause would envelop the dispute. The case, after all, involved the evolving authority of a public utility commission to alter a contractual rate when it determines that the rate has become problematic. It was a "minor" quibble, and "no one expected that it would result in an important ruling."[64] Attleboro Steam and Electric Co. (Attleboro), a Massachusetts-based utility, had contracted in 1917 with Narragansett (with RI PUC approval) to purchase electricity for twenty years at a fixed rate with a transfer of "ownership" at the state line. Seekonk Co., as an agent for Attleboro, would transmit the electricity from the Massachusetts state line to Attleboro's lines. Narragansett delivered electricity to the state line between the town of Seekonk, Massachusetts, and the town of East Providence, Rhode Island, and it was metered by Attleboro in Massachusetts.[65]

58 MURRAY ET AL., _supra_ note 48, at 32.
59 WILLIAM G. MCLOUGHLIN, RHODE ISLAND: A HISTORY 177–79 (W.W. Norton & Co. 1986). _See also Narragansett Co. Would Acquire United Railway_, HARTFORD COURANT, Sept. 10, 1926, at 19.
60 SCOTT MOLLY, TROLLEY WARS 67 (Univ. of New Hampshire Press 1996).
61 _Narragansett Not in Power Merger_, CHRISTIAN SCI. MONITOR, Jan. 19, 1926, at 4B. _See also R.I. Utility Merger Is Still under Discussion_, HARTFORD COURANT, Aug. 14, 1926, at 5 ("Evidently the great majority of the stockholders desire the Narragansett Electric Lighting Company to continue as an independent organization, free from outside control.").
62 MOLLY, _supra_ note 60, at 131–51.
63 Lincoln Steffens, _Rhode Island: A State for Sale_, 24 MCCLURE'S MAG. 337 (1905).
64 _Federal Control of Power Forecast_, NEW YORK TIMES, Jan. 16, 1927, at E13.
65 Transcript of Record at 258, Pub. Utils. Comm'n v. Attleboro Steam & Elec. Co., 273 U.S. 83 (1927) (No. 217).

World War I changed the economics of the Narragansett/Attleboro contract. The rates for electricity being sold to Attleboro became uneconomical and lower than Narragansett's rates for Rhode Island customers.[66] Indeed, "[b]y 1923 Rhode Island was a bitterly divided state, socially, economically, and politically," with a considerable portion of its dominant textile industry unable to compete with the South's industry.[67] Narragansett understandably requested that the RI PUC approve a new rate schedule. Created in 1912, the RI PUC enjoyed the typical authority to establish just and reasonable rates if it determined that a rate was unjust, unreasonable, insufficient, or unjustly discriminatory or preferential. While Attleboro protested, it did not otherwise present information and subsequently "refused to pay the new rate," filing a lawsuit to enjoin the application of the new rate.[68] Attleboro warned that it lacked sufficient access to electric generation, and absent energy from Narragansett, "the City of Attleboro would be deprived of electrical energy and power to . . . incalculable damage" to itself and the city's residents. This, according to Attleboro, was particularly unfair because Narragansett had convinced Attleboro to enter the contract rather than to construct its own additional generation.[69] Attleboro's need for generation had increased and, according to news reports, would have cost the company $630,000 to build. It became efficient, therefore, to connect with Narragansett's system and build a new 12-mile transmission line (operated by the Seekonk Electric Company) for transmitting the power.[70] Narragansett lacked authority to construct facilities in Massachusetts, and its contract with Attleboro addressed the allocation of costs and agreement with Seekonk.[71] At the hearing, Attleboro's counsel suggested that Narragansett's rate increase was to recover some of Narragansett's costs for building that line.

After a district court enjoined the RI PUC's action, generally on procedural grounds, Attleboro's counsel argued that its contract with Narragansett could not, in effect, be abrogated.[72] Indeed, Narragansett lamented how Attleboro sought to deploy its contract price as a shield rather than accept negotiating a modified rate, prompting the dispute.[73] The *Boston Globe* reported how, apparently, Narragansett offered to alter the rate to increase the annual cost by only $20,000, which met with "indignation."[74] And then as sort of a kicker, Attleboro added that the RI PUC lacked

[66] Transcript of Record at 59, 111, 120–21, Pub. Utils. Comm'n v. Attleboro Steam & Elec. Co., 273 U.S. 83 (1927) (No. 217).

[67] McLoughlin, *supra* note 59, at 191.

[68] Petition for Writ of Certiorari at 3, *Attleboro*, 273 U.S. 83 (No. 217).

[69] Attleboro Steam & Elec. Co. v. Narragansett Elec. Lighting Co., 295 F. 895, 896 (D.R.I. 1924); Transcript of Record at 117, 189–90, *Attleboro*, 273 U.S. 83 (No. 217).

[70] *Typical Benefits from Plant Interconnection*, 71 Electrical World 449 (Mar. 2, 1918).

[71] Transcript of Record at 253, *Attleboro*, 273 U.S. 83 (No. 217).

[72] *Narragansett*, 295 F. at 895. A report about the case noted that the PUC even permitted the rate to go into effect immediately, "without the statutory notice of thirty days." *See Increase in Contract Rate between Companies Authorized*, 77 Electrical World 1184 (May 21, 1921).

[73] Transcript of Record at 195–98, 213 *Attleboro*, 273 U.S. 83 (No. 217).

[74] *Rate Case Is Won by Attleboro Firm*, Bos. Globe, Jan. 4, 1927, at 14.

jurisdiction because the contract involved interstate commerce and that the courts would need to decide the matter – intimating that it was not clear whether the RI PUC could entertain the issue.[75] Attleboro presumably invoked the Commerce Clause as a mechanism for avoiding a fair consideration of its rate dispute with Narragansett – which otherwise would be a state rather than federal issue, unless it could argue that the abrogation of the contract violated the Constitution.

The RI PUC nevertheless proceeded and engaged in a more robust proceeding, concluding that Narragansett was likely to have a net loss of about $1.5 million over the life of the contract. Yet Attleboro's counsel argued that Narragansett was trying to shift its new capital costs onto Attleboro, because Narragansett's only other large (indeed largest) customer was New England Power Company and it could not determine how much fixed costs it could impose on that company. Narragansett's proposal would force Attleboro to pay about an additional $50,000 annually.[76] The RI PUC's new rate ostensibly still afforded Attleboro a reliable source of electricity at a cost below Attleboro's own cost of operation. Attleboro objected and filed a challenge before the Rhode Island Supreme Court, attacking the order as well as the RI PUC act itself, claiming that it deprived the company of its property without due process, denied it equal protection of the laws, impaired its contractual relationship, and impermissibly "interfer[ed] with interstate commerce."[77] The Rhode Island Supreme Court avoided the principal issue of whether or when it could alter a contractually established rate, opting instead to address the latter argument and finding the principles of *Missouri v. Kansas Natural Gas Co.* dispositive – concluding that the state's action amounted to an impermissible "direct" burden on interstate commerce regardless of purpose. And from that decision, the Rhode Island attorney general initiated the US Supreme Court's review.

That the case provoked a legitimate Commerce Clause issue seemed peculiar under the Supreme Court's precedent. Almost all state jurisdictions might be usurped if, for example, states were precluded completely from regulating goods produced in their state. Some of those goods might be destined for interstate markets, or perhaps not. Little suggested that the Commerce Clause would block a state from regulating products that eventually might travel in interstate commerce.[78] Also, the Court previously had placed manufacturing within the states' realm and outside the Commerce Clause.[79] It would be cumbersome to explore on a case-by-case basis the likely movement of products. Assuming that theoretical lines could be erected for distinguishing between goods likely to remain in the state and

[75] Transcript of Record at 36–37, 151, *Attleboro*, 273 U.S. 83 (No. 217).   [76] *Ibid.* at 189.
[77] Petition for Writ of Certiorari at 8, *Attleboro*, 273 U.S. 83 (No. 217).
[78] Heisler v. Thomas Colliery Co., 260 U.S. 245, 259 (1922); Coe v. Town of Errol, 116 U.S. 517, 525–29 (1886).
[79] United States v. E.C. Knight Co., 156 U.S. 1 (1895).

those destined for interstate markets, producers naturally might favor escaping regulation by tilting toward out-of-state sales – effectively discriminating against intrastate markets. This occurred many decades later once the Court oddly gave the FPC rather than states jurisdiction over natural gas production and gathering for gas intended for interstate markets, discussed in Chapter 5. The Court by this time also had permitted states and the federal government to share spheres of jurisdiction – albeit subject to Congress's paramount power.

States, therefore, enjoyed a measure of regulatory latitude over in-state activities. They could exercise their police power to regulate businesses to protect the public health and welfare.[80] In one instance, the Supreme Court allowed Florida to regulate the sale of citrus fruits destined for interstate commerce.[81] Absent an ability for states to regulate the flow of goods into what had fast become a national consumer-oriented market, consumers (at least prior to the FTC and passage of robust food and drug laws) could be deceived or, worse, defrauded. The Court consequently allowed Indiana to regulate the sale of International Stock Food – an allegedly medicinal drug for domestic animals – into the interstate market.[82] And for natural resources, including potentially wildlife, water, oil, natural gas, coal, and possibly hydroelectric power, as discussed earlier, the Court already afforded states greater latitude in their regulation, even allowing in some circumstances favoring in-state over out-of-state interests.

But dormant Commerce Clause principles throughout the pre–New Deal period were fluid, making application to a specific situation – particularly to the new electric utility industry – somewhat troubling. The Court's traditional formulas would soon thereafter be abandoned as unworkable in a consumer society ever expanding and becoming interconnected. Until then, the animating principle harkened back to the mid–nineteenth century, when the Court tried to distinguish between whether an activity was local or national in character.[83] The Court also had employed other formulaic tests, such as whether an activity directly or substantially burdened interstate commerce or only indirectly or incidentally burdened interstate commerce. And the judiciary, too, began taking a keen interest in determining whether the state or local entity was targeting and therefore discriminating against interstate commerce – an inquiry that soon would become the touchstone for most dormant Commerce Clause analyses.

---

[80] For opinions concluding both ways, see Or.-Wash. R.R. & Navigation Co. v. Washington, 270 U.S. 87, 96 (1926) (alfalfa hay); Hebe Co. v. Shaw, 248 U.S. 297 (1919) (condensed milk); Amour & Co. v. North Dakota, 240 U.S. 510 (1916) (lard); Hutchinson Ice Cream Co. v. Iowa, 242 U.S. 153 (1916); Reid v. Colorado, 187 U.S. 137 (1902) (infectious cattle); Barbier v. Connolly, 113 U.S. 27 (1884) (laundries); Patapsco Guano Co. v. Bd. of Agric., 171 U.S. 345, 354 (1898) (fertilizer inspection); Schollenberger v. Pennsylvania, 171 U.S. 1, 14 (1898) (imported oleomargarine); Plumley v. Massachusetts, 155 U.S. 461 (1894) (colored margarine).

[81] Sligh v. Kirkwood, 237 U.S. 52 (1915).   [82] Savage v. Jones, 225 U.S. 501 (1912).

[83] Cooley v. Board of Wardens 53 U.S. (12 How.) 299 (1851).

WHOSE CASE CONTROLS?

The 1924 *Missouri v. Kansas Natural Gas Co.* opinion reflected a narrow band of the Supreme Court's tortured effort to bring some coherence to Commerce Clause jurisprudence. The *Attleboro* litigants argued over the narrow question of *Kansas Natural Gas Co.*'s application, effectively championing the position expressed by the FPC. The FPC, after all, had somewhat myopically opined in 1925 that the *Kansas Natural Gas Co.* decision naturally extended to electric energy supplied in interstate commerce, leaving the only outstanding question of whether it would apply to all energy sold across state lines or only that sold at wholesale rather than directly to consumers. According to the FPC, most energy sales fell within the first category.[84] While the FPC recognized several instances of interstate transmission, it treated the interstate market as small and unlikely to grow too much; of course, this did not dissuade the FPC from encouraging resolution of who ought to regulate interstate sales. Ironically, when the FPC rejected the notion of interstate compacts, such as proposed by Frankfurter and Landis, it raised the specter of too many interstate transactions. Possibly fearful of losing influence, it challenged the idea of a compact for the superpower – commenting how it "would, in effect, have merely created for such purpose another Federal Government to serve in place of the one we now have."[85] Even so, the FPC recommended distinguishing between wholesale sales and sales directly to consumers, believing that this would "simplify the problem of regulation." It explained, in cavalier fashion and with questionable assumptions even at the time, how few wholesale sales would occur, and even when they did, they would only prompt federal involvement if the states could not resolve the matter. "Any attempt to extend Federal regulation to control over rates and services to consumers," it added, "would be both unnecessary and unwise."[86]

Attleboro's dormant Commerce Clause argument was quite simple. Because the transaction involved interstate commerce, it was outside state control unless "there is anything to take the case out of the general rule that rates for interstate service rendered by a public utility cannot be fixed by state action." And *Kansas Natural Gas Co.*, it argued, was controlling. Attleboro briefly reviewed telegraph, motor carrier, and other cases but without any appreciation for the nuances of those cases or the Court's changing approach toward the Commerce Clause.[87] Overall, the analysis rested on a simple tautology: if the activity was in interstate commerce, it was an impermissible regulation of interstate commerce, unless it was a valid exercise of a state's police power – which would only occur if it was designed to achieve a traditional police power purpose rather than a regulation of interstate commerce.

---

[84]   1926 FED. POWER COMM'N SIXTH ANN. REP. at 8–9.
[85]   1925 FED. POWER COMM'N FIFTH ANN. REP. 8–10.
[86]   1926 FED. POWER COMM'N SIXTH ANN. REP. 8–9.
[87]   Brief for the Respondent at 10–19, Pub. Utils. Comm'n v. Attleboro Steam & Elec. Co., 273 U.S. 83 (1927) (No. 217).

Rhode Island countered by describing how dormant Commerce Clause cases distinguished between direct and indirect interference with commerce, seeking to persuade the Court that public utility rate regulation fit within the latter. It treated gas and electric energy regulation similarly and emphasized how the order did not discriminate against either Attleboro or interstate commerce. According to the RI PUC, the case involved a classic example of a state regulating a matter of local concern that only indirectly affected commerce because one of Narragansett's customers happened to engage in interstate commerce. Rhode Island argued against the application of *Kansas Natural Gas Co.* That case, it asserted, involved an effort by the receiving state (which in this case was Massachusetts) to keep the price of wholesale gas lower than it had been, which was not the case here. But when purportedly articulating a line beyond which state jurisdiction could not extend, Rhode Island's brief confusingly stated that the jurisdictional line should be drawn in this case "even though prohibiting it in cases similar to the *Missouri* [*Kansas Natural Gas Co.*] case." The brief then made two Commerce Clause points: first, Narragansett was a state-franchised company, and second, the rate was for a "commodity produced within the State, as distinguished from a rate for transportation."[88]

THE COURT DECIDES

Responding to these arguments and affirming the Rhode Island Supreme Court, Justice Sanford's majority opinion avoids any serious analytical treatment of the Court's evolving struggles with the Commerce Clause. According to Sanford, either *Kansas Natural Gas Co.* or *Pennsylvania Gas Co.* controlled the outcome. He held that *Kansas Natural Gas Co.* did. With a simple ipso facto statement, he announced that the RI PUC's order establishing a new rate impermissibly directly burdened interstate commerce. With an implicit nod toward the questionable original package doctrine, he added: "[t]he forwarding state obviously has no more authority than the receiving state to place a direct burden upon interstate commerce." From there he proceeded perfunctorily to justify his conclusion.

First, he intimated that if Rhode Island could establish rates for sales in interstate commerce, then quite possibly it could discriminate in favor of local residents. The problem with this analysis is that while the RI PUC hearing explored Attleboro's claim of discrimination in favor of New England Power, the possibility of discrimination was neither the finding of the RI PUC nor of the Rhode Island Supreme Court, and as such, Sanford's suggestion could only serve as an abstraction, not a factual assessment. Of course, the IR PUC–approved "rate" itself was not a rate for interstate sales; it was a rate effectively altering Attleboro's contractual rate – for electricity that simply would be used in another state. It did not, however, on its face target interstate commerce. And while undoubtedly concern about possible

[88] Brief for Petitioners at 19–30, *Attleboro* (No. 217).

discrimination influenced his decision, the posture of the case made it difficult for Sanford to rely on precedent prohibiting states from discriminating against interstate commerce – a holding that might have been less exceptional. How, therefore, the approved rate "directly burdened" interstate commerce seems unclear. It is equally hard to assess how much it "burdened" commerce because Attleboro continued to receive service and had been paying the new rate since the IR PUC's order. In addition, the new rate cost Attleboro $50,000 annually and little suggested how it affected Attleboro or its customers.

Second, Sanford described the "interstate business" of the two companies "as essentially national in character" rather than "local to either state," and as such, neither the exporting nor importing state could regulate the rates – instead, it would be a matter "vested in Congress." His attempt to distinguish the two primary cases, *Pennsylvania Gas Co.* and *Kansas Natural Gas Co.*, suggests that he believed that the "national character" of the business operated as the critical factor. Again, though, he offered a simple conclusion. What brings it within the domain of cases employing the local/national rationale is missing. The country already had a national market-place for most goods and services. Distinguishing between what requires uniformity in treatment and what does not could not be governed simply by a product's move-ment in commerce. Surely, rates for the sale of electricity would not need uniform treatment (nor could it be possible) throughout the nation. But this is what Sanford's opinion unfortunately suggested. Perhaps, then, what he meant was that "jurisdic-tion" over the sale and delivery of electricity in interstate commerce constituted a matter of national not local interest. This would mean that it was not the order of the RI PUC changing the contractual rate for the sale but rather his belief that Attleboro's business of purchasing and transporting electricity in the interstate market through an interconnected system was beyond state interference, warranting national attention. Yet little about the Supreme Court's precedent suggested that a potentially concurrent exercise of state police power could be prohibited when it would be better if regulated by the national government. Section 20 of the FWPA expressly allowed state regulation of rates for licensees selling energy in interstate commerce, with the FPC given jurisdiction to address complaints in the absence of sufficient state authority. What appears conspicuous, therefore, is that the presum-ably conservative Sanford – a Chief Justice Taft recruit having joined the Court only four years earlier – avoided any factual inquiry or confronting the Court's consider-able jurisprudence, and instead rendered a decision seemingly designed to trigger federal legislation.

Finally, Sanford dubiously suggested the *Kansas Natural Gas Co.* "precedent" was so dispositive to warrant little discussion. Relying almost exclusively on *Kansas Natural Gas Co.*, though, had three defects. First, Justice Sutherland's short opinion in *Kansas Natural Gas Co.* treated all too cavalierly state rate regulation for sales of gas into the interstate market as beyond the traditional local police power of states, such as with various food or agricultural inspection or quarantine laws. One scholar suggests that Sutherland feared the "whims of turbulent democratic majorities controlled by political factions."[89] While accepting perceived legitimate police power measures, Sutherland, a conservative justice, protected economic freedom if he believed a state had acted inappropriately. Illegitimate state behavior necessarily surfaced when states sought to discriminate against or impose a burden on those engaged in interstate commerce. The style of his opinion mirrored and relied on nineteenth-century opinions that assumed two spheres of jurisdiction, either federal for interstate commerce or state for a police power. Only a few years after *Attleboro*, for instance, Sutherland would ignore *Attleboro* and uphold an Idaho tax on Utah Power & Light (UP&L) even though UP&L's energy was intended for an interstate market. The tax, he reasoned, was imposed on electric generation rather than on transmission.[90] Indeed, in his *Kansas Natural Gas Co.* opinion, Sutherland urged the need for "equality of opportunity and treatment among the various communities and States concerned."[91] That was not, however, the posture of *Attleboro*.

Also, Justice Sutherland's *Kansas Natural Gas Co.* opinion implicitly accepted the moribund original package doctrine, establishing a jurisdictional divide between state and federal authority once a product ceased its movement in interstate commerce. The original package doctrine, announced by Chief Justice Marshall, insulated foreign imports from state taxation until they were removed from their "original package."[92] It had been applied sporadically, possibly inconsistently, as well to interstate rather than foreign commerce. New York, for instance, could prohibit the sale of lawfully obtained foreign game because it might be confused with local game during periods when the state prohibited hunting local game.[93] Sutherland applied the doctrine when explaining how sales to consumers were local – as if an interstate article had come to rest in the state and could be regulated. Until then, wholesale transactions in interstate commerce were of a national character. Sutherland, therefore, dismissed contrary natural gas cases because he viewed them as involving local distribution of gas that had ceased its character of being in interstate commerce.

The original package doctrine nevertheless had lost its allure by 1927 and only served as at most an illustrative tool. The doctrine as a jurisdictional divide seemed doomed because state or local efforts to regulate traditional activities, now routinely part of interstate commerce and the burgeoning consumer economy, would – if applied – otherwise halt most state police power measures. A good example involved the movie industry. In the 1920s, the movie industry challenged as violating the original package doctrine the ability of states to regulate the showing of films. The US District Court for the District of Connecticut issued an impassioned

[89] Samuel R. Olken, *Justice George Sutherland and Economic Liberty: Constitutional Conservatism and the Problem of Factions*, 6 WM. & MARY BILL RTS. J. 1, 6 (1997).
[90] Utah Power & Light Co. v. Pfost, 286 U.S. 165, 181–82 (1932).
[91] Missouri *ex rel.* Barrett v. Kan. Nat. Gas Co., 265 U.S. 298, 309–10 (1924).
[92] Brown v. Maryland, 25 U.S. (12 Wheat.) 419 (1827).
[93] New York *ex rel.* Silz v. Hesterberg, 211 U.S. 31 (1908).

opinion about the authority of states under their police power to oversee the industry. Films at the time, the court opined, were created only in New York and California, and therefore the industry – with the exception possibly of those two states – was undoubtedly engaged in interstate commerce. Addressing the application of the original package doctrine, the court explained that the Supreme Court had made it clear that the "analogy between imports and articles in original packages in interstate commerce in respect to immunity from taxation fails."[94]

This description by the District Court may have overstated the clarity of the Supreme Court's opinions. Undoubtedly the Supreme Court no longer accepted the original package doctrine as a litmus test. In *Red 'C' Oil Manufacturing Co.* v. *Board of Agriculture*, it allowed North Carolina to inspect and therefore regulate imported kerosene and other oils for sale in the state. The Supreme Court accepted the lower court's judgment that North Carolina's charge was similar to that of other states and therefore implicitly not discriminatory.[95] In *Texas* v. *Brown*, a unanimous Court discussed the original package doctrine only when deciding when a state may impose a fee in excess of the cost of inspection and effectively discriminate against interstate commerce.[96] The case involved Georgia's inspection (and tax) program for petroleum and petroleum products brought into the state and then distributed throughout the state to local agencies or distribution stations. The lower court had enjoined the program for products being sold or intending to be sold in their original package. However, it upheld the program for the products being sold after leaving their original package. Justice Pitney, who would depart the Court shortly before *Attleboro*, relied on two earlier decisions to conclude that the doctrine no longer applied – the question instead was whether a state tax discriminates against interstate commerce.

The doctrine's force seemingly became settled with *Sonneborn Bros.* v. *Cureton*.[97] In an account described by Alexander Bickel, a majority of Justices in *Sonneborn Bros.* apparently were inclined to apply the original package doctrine, provoking a drafted dissent by Justice Brandeis rejecting its application and arguing that the determinative factor is whether the measure discriminates against interstate commerce.[98] His dissent became unnecessary, however, once Chief Justice Taft

---

[94] Fox Film Corp. v. Trumbull, 7 F.2d 715, 722 (D. Conn. 1925), *appeal dismissed*, 269 U.S. 597 (1925).
[95] 222 U.S. 380, 393 (1912).   [96]   258 U.S. 466, 475–76 (1922).   [97]   262 U.S. 506 (1923).
[98] *See* ALEXANDER M. BICKEL, THE UNPUBLISHED OPINIONS OF MR. JUSTICE BRANDEIS 100–18 (Belknap Press 1957). Brandeis apparently was skeptical about Justice Pitney. In *Bowman*, 256 U.S. at 642, Pitney had employed the doctrine. Yet, in *Wagner v. City of Covington*, 251 U.S. 95 (1919), Pitney upheld a local license fee imposed on peddlers of goods received from out of the state. Even Justice Holmes, although unnecessary to his opinion, had earlier discussed the doctrine as if it had force. *See* Hebe Co. v. Shaw, 248 U.S. 297, 304 (1919). *See also* Armour & Co. v. North Dakota, 240 U.S. 510, 517 (1916) (rejecting Commerce Clause challenge by noting a retail sale no longer in original package); F. May & Co. v. New Orleans, 178 U.S. 496, 503 (1900) (Justice Harlan questioning concept in case involving cigarette sales). Justice Cardozo would later invoke the doctrine for illustrative purposes in *Baldwin v. G.A.F. Seelig, Inc.*, 294 U.S. 511, 526–27 (1935). *See also* Whitfield v. Ohio, 297 U.S. 431, 439–40 (1936); James Clark Distilling Co. v. W. Md. Ry. Co., 242 U.S. 311, 325, 330 (1917). *See*

employed his reasoning and rejected the doctrine's application to the case. Taft's opinion carefully examined the doctrine, reviewed the Court's precedent, and concluded the doctrine would not apply; the touchstone would be whether the tax discriminated against interstate commerce. Sanford's *Attleboro* opinion unfortunately skirted this entire constitutional dialogue, animating the Justices before his arrival.

Sanford, moreover, too quickly accepted rhetoric from *Kansas Natural Gas Co.*, reflecting the philosophy of Justices Van Devanter, Day, and his fellow Tennessean James McReynolds, without appreciating the evolution of the constitutional narrative for the Commerce Clause. There an interstate company threatened to shut off deliveries to local distribution companies (LDCs) if the LDCs refused to pay a higher rate – an additional 5 cents per 1,000 cubic feet of gas. To protect their LDCs, each state sought to enjoin the company from placing its LDC in such a quandary.[99] Justice Sutherland and the other conservatives, such as Van Devanter, failed to appreciate that Commerce Clause jurisprudence had evolved since the nineteenth century. They adhered to rigid jurisdictional categories, asking whether something served a valid police power purpose or constituted a regulation of interstate commerce, the latter being prohibited and the former acceptable if reasonable, not discriminatory, and only indirectly (or incidentally) affecting interstate commerce.

The original package doctrine thus became a talismanic formula for distinguishing a regulation of commerce from an exercise of the police power. Illustrative is Justice Van Devanter's opinion in *Dahnke-Walker Milling Co. v. Bondurant*. That case involved the movement of wheat across state lines by a common carrier. Determining whether the transaction was in interstate commerce became dispositive of its constitutionality.[100] In another grain case, Justice Day followed *Dahnke* and asked whether North Dakota's grain inspection statute constituted a regulation of interstate commerce and added that if it regulated interstate commerce, it would fail.[101] But by 1927 it had become evident, illustrated by yet another decision, that

---

generally Noel T. Dowling & F. Mores Hubbard, *Divesting an Article of Its Interstate Character: An Examination of the Doctrine Underlying the Webb-Kenyon Act*, 5 MINN. L. REV. 100 (1921).

[99] *See* Missouri ex rel. Barrett v. Kan. Nat. Gas Co., 282 F. 341 (W.D. Mo. 1922); Cent. Tr. Co. of N.Y. v. Consumers' Light, Heat & Power, 282 F. 680 (D. Kan. 1922); State *ex rel.* Helm v. Kan. Nat. Gas Co, 208 Pac. 622 (Kan. 1922). The prior rate had been fixed by a federal court and approved by a public utility commission. *See Helm*, 208 Pac. at 622.

[100] *See* 257 U.S. 282, 292–93 (1921).

[101] *See* Lemke v. Farmers' Grain Co., 258 U.S. 50, 56 (1922). Day invoked Justice Holmes' stream of commerce concept justifying how regulating goods destined for interstate markets fell inside the federal sphere of interstate commerce. *See ibid.* at 55 (citing Swift & Co. v. United States, 196 U.S. 375 (1905)). *Attleboro* expectedly raised *Lemke* in its brief. Brief for the Respondent at 15. Justice Brandeis wrote President Wilson that in *Lemke* "a promising effort of a state to protect itself met its doom." *Letter from Louis D. Brandeis to Edward Francis McClenen* (March 3, 1922), *in* 5 LETTERS OF LOUIS D. BRANDEIS, *supra* note 35, at 47. Responding to the claim the state validly exercised its police power, Day in *Lemke* dismissed the claim as having "no application where the State passes beyond the exercise of its legitimate authority, and undertakes to regulate interstate commerce by imposing burdens upon it." 258 U.S. at 59. Three months later when the court, per Chief Justice Taft, used the

such mechanistic formulas no longer captured how to address dormant Commerce Clause challenges.[102]

Justice Brandeis's dissent in *Attleboro* illustrates why an appreciation for how Commerce Clause jurisprudence was evolving was essential – though absent from the majority's opinion. Brandeis's background, perhaps more so than any of the other justices, made him acutely aware of the public utility industry. His modern biographer, Melvin Urofsky, observes how "few people of his generation understood so well the inner workings of the economic system."[103] The "people's advocate," as he was called, Brandeis worked on high-profile gas utility matters, as well as on state-granted charters for elevated electric streetcars.[104] Indeed, he may well have come across the utility when examining the associated traction company.[105] Previous opinions by Brandeis, moreover, had explored aspects of utility regulation.[106] Dissenting in *Pennsylvania v. West Virginia*, he illustrated his predilection toward deferring to expert administrators trained in exploring facts rather than accepting the majority's willingness to second-guess an administrative judgment. In a letter to Felix Frankfurter, Brandeis posited that the West Virginia case was "decided largely on [the] ground that natural gas had been made an article of interstate com[merce]," and he feared that a state would either have to prevent its "power" from entering the

"throat of commerce" concept to uphold the Packers and Stockyards Act, Justice Day did not participate (he left the court six months later). *See* Stafford v. Wallace, 258 U.S. 495, 527 (1922).

[102] Di Santo v. Pennsylvania, 273 U.S. 34 (1927). *See generally* Sam Kalen, *Dormancy versus Innovation: A Next Generation Dormant Commerce Clause*, 65 OKLA. L. REV. 381, 392 (2013).

[103] MELVIN I. UROFSKY, LOUIS D. BRANDEIS AND THE PROGRESSIVE TRADITION 124 (Little, Brown 1981). Alpheus Mason, Brandeis' former foremost biographer, explained how the justice was "[k]eenly aware of the new industrial era's complexities." ALPHEUS T. MASON, BRANDEIS AND THE MODERN STATE 55 (Nat. Home Library Found.; reprint of Princeton ed. 1936). "The most influential critic of trusts during his generation, Brandeis served from 1912 until 1916 as Woodrow Wilson's chief economic adviser and was regarded as one of the architects of the FTC [working with George Rublee]. Above all else, Brandeis exemplified the anti-bigness ethic without which there would have been Sherman Act, no antitrust movement, and no Federal Trade Commission." THOMAS K. MCCRAW, PROPHETS OF REGULATION: CHARLES FRANCIS ADAMS, LOUIS D. BRANDIES, ALFRED E. KAHN 82, 122 (Belknap Press 1984).

[104] MASON, *supra* note 103, at 24–37. *See* Louis D. Brandeis, *How Boston Solved the Gas Problem*, AM. REV. REVS. 592 (1907); *see also Letter from Louis D. Brandeis to Edward Francis McClenen* (March 14, 1916), *in* 4 LETTERS OF LOUIS D. BRANDEIS, at 120.

[105] *Letter from Louis D. Brandeis to Charles Sanger Mellen* (Nov. 18, 1907), *in* 2 LETTERS OF LOUIS D. BRANDEIS, at 48 (searching for financial information of the "United Traction & Electric Co. of Providence"). Brandeis, in fact, fought against the Rhode Island company's effective parent, the New Haven railroad monopoly. Louis D. Brandeis, *The New Haven: An Unregulated Monopoly*, BOS. J., Dec. 13, 1912; LOUIS D. BRANDEIS, FINANCIAL CONDITION OF THE NEW YORK, NEW HAVEN & HARTFORD RAILROAD COMPANY AND OF THE BOSTON & MAINE RAILROAD 3, 7, 27 (1907). *See generally* HENRY L. STAPLES & ALPHEUS T. MASON, THE FALL OF A RAILROAD EMPIRE: BRANDEIS AND THE NEW HAVEN MERGER BATTLE (Syracuse U. Press 1947); Richard M. Abrams, *Brandeis and the New Haven-Boston & Maine Merger Battle Revisited*, 36 BUS. HIST. REV. 408 (1962). And he was familiar with traction company franchises. *See Letter from Louis D. Brandeis to Arthur H. Vandenberg* (April 1, 1911), 2 LETTERS OF LOUIS D. BRANDEIS, at 419,

[106] Galveston Elec. Co. v. City of Galveston, 258 U.S. 388 (1922); Missouri *ex rel.* Sw. Bell v. Pub. Serv. Comm'n, 262 U.S. 276 (1923) (Brandeis, J., concurring).

interstate market and risk "robbery" or secure federal legislation that delegated authority to the states to regulate the market.[107] This seemed all the more justified because Justice Holmes had, in 1905, observed how "commerce among the States is not a technical legal conception but a practical one drawn from the course of business."[108]

In his *Attleboro* dissent, Brandeis began by observing how the RI PUC had exercised a valid police power over a matter of local concern involving one of its own utilities to ensure against discrimination of rates for customers within Rhode Island. He then illustrated why resolving whether it offended the Commerce Clause required a more thorough analysis than the majority opinion suggested. Simply because the matter involved a transaction in interstate commerce and could be regulated by Congress did not, he believed, answer the question. Until Congress acted, or unless congressional silence suggested that the matter should be free from regulation until Congress acts, the state's exercise of its police power was not restrained. The principal issue, instead, was whether the order of the RI PUC somehow obstructed or directly burdened interstate commerce. Here he opined that preventing discrimination against its own citizens was "not obstruct-[ing] or plac[ing] [such] a direct burden on interstate commerce." It would be no different, he reasoned, than if the state had simply placed an added tax on the cost of a product that would then be sold into the interstate market. Nor was it, according to Brandeis, any different from the *Pennsylvania Gas Co.* case. He ended his dissent with two principles generally permeating dormant Commerce Clause jurisprudence: the state had neither discriminated against interstate commerce nor sought to regulate a business engaged solely in interstate commerce.

Justice Sanford ignored altogether Brandeis's dissent, however. Federal legislation was now necessary to regulate *any* electricity that would be transmitted in interstate commerce. A utility commission rate that applied to both intrastate and interstate sales could not be enforced against the latter. Parties might contract for such sales, but the obligation would become fortified against changes by one party or that party's utility commission. There was no distinction between retail or wholesale sales, although Sanford's indirect reliance on the questionable original package doctrine may have suggested such a distinction. It may be that Sanford was aware of the FPC's assessment and implicitly sought to trigger a federal response and issued an opinion with such a sweeping suggestion. Or it may well be that Sanford was influenced by the well-recognized need for federal involvement in protecting against abuses within the corporate structures of the electric utility industry. In January 1927, the *New York Times* reported how "[t]he efforts of some large holding companies to evade State regulation by various devices, utility men fear, may result in all being placed more

---

[107] *Letter from Louis D. Brandeis to Felix Frankfurter* (June 17, 1923), *in* 5 LETTERS OF LOUIS D. BRANDEIS, at 98.
[108] Swift & Co. v. United States, 196 U.S. 375, 398 (1905).

speedily under Federal regulation."[109] A few years earlier, the FPC observed how state commissions could not effectively establish rates because of their inability to examine the books of these multistate utilities. And perhaps he intended that the opinion would signal that not only was the FWPA constitutional – an issue some had raised – but also that a uniform federal approach would make more sense. He had, after all, ended his opinion with precisely that call. And it would be a call with some urgency because by 1930 the public was committed to, as told by David Nye, an "electrical consciousness."[110]

THE DESIRED RESULT?

The opinion ignited a push for a congressional response, particularly because the industry already had become interconnected across state lines. Only the year before, the *Washington Post* reported that Secretary of Commerce Herbert Hoover projected that "there will develop a series of superpower stations, located at strategic points, and serving vast territories over a network of transmission lines" that could be addressed by regional cooperation among states through compacts, and if monopolies spanned too many states, then those monopolies could be federally regulated.[111] This notion became moot once the Supreme Court decided *Attleboro*. Indeed, the press reported how the opinion effectively stymied efforts at regional coordination and establishing a superpower system.[112] The *New York Times* reported that *Attleboro* established a "New Principle [that] transmission of electric power across State borders is 'interstate commerce' ... not subject to regulation by State Commissions."[113] A few years earlier, the FPC had observed how state commissions could not effectively establish rates because of their inability to examine public utilities' accounts.[114] The decision, added the *New York Times*, was "particularly interesting, lawyers hold, because Congress has not attempted to vest in any Federal agency the regulation of electric power sales from one State to another."

For the FPC, *Attleboro* was a clear victory. The next year the FPC parroted its observations from a few years earlier – undoubtedly anxiously awaiting some new authority. This time it added, presumably because of the apparent importance of *Kansas Natural Gas Co.*, that its analysis of drawing a line between wholesale sales and sales to a local distribution company was the appropriate jurisdictional divide. The FPC's report suggested that such a division would make sense because only in the latter circumstance could a state arguably (the receiving or importing state) exercise jurisdiction under the – albeit moribund – original package doctrine.

---

[109]   *Federal Control of Power Forecast*, N.Y. TIMES, Jan. 16, 1927, at E13.

[110]   DAVID E. NYE, CONSUMING POWER: A SOCIAL HISTORY OF AMERICAN *Energies* 171 (MIT Press 1998).

[111]   *Interstate Power Systems*, WASH. POST, Dec. 20, 1926, at 6.

[112]   *See Federal Control of Power Forecast*, N.Y. TIMES, Jan. 16, 1927, at E13.

[113]   *Bars State Control of Exported Power: Supreme Court Decides Rhode Island Cannot Tax for Electricity Sent to Bay State*, N.Y. TIMES, Jan. 4, 1927, at 40.

[114]   1925 FED. POWER COMM'N FIFTH ANN. REP. 5.

"When," according to the FPC, "the interstate commerce consists of the importa-
tion from without a State by a corporation or other agency, which itself sells and
delivers the imported energy to its customers, the State may regulate the rates of
charges made to such customers until the subject matter is regulated by Congress."
The FPC further indicated how, under the FWPA, it enjoyed authority over interstate wholesale sales by its licensees, and it could exercise jurisdiction over local sales
of interstate electricity wherever a state lacked a commission or the commission
lacked authority. The FPC ended its review of *Attleboro* with a few conclusions and
recommendations. It proclaimed the federal government enjoyed "ultimate authority to regulate interstate commerce in electric energy," that such authority was
"exclusive" when transfers involved wholesale sales (again presumably as
a consequence of the original package doctrine), that federal regulation of all
transactions would be too cumbersome, and that too much authority in the states
might prompt "interstate conflicts or deadlocks or inaction." Eschewing any formal
recommendation, it then posited how states might be given exclusive authority over
intrastate transactions and original jurisdiction over interstate transactions subject to
the power of "some Federal agency" to supervise and act as an appellate body if
necessary.[115]

<h2 style="text-align:center">CONGRESSIONAL RESPONSE</h2>

New Dealers responded to the *Attleboro* gap and dominance of the utility holding
companies by passing the Federal Power Act and the now-repealed Public Utility
Holding Company Act of 1935 (PUHCA). "The primary purpose of Title II, Part II of
the 1935 amendments to the Federal Act," the Supreme Court wrote in 1943, "was to
give a federal agency power to regulate the sale of electricity across state lines" that
Attleboro "denied to the States."[116] It gave the FPC (which would later become the
Federal Energy Regulatory Commission [FERC]) jurisdiction over "the transmission of electric energy in interstate commerce and . . . the sale of electric energy at
wholesale in interstate."[117] And it disclaimed, except as otherwise specifically
allowed, any federal authority "over facilities used for the generation of electric
energy or over facilities used in local distribution or only for the transmission of
electric energy in intrastate commerce, or over facilities for the transmission of
electric energy consumed wholly by the transmitter."[118]

   Congress made several judgments. First, rather than either displacing state retail
regulation with federal regulation or providing states with authority to regulate

---

[115] 1928 FED. POWER COMM'N EIGHTH ANN. REP. at 8-13. Shortly after Congress passed the FPA, the
   Commission's counsel explained to a trade association that the goal of the FPA was to "strengthen and
   supplement" rather than "supplant" the "regulatory power of the states." Harry M. Miller, *State and
   Federal Regulation: Their Proper Spheres*, PUB. UTIL. FORT. 30, 33 (1950). Miller lamented that his
   understanding became shattered shortly thereafter.
[116] Jersey Central Power & Light Co. v. Federal Power Commission, 319 U.S. 61, 67-68 (1943).
[117] 16 U.S.C. § 824(b)(1).   [118] 16 U.S.C. § 824(b)(1).

wholesale transactions, it supplemented state retail rate regulation with federal regulation of interstate wholesale transactions. Congress charged the FPC with regulating sales for resale and transmission in interstate commerce of electric energy. It exempted from federal regulation generation, local distribution, and wholly intrastate sales and transmission, and it extended federal regulation "only to those matters which are not subject to regulation by the States." Along with regulating interstate transmission and wholesale sales, Congress trusted the FPC with the authority to review and, if appropriate, approve utility mergers and certain securities transactions and to set up a utility rate accounting system. Over the next thirty years, the FPC proceeded to impose comprehensive utility regulation over public utilities involved in interstate transmission and wholesale sales.

Congress also embarked on one of the most ambitious "restructuring" programs for any industry. The FTC's investigations, along with additional congressional inquiries, produced at least ninety volumes of materials addressing the problem with electric utility holding companies – the "Power Trust."[119] Characteristic of one of the many the diatribes against the industry, particularly describing how municipalities clashed with the industry, a 1932 New Republic book, *The Power Fight*, warned how "leaders of the power group [had] regard[e]d this country as their oyster."[120] Moving against the Power Trust was an item on President Roosevelt's agenda, and he enlisted the aid of FPC Commissioners Frank McNinch and Claude Draper. They were later aided by Harold Ickes, chairman of the National Power Committee and subsequently an interdepartmental committee. The result was not only draft legislation responding to *Attleboro* but also language crafted to break the trusts. This became the PUHCA, which required that the Securities and Exchange Commission (SEC) break up the massive utility holding companies controlling most of the operating electric utilities in the country and restructuring them into either individual operating companies, single-state holding companies, or SEC-regulated multistate holding companies. The New Deal's vision of its restructured utility industry transcends the twin requirements that each multistate holding company be confined to the operation of a single integrated holding company system and that it divest itself of businesses that are not functionally related to such operations. The latter targeted the concern that the large electric utilities controlled possibly 70 percent of the country's natural gas production.[121]

The public-policy assumptions animating the New Deal utility legislation were that investor-owned utilities should be operated as single, interconnected, vertically integrated systems subject to (1) retail rate regulation by the states, (2) wholesale rate regulation by the FPC, and (3) interaffiliate and corporate regulation by the SEC (if the utility operated as a holding company).

---

[119]   Ellis W. Hawley, The New Deal and the Problem of Monopoly: A Study of Economic Ambivalence 327 n.2 (Princeton Univ. Press 1966).
[120]   Stephen Raushenbush, The Power Fight 481 (New Republic 1932).   [121] *Ibid.* at 7.

Several cases since *Attleboro* and the passage of the FPA solidified federal super-intendence over all wholesale sales of power in interstate commerce (even between entities in the same state), including that its authority extended to interstate wholesale sales from generation facilities and that sales were in interstate commerce in any portion of the electricity sold and transmitted on the interstate transmission grid. Unlike natural gas, electricity cannot yet be stored economically in large amounts, and it follows the path of least resistance. This means that electricity flowing through any system tied into an interstate transmission line could travel (virtually, not literally, because we cannot track the individual electrons) in interstate commerce.

Even though the philosophy of *Attleboro* itself impliedly would be repudiated by the Supreme Court in 1983,[122] the FPC (now FERC) consequently now enjoys expansive authority over wholesale sales by utilities and generators connected to the interstate transmission grid. Early on, the Court held that federal jurisdiction followed "the flow of electric energy, an engineering and scientific, rather than a legalistic or governmental test."[123] In *Hartford Electric Light Co.*, the United States Court of Appeals for the Second Circuit, in 1942, held that even though the FPA specifically denies FERC jurisdiction over "generation," a utility's books and records relating to wholesale sales from its generation facilities were "facilities subject to the jurisdiction of the Commission" because they are used in connection with whole-sale sales.[124] Then, in 1964, the Supreme Court decided *FPC v. Southern California Edison Co.* (known as *Colton*). The case involved a wholesale sale of out-of-state power by a public utility, Southern California Edison Company (SCE), to a municipal utility in the same state (the City of Colton). SCE and California argued that *Attleboro* suggested that SCE's wholesale sale could be regulated by California and not under the FPA. The Court, however, announced that Congress had drawn "a *bright line* easily ascertained, between state and federal jurisdiction," making federal jurisdiction "plenary and extending it all wholesale sales in interstate commerce."[125] While Congress has made occasional adjustments to this "bright line" over the years, it persists as the fundamental federal/state division of labor for electric regulation in the United States. *Colton*'s interpretation of the FPA effectively froze the 1927 division of labor between federal and state utility regulation articulated in *Attleboro*.

And so today electricity traveling along the interstate grid is generally treated as involving interstate commerce. The Court even expanded what touches the interstate grid by approving a commingling test: a utility would become jurisdictional if the FPC could show that any portion of the electricity transmitted or sold at

---

[122] In Ark. Elec. Coop. v. Ark. Pub. Serv. Comm'n., 461 U.S. 375 (1983), the Court held that a state could regulate wholesale sales in interstate commerce by an electric cooperative not subject to FERC jurisdiction, essentially upending *Attleboro*.
[123] Conn. Light & Power Co. v. FPC. 324 U.S. 515, 529 (1945).   [124] 131 F.2d 953 (2d Cir. 1942).
[125] FPC v. Southern California Edison, 376 U.S. 205, 215-16 (1964) (emphasis added).

wholesale by the utility came from or went to another state.[126] The practical result was that if a generator or transmission line was connected to the interstate grid, it would be deemed in interstate commerce because the FPC (later FERC) could easily establish that at least some of the power flowed to or from another state. In Justice Douglas' words, "the comingling method will now mean that every privately owned interconnected facility [outside of Texas] is within the FPC's jurisdiction."

The New Deal paradigm of utilities operating a single, vertically integrated utility system regulated on a cost-of-service basis (retail by the state, wholesale by the FERC) provided for many years a workable but cumbersome state/federal regulatory regime. Utilities were largely vertically integrated. Power flowed from large central-station generating facilities through high-voltage transmission systems either for sale at wholesale to other utilities or for delivery through local distribution facilities to end users. It was clear which sales were at wholesale and which at retail.

A SPARK THAT WASN'T NECESSARY

It is too simplistic to suggest that the language of the FPA mirrored any line identified by Sanford in *Attleboro* or that it addressed a jurisdictional "gap." Sanford's perfunctory analysis effectively ignored the context of the case and, as such, produced a categorical holding: it required federal regulation of the industry (1) because the rate applied to a product, electricity, that was being delivered across state lines and warranted national rather than local attention and (2) because of an unstated risk that in-state residents might be favored. *Attleboro*, though, did not itself establish a line between wholesale and retail sales to customers in another state. That was a line the FPC had drawn, and it would be a line fabricated by commentators, justified merely because of Sanford's citation to the *Pennsylvania Gas Co.* case. "Thus there is a gap," now the *Attleboro* gap, which prompted the congressional response presumably filling the gap for wholesale sales.

When, therefore, the Supreme Court later held that *Attleboro* "reiterated and accepted the holding of *Pennsylvania Gas Co.* . . . that sales across the state line direct to consumers is a local matter within the authority of the agency of the importing state,"[127] it perpetuated a particular understanding of *Attleboro*, not necessarily an accurate one – the case presumably appeared too dubious to accept at face value absent the line and subsequent gap. The parties had litigated whether *Kansas Natural Gas Co.* or *Pennsylvania Gas Co.* governed, and Sanford simply accepted the former. His analysis may have intimated an acceptance of the rejected original package doctrine embedded in *Pennsylvania Gas Co.*, but that is about it.

---

[126]   FPC v. Fla. Power & Light Co, 404 U.S. 453 (1972).
[127]   United States v. Pub. Utils. Comm'n, 345 U.S. 295, 711 (1953).

His reasoning, though, rested on the asserted national character of the business and a perceived need to avoid discrimination – neither of which necessarily justifies a retail/wholesale divide. And while *Attleboro* was neither analytically sound when issued nor consistent with how dormant Commerce Clause analysis would unfold shortly thereafter, its ghost remains with us today.

4

The Gap Continues

Changing Electricity Markets

Some observers hue to *Attleboro* and argue how states may regulate wholesale transactions when the sales and consumers are located within the same state.[1] But most academic conversations about today's electric grid accept *Attleboro* and focus instead on exploring new governance structures that blur the line between state and federal authority, by encouraging regional governance and cooperation rather than any increased state authority.[2] These dialogues collectively reflect the urgency of incorporating renewable energy into the grid and displacing fossil fuel generation. Discussions about the constraints confronting the construction of interstate transmission lines are plentiful: transmission facilities capable of carrying renewable resources far from their source must overcome the hurdles of state siting, cost allocation, integration with the grid, and reliability issues for the balancing authority, and in organized markets the appropriate financial incentives and approvals.[3]

For many academics, the solution lies somewhere in establishing a new governance structure. Ashira Ostrow, for instance, posits that states and the federal government could work more effectively together when encouraging or discouraging infrastructure development and that one solution could be to establish a "National Network Coordinator" who could "coordinate – rather than replace – state regulation."[4] Hari Osofsky and Hannah Wiseman propose instead that we develop a hybrid structure that merges the governmental pyramid with other stakeholders to create a regional institution.[5] Daniel Lyons similarly encourages a regional structure

[1] Frank R. Lindh & Thomas W. Bone, Jr., *State Jurisdiction over Distributed Generators*, 34 ENERGY L. J. 499 (2013).

[2] Alexandra B. Klass & Elizabeth J. Wilson, *Interstate Transmission Challenges for Renewable Energy: A Federalism Mismatch*, 65 VAND. L. REV. 1801, 1804 (2012).

[3] Ashley C. Brown & Jim Rossi, *Siting Transmission Lines in a Changed Milieu: Evolving Notions of the "Public Interest" in Balancing State and Regional Considerations*, 81 U. COLO. L. REV. 705 (2010); Klass & Wilson, *Interstate Transmission Challenges*; Jim Rossi, *The Trojan Horse of Electric Power Transmission Line Siting Authority*, 39 ENVTL. L. 1015 (2009).

[4] Ashira P. Ostrow, *Grid Governance: The Role of a National Network Coordinator*, 35 CARDOZO L. REV. 1993, 1996 (2014).

[5] Hari M. Osofsky & Hannah J. Wiseman, *Hybrid Energy Governance*, 2014 ILL. L. REV. 1, 12 (2014). *See also* Hari M. Osofsky & Hannah J. Wiseman, *Dynamic Energy Federalism*, 72 MD. L. REV. 772 (2013).

embodying "cooperative federalism" rather than what he sees as the "dual federalism approach embodied by the Federal Power Act [that] offers a false dichotomy between state and federal regulation."[6] Robin Craig accepts the trend toward regional governance and explores the constitutional issues confronting state and local governments when they do so.[7] These suggestions by Ostrow, Osofsky, Wiseman, and others were, in some form or another, also discussed around the time of *Attleboro* but shelved once *Attleboro* forced Congress's hand.[8]

In practice, however, an effective transition to a different energy grid may necessitate reexamining or abandoning *Attleboro*'s purportedly simplistic "bright line" and quite possibly further amending the Federal Power Act (FPA). An advisor to a Federal Energy Regulatory Commission (FERC) commissioner wrote in 1986 that

> much of the debate ... centers on which side of the "bright line" one thinks the regulatory function in question should reside. That thinking, of course, underlies most of the strong positions take on the Narragansett doctrine, which really comprises the effort to legally police the *Attleboro* "bright line."[9]

Charles Curtis, the first chairman of the FERC, when the agency changed from the Federal Power Commission (FPC) to the FERC in the 1970s, along with other prominent energy experts, expressed the sentiment that "federal and state regulators will 'muddle through'" the jurisdictional divide.[10] This muddling includes – so far unsuccessful – efforts by states to wrest from FERC's jurisdiction the ability to control aspects of local or regional electric generation capacity markets. The Fourth Circuit invalidated Maryland's program for encouraging new capacity in the wholesale market, reasoning that the *Attleboro* line and resulting FPA placed that authority exclusively within FERC's domain, with the Supreme Court concluding that the FPA preempted Maryland's program.[11] The Third Circuit held that the FPA similarly preempted New Jersey's program for incentivizing the construction of new electric generation facilities.[12] The Second Circuit rejected New York's challenge to FERC's presumption for the dividing line between the bulk power system under its domain and local distribution under

6   Daniel A. Lyons, *Federalism and the Rise of Renewable Energy: Preserving State and Local Voices in the Green Energy Revolution*, 64 CASE WESTERN RES. L. REV. 1619, 1624 (2014).

7   Robin K. Craig, *Constitutional Contours for the Design and Implementation of Multistate Renewable Energy Programs and Projects*, 81 U. COLO. L. REV. 771 (2010).

8   Felix Frankfurter & James M. Landis, *The Compact Clause of the Constitution – A Study in Interstate Adjustments*, 34 YALE L. J. 685, 709 (1925).

9   Reinier H.J.H. Lock, *Models for Bulk Power Deregulation: What Promise for the Future?*, 38 ADMIN. L. REV. 349, 358 (1986).

10   Rod Kuckro, *Without Congress Acting, Electric Markets Will "Muddle Through" – Panel*, E&E NEWS, Sept. 8, 2014.

11   PPL Energyplus, LLC v. Nazarian, 753 F.3d 467 (4th Cir. 2014); Hughes v. Talen Energy Mktg., LLC, 136 S. Ct. 1288 (2016).

12   PPL Energyplus, LLC v. Solomon, 766 F.3d 241 (3d Cir. 2014). *See also* N.J. Bd. of Pub. Utils. v. FERC, 744 F.3d 74, 80 (3d Cir. 2014) (discussing *Attleboro*, Congress's response, and the modern jurisdictional divide when deciding challenge to tariff for PJM).

state jurisdiction.[13] State programs for enticing renewable energy generation are similarly being challenged as transgressing some line. The Eighth Circuit rebuffed Minnesota's attempt to restrict sales from out-of-state coal-fired generation into its state.[14] And along with these challenges, there is the escalating chorus of scholarship fearful that the dormant Commerce Clause is chilling state and local efforts to reduce greenhouse gas emissions. The dormant Commerce Clause even surfaced as an issue in the initial stages of the highly publicized and now defunct Cape Wind offshore wind project, when Massachusetts originally required utilities within the state to acquire renewable energy generation located "within the jurisdictional boundaries of the commonwealth."[15]

The continued resonance of the *Attleboro* jurisdictional line surfaced in FERC's defense of its effort to promote demand response and reduce greenhouse gas emissions. In Order No. 745, FERC required that certain large customers, including factories and commercial facilities, receive full market prices when they reduce their electric consumption.[16] The concept is simple. Instead of increasing generation of electricity to meet consumer demand, possibly from fossil fuel–fired plants, the grid operator can request that certain consumers reduce their demand and thus avoid the need for additional energy generation. Demand response, therefore, provides an attractive option for greening the grid. One of the leading scholars on demand response, Joel Eisen, writes about the importance for FERC to possess the authority to require demand response.[17] The grid is becoming "smarter," allowing enhanced and two-way communication between consumers and energy suppliers, and accompanying this evolution of the electric grid is the ability to manage our electricity needs with more precision and deliberation than we have in the past.[18] FERC has promoted this in the wholesale market. Put simply, FERC provided a compensation mechanism for enticing entities that regulate the grid and operate wholesale markets (independent system operators and regional transmission organizations) "to use demand-side resources to meet their systems' needs for wholesale energy, capacity,

[13]   New York v. FERC, 783 F.3d 946 (2d Cir. 2015) (New York questioned the presumptive threshold for local distribution lines at 100 kV, adopted for implementing reliability standards under the Energy Policy Act of 2005, Pub. L. No. 109–58, 119 Stat. 594).

[14]   North Dakota v. Heydinger, 825 F.3d 912 (8th Cir. 2016).

[15]   Town of Barnstable v. O'Connor, 786 F.3d 130 (1st Cir. 2015) (describing program and noting geographic limitation subsequently removed). *See also* Energy & Envtl. Legal Inst. v. Epel, No. 14–1216, 2015 WL 4174876 (10th Cir. July 13, 2015) (rejecting challenge to Colorado renewable standard).

[16]   Demand Response Compensation in Organized Wholesale Energy Markets, 134 FERC ¶ 61,187, 2011 WL 890975 (2011).

[17]   Joel B. Eisen, *Who Regulated the Smart Grid? FERC's Authority over Demand Response Compensation in Wholesale Electricity Markets*, 4 SAN DIEGO J. CLIMATE & ENERGY L. 69 (2012–13).

[18]   Joel B. Eisen, *An Open Access Distribution Tariff: Removing Barriers to Innovation on the Smart Grid*, 61 U.C.L.A. L. REV. 1712 (2014); Joel B. Eisen, *Smart Regulation and Federalism for the Smart Grid*, 37 HARV. ENVTL. L. REV. 101 (2013).

and ancillary services."[19] The United States Court of Appeals for the DC Circuit, however, held that FERC intruded into the states' authority to regulate retail sales – embodied in the FPA. After the Supreme Court accepted certiorari, the Solicitor General argued that *Attleboro* established "that the Commerce Clause bars States from regulating *certain* interstate electricity transactions, such as wholesale power (*i.e.*, a sale for resale)" by a utility "across state lines."[20] In upholding FERC's program, the Court nonetheless echoed how it had previously prohibited states from regulating wholesale interstate sales when it "created what became known as the '*Attleboro* gap.'"[21] However, that is an illusion. It was neither accurate then nor now.

Much has happened since *Attleboro* and Congress's 1935 response. To begin with, Richard Hirsch, in *Technology and Transformation*, chronicles how technology changed dramatically between the early 1900s and the 1970s. Generators blossomed in size and became singularly more efficient, while transmission lines straddled the landscape farther and farther. The postwar economy touted using more electricity and the many new appliances and toys driven by electric power. To be sure, the utilities witnessed grid reliability problems in the 1960s and were forced to develop more elaborate arrangements for interconnecting their systems and pooling resources. And, of course, the North American Electric Reliability Council (NERC) was born following the dramatic Northeast blackout in 1965, with FERC forty years later finally receiving from Congress actual authority to supervise the reliability of the nation's bulk power system.[22]

But the seeming stability of the utilities' world shattered by the 1970s, when utilities otherwise comfortable with their monopoly and the growing post–World War II economy confronted the energy crisis, inflation, increased cost of capital, rising energy costs for consumers, and new environmental concerns, many of which are discussed in later chapters. Demand for energy, too, tapered off; annual energy growth at its prior nice clip was replaced by utilities having excess capacity and investments in new plants that could only be recovered by higher costs to consumers. Average annual residential electricity prices increased by roughly 25 percent, adjusted for inflation, between 1970 and 1985. In 2016 congressional testimony on

[19]   Elec. Power Supply Ass'n v. FERC, 763 F.3d 216, 219 (D.C. Cir. 2014), *rev'd*, 136 S. Ct. 760 (2016). *See generally* Sharon B. Jacobs, *Bypassing Federalism and the Administrative Law of Negawatts*, 100 Iowa L. Rev. 885 (2015).

[20]   Brief for Petitioner at 3, FERC v. Elec. Power Supply Ass'n, 136 S. Ct. 760 (2016) (No. 14-840) (emphasis added), 2015 WL 4237680, at *3.

[21]   FERC v. Elec. Power Supply Ass'n, 136 S. Ct. 760, 767 (2016). While endorsing the divide between retail and interstate wholesale rates, the Court nonetheless, according to Jim Rossi and former commissioner Wellinghoff, "approached FERC's jurisdiction in a functional manner, endorsing pragmatism over formalism in the regulation of energy markets." Jim Rossi & Jon Wellinghoff, *FERC v. EPSA and Adjacent State Regulation of Customer Energy Resources*, 40 Harv. Envtl. L. Rev. F. 23, 24 (2016).

[22]   For an account of the blackout and response, see Phillip F. Schewe, The Grid: A Journey through the Heart of Our Electrified World 115–66 (Joseph Henry Press 2007).

energy markets, former FERC general counsel, Susan Tomasky, explained how these increasing costs, "due primarily to the escalating costs of new nuclear power plants in some parts of the country," contributed to disputes about how to recover those costs and "plagued regulatory proceedings at the state and Federal level." Beneficially, though, she added, how these higher costs prodded industrial customers to look for cheaper energy resources – along with the flexibility for purchasing from another supplier and an ability to have that energy transmitted – facilitating innovation in natural gas plants that could be built quicker and cheaper. The resulting "need for a competitive wholesale market" from new, possibly independent market entrants required an industry restructuring that could not be accomplished on a case-by-case basis.[23] That restructuring is now upon us.

And so today the New Deal regulatory regime no longer exists at the federal level, and it has been abandoned in many states – replaced by significant shifts in federal policy and a patchwork of regulatory approaches at the state level. With repeal of the Public Utility Holding Company Act (PUHCA) in 2005, holding companies are no longer required to operate a single integrated utility system. FERC no longer regulates most wholesale power transactions on a cost-of-service basis. Rather, sellers, if they lack market power, may sell at competitive "market-based" rates. FERC-regulated regional transmission organizations or independent system operators (collectively RTOs) operate organized regional energy and capacity markets. Interstate wholesale sales and interstate transmission services until the 1990s were but a small part of the typical integrated utility's business.

At the state level, many states required that utilities divest their generation facilities and turn over operation of transmission facilities to RTOs, whereas others retained the vertically integrated utility model. Several states now permit retail competition, dispensing with exclusive service territories and leaving many sellers at retail unregulated. The resulting "vertical disintegration" of much of the industry into independent generators, RTOs operating regional transmission systems, and local distribution companies meant a massive increase in FERC's role as it regulated the upstart independent generators and the newly created RTOs.

"DEREGULATION" AND THE CALIFORNIA ENERGY CRISIS

Congress, in the Public Utility Policies Act of 1978 (PURPA), took a small but crucial initial step toward sweeping in these eventual changes to the prevalent regulatory model by exempting small power producers and cogeneration (also known as *combined heat and power*) from the FPA. Section 210 of PURPA permitted FERC to exempt certain cogenerators and renewable power producers from the FPA, PUHCA, and state utility regulation. PURPA encouraged market entry by

---

[23]   Testimony of Susan Tomasky before the United States House of Representatives Committee on Energy and Commerce, Subcommittee on Energy and Power, Sept. 7, 2016.

cogenerators as well as "qualifying facilities" (QFs), generally non–fossil fuel–burning generators producing 80 MW or less, by requiring that utilities inter-connect (within the utility's service territory) and purchase the output of those facilities at what is called an *avoided cost rate*. One court observed that PURPA was designed to redress "traditional electric utilities' reluctance to deal with these nontraditional facilities" by charging "the Commission with implementing manda-tory purchase and sell obligations, requiring electric utilities to purchase electric power from, and sell power to, qualifying cogeneration and small production facilities."[24] The state would establish the avoided cost (with a complicated mechan-ism for state, federal, and judicial oversight to ensure compliance) in an amount commensurate with the incremental cost a utility would incur to provide that additional amount of power. The utility, in effect, would be paying the PURPA facility for the utility's avoided cost of generating or purchasing the additional amount of electricity. This led to long-term contracts between PURPA facilities and utilities for the sale of energy at avoided costs, generally at above market-based rates. "Congress," in the Supreme Court's words, "did not intend to impose tradi-tional ratemaking concepts on sales by qualifying facilities to utilities."[25] And, moreover, the Court rejected a challenge to PURPA's constitutionality.[26]

These QFs and cogenerators also were exempted from some of the FPA and PUHCA limitations. As such, owning one of these types of facilities would not subject the owner to the PUHCA's draconian ownership rules. But an important caveat, one that consumed many lawyers during PURPA's early years, was that a regulated utility (or its affiliate) could not have more than a 50 percent interest in a QF – eliminated in 2005, along with affording FERC authority to terminate the mandatory purchase and sale obligation if a facility would otherwise have access to competitive electric markets – a determination the Commission has made for certain sized QFs in identified organized markets.

Prior to PURPA, the FPA did not impose any obligation on an electric utility to transmit another party's energy on its transmission system. Generators lacking transmission capacity therefore would need to negotiate the right to use another party's lines. And so when the claim was made that the Commission should require wheeling as part of its approval of the agreement for the New England Power Pool, the region's utilities' arrangement for interconnecting and coordinating their sys-tems, the Commission declined by suggesting that there was no evidence of dis-criminatory or anticompetitive behavior. Of course, alternatives existed for forcing transmission access, or *wheeling,* such as federal antitrust principles designed to arrest transmission bottlenecks that constricted the flow of energy, as well as looking at how the Nuclear Regulatory Commission imposed a wheeling obligation when necessary to correct anticompetitive behavior, or if electric utilities were seeking

[24] So. Cal. Edison Co. v. FERC, 443 F.3d 94, 95 (D.C. Cir. 2006).
[25] American Paper Inst., Inc. v. American Elec. Power Service Co., 461 U.S. 402, 414 (1983).
[26] FERC v. Mississippi, 456 U.S. 742 (1982).

approval to merge, the Commission could condition the merger on the company's agreement to provide open access.[27] Then, with PURPA's passage, an electric utility could apply to FERC requesting an order directing another electric utility to provide transmission service, and while QFs could have used this provision to require wheeling as well, it largely went unused because of its complexity. Indeed, an early energy treatise observed that PURPA's wheeling provision was "so ineptly drafted that it is difficult to tell precisely how many findings are necessary before a Wheeling Order may issue."[28]

In a 357-page Energy Policy Act of 1992, Congress expanded beyond PURPA and removed a few more barriers to wholesale competition in the electric industry. Throughout its various titles, the Act targeted a host of programs ranging from climate change, federal automobile fleet requirements, nuclear energy, research and development (R&D) to the Strategic Petroleum Reserve. Yet fundamentally, this Act, according to a former FERC economist, "increased the pace of change in American electric power industry."[29] Then President George H. W. Bush described the electricity component as a "landmark" event destined to infuse competition into electric markets and change "the way electricity is generated and sold."[30] One way was by removing PUHCA obstacles.

At least by the late 1980s, the 1935 PUHCA enjoyed the dubious distinction of having stymied innovation and diversification among the players in the electric grid, effectively hindering by whom and how our electricity would be generated and sold. A former FERC general counsel, Douglas Smith, wrote along with a colleague about how PUHCA's ownership restrictions stifled "opportunities for non-utility generation" and scared off investors and even lenders who feared investing in projects and falling under PUCHA's unworkable umbrella.[31] In response, the 1992 Energy Policy Act exempted certain wholesale electric generators, called *EWGs*,

---

[27] Municipalities of Groton v. FERC, 587 F.2d 1296 (D.C. Cir. 1978) (power pool). *See also* Utah Power & Light, 47 FERC ¶ 61,209 (1989) (merger). *See generally* GAO, Electric Supply: Regulating Utility Holding Companies in a Changing Electricity Industry (1992).

[28] WILLIAM F. FOX, JR., FEDERAL REGULATION OF ENERGY 769 (Shepard/McGraw-Hill 1983). The language reflected a difference between the House and the Senate; the former favored broad wheeling authority consistent with the Carter administration, whereas the Senate opposed it. *See* Southeastern Power Admin. v. Kentucky Utilities Co., 25 FERC ¶ 61,201 (1983). Richard Hirsch proffers one version of PURPA's history in *Power Loss*. RICHARD HIRSCH, POWER LOSS: THE ORIGINS OF DEREGULATION AND RESTRUCTURING IN AMERICAN ELECTRIC UTILITY SYSTEM 83–88 (MIT Press 1999). In some instances, requests for wheeling became moot once the parties negotiated an arrangement. E.g., The City of Manti, Utah v. Utah Power & Light Co., 40 FERC ¶ 61,004 (1987). Additional potential options for wheeling existed for both federal and private hydroelectric projects, as well as for projects crossing federal property.

[29] RICHARD P. O'NEILL and CHARLES S. WHITMORE, *Network Oligopoly Regulation: An Approach to Electric Federalism, in* REGULATING REGIONAL POWER SYSTEMS: CASE STUDIES AND PERSPECTIVES ON EMERGING COMPETITION 99 (Clinton J. Andrews ed., IEE Press 1995).

[30] President's Statement on the Energy Policy Act, White House Release, 28 Weekly Comp. Pres. Doc. 2094 (Oct. 24, 1992).

[31] Jeffery D. Watkiss & Douglas W. Smith, *The Energy Policy Act of 1992: A Watershed for Competition in the Wholesale Power Market*, 10 YALE J. REG. 447, 465 (1993).

from the PUHCA, although it left their wholesale sales subject to the FPA. PURPA, after all, contributed toward having all new non-utility-generated capacity in the country shift from 14.8 percent in 1986 to roughly 88.4 percent of all new capacity in 1992.[32] With these reforms, utilities could now invest in projects outside their service territory, even across the country. EWGs were nonutility players that, whether by owning or leasing generating capacity, could sell wholesale electric energy. Congress also amended the FPA by giving FERC effective authority to require transmitting utilities to provide wholesale transmission services, while states could, if they so chose, order retail wheeling. It even ostensibly authorized the Commission to require the construction of new transmission capacity for providing wholesale capacity to additional markets if necessary (at just and reasonable rates sufficient to cover costs).[33]

On the heels of the deregulation movement of the 1980s and consistent with the 1992 legislation's goal of opening capacity markets, FERC in the early 1990s embarked on a suite of maneuvers to fundamentally alter its regulation of interstate transmission and wholesale sales. Most of the industry was still vertically integrated. FERC, exercising its authority under the FPA to ensure "just and reasonable" rates, began to allow jurisdictional "public utilities" to make wholesale sales and provide transmission services at market-based (rather than cost-based) rates on a showing that they lacked market power over the buyer or have adequately mitigated that market power. FERC, at first, toyed in the late 1980s and early 1990s with interpreting its ratemaking authority a bit more broadly to promote negotiated or market-based rates for wholesale sales rather than rates based on a utility's cost of service (including a fair rate of return), if a utility would agree to afford open access to its transmission system. In May 1985, for instance, the Commission released a notice that it was exploring alternatives for increasing efficiency in the electric industry, such as using market forces.[34] Later, the FERC began approving wholesale market rates in return

[32] Edison Electric Institute, Capacity and Generation of Non-Utility Sources of Energy, 1989 and 1992, referenced in DAVID FREEMAN, *Competition in the Electric Industry: An Unguided Missile?, in* THE ELECTRIC INDUSTRY IN TRANSITION 15, 24 n.3 (P.U. Reps. 1994). Inflation and conservation left the country with more electric power generation capacity than necessary by the mid-1980s, with little need for utility investment in new plants. *See* Richard J. Pierce, Jr., *The Regulatory Treatment of Mistakes in Retrospect: Canceled Plants and Excess Capacity,* 132 U. PA. L. REV. 497 (1984).

[33] Energy Policy Act of 1992, Pub. L. No. 102–486, 106 Stat. 2776. *See generally* DAN R. WILLIAMS, GUIDE TO THE ENERGY POLICY ACT (Pennwell Corp. 1994); Donald Santa and Patricia Beneke, *Federal Natural Gas Policy and the Energy Policy Act of 1992,* 14 ENERGY L. J. 10 (1993); THE NATIONAL REGULATORY RESEARCH INSTITUTE, A SYNOPSIS OF THE ENERGY POLICY ACT OF 1992: NEW TASKS FOR STATE PUBLIC UTILITY COMMISSIONS (NRRI June 1993).

[34] 50 Fed. Reg. 23,445 (May 30, 1985); Wisconsin Electric Power Co., 33 FERC ¶ 61,322 (1985); Wisconsin Electric Power Co., 34 FERC ¶ 62,286 (1986). The effort intensified thereafter. *See* Heartland Energy Services, Inc., 68 FERC ¶ 61,223 (1994). Regulations Governing Bidding Programs, 53 Fed. Reg. 9,324 (March 22, 1988); Regulations Governing Independent Power Producers, 53 Fed. Reg. 9,327 (March 22, 1988). Early decisions skirted defining the breadth of such authority. Richmond Power and Light Co. v. FERC, 574 F.2d 610 (D.C. Cir. 1978); New York State Electric & Gas Corp. v. FERC, 638 F.2d 388 (2nd Cir. 1980). The Commission later expressed a willingness, regardless, to order wheeling to remedy anticompetitive behavior.

for transmission system access.[35] Of course, this all occurred amid a brewing debate surrounding the efficacy of relying on the market, along with deregulating the industry.[36] And a long-term FERC administrative law judge observed around this time how the "anachronistic" jurisdictional divide was rearing its infuriating head.[37]

In 1996, drawing on its experience with opening up access to natural gas pipelines, the Commission issued Order No. 888, styled as an order "*Promoting Wholesale Competition through Open Access Non-discriminatory Transmission Service by Public Utilities; Recovery of Stranded Costs by Public Utilities and Transmitting Utilities.*"[38] FERC discussed how significant changes in the electric industry had occurred since the late 1960s and 1970s, principally shifting utility interest toward competitive markets. That utilities favored some form of open access to transmission systems was confirmed, according to FERC, by having almost 64 percent of the public utilities with transmission facilities file some form of open access tariff as of the Order's finalization. FERC concluded that it could unbundle wholesale transactions and ensure open access to transmission service. And that it had the authority to do so under the FPA's Sections 205 and 206, which gave the Commission authority to prevent undue discrimination or preference. While FERC claimed that it could exercise jurisdiction over unbundled retail electric transmission, it avoided asserting any power over bundled retail transmission service – and potentially intruding into the states' domain. Unbundling service, that is, separating generation, marketing, transmission, and retail service, was critical – provided that sufficient oversight and transparency existed to prevent market manipulation by unbundled affiliated entities. Eight years later and after several clarifications by FERC of its program, the Supreme Court treated FERC's choices as reasonable and permissible under the FPA.[39] The United States Court of Appeals for the Ninth Circuit

---

[35] E.g., Public Serv. Co. of Indian, 51 FERC 61,367 (1990), *reh'g* 52 FERC 61,260 (1990); Tex-La Electric Cooperative of Texas, Inc., 67 FERC ¶ 61,019 (1994); Florida Municipal Power Agency, 65 FERC ¶ 61,125 (1993).

[36] See PAUL JOSKOW & RICHARD SCHMALENSEE, MARKETS FOR POWER: AN ANALYSIS OF ELECTRIC UTILITY DEREGULATION (MIT Press 1983); OFFICE OF TECHNOLOGY ASSESSMENT, ELECTRIC POWER WHEELING AND DEALING: TECHNOLOGICAL CONSIDERATIONS FOR INCREASING COMPETITION (May 1989); Richard Pierce, *A Proposal to Deregulate the Market for Bulk Power*, 72 VA. L. REV. 1183 (1986); Benjamin Holden, *Total Deregulation in Electricity Sector Would Hurt Customers, A Report Says*, WALL ST. J., Aug. 4, 1995, B4.

[37] Isaac D. Benkin, *Who Makes the Rules? Federal and State Jurisdiction over Electric Transmission Access*, 13 ENERGY L. J. 45 (1992).

[38] Promoting Wholesale Competition through Open Access Non-Discriminatory Transmission Services by Public Utilities; Recovery of Stranded Costs by Public Utilities and Transmitting Utilities, 61 Fed. Reg. 21,540, 21,541, 75 FERC ¶ 61,080 (Apr. 24, 1996). Another order required that utilities file tariffs with the Commission outlining the utility's information for access to its system, including its rates. 75 FERC ¶ 61,078 (Apr. 24, 1996). The FERC later revised that order in 2007.

[39] New York v. FERC, 535 U.S. 1 (2002).

also concluded that FERC's approach to allowing market-based rates was permissible.[40]

Order No. 888 laid the seeds for significant additional market refinements. It hinted, for instance, that the future lay in developing organized markets and independent entities that could collectively approach transmission planning and access. Regional entities, or independent system operators (ISOs), could make it easier for generation resources to sell into the market by being able to contract with a single entity rather than contract with multiple transmission providers.

Then, in December 1999, explains energy firm Navigant Consulting, "FERC released Order No. 2000 calling for the voluntary formation of RTOs" designed to "facilitate the continued development of competitive wholesale power markets" and to improve the "reliability and management of the transmission system."[41] Transmission line owners in these RTOs would transfer their ability to control the transmission system to the RTO. These organized markets, further refined by FERC in 2008 with Order No. 719, allow generators to bid into an RTO-managed system at a cost that considers the location of the generation facility – called *locational marginal pricing* – and generally comprising generation cost, cost arising from congestion in the system, and costs associated with transmission losses. Bids might be based on an hour- or day-ahead spot market. The largest RTO, PJM, for instance, operates a day-ahead, real-time, reliability pricing model capacity market, a regulation market, a synchronized reserve market, and a day-ahead scheduling reserve market and financial transmission rights market.[42] Each of these markets is for unique services. Successful bidders in the typical situation receive the market-clearing price or the highest accepted bid for the service. Two-thirds of the nation's electric load is now served by seven of these markets, generally covering all but the Intermountain West and the Southeast – and proposals have been floated for having the Intermountain West become part of the system operating out of California – the California Independent System Operator (CAISO). This is all distinct from the traditional, historical bilateral transaction, where utilities negotiate contracts to sell energy or capacity. This can still be done, though, for companies serving the customer base, or the load, within the RTO territory.

To address transmission constraints confronting renewable resources' access to the market, FERC, in 2011, issued Order No. 1000. FERC described the order as "continu[ing] the evolutionary reform process the Commission began with the

---

[40]   California *ex rel.* Lockyer v. FERC, 383 F.3d 1006 (9th Cir. 2004). The court further concluded that the FERC could order retroactive refunds to recover unjust or unreasonable rates, an interpretation that surprised some at FERC. Hon. Joseph T. Kelliher & Maria Farniella, *The Changing Landscape of Federal Energy Law*, 61 ADMIN. L. REV. 611, 630 (2009).

[41]   NAVIGANT CONSULTING, INC., EVOLUTION OF THE ELECTRIC INDUSTRY STRUCTURE IN THE U.S. AND RESULTING ISSUES 13 (Oct. 8, 2013).

[42]   Monitoring Analytics, LLC, Independent Market Monitor for PJM, State of the Market Report for PJM, 1 (March 9, 2017).

functional unbundling of the electric industry in the mid-1990s."[43] The order charged managers of organized markets with considering state renewable policies when performing regional transmission planning. The order, observes Navigant, also imposed "requirements for regional and interregional planning, cost allocation, consideration of public policy requirements, and elimination of" a utility's ability to reserve a right of first refusal for constructing new facilities – albeit retaining some benefit to an incumbent transmission provider interested in participating in a new transmission project.[44] But, aside from what these managers might decide, each state where a transmission line might transect could decide not to allow the transmission owner the authority to condemn the necessary rights of way for construction. Unlike natural gas pipelines that enjoy federal eminent-domain authority when FERC issues them a certificate of public convenience and necessity, electric transmission lines lack any such benefit. Order No. 1000, moreover, skirted its policy toward merchant transmission lines, those non-incumbents willing to build transmission lines and recover the costs of construction through negotiated rates. One of the nation's largest merchant developers, Clean Line, chastised FERC by suggesting that the order only requires coordination among neighboring planning regions, but Clean Line's projects span considerable distances, and as such, "Order [No.] 1000 perpetuates a free rider problem."[45] This federal/state dynamic prompts energy law professor Steven Ferry to ask "whether it is the federal government or the states that can better regulate multistate energy projects."[46]

In the late 1990s, a few states, led by California, deregulated their electric utilities by requiring them to divest most of their generators, to turn over control of their transmission facilities to RTOs, and to allow retail competitors to use their distribution facilities. The state already had embraced PURPA, and by 1991, about a third of the state's energy was produced by independents.[47] California's restructuring program required its three investor-owned utilities (IOUs) to open up their service territories to retail competition, to divest most of their fossil fuel generation within the state, to turn over operation of their transmission facilities to a private, nonprofit

[43] Brief of Respondent Federal Energy Regulatory Commission, South Carolina Pub. Serv. Auth. v. FERC, Nos. 12–1232 3 (Sept. 25, 2013). *See* FERC Order No. 1000, Transmission Planning and Cost Allocation by Transmission Owning and Operating Public Facilities, 76 Fed. Reg. 49,842 (Aug. 11, 2011).

[44] Navigant Consulting, Inc., Evolution of the Electric Industry Structure in the U.S. and Resulting Issues, vi (Oct. 8, 2013). *See also* Shelley Welton & Michael B. Gerrard, *FERC Order 1000 as a New Tool for Promoting Energy Efficiency and Demand Response*, 42 ENVTL. L. REP. NEWS & ANALYSIS 11025 (2012); *e.g.*, South Carolina Public Serv. Auth. v. FERC (D.C. Cir. 2014); MISO Transmission Owners v. FERC, 819 F.3d 329 (7th Cir. 2016); Emera Maine v. FERC, 854 F.3d 662 (D.C. Cir. 2017).

[45] Louis Pitre, *What We're Thinking: FERC Order 1000, What Does It Mean to Clean Line?*, post on cleanlineenergy.com, June 18, 2012.

[46] Steven Ferry, *Efficiency in the Regulatory Crucible: Navigating 21st Century 'Smart' Technology and Power*, JOURNAL OF ENERGY & ENVTL. L. 1, 12 (Winter 2012).

[47] RICHARD F. HIRSCH, POWER LOSS: THE ORIGINS OF DEREGULATION AND RESTRUCTURING IN THE AMERICAN ELECTRIC UTILITY SYSTEM 93–100 (MIT Press 1999).

corporation, the CAISO, and to purchase nearly all of their wholesale power from the newly established California Power Exchange (PX) or from the CAISO auction markets.[48] The CAISO operates the investor-owned utility transmission facilities in California, schedules generation and transmission over the grid, manages transmission congestion, and operates single-price auction markets for real-time energy, ancillary services, and firm transmission rights. The real-time energy market balances generation and load in "real time." The "forward markets" permit buyers and sellers to balance generation and load in advance of actual delivery, i.e., hour ahead, day ahead, or months ahead. The single-price auction market pays all bidders whose bids are accepted, a market-clearing price equal to the highest accepted bid. The PX, before its untimely demise (see below), operated single-price auction markets for forward energy – hour-ahead, day-ahead, and "block forward" markets (a market for blocks of power over a future period). The IOUs retained their distribution systems and an obligation to continue to provide a "default retail" sales service at rates that were frozen at about 10 percent lower than their pre-restructuring rates. They were permitted to recover their "stranded costs" through a competitive transition charge equal to the amount by which their frozen retail rates exceeded their wholesale power and other costs.

The California experiment turned out poorly, to say the least. Starting in June 2000, wholesale rates far exceeded the frozen retail rates for the state's two largest utilities, ultimately resulting in PG&E, the state's largest utility, and the PX petitioning for relief under Chapter 11 of the Bankruptcy Code and the state's second-largest utility, Southern California Edison Company, becoming insolvent. During the first quarter of 2001, wholesale prices for energy in the spot market averaged over 10 times higher than in 1998 and 1999. Yet the California utilities purchasing that energy could not pass through all the higher costs to their retail customers. Consumers nevertheless experienced a large increase in retail rates and rolling blackouts during the winter and spring of 2001. The state itself incurred massive indebtedness as the backup purchaser for electric power in the state, and the California Public Utilities Commission responded by decreeing an end to retail competition in the state.[49]

As the ill-fated California program unfolded, it became increasingly evident that not only were wholesale prices exceeding levels that would be expected in a competitive market but also that the CAISO and the FERC were unable to take effective steps to ensure that the wholesale market was workably competitive. In October 1999, the CAISO Market Surveillance Committee (MSC), of which

[48]   Richard J. Pierce, Jr., *How Will the California Debacle Affect Energy Deregulation?*, 54 ADMIN. L. REV. 389 (2001); *See* Eric Hirst, The California Electricity Crisis: Lessons for Other States, 3 & 4 (Prepared for Edison Electric Institute July 2001).

[49]   JAMES L. SWEENEY, THE CALIFORNIA ELECTRICITY CRISIS (Hoover Inst. Press 2002); Paul J. Joskow, *California's Electricity Crisis*, 17 OXFORD REV. OF ECON. POL'Y; Congressional Budget Office, Causes and Lessons of the California Electricity Crisis (CBO Sept. 2001).

one of the authors, Robert Nordhaus, was a member between 1998 and 2001, reported how in the summer months of 1998 and 1999 average wholesale prices were significantly above prices that would be expected in a fully competitive market.[50] Subsequent reports of the MSC indicated that the performance of California's market was inconsistent with what could be expected in a fully competitive market.[51] The MSC concluded that California's market design and California and federal regulatory policies permitted ready exercise of market power in periods of high demand. The CAISO market structure had the effect of allowing "pivotal bidders" to drive up market-clearing prices by withholding output or by pricing it well in excess of marginal (running) cost. In addition, information made public in the coverage of the 2001 Enron bankruptcy showed how Enron had engaged in a series of market-manipulating strategies that exacerbated the already serious price impacts of the pivotal bidders. The result, as the MSC reported, was that in June 2000, average wholesale prices were almost *three* times the level that would be expected in a competitive market.[52] For the entire 2000 calendar year, wholesale prices in the California market exceeded PG&E's frozen retail rates by 40 percent and Southern California Edison's by 30 percent.

FERC AND THE STATES RESPOND TO THE CALIFORNIA ENERGY CRISIS

Both California and federal regulators eventually responded to the wholesale price explosion in the California market. FERC belatedly reined in runaway wholesale prices both in California and in other western states. It reregulated the deregulated western states wholesale markets and reexamined its long-standing policies toward market-based rates. Specifically, FERC required that generators inside California make unscheduled capacity available in the CAISO real-time energy market. FERC also imposed limits (based on the generation unit running cost) on generator's bids into the CAISO's spot markets and ultimately commenced a massive administrative proceeding to determine refunds due for spot sales at prices above a "mitigated market clearing price" that was set at a level intended to replicate the price expected in a workably competitive market. Similar rules were subsequently imposed for the other western states.

Also, because of the 2000–1 experience in California and the western states, FERC reexamined its policies for market-based rates. FERC envisioned a more sophisticated test for market power, broadening the circumstances when refunds under market-based rates may be collected.

---

[50] Frank A. Wolak, Chairman, Mkt. Surveillance Comm. of Cal. Indep. Sys. Operator, Report on Redesign of California Real-Time Energy and Ancillary Services Market, 64 (1999).
[51] Frank A. Wolak, Chairman, Robert R. Nordhaus, Member, & Carl Shapiro, Member, Mkt. Surveillance Comm. of Cal. Indep. Sys. Operator, Long-Term Price Cap Policy, 3 (2000).
[52] *Ibid.* at 3 (stating how at that time the California energy market was not "workably competitive").

In the longer term, both FERC and states also adopted policies for shaping both competitive RTO markets and state regulation. At the federal level, FERC revamped its methodology for determining whether applicants for market-based rates exercised market power. The Commission also required that RTOs redesign their energy, ancillary service and capacity markets to make them less susceptible to the exercise of market power and manipulation and armed RTOs' market monitors with the tools necessary to detect and remedy an exercise of market power and manipulation.

Congress also intervened by strengthening federal supervision to thwart market manipulation. In the Energy Policy Act of 2005, Congress invested the FERC with new tools for policing its markets, including civil remedies to punish market manipulation (criminal penalties would be pursued to the Department of Justice), limited authority over otherwise exempt public power entities' wholesale sales and transmission, electricity market transparency rules, and earlier effective dates for refund orders. A former FERC commissioner described this authority as having been modeled after the 1934 Securities Exchange Act and embodied a significant change to the Federal Power Act Part II.[53] Two years later, Congress again visited energy policy, passing this time the Energy Independence and Security Act. This Act contains a host of programs, including charging the FERC with exploring how to assist states with encouraging demand response.[54] It "continued," explains one energy attorney, "the trend of putting federal policy-makers in a more prominent role with respect to matters also within state jurisdiction."[55]

The net result, twenty-five years after FERC commenced "deregulation" of wholesale markets, is that today we have a group of organized wholesale markets run by RTOs that in some respects are more heavily regulated than wholesale transactions ever were under cost-of-service regulation. We now have complex tests for generator market power, intricate rules for bidding in and setting prices in these markets, and the authority to monitor markets and undo transactions to mitigate market power or market manipulation.

The California crisis also had major implications at the state level. As discussed earlier, California increased retail rates, was forced to purchase power on behalf of its utilities, and essentially ended its retail competition policy. Until 2001, many other states were moving (or had moved) toward "deregulation" programs like California's. But California's difficulties led some states that had not taken irreversible steps to restructure their utilities to suspend or terminate their restructuring programs. States that had required their utilities

---

[53] Kelliher & Farniella, *supra* note 40, at 627.
[54] Pub. L. No. 110–140, 121 Stat. 1492 (Dec. 19, 2007).
[55] Jeffery S. Dennis, *Twenty-Five Years of Electricity Law, Policy, and Regulation: A Look Back*, 25 NAT. RES. & ENV'T 33 (Summer 2010).

to divest generation or turn operation of the utility transmission over to RTOs were not able as a practical matter to reverse course even if they wanted to because FERC – not the state – was now in charge of generation and transmission. The result was a patchwork of state regulatory schemes – some largely retaining the New Deal model of vertically integrated utilities regulated on a cost-of-service basis, others restructuring their utility systems using the more successful model developed by the Northeast states and RTOs. At present, many states in the Southeast and Northwest have rejected RTOs and retained some version of the New Deal model. Most other states have permitted (or required) their utilities to join RTOs and, in some instances, have required divestiture of utility-owned generation and embraced retail competition.

THE "WHO IS IN CHARGE" ISSUE

Changes in use of the grid, including its transformation into a "smart grid," the deployment of distributed generation (small-scale generation facilities such as rooftop solar, usually on customer premises) and associated net-metering policies, the development of FERC-regulated organized wholesale markets, new market entrants such as merchant transmission owners and nonutility storage facilities, and demand response policies in those markets collectively render *Colton's* wholesale/retail "bright line" increasingly difficult to apply. This difficulty is unlikely to dissipate as the FERC explores how its supervised RTO and ISO organized markets can accommodate state policymakers' preferences for a resource, such as zero- or low-carbon generation. The same entity may be both a retail purchaser from and a seller at wholesale to an electric utility (or may otherwise participate in FERC-regulated wholesale markets). For instance, distributed generation, net metering, and demand response programs defy the notion that there is a clear distinction between wholesale and retail markets. Retail purchasers of electricity sell electricity at wholesale; they also sell demand response (reductions in retail demand) into wholesale markets. Moreover, in regulating utilities selling electricity at retail, states frequently direct them to enter into purchase-power agreements (PPAs) with new or existing generating facilities. These PPAs lower market-clearing prices in FERC-regulated wholesale markets, and several courts have held that these arrangements constitute wholesale price setting preempted by the FPA.

Distributed Generation.   Distributed generation reverses the Edison/Insull model of a central service station and instead localizes the generation facilities by having them located near their load, or customers. The increasing deployment of distributed generation resources (such as rooftop solar or photovoltaic [PV]) capable not only of supplying the load of the host customer but also of sending power into the grid triggers a series of intriguing questions with respect to who regulates these transactions. The distributed-generation resource is still connected to the grid, because the utility continues to deliver power to the customer when the distributed resource is unavailable or is insufficient to meet its load. On the one hand, this service would ordinarily be regarded as a retail transaction. On the other hand, the sale of surplus power from the distributed-generation facility to the utility to which it is connected could, at least in theory, be treated as a sale for resale in interstate commerce if the utility is connected to the interstate grid.

Meanwhile, although to date these transactions have been subject to state rather than federal authority, states have wrestled with how the energy sold back into the grid ought to be priced. States have developed net metering policies that allow a customer to net out sales to the utility against retail sales to the customer.[56] These policies effectively require that distribution utilities purchase surplus output of rooftop solar generation and similar resources at the utility's retail rate – usually more than avoided cost – even though this too was a wholesale sale seemingly subject to FERC jurisdiction if the utility is connected to the interstate grid. "Net metering," explains a DOE study, "allows homes and businesses with onsite PV systems to offset their electricity consumption regardless of the temporal match between PV production and electricity consumption."[57] Some opposition to net metering persists, with some utilities arguing that net metering customers are not paying their share of utilities' capital costs and instead are forcing others in the system to shoulder those costs. Congress amended Title I of PURPA in 2005 to require that state commissions and nonregulated utilities consider and determine whether to implement net metering.

A series of net metering cases have attempted to define the jurisdictional line between retail sales to end users and wholesale sales by end users to the grid. The result of these cases is that if distributed generation deliveries into the grid are less than consumption by the end user during the applicable billing period, they are subject to state jurisdiction.[58] If, however, a net surplus is delivered into the grid during the billing period, the FERC exercises jurisdiction.[59] Also, states have implemented feed-in tariffs allowing distribution utilities to purchase the output of renewable generation facilities at a standard rate set by statute or state regulators, again, a seemingly wholesale sale to the utility.[60] While the FERC initially rejected state-required feed-in tariffs at purchase rates above the purchasing utilities' system-

---

[56] Richard Revesz & Burcin Unel, *Managing the Future of the Electricity Grid: Distributed Generation and Net Metering*, 41 HARV. ENVTL. L. REV. 43 (2017).

[57] NAÏM R. DARGHOUTH, RYAN WISER, GALEN BARBOSE & ANDREW MILLS, NET METERING AND MARKET FEEDBACK LOOPS: EXPLORING THE IMPACT OF RETAIL RATE DESIGN ON DISTRIBUTED PV DEPLOYMENT 2 (Ernest Orlando Lawrence Berkeley National Laboratory July 2015).

[58] Southern Cal. Edison Co. v. FERC, 603 F.3d 996 (D.C. Cir. 2010), *remanded sub nom.* Duke Energy Moss Landing v. Cal. Indep. Sys. Operator Corp., 132 F.E.R.C. ¶ 61,183 (2010), *reh'g denied*, 134 F.E.R.C. ¶ 61,151 (2010), *aff'd sub nom.*, Calpine Corp. FERC, 702 F.3d 41 (D.C. Cir. 2012).

[59] Sun Edison LLC, 129 F.E.R.C. ¶ 61,146 at P 18 (2009).

[60] Southern Cal. Edison Co., 603 F.3d at 996 (rejecting as inconsistent with PURPA's avoided cost rules).

wide avoided cost, it eventually settled on a rule that permitted a resource-specific avoided cost (e.g., avoided cost for solar generation).

These evolving rules seemingly make little policy sense. FERC has little incentive for acting under federal law to bar state policies that may require above-avoided-cost purchases of distributed generation output as long as ratepayers in the state bear the economic burden of the higher price. Those ratepayers, after all, have the state political process available to them to decide whether to accept or reject the consequences.

New York, for instance, has been engaged in reforming capacity markets. It has decided to tilt more toward promoting distributed generation, potentially pushing the envelope of the federal/state divide. New York's program, called Reforming the Energy Vision (REV), explores how best to promote customer choice, incentivize low-carbon energy capacity, offer consumers low energy costs, and ensure resiliency in the electric power system. The state's public utility commission, when examining traditional cost-of-service regulation, reasons that "its core statutory duties can no longer be met with the utility regulatory model of the previous century."[61] A principal thrust is having a renewable-energy decentralized system providing electricity.[62] The objective, though, is to be even more transformative: in the words of the state commission, "to establish markets so that customers and third parties can be active participants, to achieve dynamic load management on a system-wide-scale, resulting in a more efficient and secure electric system including better utilization of bulk generation and transmission resources." To accomplish this, though, will require that utilities in the state "serve as a seamless interface between aggregated customers and the" FERC-regulated New York ISO. This naturally straddles the federal/state divide, even though the state assiduously is targeting only the state side of that line. And so too, another component of REV will likely include solar power–driven microgrids, including through a Community Solar Program, that will allow customers to aggregate solar energy and then have that energy sold into the community – all seemingly on the state side of the *Attleboro* line but not without some question.[63]

---

[61] PSNY, Case 14-M-0101, Order Adopting a Ratemaking and Utility Revenue Model Policy Framework, May 19, 2016, at 1.

[62] New York Public Service Comm'n, Case 14-M-0101, Order Adopting Regulatory Policy Framework and Implementation Plan (Feb. 26, 2015); Jonathan A. Binder and Patrick E. Foster, *Comparing Ambitious Energy Reforms: The German Energiewende and New York State REV*, 30 NAT. RES. & ENVT. 8 (Spring 2016). The Brattle Group prepared a detailed report suggesting that the New York ISO could incorporate a carbon price into its wholesale market to assist New York in decarbonizing its energy market. Samuel A. Newell et al., Pricing Carbon into NYISO's Wholesale Energy Market to Support New York's Decarbonization Goals (Aug. 10, 2017).

[63] Southern Maryland Cooperative, Inc., 157 FERC ¶ 61118 (2016) (Maryland's community solar pilot program and arguments about whether the state had the authority).

Organized Markets.   In the United States, about two-thirds of electric power today is delivered through RTOs and ISOs, which operate the transmission grid within a defined region, provide transmissions services, and operate wholesale energy markets (and in some cases capacity markets) for their respective region. RTOs, the transmission services they provide and the energy capacity markets they operate (outside of Texas), might appear to be subject to the FERC's exclusive jurisdiction over transmission and wholesale sales in interstate commerce, but here, as with distributed generation, drawing the line between wholesale and retail has become increasingly difficult. Several recent controversies and the litigation they have engendered illustrate this difficulty.

Demand Response.   RTO tariffs for several years have permitted end users to offer demand response (a temporary reduction in an end user's electric load) into whole-sale energy and capacity markets as if it were generation. The FERC, in its Order No. 745, required that RTO energy markets that allowed demand response partici-pation to provide the same price to demand response as they did for energy offered by electric generators.

In *EPSA* v. *FERC*, the DC Circuit held not only that FERC's pricing rule in Order No. 745 was arbitrary and capricious but also that it lacked authority to regulate demand response offered into FERC-regulated wholesale markets because the Commission was trying to regulate retail markets. The Supreme Court correctly disagreed and affirmed FERC's authority, reasoning that the Commission possesses the authority to regulate activities that directly affect wholesale rates. But the controversy illustrates the difficulty the FERC, states, and courts confront when applying the "bright line" to today's grid, in circum-stances where end users are both retail customers and participants in wholesale markets.[64]

This is more than merely a pedantic concern. If the Court had held otherwise, it would have removed a key element of elasticity of demand that could moderate prices in organized energy markets, resulting in higher market-clearing prices and, in some cases, unnecessary dispatch of fossil fuel generators that would otherwise operate less in these markets. In these auction markets, the market-clearing price is set by the highest accepted bid. Demand response bids that undercut fossil generation bids result in a lower market-clearing price and

---

[64]   Order No. 745, *Demand Response Compensation in Organized Wholesale Energy Markets*, 76 Fed. Reg. 16,658 (2011) [Order No. 745]; *order on reh'g*, Order No. 745-A, 137 F.E.R.C. ¶ 61,215 (2011); *reh'g denied*, Order No. 745-B 138 F.E.R.C. ¶ 61,148 (2012); *vacated sub nom.*, Elec. Power Supply Ass'n v. FERC (*EPSA*), 753 F.3d 216 (D.C. Cir. 2014), *reversed*, FERC v. Elec. Power Supply Ass'n, 136 S. Ct. 760 (2016). *See generally* Joel B. Eisen, *Who Regulates the Smart Grid? FERC's Authority over Demand Response Compensation in Wholesale Electricity Markets*, 69 SAN. DIEGO J. CLIMATE & ENERGY L. 69 (2013); James J. Hoecker & Douglas W. Smith, *Regulatory Federalism and Development of Electric Transmission: A Brewing Storm?*, 35 ENERGY L. J. 71 (2014); Sharon B. Jacobs, *Bypassing Federalism and the Administrative Law of Negawatts*, 100 IOWA L. REV. 885 (2015); Jim Rossi, *The Brave New Path of Energy Federalism*, 95 TEX. L. REV. 399 (2016).

less fossil fuel generation. Higher market-clearing prices and unnecessary fossil fuel generator dispatch will, in turn, raise consumer electric rates and could increase emissions of carbon dioxide (CO_2) and other pollutants. But the emissions-related consequences of demand response are complicated and may depend on several variables.

Capacity Markets.   As noted earlier, all RTOs operate the transmission system within their footprint, and all operate energy and ancillary service auction markets. Three Northeast RTOs (New York Independent System Operator, Inc., PJM Interconnection, L.L.C., and ISO New England, Inc.) also operate mandatory auction-based capacity markets through which retail sellers of electricity must acquire capacity rights sufficient to cover their peak demand. As in the energy markets, generators bid into the capacity markets, and the highest accepted bid sets the market-clearing price. These capacity markets were developed, among other reasons, because bid caps in RTO energy markets and other constraints on wholesale energy prices limited generator revenues and were thought to imperil continued operation of existing generation facilities and discourage construction of new facilities.

After some experience with the Northeast capacity markets, several states and many utilities complained that these markets unnecessarily raised consumer prices (by imposing high capacity costs on retail electricity sellers) but were ineffective in eliciting investment in needed new generation. As a result, they took steps to ensure that new generation facilities they regarded as necessary either for environmental reasons or for consumer protection would be built. Because the addition of this new generation capacity into RTO markets would reduce ("suppress" in FERC parlance) capacity prices in those markets, the FERC developed "buyer-side mitigation" (BSM) measures that imposed minimum offer price requirements, which had the effect of excluding many of these new resources from the capacity market auction.[65]

These state generation development strategies also triggered preemption challenges from incumbent generators. For example, when Maryland and New Jersey attempted to direct utilities under their jurisdiction to offer competitive solicitations for new generation capacity (gas-fired plants) in their respective states, incumbent generators sued to enjoin those arrangements. The Fourth Circuit, in *PPL Energy, LLC v. Nazarian*, held the FPA preempted Maryland from directing its distribution utilities to enter into contracts with a merchant generator that would, in the court's view, subsidize the generator's entry into, and suppress prices in, FERC-regulated wholesale capacity markets, which the court observed are "quite sensitive to external

---

[65] *New England Power Generators v. FERC* and related cases upheld FERC's BSM policies. New England Power Generators Ass'n v. FERC, 757 F.3d 283 (D.C. Cir. 2014); N.J. Bd. of Pub. Utils. v. FERC, 744 F.3d 74 (3rd Cir. 2014).

tampering."[66] A companion New Jersey case in the Third Circuit reached a comparable result.[67] These cases threatened to go beyond excluding "subsidized" resources from capacity markets – they bar their construction and operation altogether.[68]

These cases, though, have become less problematic as other courts have begun interpreting the Supreme Court's admonition in *Hughes*. *Hughes* involved Maryland's program, and the Fourth Circuit's decision that the FPA preempted the program made its way to the Supreme Court.[69] The Court issued a narrowly crafted opinion agreeing that Maryland's program conflicted with the Commission's jurisdiction over wholesale rates in the regional capacity market. But the Court further signaled that not all local subsidies affecting capacity markets would run afoul of the federal/state divide.

This led the Second Circuit to feel comfortable in upholding Connecticut's program.[70] Connecticut's legislature prompted the state's energy regulator, in the courts words, "to solicit proposals for renewable energy generation, to select winning bids from such solicitations, and then to 'direct' Connecticut's utilities to 'enter into' wholesale energy contracts with the winning bidders." A disappointed bidder challenged the program, claiming in part that it violated the dormant Commerce Clause and was preempted by the FPA. The court rejected these claims, reasoning on the latter that the state was not really compelling the winning bidder to sign a wholesale contract with a utility (for an entity that would not qualify as a PURPA QF). Connecticut's program, the court explained, acceded to FERC's review of the bilateral contract between the utility and the successful bidder and did not, as in *Hughes*, establish a guaranteed price for wholesale sales that effectively altered the functioning of the regional organized market. The successful bidder explained how Connecticut's program was important for renewable projects because otherwise such projects would "fare poorly in FERC's multi-state, market based system. Renewable energy [as of 2014] is generally more expensive than power generated by non-renewable resources," and because they would not necessarily be delivering their power directly to a Connecticut utility, they might not want to "take on Enron-style energy risks because of the potential difference between the locational marginal price of energy" where the project would be constructed and the locational marginal price in Connecticut. And once the court affirmed Connecticut's program, courts elsewhere immediately

[66] PPL Energyplus, LLC v. Nazarian, 753 F.3d 467, 473 (4th Cir. 2014).
[67] PPL Energy Plus, LLC v. Solomon, 766 F.3d 241, 246 (3d Cir. 2014).
[68] In 2014, the FERC declined to enter the controversy, reasoning that the courts had already determined the involved contracts were void. CVP Shore, L.L.C., 148 F.E.R.C. ¶ 61,096 (2014).
[69] Hughes v. Talen, 136 S. Ct. 1288 (2016).
[70] Allco Finance Ltd. v. Klee, 861 F.3d 82 (2nd Cir. 2017).

upheld state subsidies for nuclear power generation in regional organized markets.[71]

In the spring of 2017, the dilemma confronting state policies and regional markets prompted the FERC to convene a technical conference. Participants generally addressed a thematic question implicitly posed by the Commission. How should regional wholesale capacity markets, not geared toward focusing on any one type of generation resource, "select resources of interest to state policy makers while preserving the benefits of regional markets and economic resource selection"?[72] While the participants engaged on an array of issues, William Hogan from the Harvard Kennedy School perhaps captured the fundamental problem about energy markets in "stress": "[t]he increasing impact of federal and state policies to support technologies, or specific facilities, raises questions about the viability of wholesale power markets. There are regular expressions that the Commission and competitive wholesale power markets are not up to the task."[73] He favored appropriate price tools–signaled subsidies, and even the Commission's demand response pricing and cost allocation rules, as poor examples of tinkering with capacity markets in the wrong way.

It should be now somewhat self-evident that the "bright line" is no longer "easily ascertained." More significantly, even if one's glasses were so finely tuned, it would make little sense for today's grid, and even less for tomorrow's. RTOs and multistate utility systems (such as the Southern Company), after all, operate much of the grid. RTOs operate most organized wholesale markets under FERC supervision. However, key management decisions on siting of generation and transmission facilities and on generation mix are made on a state-by-state basis. States have, and will continue to have, the major responsibility for protecting the interests of retail electric consumers, regulating land use (for nonfederal lands), and protecting air and water quality in the state, subject to minimum federal standards under the Clean Air Act and the Clean Water Act. States' ability to implement these responsibilities is unnecessarily cabined by the potentially preemptive capacity of the current jurisdictional arrangement under the FPA. Either states ought to be given clear authority to carry out their consumer protection and environmental responsibilities, or those responsibilities should be vested elsewhere.

---

[71] Coalition for Competitive Electricity, Dynegy, Inc. v. Zibelman, 272 F. Supp.3d 554 (S.D. N.Y. July 25, 2017); Village of Old Mill Creek v. Star, 2017 WL 3008289 (N.D. Ill. July 14, 2017). *See generally* Ari Peskoe, *Easing Jurisdictional Tensions by Integrating Public Policy in Wholesale Electricity Markets*, 38 ENERGY L. J. 1 (2017); Joel B. Eisen, *Dual Electricity Federalism Is Dead, But How Dead and What Replaces It?*, 8 GEO. WASH. J. OF ENERGY & ENVT. L. 3 (2017).

[72] Technical Conference, State Polices and Wholesale Markets Operated by ISO New England Inc., New York Independent System Operator, Inc., and PJM Interconnection, L.L.C., Docket No. AD17-11–000, May 1, May 2, 2017.

[73] Comments of William Hogan, Docket No. AD17-11–000, May 2, 2017.

Moreover, trying to apply the "bright line" to tomorrow's grid may be even more problematic than applying it to today's. New technologies and new commercial practices, include

- **Microgrids** – where retail customers in an area take power from, and deliver the output of distributed generation into, a local network, which, in turn, may purchase or sell at wholesale to a distribution utility;
- **Smart Grids** – where the relationship between the utility and customer is redefined and information flows bidirectionally, and the parties can instantly monitor and respond[74];
- **Energy Storage** – where end users may charge storage at retail and discharge and sell at wholesale;
- **Automated Demand Response** – where an RTO can signal retail customers to reduce demand or charge or discharge batteries or other storage; and
- **Real-Time and Dynamic Pricing** – which permits customers to increase or decrease energy use based on price.

These developments all challenge the assumption that wholesale and retail populate different worlds. For example, those promoting energy storage, possibly the future for any electric grid – whether distributed or otherwise, already are engaged in dialogues about whether the existing regulatory structure adequately sends the right signals and allocates authority appropriately between the states and the federal government. How this conversation unfolds could have profound effects because energy storage costs have decreased considerably over the last 10 years, and according to some at McKinsey & Company, the technology is "entering a dynamic and uncertain period."[75] One energy lawyer, consequently, observes that "[b]ecause energy storage facilities have attributes of generation, transmission, and distribution assets, they do not rest solely within one federal jurisdiction or state jurisdiction, let alone fit neatly into traditional ratemaking categories."[76]

In November 2016, the FERC at least accepted the cudgel and signaled its interest in removing barriers present in FERC-regulated organized markets to energy storage at the wholesale level.[77] It is proposing to do so by requiring that RTOs and ISOs "establish distributed energy resource aggregators as a type of market participant and allow the distributed energy resource aggregators to register distributed energy

---

[74] Congress provided its own definition in 2007. Energy Independence and Security Act of 2007, Pub. L. No. 110–140, 121 Stat. 1492, § 1306(d).

[75] David Frankel and Amy Wagner, Battery Storage: The Next Disruptive Technology in the Power Sector, McKinsey & Company, June 2017.

[76] Michael J. Allen, Energy Storage: *The Emerging Legal Framework (And Why It Makes a Difference)*, 30 Nat. Res. & Envt. 20, 21 (Spring 2016). *See also* Amy L. Stein, *Reconsidering Regulatory Uncertainty: Making a Case for Energy Storage*, 41 Fla. St. U. L. Rev. 696 (2014).

[77] Electric Storage Participation in Markets Operated by Regional Transmission Organizations and Independent System Operators, 157 FERC ¶ 61121 (Nov. 2016).

resource aggregations." By aggregating their storage capacity, energy storage facilities can more effectively participate in an organized market. But is energy storage that occurs behind the meter really a wholesale transaction, or should it be treated like home PV sales back into the grid? FERC concluded that "the sale of energy from the grid used to charge electric storage resources for later resale" is a wholesale transaction when resold, but the FERC appreciated that more work was necessary to figure out what happens if those behind the meter energy storage facilities distribute their power at the retail level but at wholesale rates. So, too, Joel Eisen, one of the nation's top energy law experts, notes how deploying smart grid technology will likely "require [] coordination of efforts between the different levels of government, and perhaps even a new distribution of regulatory authority."[78] As such, energy storage, smart grid technologies, and the host of other developments may require new approaches to regulation that cannot easily be accommodated by the existing wholesale/retail division of labor.

FERC and the judiciary, of course, can try to muddle through and make the existing framework function. Whether this is even possible is a significant question, but in any case muddling through will entail litigation, uncertainty, and delay, as the saga of the *EPSA* controversy illustrates. The FERC proposed its Order No. 745 rule in March 2010 and finalized it in March 2011. The DC Circuit overturned the rule in May 2014. The Supreme Court issued its decision in 2016, six years after the rule was proposed and five years after it was finalized. Even though the FERC ultimately prevailed on its effort, the jurisdictional challenges precipitated considerable uncertainty and unnecessarily delayed the full consumer benefit of demand response in organized RTO markets.

ELECTRIC POWER REGULATION FOLLIES AND SUCCESSES

Looking back over the last century of utility regulation, several choices stand out as acutely problematic. The first is the *Attleboro* ruling itself, discussed in Chapter 3, which was broader than it needed to be and whose analysis was later abandoned by the Supreme Court. This decision set the stage for Congress to prescribe a division of labor between state and federal regulators that, thanks to the Supreme Court's later intervention in the *Colton* case, locked in a jurisdictional "bright line" that neither the FERC nor the states can change. As use of the grid has changed with distributed generation, demand response, and the need for a rapid shift to low-carbon resources, jurisdictional disputes arising from the inability to apply the "bright line" threaten to invalidate key federal or state initiatives and will continue to invite uncertainty and litigation that will delay modernization of the electric power system.

---

[78] Joel B. Eisen, *Smart Regulation and Federalism for the Smart Grid*, 37 HARV. ENVTL. L. REV. 1, 2 (2013); *see also* Joel B. Eisen, *Open Access Distribution Tariff: Removing Barriers to Innovation on the Smart Grid*, 61 U.C.L.A. L. REV. 1712 (2014).

The second decision point was the design and implementation of the California deregulation program. The design flaws in the California program and the failure of state and federal regulators to promptly repair those flaws led not only to a massive failure of the California experiment (with rolling blackouts and massive rate increases in California and other western states) but also impelled many states to abandon the California model and revert to traditional cost-of-service regulation. The result is a patchwork of state regulatory policies under which states decide whether utilities they regulate remain vertically integrated or must divest their generation and join RTOs. This patchwork makes it difficult to attain the economies of scale and efficiencies of regional dispatch of generation that could occur under a more uniform system of state regulation.

A third choice (really a series of decisions by the FERC and the courts) is the design of RTO energy and capacity markets, which appear mind-numbingly complex, incapable of keeping needed existing generation running, and rather than incentivizing new generation arguably erect barriers to entry into RTO markets. Of some concern are the FERC's capacity market policies. First, as discussed earlier, there are continuing "who is in charge" issues as the use of the grid and commercial practices develop and change. Second, in the case of BSM policies, even though the FERC oversees this aspect of RTO regulation, the BSM policies sometimes make little sense. The fundamental objective of the RTO capacity markets is to supplement revenues from energy markets so that needed new capacity will be constructed. However, because the BSM minimum offer price rule can exclude new generation from the capacity market even if the owner is willing to be a "price taker," it presents a substantial barrier to entry of new generation into RTO markets. Third, even where new generation can bid into the capacity market, the revenue stream (one to seven years, depending on the RTO) is not long enough, or certain enough, to finance a new generation facility.

Thus, closing in on a century after *Attleboro*, the division of regulatory authority over the electric power industry is still largely dictated by *Attleboro's* wholesale/retail distinction. But, for much of today's grid, the wholesale/retail distinction is increasingly unworkable. And even where it is clear who is in charge, the patchwork of state regulation and the FERC's difficulties in regulating RTO-organized markets make the existing system increasingly problematic. Congress, federal and state regulators, and the courts need to look at ways of combining state and federal regulation under a single regional agency or a single regional regulatory proceeding or to redraw the "bright line" in a manner that is better suited to management of today's and tomorrow's grid. Regional regulation will also help in dealing with the patchwork problem and make RTO regulation more workable. But unless these issues are addressed meaningfully, electric power regulation is likely to become an obstacle rather than an enabler of efficient and reliable delivery of low- or zero-carbon electricity to consumers.

5

Natural Gas's Tortured Road from Regulation to Decontrol

The 1938 Natural Gas Act (NGA), like its 1935 predecessor the Federal Power Act (FPA), sought to establish at the federal level the regulatory authority the US Supreme Court eliminated at the state level. In 1924, the Supreme Court decided *Missouri* v. *Kansas Natural Gas Company*, the natural gas counterpart of – and precursor to – the *Attleboro* case discussed in Chapter 3. The *Kansas* Court held that state utility commissions lacked authority to regulate rates for sale of natural gas by interstate pipelines to local distribution companies for resale. In removing what it regarded as state barriers to interstate trafficking of natural gas, the Court effectively removed state regulation of interstate transportation and sales for resale of natural gas. Although the country's first 100-mile-plus pipeline was constructed in 1891 in the Midwest, when the Court issued the *Kansas Natural Gas* opinion, only a few interstate pipelines existed, and it would be another year before seamless pipes would be developed to allow greater interstate transportation.

By 1938, this had all changed: along with advances in gas compression technology, reportedly over 50,000 miles of pipelines transported over 400 billion cubic feet of gas across state or international borders.[1] And with this growth, the Federal Trade Commission issued a scathing roughly 600-page report chronicling the gas industry's monopolistic practices – propelling congressional action. This mirrored the parallel inquiry into electric utility holding companies, leading to passage of the Public Utility Holding Company Act of 1935. Again, mirroring the electric power industry, Congress chose to regulate the gas industry under a public utility–type model rather than merely as common carriers that would need to provide access to their pipelines. As Justice Douglas explained, "the 'basic purpose' of this legislation was 'to occupy' the field in which such cases as *Missouri v. Kansas Gas Company* and *Public Utilities Commission v. Attleboro Steam and Electric*, had held the states might not act."[2]

---

[1] Dozier A. DeVane, *Highlights of Legislative History of the Federal Power Act of 1935 and the Natural Gas Act of 1938*, 14 GEO. WASH. L. REV. 30, 33 (1945–46). *See also* ARLON R. TUSSING & BOB TIPPE, THE NATURAL GAS INDUSTRY: EVOLUTION, STRUCTURE AND ECONOMICS (Ballinger Publishing 1995).

[2] Federal Power Comm'n v. Hope Natural Gas, 320 U.S. 591, 609–10 (1944).

The NGA delegated to the Federal Power Commission (FPC) authority to establish just and reasonable rates for interstate transportation and interstate sales for resale of natural gas and to grant certificates authorizing the transportation and sale of natural gas in interstate commerce, as well as for the construction and operation of facilities for such sale and transportation. Regulated companies cannot cease operating such facilities or terminate certificated transportation and sale unless granted abandonment by the Commission. And retail sales for ultimate public consumption and "production and gathering" were specifically exempted from the Commission's jurisdiction.[3]

The regulatory scheme the FPC implemented in the fifteen years following the NGA's enactment filled the gap the Supreme Court created in its pre-1938 decisions.[4] To be sure, the Court in the years following the NGA still acknowledged the legitimate state interest in conserving its natural resources, such as natural gas (a distinct difference between the electric utility industry and the gas industry), even allowing states the ability to employ conservation laws designed to avoid, in the words of the Court, "preventing rapid and uneconomic dissipation of one of its chief natural resources."[5] The FPC, conversely, during this period established its uniform system of accounts, original cost-rate-base regulation, its cost-allocation and rate-design methodology, and its program for regulating interstate pipelines' own production of natural gas. It declined, however, to regulate independent (non-pipeline) natural gas producers who sold gas to interstate pipelines. The Commission was ill equipped, after all, to regulate the price of natural gas produced at the well, and any suggestion otherwise threatened to overwhelm the agency and adversely affect the industry. The Supreme Court, though, disagreed and in *Phillips Petroleum Co. v. Wisconsin* set the Commission on a decades-long exercise of gas producer regulation described later, eventually contributing significantly, and unnecessarily so, to the 1970s' energy crisis.

DIVERGENT PATHS FOR ELECTRIC AND NATURAL GAS REGULATION

While much of the structure and basic regulatory provisions of the original FPA and NGA are strikingly similar, the regulatory evolution for the two industries diverged.

---

[3] Natural Gas Act §§ 1(b), 4, 5, 7, 15 U.S.C. §§ 717c, d. The NGA confers jurisdiction on the FPC to regulate, *inter alia*, "the sale in interstate commerce of natural gas for resale for ultimate public consumption." Normally, such transactions involve sales by interstate pipeline companies to intrastate distributors who resell the gas to consumers. Direct sales entail one transaction between the interstate carrier and the ultimate consumer and are subject only to limited Commission jurisdiction. *See, e.g.,* FPC v. Transcontinental Gas Corp., 365 U.S. 1, 4 (1961).

[4] The Supreme Court easily upheld the Act's constitutionality. *See* Illinois Natural Gas Co. v. Central Illinois Pub. Serv. Co., 314 U.S. 498 (1942); Federal Power Commission v. Natural Gas Pipeline Co., 315 U.S 575 (1942).

[5] Cities Service Gas Co. v. Peerless Oil & Gas Co., 340 U.S. 179 (1950). The Court, though, caveated its holding by observing how no party suggested that the NGA preempted the state conservation measure, and consequently, it avoided the question. *See also* Hunter Co. v. McHugh, 320 U.S. 222, 227 (1943); Thompson v. Consol. Gas Util. Corp., 300 U.S. 55, 76–77 (1937). But, after *Phillips*, such laws fared less well. *E.g.*, Natural Gas Pipeline Co. of America v. Panoma Corp., 349 U.S. 44 (1955); Natural Gas Pipeline Co. of America v. Corp. Comm'n of Oklahoma, 349 U.S. 44 (1955).

The *Phillips* case (described later) and the *Hartford Electric Light* case held that the FPC could regulate interstate wholesale sales by gas producers and electric generators, respectively, notwithstanding the respective statutory exemptions for producing and gathering and for generation. And both industries became subject to 1960s' "commingling" rules, applying federal jurisdiction when inter- and intrastate commodities were commingled. But here the similarly ends. Until recently, grid operators could not direct the flow of electricity over specific transmission lines, nor could they prevent electricity from flowing out of state. The practical result was that if a generator or transmission line was connected to the interstate grid, the FPC would deem the line as engaged in interstate commerce because the Commission could claim that at least some of the power flowed to or from another state. Natural gas, by contrast, is transported by pipeline, and a pipeline system can be a designed to preclude out-of-state flows by not connecting with any pipeline serving another state. This made it possible for pipeline operators to escape federal jurisdiction under the NGA merely by establishing that none of the gas transported by the pipeline flowed in interstate commerce.

Because of these engineering differences and their jurisdictional consequences, the natural gas industry developed differently from its sister utility – the electric power industry. Electric utilities, if they wanted access to the eastern or western interstate transmission grid, would have to subject their transmission and wholesale sales to federal jurisdiction. The natural gas industry, conversely, could bifurcate into separate interstate and intrastate pipeline systems – allowing producers to choose whether to sell their gas in the state of production or in interstate markets. Reacting to the prospect of producer regulation under the *Phillips* decision, many producers opted to avoid the interstate market.

In June 1954, the Supreme Court issued a landmark, some might say infamous, natural gas decision – *Phillips Petroleum Co. v. Wisconsin*. In *Phillips*, the Court required the FPC to regulate independent natural gas producers' wholesale sales of natural gas in interstate commerce. The *Phillips* decision, issued just weeks after the Warren Court's landmark *Brown v. Board of Education* decision, became immediately controversial in gas-producing states – the "Impeach Earl Warren" bill boards that appeared in western states with small African-American populations and little or no history of segregation, some have speculated, were possibly triggered more by *Phillips* than by *Brown*.

Phillips marks the birth of a twenty-five-year regulatory experiment that ended in abject failure. It propelled the FPC on a path of natural gas producer regulation with unforeseen and extraordinarily disruptive consequences for the natural gas industry, for the economies of gas-consuming states, and ultimately for US energy security (since natural gas is a partial substitute for petroleum). It triggered interstate natural gas shortages, unworkable FPC gas "curtailment" (i.e., shortage-management) policies, and eventual intervention by Congress with the passage in 1978 of the Natural Gas Policy Act (NGPA). While the NGPA solved the shortage problem, it created perverse market distortions. Decades would lapse before natural gas, the cleanest fossil fuel, could be widely available for purposes of environmental compliance.

In *Phillips*, Phillips Petroleum Co. had been producing and gathering natural gas for sale to nonaffiliated interstate pipelines for resale. The company produced about half this gas from oil wells as casinghead gas – and Phillips, moreover, did not itself produce most of its gas but instead contracted with independent producers who would sell the gas to the company. Until after World War II, most natural gas was produced along with the discovery and production of oil – and, of course, oil prices were not regulated by the FPC. And notably, Phillips was not transporting any of its casinghead gas across state lines; instead, it was transferring title to the gas at its processing plants (either before or after the processing). The natural gas–producing states of New Mexico, Oklahoma, and Texas claimed that Phillips' sales were not subject to federal jurisdiction, while the receiving states of Wisconsin, Missouri, and Michigan sought to persuade the FPC to regulate Phillips' transactions.

The lawsuit presented the question of whether Phillips was a federally "regulated natural gas company." The natural gas industry then was organized along three economic sectors: those initially producing and gathering natural gas, those transporting the gas across state lines, and those distributing the gas locally to consumers, whether commercial, industrial, or household users. While some companies performed all three functions, as vertically integrated entities, most did not. Congress's purpose in passing the NGA, along with its language and structure, hinted that the Act only applies to the second industry category – those roughly 115 entities that are transporting for resale natural gas across state lines. Indeed, Congress expressly provided in Section 1(b) that the Act would not apply "to any other transportation or sale of natural gas or to the local distribution of natural gas or to the facilities used for such distribution or to the production or gathering of natural gas."

Phillips' lawyers explained that, as of 1947, the FPC had reported that there were 115 federally regulated interstate transportation companies, 2,300 independent producers selling produced and gathered gas directly to interstate pipelines, and several thousand others not selling their gas directly to an otherwise regulated interstate pipeline company. What they might have added is that in 1949, natural gas pipeline companies were described by *Fortune Magazine* as the "darling of Wall Street." Between 1948 and 1948, the volume of gas moving through interstate pipelines doubled, and it was increasing exponentially. Residential users and industries were hungry for more gas to heat their homes and businesses. Natural gas, by 1942, had become more price competitive than either oil or coal. Larger-diameter steel pipelines made it possible to move gas over 1,500 miles and remain competitive with either oil or coal.[6]

In a 1949 Supreme Court opinion in *Federal Power Commission v. Panhandle Eastern Pipeline Line Co.*, Justice Reed explained how Congress did not "envisage

---

[6] *Natural Gas – Woosh!*, FORTUNE, Dec. 1949, at 107.

federal regulation of the entire natural-gas field to the limit of constitutional power" but instead extended regulation to the "interstate segment which the states were powerless to regulate because of the Commerce Clause of the Federal Constitution." The Court in *Panhandle Eastern* concluded that the FPC lacked jurisdiction over production and gathering and therefore could not assert regulatory authority over transfers of leases. Two years earlier, in another *Panhandle Eastern* case, the Court explained how the NGA established a cooperative federal/state regulatory regime ensuring against having companies structure operations to avoid regulatory oversight. And there the Court allowed Indiana to regulate an interstate pipeline company's sale of natural gas to industrial customers.[7]

Prior FPC precedent similarly suggested that states and not the Commission could regulate sales such as those by Phillips. After an investigation producing almost 11,000 pages, with close to 5,800 pages of testimony and 4,000 pages of exhibits, the FPC concluded that Phillips was not a natural gas company subject to NGA jurisdiction. It reasoned that Phillips' sales involved exempt production and gathering processes. The Commission struggled with spotty Supreme Court precedent and distinguished the one principal instance where jurisdiction had attached. Over a dissent by Justice Douglas and two other colleagues, a majority of the Court declared that "sales in interstate commerce for resale by producers to interstate pipeline companies do not come within the 'production and gathering' exemption." Phillips engaged in sales of gas that would travel in interstate commerce for resale, and the fact that it was not affiliated with any natural gas company otherwise subject to FPC jurisdiction was not dispositive. Despite the company lawyers' extensive discussion of the legislative history surrounding the passage of the NGA suggesting otherwise, the Supreme Court discerned a congressional intent to confer "Commission jurisdiction over the rates of all wholesales of natural gas in interstate commerce, whether by a pipeline company or not and whether occurring before, during, or after transportation by an interstate pipeline company."[8]

Reaction was swift. The next day the *New York Times* reported how the cost of natural gas to consumers in fourteen states might be affected. The company, though, apparently was not surprised by the decision and counted on Congress weighing in.[9] The dissenting Justices in *Phillips* observed how the Court expressed

[7] Federal Power Comm'n v. Panhandle Eastern Pipe Line Co., 337 U.S. 498 (194); Panhandle Eastern Pipe Line Co. v. Public Service Comm'n of Indiana, 332 U.S. 507 (1947). The 1947 Court held that Congress's passage of the NGA did not strip states of their jurisdiction over sales of gas (even produced out of state) to consumers. *Cf.* Interstate Natural Gas Co. v. Federal Power Comm'n, 331 U.S. 682 (1947) (gas comingled with other gas after gathering and moving in interstate commerce subject to federal jurisdiction). For a history of jurisdictional issues prior to *Phillips* by two contemporary lawyers at the Commission, see Bradford Ross and Bernard A. Foster, Jr., *Phillips and the Natural Gas Act*, 19 LAW & CONTEMP. PROBLEMS 382 (1954).

[8] *Ibid.* at 680–85. The Court accepted the states' argument that the national interest of protecting consumers removed state jurisdiction and consequently required federal regulatory oversight of sales for resale.

[9] *High Court Voids F.P.C. Gas Decision,* N. Y. TIMES, June 8, 1954, p. 35.

choices, just like it recently did in *Brown* v. *Board of Education*, and hinted toward congressional action.[10]

Congress indeed responded by passing corrective legislation. But while it was doing so, a possible bribery incident derailed the bill. Senator Case (R-S.D.), described as a man of "unpeachable integrity," announced on the floor of the Congress that he had received a $2,500 cash donation, presumably if he would support the legislation. This led to a Senate and FBI investigation. More important, as the press pointed out, it "threw a bombshell into the otherwise dull proceedings." Case returned the money and even switched his vote. Of course, the legislation already appeared likely to pass when he received the donation – and Case dutifully alerted his colleagues to this brazen attempt by an oil and gas lobbyist/attorney interested in the bill. The attorney, John M. Neff, later denied he was attempting to influence the vote. Yet Senators feared that the incident clouded their support and "may defeat the bill, which otherwise was expected to pass by a few votes." A similar measure already had passed the House the previous year. The bill barely passed the Senate and avoided having to go back to the House, but these precarious circumstances surrounding its passage forced a veto by the White House, even though the measure originally had been supported by the Eisenhower administration.[11]

This left it up to an ill-equipped FPC. The FPC's early efforts were subsequently described as "Sisyphean labors . . . as it marche[d] up the hill of producer regulation only to tumble down again with little undertaken and less done."[12] In 1960, the incoming Kennedy administration treated the Commission's efforts at producer regulation as a prime illustration of the failure of the administrative process. Responding, Kennedy's appointees to the Commission commenced a series of "area rate" proceedings, where the Commission would avoid reviewing individual rates for specific companies and instead determine maximum producers' rates for each of the major gas-producing areas.

In the 1964 *Permian Basin Area Rate* case, the FPC established a two-tier rate structure for Permian Basin natural gas – the producing area in West Texas and Southeast New Mexico. For nonassociated gas (gas not produced in association with oil) dedicated to interstate commerce after 1960, the Commission devised an incentive price based on national estimates of the cost of finding and producing nonassociated gas first produced in 1960. Correspondingly, the Commission adopted a relatively low price for all other natural gas produced in the Permian Basin because price could not serve as an incentive, and any price above average historical costs, plus an appropriate return, would merely confer windfalls.

[10] Arthur Krock, *In the Nation: The Dissents in the Natural Gas Case*, N. Y. TIMES, June 10, 1954, at p. 30.
[11] *See* Hal Levy, *Senate Votes Gas Bill; Probe Pressed*, NEWSDAY, Feb. 7, 1956, at 1; *FBI, Senate Probe Gas Bill "Donation"; Special Biparty Panel Lined Up by Johnson*, THE ATLANTA J. & ATLANTA CONST., Feb. 5, 1956, at 1A; *Probe Called by Knowland: Would See if Case Offer Concerned Gas Vote*, THE SUN, Feb. 6, 1956, at 7.
[12] Wisconsin v. FPC, 373 U.S. 294, 315 (1963) (Clark, J., dissenting).

Associated gas and gas already flowing in interstate commerce before 1961 received a lower rate based on the costs over the years of finding and producing nonassociated gas flowing in 1960 in the Permian Basin. By 1973, the Commission extended the area-rate methodology to all the major producing areas of the country. Then, in 1974, the Commission established a new, higher national rate for natural gas,[13] which generally applied to natural gas first flowing in interstate commerce in 1972 or thereafter. The FPC in 1976 established a second, higher national rate for gas first flowing in 1975–76.

While the Commission ultimately responded to the Supreme Court's *Phillips* mandate, the response seemed excruciatingly slow: the Commission issued its *Permian* opinion eleven years after *Phillips*; area rates were not prescribed for all major producing areas in the United States until 1973, some nineteen years after *Phillips*; and the first national rate was prescribed twenty years after the decision. More important, the eventual success of the Commission's area and national rate policy led to the unraveling of the entire producer regulation scheme under the NGA. As one commentator noted in 1976:

> Since 1946 . . . the amount of newly discovered gas supplies had always exceeded the amount of gas produced in any one given year. In 1968, however, production was greater than were additions to reserves, indicating a net decline in available gas resources. By 1970, interstate pipelines began experiencing difficulties in meeting their contract commitments because not enough gas was being sold on the interstate market.[14]

The source of the problem, added this same commentator, followed from the FPC's producer regulation that "not only discouraged exploration and production but had also channeled supplies into the intrastate market, where prices were several times what they were in the interstate market."[15] The effect became further compounded by what are called "commingling rules." Under the 1965 Supreme Court case of *California v. Lo Vaca*, if a pipeline commingled gas for in-state consumption with gas for out-of-state consumption, the entire gas stream and the pipeline itself became subject to federal jurisdiction under the NGA.[16]

Nixon's 1971 clean energy message observed how natural gas demand had escalated but warned that "[o]ur present supply of natural gas is limited . . . and we are beginning to face shortages which could intensify." Indeed, during the 1900s, it became apparent that natural gas consumption and production effectively peaked by the early 1970s. Both production and consumption climbed significantly between 1950 and the early 1970s, and then declined until more recently (Figure 5.1).

---

[13]   51 F.P.C. 2212 (1974).
[14]   Daniel J. Fiorino, *Regulating the Natural Gas Industry: Two Decades of Experiences, in* ECONOMIC REGULATORY POLICIES 89, 94–95 (Lexington Books, J. Anderson ed., 1976).
[15]   *Ibid.*   [16]   379 U.S. 366 (1965).

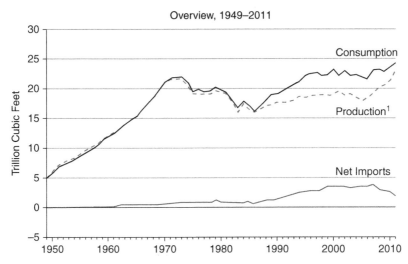

FIGURE 5.1 US Energy Information Administration, *Annual Energy Review* 2011 (September 2012)

Eerily, this was the famed prediction of Shell geologist M. King Hubbert in his classic 1956 paper, "Nuclear Energy and the Fossil Fuels," where he predicted that natural gas production would peak around then (only more recently discredited with the advent of unconventional natural gas development). Future supplies of gas from Canada, which were about 3.55 percent of our total requirements, seemed unclear – and Secretary Morton even suggested that we would, consequently, need a "continental energy policy."[17] Nixon then added how increasing gas supplies would be "one of our most urgent energy needs in the next few years." As we explain in Chapter 6, Congress eventually responded by incentivizing the use of coal rather than gas or oil.

The FPC also responded. Addressing the interstate pipelines' limited access to sufficient natural gas supplies to satisfy the needs of their customers, the Commission developed "curtailment" policies for the rapidly developing natural gas shortages. The DC Circuit explained how the natural gas shortage "necessitates the curtailment of supplies to certain customers during peak demand periods. The problem confronting many pipeline companies is whether to curtail on the basis of existing contractual commitments or on the basis of the most efficient end use of the gas." And the pipelines were concerned that "withholding gas due under existing contracts may subject them to civil liability."[18] In 1971, the FPC directed that each interstate pipeline report to the Commission whether curtailment of deliveries to customers would be necessary because of inadequate gas supply and, if such

---

[17] The President's Energy Message, Hearing before the Committee on Interior and Insular Affairs, U.S. Senate, Pursuant to S. Res. 45, A National Fuels and Energy Policy Study, Serial No. 92–1, 92nd Cong., 1st Sess., 13–14, June 15, 1971.
[18] Pacific Gas and Electric Co. v. FPC, 506 F.2d 33, 35 (D.C. Cir. 1974).

curtailment were necessary, to file a new tariff governing deliveries to its wholesale customers and its direct (large retail) customers.[19]

Two years later, promoting some uniformity for pipeline curtailment practices, the Commission spelled out its end-use curtailment policy, directing curtailment on the basis of end use rather than on the basis of contract. The end-use policy gave priority, notwithstanding contract provisions to the contrary, to gas consumers such as schools, homes, and businesses that lacked access to alternative fuels. The major losers under the policy were "boiler fuel users" such as gas-fired electric generators that could substitute oil for natural gas. The Commission reasoned how, in times of shortage, "performance of a firm contract to deliver gas for an inferior use, at the expense of reduced deliveries for priority uses, is not compatible with consumer protection."[20] This focus on end use stretched back decades, such that during smog-laden 1950s in Los Angeles the Commission reasoned that California would have to decide whether a particular company's "use of gas in place of fuel oil would be more beneficial than the conversion to gas by numerous other, less efficient users of fuel oil in the area or that gas is not needed more vitally for household and commercial uses." The Commission, consequently, reasoned in this 1959 order that it would make the subject gas "generally available to all so that the state and local agencies, who have the best knowledge of the smog problems can see that the gas is used in a manner most beneficial to the whole area."[21]

Desperate to diminish the pernicious effects of the dual market, the FPC explored its options for increasing the flow of natural gas to interstate pipelines and their customers – thereby allowing interstate pipelines to compete for gas supplies on a more equal footing with the intrastate market. The Commission, for instance, experimented with several programs allowing interstate pipelines to obtain new long-term commitments of gas to the interstate market and permitting interstate pipelines to make short-term purchases from the intrastate market. In one experiment, the Commission tried to exempt small producers from rate regulation under the Act, only to be chastised by the Supreme Court that it could not avoid ensuring that the small producers' rates were just and reasonable as prescribed by the NGA.[22] The FPC also permitted interstate pipelines to make advance payments to producers for exploration and development and to make unregulated sixty-day emergency purchases from producers and intrastate pipelines, as well as various other short-term transportation and sales services.[23]

---

[19]   45 F.P.C. 570, 571–72 (1971). In *FPC v. Louisiana Power and Light*, 406 U.S. 621 (1972), the Supreme Court upheld the Commission's authority to regulate curtailment of direct-sales customers.

[20]   Order No. 467, 49 F.P.C. 85, 86 (1973). The Commission reasoned that "curtailment should first fall on those ... best prepared to accept uninterrupted service for protection of life or property." *See also* Arkansas Louisiana Gas Company, 49 F.P.C. 53, 66–67 (1973).

[21]   El Paso Natural Gas Co., 22 F.P.C. 900 (1959).   [22]   FPC v. Texaco Inc., 417 U.S. 350 (1974).

[23]   An NGA certificate holder normally provides service without any durational limit. If that holder subsequently wants to discontinue service, it must apply for abandonment authorization under Section 7(b). However, under its limited-term certificate program, the Commission certified

Though these programs enjoyed mixed success when reviewed by judges, they met with even less success in the marketplace. By 1974, additions to natural gas reserves constituted only 40 percent of marketed production of natural gas on a national basis.[24] More important, most additions to natural gas reserves went to the intrastate rather than interstate market. Between 1964 and 1969, 67 percent of reserve additions were committed to the interstate market, and by 1970–74 (as a result of the change in the relative prices in the two markets), less than 5 percent of reserve additions was committed to the interstate market.[25] And, for whatever gas went into the interstate market, the average field price for gas had been steadily rising since the 1960s and witnessed a "pronounced" increase in 1973.[26] A seminal article by soon to be Justice Stephen Breyer and an economist colleague at MIT blamed the FPC's producer price regulation for contributing to the natural gas shortages, ostensibly to benefit residential consumers. But consumers, they argued, were hurt, not helped.[27] Subsequent efforts by the FPC and the Federal Energy Administration (FEA) to increase the supply of interstate natural gas floundered as the agencies tepidly sought to avoid a price shock to consumers and increased costs to interstate pipelines. In July 1976, for instance, the FPC raised the "nationwide ceiling price for new interstate gas produced or contracted for after 1974."[28] Of course, by 1976, natural gas supplied roughly 37 percent less electric generation than oil.[29]

The increasingly debilitating supply situation confronting interstate pipelines and the FPC's seeming inability to remedy the problem administratively prompted a recommendation by the Ford administration and the FPC that Congress deregulate "new natural gas" (generally, gas first sold in interstate commerce in 1975 or thereafter).[30] This effort, however, "foundered on the twin rocks of intransigence and a refusal to believe that natural gas shortages were other than contrived," explains Neil De Marchi.[31] A major political battle ensued between producing and

producer sales into the interstate market for a fixed period and at the same time authorized ("pregranted") abandonment of the service at the end of the fixed period. The Commission also tried to permit high-cost producers to apply for and collect (net subject to refund) a rate higher than the national rate and to abandon the service if the higher rate was not ultimately approved by the FPC.

[24] H. R. Rep. No. 543, 95th Cong., 1st Sess. 387 (1977).

[25] *Ibid.* at 388. *See* Federal Energy Administration, *National Energy Outlook* 122 (1976).

[26] Foster Associates, Inc., Energy Prices 1960–73: A Report to the Energy Project of the Ford Foundation 18 (1973).

[27] Stephen Breyer & Paul W. MacAvoy, *The Natural Gas Shortage and the Regulation of Natural Gas Producers*, 86 Harv. L. Rev. 941 (1973).

[28] Neil De Marchi, *The Ford Administration: Energy as a Political Good, in* Energy Policy in Perspective: Today's Problems, Yesterday's Solutions 508–9 (Craufurd D. Goodwin et al. eds., 1981).

[29] Charles King Mallory, III, *The Phasing Out of Oil and Gas Used for Boiler Fuel: Constraints and Incentives*, 13 Tulsa L. Rev. 702 705 (1978).

[30] Federal Power Commission, National Gas Survey (vol. 1 1975); Address before a Joint Session of the Congress Reporting on the State of the Union, I Pub. Papers 41 (1975).

[31] De Marchi, *supra* note 28, at 508.

consuming states. Producing states threatened to let consumers in the Northeast "freeze in the dark," and some producer representatives privately referred to advocates of continuing price controls as "cheap gas queers."

The Senate, on October 22, 1975, passed the Pierson-Bentson amendment (S. 692). This amendment would have deregulated sales in interstate commerce of new natural gas. In a dramatic series of close votes, the House in February 1976 defeated the amendment and substituted for it one that would deregulate interstate sales of natural gas by small producers, retaining rate regulation of interstate sales by large producers and extending federal regulation to large-producer sales into the intrastate market. Both the House and Senate bills died at the end of the 94th Congress, but the political controversy remained.

The 95th Congress opened during an extraordinarily serious natural gas shortage in the interstate market, resulting from the coldest winter in many years. A *New York Times* reporter would later describe it as the "worst winter of the century," closing factories and fueling inflation.[32] The Carter administration and Congress responded immediately by enacting the second bill of the term, the Emergency Natural Gas Act of 1977 (ENGA), a temporary measure authorizing the president to allow interstate pipelines and local distribution companies to purchase natural gas from producers, intrastate pipelines, and local distribution companies – subject to terms and conditions imposed by the president (or his delegate, the chair of the FPC). Under the ENGA, NGA jurisdiction did not attach to any authorized sale or to any intrastate pipeline transportation in connection with such a sale. ENGA also gave the president the power to allocate natural gas among interstate pipelines to satisfy designated high-priority uses. That authority, however, went unused.[33]

Only months after Congress passed the emergency gas bill, President Carter unveiled the administration's National Energy Plan (NEP). On April 20, 1977, Carter proposed his plan for resolving the nation's ostensible energy crisis, introduced in the House as H.R. 6831. In the words of the transmittal accompanying the plan, Carter was submitting a "complicated" plan containing nine chapters. Many aspects of the plan are discussed in more detail in subsequent chapters. But undeniably the crisis centered on the administration's concern that oil and gas constituted three-quarters of the nation's energy consumption while "constitut[ing] less than 8 percent of domestic reserves." Our experience, the report explained, reflected an "erratic, complex, and ineffective" approach to regulating both resources.

The plan's natural gas provisions were shaped by the difficulties attendant with the jurisdictional limitations of the NGA and by the more immediate experience of the 1976–77 winter. Writing in the fall, economist Robert Samuelson echoed the prevailing sentiment of how gas scarcity flowed from the *Phillips* decision tying the

---

[32] Thomas E. Mullaney, *An Energy Policy – At Last*, N. Y. TIMES, Apr. 24, 1977, at F15.
[33] Pub. L. 95–2, 91 Stat. 4, Feb. 2, 1977.

Commission's hands and keeping natural gas prices unreasonably low, stimulating demand while hindering production.[34] This meant, according to the NEP, that natural gas was being diverted to industrial and utility uses rather than being delivered to consumers dependent on gas for heating. The solution was apparent: remove aspects of meddlesome cost-based regulation and the artificial barrier inhibiting the movement of natural gas into the interstate market.

The natural gas title of Carter's legislative proposal – the National Energy Act – was designed to tilt the country "toward a single national market for gas." It retained, though, price controls, what it termed *commodity value pricing*. "[P]rices [according to the plan] should reflect the costs and the degree of risk associated with finding replacement supplies." It established ceiling prices for all producer sales of natural gas produced in the United States, whether in the intrastate or interstate market – thus eliminating the distinction in the two markets. And it linked the ceiling price for new natural gas (whether sold interstate or intrastate) to the price of domestic crude oil – establishing effectively a Btu-equivalent price. Ceiling prices for gas other than new natural gas were lower than those for new gas and were determined under a complicated set of pricing rules.[35] Robert Samuelson found this continued affinity for price controls troubling and potentially problematic because it promoted dirtier coal and threatened to increase the nation's need for expensive imported natural gas, from countries such as Canada, Algeria, and Mexico. He cautioned that "environmentalists may most regret Carter's policy. Natural gas is the nation's cleanest fuel, coal the dirtiest. Carter hopes to cure the natural gas scarcities through a rush to coal." Some in the natural gas industry also expressed concern with Carter's proposal, labeling it as a "serious backward step."[36] This rush to coal is discussed in Chapters 7 and 8, but strikingly, Samuelson presciently hinted how untapped reserves of tight natural gas – what would later be unleashed with the development of fracking and horizontal drilling – might make all this unnecessary.[37] Of course, the General Accounting Office's analysis suggested that even with full deregulation of natural gas, it would be unlikely that the 1977 level of natural supplies would increase at least before 1985.[38] To be fair, though, the administration did not project much of an increase in new natural gas supplies until between 1983 and 1985.[39]

The president's natural gas proposal emerged from the House largely intact but fared poorly in the Senate.[40] One proposal floated in the Senate by the

[34] Robert J. Samuelson, *Gas Deregulation vs. Price Controls Plan*, WASH. POST, Sept. 13, 1977, at D8.

[35] Executive Office of the President, The National Energy Plan 53 (1977).

[36] Robert D. Hershey, *Oilmen Attack Lack of Incentive in Carter Plan to Increase Output*, N. Y. TIMES, April 22, 1977, at pg. 28.

[37] Samuelson, *supra* note 34.

[38] GAO, Report to Congress: An Evaluation of the National Energy Plan 4–18 (July 25, 1977).

[39] Hearings before the Ad Hoc Committee on Energy, National Energy Act, 95th Cong., 1st Sess., May 4, 5, and 12, 1977, at 196.

[40] H.R. Rep. No. 543, 95th Cong., 1st Sess. 45 (1977).

Governmental Affairs Committee contemplated establishing an Energy Department and then assigning to a three-member board inside the department the authority to establish wellhead natural gas prices – allowing the Secretary to propose prices for the board. However, the eventual Senate bill, as the NGPA conferees drily noted, "embodied a significantly different approach to the natural gas pricing issue than that adopted by the House." The Senate bill eliminated federal price controls on new natural gas produced onshore in two years. Price controls were retained for other interstate natural gas, but intrastate natural gas would remain outside federal regulation.[41]

The compromise emerging from a contentious House/Senate conference – the NGPA – retained most of Carter's proposed elements, particularly the extension of price controls. The Senate conferees had been deadlocked by December 1977, and it took ninety minutes of debate before they could agree, according to a *New York Times* reporter, that "they really did want a natural gas bill."[42] When they went into conference, the staff supporting the conferees worked hard to secure a consensus, particularly Elizabeth Moler (who would later become a FERC commissioner), as the conferees themselves debated natural gas curtailment policies and such minutiae as whether dog and cat food might be included as essential animal feed for the American people. The orchestrator for deregulating the industry, Senator Bennett Johnston (D.-LA), lamented at a March 1978 conference committee meeting on the difficulties of reaching a consensus between the two bodies, at one point invoking the Humpty-Dumpty metaphor, only to be asked by Senator Jackson if the proposal now before the conferees was a "new turkey." This prompted Senator Johnston to respond that some turkeys, if "properly seasoned," might "become more delectable." And yet what the conferees had so far "is no Thanksgiving turkey," Senator Johnston added. "There is no praise, there is no jubilation about this bill, in my state," he continued, "but it is a bill that I think at last count" might have enough votes. What emerged from this conference, though, retained the key component of the Senate proposal – phased deregulation of new natural gas. More important, it purportedly provided interstate pipelines and their customers "parity of access" to new supplies of natural gas and to gas presently flowing in the intrastate market. Congress anticipated that the parity-of-access policy would permit interstate pipelines to purchase, and producers and intrastate pipelines to sell, gas not then committed to the interstate market under the same pricing, certification, and abandonment rules that apply to buyers and sellers in the intrastate market.

Under the phased-deregulation policy, ceiling prices under the NGPA initially applied to all producer sales of natural gas produced in the United States. One year later, certain high-cost gas was removed from NGPA price controls. In 1985, new

---

[41]   H. R. Rep. No. 1752, 95th Cong., 2nd Sess. 68 (1978).
[42]   Edward Cowan, *Conferees on Gas Take a Step Ahead*, N. Y. TIMES, Dec. 9, 1977, at pg. D1.

natural gas and certain intrastate gas were removed from NGPA price controls, and in 1987, another increment of gas production was deregulated.

This complex pricing scheme contained eight statutory ceiling-price categories for producer sales. Congress expected that this scheme would incentivize new production while maintaining then-current prices (with periodic increases) on gas committed to the interstate market or under contract to the intrastate market. Even though ceiling prices under the scheme would be determined by reference to the market into which the gas was flowing *on or before* date of enactment, ceiling prices were determined without regard to the market into which the gas flowed *after* the enactment date. If, therefore, an interstate pipeline bought gas under a successor to an existing intrastate contract, or rollover of an existing intrastate contract, that gas would be subject to the same pricing rules as if it had been purchased by an intrastate pipeline.

In many ways the NGPA operated as an overlay on the NGA. The NGA, after all, still applied to interstate transportation and interstate sales for resale, absent an exclusion. And Title VI of the NGPA contained several such exclusions. For instance, it eliminated much of the NGA's price and "nonprice" producer regulation and made the NGA inapplicable to producer sales of natural gas neither committed nor dedicated to interstate commerce at the time of the NGPA's enactment, along with certain gas from new wells and "high-cost" gas. Moreover, under the NGPA's "guaranteed pass-through" provision, interstate pipelines could pass through to their customers amounts paid in producer sales that did not exceed applicable ceilings without being subject to FERC prudence review.

The NGPA removed the FPC's authority to establish just and reasonable prices under the NGA for producer sales into the interstate market, as well as any authority to indirectly regulate those sales through control of the interstate pipeline purchaser's pass-through of purchase gas costs. It further relieved producers of gas not then flowing in interstate commerce from "nonprice" regulation under the NGA – that is, requirements to obtain certification or abandonment authorization, or make rate filings under the NGA. The next year the Commission issued simplified rate-filing procedures for producer sales that remained subject to Section 4 of the NGA. These procedures permitted producers to file a "blanket affidavit" that permitted collection of certain NGPA rates without the necessity of monthly rate-change filings. The NGPA also contained provisions removing regulatory deterrents to transportation for, and sales into, the interstate market by intrastate pipelines and to the development of a national transportation system for natural gas. The NGPA, consequently, effectively eliminated the principal barriers to producer sales into the interstate market of natural gas not committed to that market at the time of the NGPA's enactment.

As it turned out, shortly after the NGPA became law, the country enjoyed a glut of natural gas – projected to remain for the next few years. The *Washington Post* reported how "[t]his dizzying shift from shortage to glut has left consumers, to say nothing of some members of Congress who just finished the often acrimonious legislative battle, confused."[43] Arthur Schlesinger predicted that higher prices would release a considerable amount of additional otherwise shut-in gas into the market.[44] Correspondingly higher oil prices led to more overall development that further increased the nation's proved reserves, and that was on top of Mexico and Canada producing more gas.

POST-NGPA: MARKET DISRUPTION AND INDUSTRY RESTRUCTURING

The NGPA, much like the area-rate policy, was a victim of its own success. The NGPA's parity of access policies that removed disincentives to sell gas into the interstate market and, after 1979, the availability of deregulated high-cost gas permitted interstate pipelines to rapidly replenish their depleted gas supplies. Many of them embarked on what could only be described as a shopping spree, buying up large quantities of high-cost gas in transactions that included high take-or-pay requirements. Take-or-pay contracts require the buyer either to take a minimum quantity at the contract price or pay the seller for amounts not taken. Minimum bills in transactions between pipelines had a similar effect. Pipelines agreed to these contract terms in reliance on the NGPA's guaranteed pass-through provisions and what was then referred to as the "cheap gas cushion," which permitted them to average expensive new gas supplies with older price-controlled gas. The problem, explains, Paul Joskow, is that "real crude oil prices peaked in 1981 and fell by nearly two-thirds by 1986 making gas less economical compared to oil at the now higher regulated bundled price charged by the pipelines."[45] As a result, interstate pipeline rates increased by about 50 percent between 1980 and 1982, while at the time their sales dropped by 20 percent. End-use customers switched to fuel oil (the price of which was rapidly dropping) if they had dual fuel capacity and cut back on gas use even if they didn't.

As interstate pipeline gas became increasingly unmarketable, and the pipelines were unable to cut back on purchases of high-cost gas because of onerous take-or-pay requirements, they resorted to various strategies (mostly unsuccessful) to extricate themselves from their looming financial difficulties. These strategies included

1. Special marketing programs, with pipelines transporting gas sold by producers to industrial customers in return for take-or-pay relief from those producers;
2. Off-system sales programs, with pipelines selling or transporting natural gas to end users who were not regular direct or indirect customers of the pipeline;
3. Attempts to change pipeline rate design by loading more pipeline costs on fixed-demand charges and less to variable-commodity charges; and

---

[43] J. P. Smith, *Natural Gas Glut: Experts Agree That Outlook Has Changed Dramatically*, WASH. POST, Oct. 30, 1978, A1.
[44] *Ibid.*
[45] Paul L. Joskow, *Natural Gas: From Shortages to Abundance in the United States*, 103(3) AMER. ECON. REV.: PAPERS AND PROCEEDINGS 338–43, 339 (2013).

4. Attempts to modify pipeline-to-pipeline minimum bills.

These strategies, however, elicited a lukewarm reception before the FERC and the courts and eventually became overshadowed by the Commission's decision to entice a restructuring of the industry. As a prominent energy jurist would later write, "[i]n the Spring of 1985, as Mikhail Gorbachev was assuming the duties of General Secretary and inaugurating *perestroika*, the Federal Energy Regulatory Commission launched its own restructuring of the natural gas industry."[46] This is when the Commission issued Order No. 436. This order afforded interstate pipelines broad, flexible authority to provide various types of transportation services, but only if they offered these services on a nondiscriminatory, open-access basis. For pipelines electing open-access transportation, Order No. 436 provided a simplified procedure for authorizing new pipeline construction. In *Associated Gas Distributors v. FERC*, the DC Circuit largely upheld the substance of Order No. 436 but vacated the rule principally because the Commission failed to deal with pipeline take-or-pay liabilities.[47] The Commission, in a series of subsequent rulemakings known as Order No. 500, retained Order No. 436's open-access transmission features and addressed pipeline take-or-pay issues through a package of provisions that, for the most, part satisfied the DC Circuit.[48] The Commission's solution, for instance, consisted of allowing pass-through of transition costs (mostly take-or-pay) and requiring that producers credit transportation volumes. The net result, as noted by two contemporary energy hill staffers, was that pipeline companies went from transporting, in 1984, about 92 percent of their own gas to, in 1992, transporting 21 percent of their own gas.[49]

As the FERC struggled with transportation policy and pipeline take-or-pay obligations, the Reagan administration and Congress shifted their attention to cleaning up the remnants of the NGPA price-control scheme. In 1985 and 1987, most natural gas producer sales were deregulated under the NGPA, but a substantial amount of pre-NGPA gas dedicated to interstate commerce [and of pre-NGPA intrastate contract gas] remained subject to NGPA ceiling prices, some of which were well below market levels. The retention of partial producer regulation impeded the development of a truly national natural gas market. At the Energy Department's behest, the FPC first attempted to address the market distortions resulting from the NGPA vintaging policy by raising all ceiling prices to the level of the highest remaining NGPA ceiling price (the price for post-1974 interstate gas). Then, in 1987, Congress removed the NGPA's incremental pricing scheme (forcing too-high prices for industrial sales) and repealed the limitations on gas imposed in the Fuel Use Act.

---

[46] American Gas Ass'n v. FERC, 912 F.2d 1496, 1503 (D.C. Cir. 1990).

[47] 824 F.2d 981 (D.C. Cir. 1987). *See also* American Gas Ass'n v. FERC, 888 F.2d 136 (D.C. Cir. 1989); Associated Gas Distributors v. FERC, 893 F.2d 349 (D.C. Cir. 1989); Transwestern Pipeline Co. v. FERC, 897 F.2d 570 (D. C. Cir. 1990).

[48] American Gas Ass'n v. FERC, 912 F.2d 1496 (D.C. Cir. 1990), *cert. denied*, 111 S. Ct. 957 (1991).

[49] Donald F. Santa, Jr. & Patricia J. Beneke, *Federal Natural Gas Policy and the Energy Policy Act of 1992*, 14 ENERGY L. J. 1, 7 (1993).

The following year, Congress further removed limitations on gas produced from the Outer Continental Shelf. And finally, Congress enacted the Wellhead Decontrol Act of 1989, fully deregulating (effective at the end of 1992) all producer sales under the NGPA such that producer prices were fully market determined.

Anticipating the 1992 wellhead decontrol, awash in its travails of wrestling with pipeline take-or-pay problems, and attempting to fashion a workable gas transportation policy, the FERC unfolded its more comprehensive program for restructuring the natural gas industry. The end product of this restructuring, Order No. 636 issued in mid-1992, contained several salient features: to begin with, it required mandatory unbundling, with only a limited ability for pipelines to market their own gas; it provided for blanket pipelines sales certificates, with "pre-grand of abandonment"; and it included a capacity-reallocation mechanism, a comparability standard, and a confirmation of straight fixed/variable-rate design, along with transition-cost recovery.

The combination of wellhead decontrol and Order No. 636 effectively transformed the natural gas industry from one where pipelines bought natural gas (some of it at regulated prices) and then resold it in a bundled transaction that included both gas acquisition costs and pipeline transportation to a regime where pipelines were primarily transporters (at regulated rates) of gas produced and sold entirely outside the ambit of price regulation. This regime established what eventually became a national market for natural gas. A history of this regulatory period posits that "[i]t is hard to think of an established industry at any time in any country whose market structure and dynamics, intellectual environment, and business culture changed as radically within a single generation as the natural gas industry of North America."[50]

Congress facilitated this transition by including several gas-related provisions in what has since become the first of now three (likely four) major omnibus energy bills – this one the Energy Policy Act of 1992. Independent producers, for instance, were relieved of the alternative minimum tax. Congress, also, notably considering subsequent developments, sought to promote unconventional gas development. Natural gas received an implicit additional boost through Title XVI, on Global Climate Change, where Congress called for developing a least-cost and reduced greenhouse gas energy strategy. And this all occurred as the use of natural gas increased annually, coinciding with increased industrial as well as residential use of natural gas and an economy (on the non-service-oriented side) that would soon become stronger in the early 1990s. In the electric energy sector, by comparison, however, natural gas use ranked third in consumption at the outset of the decade – although "major growth" was expected over the decade.[51] That growth occurred as low gas prices and coal-fired generation decreased (Figure 5.2).

---

[50]   ARLON R. TUSSING & BOB TIPPEE, THE NATURAL GAS INDUSTRY: EVOLUTION, STRUCTURE, AND ECONOMICS 249 (PennWell Books 1985).

[51]   A somewhat contemporary article on natural gas policy at the time is Donald F. Santa, Jr., and Patricia J. Beneke, *supra* note 49. Both authors served on the Senate Committee on Energy and Natural Resources and worked on the 1989 Wellhead Decontrol Act.

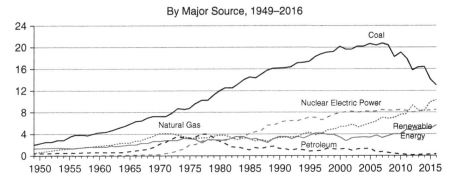

FIGURE 5.2 US Energy Information Administration, *Monthly Energy Review 2016* (August 2017)

By the end of the first decade of the twenty-first century, natural gas became the nation's primary source of energy production, overtaking coal, and it likewise became the second primary source of energy consumption, again overtaking coal but less than petroleum.[52] While both consumption and production increased at the end of the twentieth century, a more robust gas market, of course, did not eliminate price volatility and, in fact, probably increased it. Wellhead natural gas prices that had been below $1 per thousand cubic feet (tcf) throughout the 1970s hovered around $2 to $3/tcf during the 1990s, rising to an average of closer to $4/tcf by 2000–1, and, while decreasing somewhat thereafter, rocketed again to even higher levels and then tapered off with the advent of sharply increasing shale gas production, settling back to their early 1990s levels. Paul Joskow explains how prices became more volatile around 2000, precipitating the California energy crisis, because according to the "received wisdom . . . there had been a gas supply 'overhand' during the 1990s and . . . as demand caught up with supply more expensive gas production sources would have to be relied upon to balance supply and demand, including more imports from Canada, the construction of a large pipeline to being new supplies of gas from Northern Alaska through Canada to the United States, and a large expansion of liquid gas (LNG) imports from the rest of the world."[53] Of course, today's continuing shale revolution has led to a shift from LNG imports to LNG exports, lingering doubts about the viability of Alaska's natural gas pipeline, and an electric utility industry that considers natural gas "king" – at least until renewable energy and battery storage overthrow it.

The advent of our current shale gas revolution and seeming abundance, to some extent, likely was a result of the gas restructuring of the 1990s. It sent clear market signals to producers and afforded incentives for cost-effective new technologies. Natural gas also became more economical with the advent of efficient

---

[52] EIA, *Monthly Energy Review 2016*, August 2017, at 4, 6.   [53] Joskow, *supra* note 45, at 340.

combined-cycle gas turbines capable of serving as base-load generation (available to run more often rather than just during peak hours when electricity is in higher demand). The Energy Policy Act of 2005 added even further carrots for the industry, such as streamlining provisions and allowing companies to provide storage at market-based rates – to be sure, also directing price transparency and strengthening rules against market manipulation. But the principal cause of the increase in supply and decrease in price was a once-in-a-generation technological development – the combination of directional drilling and fracking, which collectively fostered the development of the nation's vast shale gas resources.

NATURAL GAS FOLLIES AND SUCCESSES

In the ninety years since *Missouri* v. *Kansas Natural Gas Co.*, natural gas regulation has witnessed a series of judicial interventions, attempts by the states and the FPC to accommodate gas regulation to these interventions and on three occasions congressional action to rectify what became an unworkable regulatory scheme. The Court's holdings during the period before the enactment of the NGA left interstate transportation and interstate wholesale sales of natural gas unregulated. Producing states could not reserve their own production for consumers within the state, nor could consuming states regulate the price that their own utilities paid for gas purchased from interstate pipelines. The 1938 enactment of the NGA filled this regulatory gap by requiring the FPC to impose on interstate transportation and interstate wholesale sales the same type of utility regulation other states imposed on intrastate transportation and on retail sales of natural gas. Once the gap was filled, both the interstate and intrastate markets were subject to similar regulatory schemes. This parity of regulation removed whatever perverse incentives may have predated NGA and chilled producers and pipelines from selling in the interstate rather than the intrastate market.

The *Phillips* decision removed this regulatory parity and created a new gap, this one in the intrastate market. Producer sales into the interstate market were subject to regulation under the NGA, even though intrastate producer sales were not then subject to ceiling-price regulation under state law. The gap was one states (other than New Mexico) were unwilling to fill. The imposition of producer regulation in the interstate market resulted in the supply difficulties the interstate pipelines experienced in the 1970s. These difficulties arguably mirror the intrastate market difficulties between 1910 and 1938, when the interstate market was not regulated and producing states could not effectively ensure supply to their own consumers. The NGPA represented a congressional response to the disparity of regulatory treatment created by *Phillips* in much the same way the NGA responded to the discrepancy created by *Missouri* v. *Kansas Natural Gas Company*. But the NGPA created its own market disruptions, remedied only after Congress passed the 1989 Wellhead Decontrol Act and FERC issued its now-classic Order No. 636.

This history of natural gas regulation shows how judicial misjudgment (the *Kansas Natural Gas* and *Phillips* cases) and clumsy remedial legislation by Congress retarded for many years a fully functioning natural gas market that otherwise could have developed sooner and averted, if not at least mitigated, some of the pernicious effects from coal-fired generation.

6

Oil Shocks, Gas Lines, and Energy Policy

The 1973 Arab oil embargo is a watershed event for energy policy and energy law: it effectively marks the beginning of what we now call "energy policy." Before then, few, if any, discussed "energy law" as such; rather, attention focused on individual statutes and rules targeting specific forms of energy, such as the Natural Gas Act (NGA) and the Federal Power Act (FPA). Conversations about energy therefore generally targeted one of these individual statutory programs. When the embargo hit, the fractured regulatory structure made it almost virtually impossible to implement a coherent energy policy – even if policymakers could figure out what such a policy ought to be. And over the next roughly decade, policymakers would struggle with how to craft an integrated energy policy, only to fall woefully short and force the need for more tinkering.

BEFORE THE EMBARGO: STUDIES, REPORTS, AND POLICY DISARRAY

Prior to the embargo, federal policymakers exhibited only fleeting appreciation of the interrelated nature of what we now term "energy regulation." As one commenter explained, each energy resource enjoyed its own "protective belt of policies and bureaucratic apparatus."[1] To be sure, the need for planning was not lost on policymakers, even though there was little inclination or ability to translate plans into action. For instance, World War I demonstrated the importance of oil to the war effort and the need for planning for future supplies – particularly because consumption of petroleum increased by 50 percent in just the four years between 1914 and 1918.[2] Although focused on coal more than oil, Wilson's 1917 Federal Fuel Administration was an early type of planning effort. Later, as the automobile and crude consumption skyrocketed in the 1920s, Commerce Secretary Herbert Hoover

---

[1]   James L. Cochrane, *Energy Policy in the Johnson Administration: Logical Order versus Economic Pluralism, in* ENERGY POLICY IN PERSPECTIVE: TODAY'S PROBLEMS, YESTERDAY'S SOLUTIONS 337, at 338 (Craufurd D. Goodwin et al. eds., 1981).
[2]   BLAKE C. CLAYTON, MARKET MADNESS: A CENTURY OF OIL PANICS, CRISES, AND CRASHES 50 (Oxford Univ. Press 2015).

persuaded President Coolidge to establish a Federal Oil Conservation Board, capable of examining allegedly wasteful production practices by the oil industry. The Board's 1926 report highlighted the need for legislation to prevent both physical and economic waste, but little came of the effort.[3]

Then, as World War II loomed, President Roosevelt established various committees and boards that, in an exception to the general pattern of inaction, successfully coordinated wartime energy planning. By the early 1930s, a National Planning Board emerged (its name later changed to the National Resources Board and then to the National Resources Planning Board [NRPB]).[4] At one point chaired by Interior Secretary Harold Ickes, the NRPB held promise as an advisory board to the White House. A 1939 report by the Energy Resources Committee and submitted to the NRPB acknowledged the interrelated nature of energy resources and the corresponding necessity of governmental planning. While the NRPB produced a cadre of future experts and illustrated the need for coordinated resource planning by the federal government, it ultimately fizzled as Congress withdrew its funding.

After the war, analysis of the interaction of energy, natural resources, environment, geopolitics, and economic policy continued – but with minimal action by the government. In 1946, the Interior Department established both an Oil and Gas Division to, among other things, gather information and coordinate energy policy, and the National Petroleum Council (NPC). This was followed in 1947 with the passage of the National Security Act of 1947 and creation of the National Security Resources Board. A 1949 report to President Truman complained that "we are still considering energy policies separately through particularized agencies, committees, advisory groups, and working parties, usually attempting to work out a specific problem."[5] Then came the prominent Materials Policy, or Paley Commission, and later Eisenhower's 1955 Cabinet Committee on Energy Supplies and Resources Policy. The Paley Commission report advocated for less (but not no) government interference with the market, geared toward ensuring an adequate supply of resources to match projected demand.

Similar efforts surfaced during the 1960s. In Congress, for instance, the Senate established a National Fuels and Energy Study Group, while in the White House, President Kennedy prompted the creation of an Interdepartmental Energy Steering Committee, with President Johnson following suit and commissioning a Natural

---

3   RICHARD H. K. VIETOR, ENERGY POLICY SINCE 1945: A STUDY OF BUSINESS-GOVERNMENT RELATIONS 21–2 (Cambridge Univ. Press 1984). A decade later, in the throes of the Great Depression, Congress passed the Connolly Hot Oil Act and approved the Interstate Oil Compact Commission, which "stabiliz[ed]," petroleum output until" roughly 1972. *Ibid.* at 24.

4   For an excellent history of the NRPB, *see* MARION CLAWSON, NEW DEAL PLANNING: THE NATIONAL RESOURCES PLANNING BOARD (Johns Hopkins Univ. Press 1981). In 1934, the president established a National Power Policy Committee as well. *Ibid.* at 121.

5   Craufurd D. Goodwin, *The Truman Administration: Toward a National Energy Policy*, in ENERGY POLICY IN PERSPECTIVE: TODAY'S PROBLEMS, YESTERDAY'S SOLUTIONS 1, 40 (Craufurd D. Goodwin et al. eds., 1981). For a detailed account of the nation's fuel policies prior to 1946, *see* JOHN C. CLARK, ENERGY AND THE FEDERAL GOVERNMENT: FOSSIL FUEL POLICIES, 1900–1946 (Univ. of Illinois Press 1987).

Resources Task Force that talked about a "new frontier" in energy and the need for new funding opportunities and government-wide efforts.[6] Primarily, this task force championed the importance of research and development (R&D), along with the urgency of ensuring that economic growth did not come at the cost of "pollution and environmental degradation." And it promoted establishing an Energy Policy Commission capable of "examin[ing] trends and issues" and signaling the path toward executive and congressional policies for improving and rendering our energy polices "more consistent." Presidential Science Advisor Donald Horning, in particular, unsuccessfully pleaded personally with President Johnson for a broad enough study that could inform sound energy policy "because so much time had elapsed since the Paley Commission report; the technology of energy production and consumption had changed so much; nuclear energy development had been plagued by so many problems; and the oil import policy, shale oil development, fossil fuel combustion pollution of atmosphere, and so on were such pervasive problems."[7] In 1966, an interdepartmental study group created several years earlier released its report on the nation's future energy supply: available energy resources were sufficient to satisfy our needs until the end of the century at roughly the same cost, though the resource mix might need to change.[8]

But that assessment overlooked several critical dynamics: natural gas shortages, oil import policies, and brownouts in the Northeast all signaled by the end of the 1960s the need to focus on energy policy. In a May 1970 memorandum, Nixon's Ash Council echoed earlier recommendations that the Interior Department be renamed the Department of Natural Resources (DNR). The purpose for a new DNR, Nixon explained in March the following year, would be to bring "natural resource responsibilities now scattered throughout the federal government" under the ambit of a DNR. Presumably fostering coordination was implicit in such a reorganization, an objective made explicit in an accompanying Office of Management and Budget memoranda.[9] The reorganization effort, however, languished in Congress – albeit resurrected occasionally, including most recently in thoughts expressed by President Trump's Interior Secretary Ryan Zinke. But the focus on energy policy persisted, and federal policymakers by 1971 had begun to understand that the nation was confronting an energy crisis. In the spring of 1971,

---

[6] REPORT TO THE PRESIDENT BY THE TASK FORCE ON NATURAL RESOURCES, RESOURCE POLICES FOR A GREAT SOCIETY (Nov. 11, 1964).

[7] Cochrane, *supra* note 1, at 363 (quoting Horning Papers).

[8] *Ibid.* at 353–54. The report opined how the United States could exhaust its natural gas and petroleum resources, but those losses might be offset by shale or even liquefied coal and "a reasonable level of effort to develop advanced nuclear power plants with improved fuel utilization." The Federal Power Commission's 1964 *National Power Survey*, "the first comprehensive study of the industry as a whole, covering the entire Nation and all ownership segments," already had suggested that through coordinating and integrating the electrical grid, the nation could better satisfy its energy demand.

[9] This is described in DENNIS C. LE MASTER, DECADE OF CHANGE: THE REMAKING OF FOREST SERVICE STATUTORY AUTHORITY DURING THE 1970S 109 (Greenwood 1984).

Congress adopted Senate Resolution 45, concluding that "it appears that a Senate committee study of the fuels and energy industries is indicated to determine what, if any, changes in the implementation of existing and prospective Government policies and laws may be desirable in order to coordinate and provide an effective national policy."

On June 4, 1971, President Nixon delivered his "Special Message to the Congress on Energy Resources." Nixon warned how the nation could no longer "take our energy supply for granted." He recounted blackouts and then brownouts, natural gas shortages, rising fuel prices, and the need for protecting our environment as factors warranting attention. His message promoted clean energy, from nuclear power to clean coal (coal gasification and sulfur oxide control), along with nods toward geothermal and solar energy. He directed accelerating resource development from federal lands, including an offshore oil and gas leasing program, along with an oil shale program, and he encouraged more R&D funding as well as energy conservation. At one point, of acute relevance as the Trump administration shies away from examining the social cost of energy, Nixon expressly endorsed appreciating the "full costs to society" of producing and consuming energy. And he continued to push for a DNR. During the subsequent hearings in the Senate, Senator Jackson observed how "develop[ing] a national energy policy which is coherent and consistent, realistic and rational, is one of the most pressing [problems] facing the Nation today." Nixon's Council of Economic Advisers' chair, Paul McCracken, testified how an "organization key to a national energy policy is a single agency that can administer the programs now handled by a number of separate authorities."[10] Nixon's energy policy expert, S. David Freeman, similarly promoted (unsuccessfully) enhanced coordination of energy policy through the creation of a DNR, believing that energy-related decisions were driven by narrow responses addressing outdated circumstances and did not necessarily mesh well with one another.[11]

This dynamic became abundantly clear as the nation's oil import program unfolded. By the 1930s, industry became alarmed with the federal/state dynamic for addressing US oil production. Independent producers objected to inexpensive imported foreign oil.[12] Once the war ended and available oil supplies ostensibly shrank, the focus on imports intensified. Yale Law School Professor Eugene Rostow published a seminal monograph, *A National Policy for the Oil Industry*, concluding that the nation's "foreign and our domestic oil policies would be powerfully served by the transfer of petroleum products to the free list, and the elimination of all quotas

---

[10] The President's Energy Message, Pursuant to S. Res. 45: A National Fuels Policy Study, Hearing before the Committee on Interior and Insular Affairs, U.S. Senate, 92nd Cong., 1st Sess., June 15, 1971, Serial No. 92–1, at 1 (Senator Jackson), 7 (Paul McCracken).

[11] Neil De Marchi, *Energy Policy Under Nixon: Mainly Putting Out Fires, in* ENERGY POLICY IN PERSPECTIVE: TODAY'S PROBLEMS, YESTERDAY'S SOLUTIONS 395, at 404–6, 410, 412, 450 (Craufurd D. Goodwin et al. eds., 1981).

[12] Rachel A. Schurman & Paul E. Sabin, Public Policy, Oil Production, and Energy Consumption in Twentieth Century California, Final Study Report, at 212–13 (MMS Oct. 2003).

or other quantitative limits on imports."[13] Several years earlier, the State Department had issued a policy paper advocating for enhanced programs and incentivizing greater development in the Middle East. Michael Klare explains how, although during the early years of World War I it was "estimated that the United States possessed approximately 20 billion barrels of oil – at that time the greatest concentration of known reserves on earth" – that soon changed by 1942 as the "nation was drawing on these reserves at a rate of about 4 million barrels a day, or 1.45 billion barrels a year."[14] By 1948, oil capacity seemingly became strained as the automobile became an American staple: the country went from 26 million cars in 1945 to about 40 million cars a mere five years later. "No one in the oil industry," according to Daniel Yergin, "was prepared for the explosion of demand for all oil products."[15] The National Petroleum Council in 1949 submitted it's "A National Oil Policy for the United States" report to the Interior Secretary, favoring policies for enhancing domestic production. Established in 1946, this Council served as an industry advisory group on petroleum policy for the Secretary of the Interior.

The industry followed with a lively debate about how rising imports threatened domestic production, a dialogue that escalated following the Korean War and an increase in both domestic exploration activities as well as oil imports. After all, the United States went from being, in 1938, the world's largest exporter to barely a player by the mid-1950s – with a 30 percent reduction in exports (and constituting only a small percentage in the world export market).[16] By 1954, "the growth of imports exceeded that of domestic production by a factor of six, and spare productive capacity ... doubled." US oil consumption, at almost 6 million barrels a day in 1948, rose steadily after the war, increasing significantly between 1960 and 1972, with the United States consuming roughly 16 million barrels a day by the early 1970s.

Successive administrations attempted to balance coal's declining market share for electric generation and increased oil consumption, insufficient domestic oil supply,

---

[13] EUGENE V. ROSTOW, A NATIONAL POLICY FOR THE OIL INDUSTRY 147 (Yale Univ. Press 1948). By the mid-1930s, state portioning or "conservation" programs constrained oil production. Only a few decades earlier, reports of oil's scarcity had captured attention. CLAYTON, *supra* note 2, at 37–45. Of course, contemporary conversations about scarcity cannot be divorced from the widespread dialogues about big oil trusts. These programs nevertheless limited how much oil could be produced, largely to raise or stabilize domestic crude prices. (The federal 1935 Connolly Hot Oil Act prohibited shipping oil in interstate commerce if produced in violation of any state pro-rationing laws, and the 1935 Interstate Oil and Gas Compact Commission permitted interstate coordination.) New Deal programs (the National Industrial Recovery Act – invalidated by the Supreme Court) then gave Interior Secretary Harold Ickes authority over an oil program. *See* DANIEL YERGIN, THE PRIZE: THE EPIC QUEST FOR OIL, MONEY & POWER 252–59 (Free Press 1991).

[14] MICHAEL T. KLARE, BLOOD AND OIL: THE DANGERS AND CONSEQUENCES OF AMERICA'S GROWING PETROLEUM DEPENDENCY 29 (Henry Holt & Co. 2004).

[15] YERGIN, *supra* note 13, at 409. *See also* CLAYTON, *supra* note 2, at 73–94 (noting, though, that concerns about supply shortage are not accurate).

[16] JOHN H. LICHTBLAU & PETROLEUM INDUSTRY RESEARCH FOUNDATION, INC., UNITED STATES OIL IMPORTS: A CASE STUDY IN INTERNATIONAL TRADE 8 (1958). Chapter II of Lichtblau's report traces the history of imports until the mid-1950s.

and domestic oil producers' competitive disadvantage against inexpensive imported oil. While oil primarily served as a principal fuel for transportation, thermal power plants could burn oil as well. But the oil generally being used in power plants was what is called "residual oil," or the oil remaining after refineries refined and sold off the more valuable product for other uses. Sales of residual fuel for power generation rose throughout the 1950s and 1960s. More residual oil to feed power plants, of course, meant a smaller market for coal. A general counsel of the coal industry unabashedly stated that "uncontrolled imports of residual oil" would cause coal production to "disappear" and that "unrestricted imports of crude oil" would retard synthetic gas technological developments.[17] Oil import quotas helped to preserve coal's electric generation market.

In 1959, after twenty months of a voluntary oil import program, President Eisenhower acted under the authority of the Trade Agreements Extension Act of 1955 and inaugurated the Mandatory Oil Import Program (MOIP) limiting oil imports, including incoming residual fuel oil (the lesser-quality by-products of refining oil for use as gasoline and other such products). Eisenhower's MOIP accepted the warnings of his Advisory Committee on Energy Supplies and Resources Policy, which reported in 1955 that imported crude and residual oil would retard domestic exploration and production, threatening industrial growth and national security.[18] Originally, oil imports were limited to 9 percent of US demand, later changed to 12.2 percent of estimated production. The residual oil, a good portion of it from Venezuela and unable to compete in European markets, could compete for coal as a generation resource, but it, too, contained high amounts of sulfur – depending on its peculiarities. Eisenhower expected that incoming residual fuel above certain limits would be permissible, if necessary, to satisfy refinery demands or pipeline companies using the oil as a fuel source. He later announced that such imported oil was primarily used for fuel along the East Coast and tasked the Interior Department with establishing an equitable program for distribution. But this came with a significant caveat: the residual fuel oil could not be refined – or desulfurized – unless the refiner accepted a reduction in its allocation (unlikely because the allocation reduction would count against a higher-quality product).

---

[17] Oil Import Controls, 91st Cong., 2nd Sess., Serial No. 91–17, at 329 (March and April 1970).

[18] Presidential Proclamation No. 3279, March 10, 1959; S. Rep. No. 232, 84th Cong., 1st Sess. 4, *reprinted in* 1955 U.S. Code Cong. & Admin. News 2101, 2014. For a contemporary account of the genesis of the MOIP, see Testimony of Assistant Secretary Moore, Mandatory Oil Import Control Program, Its Impact Upon the Domestic Minerals Industry and National Security, 90th Cong., 2nd Sess., Serial No. 90–25, at 34 (May 1968). The story of how companies in 1960 flooded the international market with oil (at low prices) and prompted the formation of the Organization of Petroleum Exporting Countries (OPEC) has been told by many. *See* ANTONIA JUHASZ, THE TYRANNY OF OIL: THE WORLD'S MOST POWERFUL INDUSTRY – AND WHAT WE MUST DO TO STOP IT (HarperCollins 2008); YERGIN, *supra* note 13. For some excellent sources on the oil import program, see DOUGLAS R. BOHI & MILTON RUSSELL, LIMING OIL IMPORTS: AN ECONOMIC HISTORY AND ANALYSIS (Johns Hopkins Univ. Press 1978); VIETOR, *supra* note 3, at 91–145.

While the MOIP was conceived, in the words of Congressman Edmondson, chair in 1968 of the congressional subcommittee on mines and mining, "to ensure the national security by safeguarding a vigorous healthy domestic petroleum industry," congressional hearings from the late 1960s through the early 1970s confirmed that constraints on imports were hurting some regions and having a perverse effect on domestic supply.[19] It was widely recognized that certain regions, particularly along the east coast, received more exceptions to the quotas, and eventually the program became overly complex in its administration. In May 1969, a Cabinet Task Force on Oil Import Control solicited public input on the program, including asking whether an import program should be maintained. Although in 1970 Nixon rejected its principal recommendation, the task force concluded that the program was no longer effective.[20] Notably, industry opposed its recommendations. The NPC's 1969 report to the Secretary favored maintaining the program, although promoting uniformity and consistency in application.[21] By 1970, oil imports, according to some accounts, constituted upwards of around 20 percent of the nation's "consumption," and it would almost double that percentage by early 1973.[22]

Yet enough signals warned of a looming energy crisis. The 1969–70 winter had been one of the coldest in recent times; 1970, as the initiation of the environmental decade, was witnessing an ever-increasing focus on environmental protection that could significantly affect the energy sector. Although the United States was still the leading oil producer in the world until roughly around 1974 (with peak production generally identified as occurring in 1970), it no longer had the spare production

[19]   Mandatory Oil Import Control Program, Its Impact Upon the Domestic Minerals Industry and National Security, 90th Cong., 2nd Sess., Serial No. 90-25, at 1 (May 1968). Congressman Wayne Aspinall added that "[w]hat started out as a simple, straightforward program, has become a complex administrative wilderness clouded by rules and procedures that few understand and even less approve." *Ibid*. at 3. However, the Interior Department, administering the MOIP, defended the need to restrict imports to incentivize domestic production. *Ibid*. at 8, 16. He claimed that so far over the life of the program, that has occurred. *Ibid*. at 164 (imports increased by only 200,000 barrels while US production increased by 1.5 million barrels). When Congressman Saylor pressed the Interior Department about whether the program operated effectively when the Department was off by about 50 million barrels at the outset of the 1967 six-day Arab-Israeli war, the Departmental official responded that the agency met that type of unexpected contingency. *Ibid* at 37.

[20]   For the Task Force's solicitation, see Mandatory Oil Import Control Program Procedure and Inquiry, 34 Fed. Reg. 8,055 (May 22, 1969). The Nixon Library contains boxes on the Task Force, a subject that admittedly this book only touches on in passing.

[21]   A Report of the National Petroleum Council to the Secretary of the Interior, U.S. Petroleum Imports (1969); De Marchi, *supra* note 11, at 402–3. Nixon accepted the Task Force's recommendation to establish an Oil Policy Committee, headed by one of the administration's energy experts, Brigadier General George A. Lincoln. That committee, along with a newly formed interagency Joint Board on Fuel Supply and Transportation, presumably sought to promote a more coordinated energy policy.

[22]   The Nixon administration, in 1971, suggested that oil imports accounted for roughly 10 percent of US energy consumption. The President's Energy Message, Pursuant to S. Res. 45: A National Fuels Policy Study, Hearing before the Committee on Interior and Insular Affairs, U.S. Senate, 92nd Cong., 1st Sess., June 15, 1971, Serial No. 92-1, at 9 (testimony of George Lincoln, director of Office of Emergency Preparedness). *See also* Malcolm F. Baldwin, *Public Policy on Oil: An Ecological Perspective*, 1 Ecology L. Rev. 245, 249 (1971).

capacity to provide oil to Europe in the event of a Middle East crisis, as it had in the 1956 Suez crisis and the 1967 Arab-Israeli war. As summarized by David Painter, "[t]he United States no longer had the spare capacity to help compensate for a cutoff of oil supplies to Europe and could free oil for Europe in the event of a crisis only by rationing oil domestically. Disruptions in oil supply could also damage the international economy, lead to the nationalization of U.S. oil company holdings, impair European security, and increase pressure on the United States to change its policies toward Israel."[23] The Texas Independent Producers and Royalty Owners Association warned in 1970 of a diminishing cushion in production.[24] And administration officials at the time already were discussing potentially unfolding energy demand/supply scenarios. The NPC, in an initial analysis during the summer of 1971, projected that demand for crude oil might double by 1985, with reliance on imports increasing dramatically. The NPC assumed that imports in 1970 were about 23 percent of total demand and that they would rise to 39 percent by 1975, 47 percent by 1980, and – if those numbers were not scary enough – 57 percent by 1985. To be sure, the NPC miscalculated, but its projections reflected a faction of the prevailing sentiment.[25]

In what was touted as the first message to Congress on energy, Nixon's June 4, 1971 "Remarks About a Special Message to the Congress on Energy Resources" referenced the recent brownouts in the Northeast, the increase in fuel prices, and the environmental externalities of energy use and acknowledged that the nation's assumption of sufficient energy supplies had "been brought sharply into question." Also in June, Nixon appointed John Love as a White House energy czar. And while Nixon's message contained a host of policy proposals and precipitated an array of energy supply studies, De Marchi suggests his message was "ignored" by Congress and "within the administration" and, as such, "was quietly laid aside."[26] Of course, by the fall of 1971, wage and price controls became popular, and the Economic Stabilization Program supported controls for petroleum products.

By 1973, the United States and the Western economies had become increasingly vulnerable to interruption of imported oil supplies, but there was neither a strategy nor a regulatory mechanism for dealing with this vulnerability. This had been the

[23] David S. Painter, *From the Nixon Doctrine to the Carter Doctrine: Iran and the Geopolitics of Oil in the 1970s, in* AMERICAN ENERGY POLICY IN THE 1970S 61, at 69 (Robert Lifset ed., Okla. Univ. Press 2104). By 1978, US oil consumption would increase by roughly 2 million barrels per day from four years earlier, and imports would grow from approximately 37 to 45 percent during this same period. *Ibid.* at 76.

[24] De Marchi, *supra* note 11, at 406. Louisiana and Texas production levels had fallen by early 1972. *Ibid.* at 422. Vietor suggests that estimates of spare production capacity were overstated in the late 1960s, which is why "scarcely anyone recognized [the] decline in spare capacity until it had occurred." Vietor, *supra* note 3, at 198–99.

[25] World Oil Developments and U.S. Oil Import Policies: A Report Prepared for the Committee on Finance by the U.S. Tariff Commission, Committee on Finance, U.S. Senate, 93rd Cong., 1st Sess. 10 (Dec. 12, 1973).

[26] De Marchi, *supra* note 11, at 411.

State Department's concern starting two years earlier and growing even stronger by 1972.[27] The administration ostensibly recognized the risk that oil supply disruption posed to national security and established in the White House a Special Energy Committee, which included National Security Advisor Henry Kissinger, along with Treasury Secretary George Schultz and White Advisor John Ehrlichman.[28] And a 1973 congressional background paper warned that "[r]ecent forecasts of U.S. fuels imports in 1980 have ranged from 11 to 17 million barrels per day (crude oil equivalent), in contrast to less than 4 million barrels," or 22 percent of total US oil consumption, in 1970.[29] But the cast of many characters engaged in energy supply discussions could not reach any widespread consensus on whether free-market solutions would work or whether or how best to tinker with markets.

President Nixon's April 18, 1973, "Special Message to Congress on Energy Policy" warned the public about future energy shortages; encouraged additional reliance on coal, hydroelectric energy, and nuclear power; and promoted new exploration and production of more natural gas and oil (particularly shale oil, offshore oil and gas development, and Alaskan resources), albeit with nods toward energy efficiency, conservation, and R&D. He promoted decontrolling natural gas (initially for new natural gas wells and then separately for gas under existing contracts). He labeled MOIP as having "virtually no benefit any longer" and removed the import restrictions and changed MOIP into a license-fee quota system, leading to a rise in imports just months before the Arab oil embargo. A few weeks after his April message, he signed the Economic Stabilization Act Amendments, where he again, this time in the context of addressing inflationary trends, observed that "if prices are frozen or rolled back," then "supplies will not be available."[30] And he once again pressed for an "integrated national energy policy" and a DNR (in the interim establishing new offices). It was during this same month, moreover, that a State Department official published a provocative article in *Foreign Affairs* warning how we were becoming too dependent on foreign (Middle East) oil and were on the cusp of a real supply crisis.[31]

---

[27] CLAYTON, *supra* note 2, at 102–3.

[28] De Marchi reports that Kissinger did not participate in Nixon's April energy message. With Charles J. DiBona at the helm, the administration also established a National Energy Office. The State Department's interest in energy policy reportedly surfaced only after Thomas O. Enders became an advisor to Kissinger once he became Secretary of State. While Kissinger supported energy independence, Enders apparently persuaded him of the need for an energy policy. De Marchi, *supra* note 11, at 446, 416–17, 526.

[29] Toward a Rational Policy for Oil and Gas Imports: A Policy Background Paper, Prepared at the Request of Senator Henry M. Jackson, Pursuant to S. Res. 45, A National fuels and Energy Policy Study, Serial No. 92–34, 2 (1973).

[30] Economic Stabilization Act Amendments of 1973 (S. 398), Pub. L. 93–28, April 30, 1973; Statement by the President after Signing the Bill to Extend the Economic Stabilization Act and Directing Additional Steps in the Price Control Program, May 2, 1973, 9 Presidential Documents: Richard Nixon, 1973, at No. 18, at 444.

[31] James E. Aiken, *The Oil Crisis: This Time the Wolf Is Here*, 51(3) FOREIGN AFF. 462–490 (April 1973).

Then, late in 1973, Nixon established a Federal Energy Office (FEO) inside the Executive Branch charged with coordinating oil and petroleum policy. Under the leadership of William Simon and his deputy, John Sawhill, the agency quickly grew. But Simon, a free-market advocate, exhibited little affinity for his new agency or, for that matter, even his deputy.[32] One agency official indicated that it would need legislation to implement necessary changes, such as addressing the shortage by requiring that power plants convert from oil to coal. Simon, however, merely indicated that legislation was "desirable," and after the embargo, for instance, he implemented some measures such as diverting 1.5 million barrels of military jet fuel to civilian use.[33] Within months of the agency's creation, *Washington Post* columnist Jack Anderson wrote about Simon's brusque management style and how the agency was in "disarray" and even, in one case, made a decision that led to less crude oil imports.[34]

Many Democrats, as well as the public, thought that Nixon missed the mark. They faulted his failure to emphasize conservation rather than promote production, as well as his administration's lack of appreciation for sufficient R&D funding. Congressman Moss, for instance, reportedly wrote how the immediate energy problems were from a "man-made shortage of natural gas, an inadequate oil-refining capacity and an ever increasing demand for energy by the American public."[35] Democrats who were part of the 1972 Joint Economic Report previously had warned how the nation needed more "clean energy" resources (at the time, many assumed, for instance, coal gasification and the fast breeder nuclear reactor) to support the nation's energy growth needs.[36]

THE EMBARGO AND CONGRESS'S RESPONSE

The first oil shock, the Arab oil embargo, was triggered by the 1973 (October) Yom Kippur war. It threw world oil markets into turmoil. Saudi Arabian King Faisal had warned the United States in May that the US support for Israel could force his country to cut off oil to the United States. This is what happened. During the ensuing embargo, a portion of US oil supply was cut off by the Organization of Petroleum Exporting Countries (OPEC), and the United States experienced fuel

---

[32] MEG JACOBS, PANIC AT THE PUMP: THE ENERGY CRISIS AND THE TRANSFORMATION OF AMERICAN POLITICS IN THE 1970S 69, 107–108 (Hill & Wang 2016). Sawhill would soon be fired when he supported a gasoline tax over the objection of James Schlesinger. Yanek Mieczkowski, *"The Toughest Thing": Gerald Ford's Struggle with Congress over Energy Policy, in* AMERICAN ENERGY POLICY IN THE 1970S 19, 24 (Robert Lifset ed., Okla. Univ. Press 2014).

[33] Tim O'Brien, *Energy Chief Optimistic on U.S. Ability to Cope,* WASH. POST, Dec. 25, 1973, at A1.

[34] Jack Anderson, *Disarray at the Federal Energy Office,* WASH. POST, March 10, 1974, at B7. *See also* Mike Causey, *Fuel Office Has People Shortage,* WASH. POST, Jan. 4, 1974, at D13 (describing lack of funds, personnel transfers from other agencies, and the agency application process).

[35] 119 Cong. Rec. 17182 (May 29, 1973) (Statement of Hons. Aspin and Moss).

[36] Minority Views on the 1972 Economic Report of the President, Report on the January 1972 Economic Report of the President, Rep. No. 92–708, 92nd Cong., 1st Sess., 105–7 (March 23, 1972).

shortages, gasoline lines, and increased prices – OPEC effectively caused the price of oil to increase by roughly 468 percent from 1970. Predictions had some regions likely short between 20 and 25 percent of demand for residual fuel oil.[37] By February 1974, according to Meg Jacobs, "the gas crisis had become acute."[38] And between 1973 and 1975, gasoline prices, in turn, would increase by roughly 30 percent. The net result was a significant economic disruption, followed by a massive recession. The embargo, though, did not create the energy crisis; rather, it confirmed what "experts had been pointing out for some time" – that the country was becoming too dependent on foreign oil as US production was declining and consumption climbing.[39]

An effective response required overcoming how, before the embargo, the United States had neither an organized energy policy nor "energy law." Energy policy, to the extent it can be called such, addressed how to incentivize production, stimulate technological development, and monitor the nation's resource needs.[40] Individual statutes and rules dealt with different forms of energy – the Natural Gas Act and the Federal Power Act for gas and electricity, the Atomic Energy Act for licensing nuclear power plants, and such statutes as the Connolly Hot Oil Act of 1935 and the Public Utility Holding Company Act of 1935. Federal lands were leased for onshore and offshore oil and natural gas production under different statutes, such as the Mineral Leasing Act and the Outer Continental Shelf Lands Act. In short, prior to the embargo, "it was customary to think of individual fuels, not of 'energy.'"[41] The Clean Air Act (CAA) also was in the early stages of its implementation. And separately there was the Economic Stabilization Act of 1970 authorizing price controls on crude oil and refined petroleum products.

Until the embargo, each of these programs operated within its own bureaucratic world: there was little appreciation for how they interacted with one another. The embargo demonstrated not only that the United States was totally unprepared for a significant interruption of oil supply but also that the growing US dependence on imported oil resulted in significant part from a fractured regulatory structure, under which it was difficult, if not impossible, to implement a coordinated national energy policy. More important, several then-existing regulatory policies increased oil use and decreased domestic oil production. In the words of a 1973 staff paper prepared for Senator Jackson, "[t]he present situation is a logical outcome of past policy decisions."[42]

For example, in the late 1960s and early 1970s, the electric power industry was in the process of shifting away from coal-fired generation and toward low-sulfur oil

---

[37]   Thomas O'Toole & Peter Milius, *Nixon Defers Decision on Gas Rationing*, WASH. POST, Dec. 1973, at A1.

[38]   JACOBS, *supra* note 32, at 110.   [39]   Congressional Quarterly, Energy Policy, at 3-A (1979).

[40]   De Marchi, *supra* note 11, at 399.   [41]   *Ibid.*

[42]   Toward a National Policy for Oil and Gas Imports: A Policy Background Paper, 19. The paper added that the import policy, for instance, was "unworkable" and required "major changes," and yet "[m]ajor changes are indeed taking place on an *ad hoc* basis without clear policy direction." *Ibid.* at 213.

and natural gas. This drove up oil use and imports. The conversion to oil was driven by three different regulatory regimes that few, if any, at the time realized were interrelated. First, in the early days of state air-quality abatement programs and the CAA, one of the principal compliance strategies under state implementation plans (SIPs) was to convert coal units to lower-sulfur oil.[43] Second, as Chapter 5 recounts, wellhead price controls on natural gas resulted in an extraordinary natural gas shortage outside the gas-producing states. Under FPC gas curtailment policies, electric generators were not permitted to use natural gas to run their generators during much of the year. They had to switch to oil. Yet, simultaneously, natural gas supplies were further constrained because natural gas's low price, and low sulfur, made it highly attractive as a boiler fuel.[44] A third regulatory regime was state public utility regulation, which in many states permitted fuel adjustment clauses and, in turn, made it much easier to pass through the increased fuel costs rather than to recover capital costs of new, more efficient generation.

Without a full appreciation for these historical dynamics, Congress's and the Nixon administration's responses were poorly designed. The administration's October 1973 allocation of petroleum products upset distribution chains and failed miserably. In his analysis of energy policy during the Nixon years, Neil De Marchi concludes that "the programs adopted and the authority granted to deal with the crisis were not those best suited to resolving the long-run energy problems of the nation."[45] In her book on oil and politics, Meg Jacobs opines that the 1973 "problems were new, but the policy solutions came right from the era of Franklin Roosevelt."[46] Nixon's price controls on oil and petroleum products, for instance, compounded matters by impeding domestic oil production and encouraging additional consumption. One estimate posited that federal price-control programs may have cost the country 1.4 million barrels a day of production.[47] Moreover, when the administration terminated Eisenhower's oil import quota program in early 1973, oil imports rose (particularly from the Middle East). The country became

---

[43]   The vice president for the New England Electric System testified in 1975 how "air pollution control restrictions in the late 1960's and the acceleration of that process by the passage of the Clean Air Act in 1970" contributed to the "decline in coal's percentage of production of electricity." He added that because of "fuel composition availability and cost and the uncertainties and costs of alternative control technologies, many utilities shifted from coal to oil at existing plants with built-in conversion capability and elected to build new plants fired by oil instead of coal." Greater Coal Utilization, Joint Hearings before the Committee on Interior and Insular Affairs and Public Works, Pursuant to S. Res. 45, The National Fuels and Energy Policy Study, on S. 1777, 94th Cong., 1st Sess., Serial No. 94–18 (92–108), 863, June 1975. The embargo chilled at least some planned conversions. *Ibid* at 1468 (planned conversion of coal to oil by Potomac Electric Power Co.).

[44]   Toward a National Policy for Oil and Gas Imports: A Policy Background Paper, 12, 20. The FPC, absent legislative intervention, had begun to allow natural gas price increases. JACOBS, *supra* note 32, at 35.

[45]   De Marchi, *supra* note 11, at 397.   [46]   JACOBS, *supra* note 32, at 49.

[47]   Mieczkowski, *supra* note 32, at 37.

"increasingly vulnerable to short-term supply interruptions,"[48] the first of which occurred a few months later with the embargo. Gas rationing, in turn, quickly captured the attention of the media and the public.[49]

Many of these policies arguably seemed credible on a stand-alone basis, but their cumulative impact – only marginally examined at the time – was to substantially increase oil imports and US vulnerability to interruption of those imports. The overall impact of these regulatory programs is difficult to assess, but upper-bound estimates are possible. Coal-to-oil conversions are estimated to have increased oil consumption by about 0.6 million barrels per day,[50] natural gas curtailments may have increased oil use by as much as 0.5 million barrels per day,[51] and oil price controls reduced domestic oil production by 1.4 million barrels per day, according to one estimate. Adding up the impact of these three regulatory programs, they could have contributed as much as 2.5 million barrels per day to US oil imports, about one-third of total imports. To put this in context, net world oil production decreased during the embargo at about 4.4 million barrels per day, and the Nixon administration concluded that US imports decreased by about 2.7 million barrels a day by January 1974 (about 14 percent of total supply), although other estimates are as low as 900,000 barrels.[52] Presumably such low numbers and little change in US stockpiles led Blake Clayton to conclude that "the reality of the 1973 oil crises was that physical shortage of oil had never in fact occurred – "crisis notwithstanding." The story, though, is much more complex than asking if, in fact, only 900,000 barrels didn't reach the United States. The story is, as Clayton acknowledges, "bad domestic economic policy."[53]

When the embargo occurred, for instance, Congress's initial reaction, after a series of raucous late-night debates, was to extend the life of Nixon's price controls on oil and impose an economy-wide allocation system for oil and petroleum products. The resulting statute, the 1973 Emergency Petroleum Allocation Act

---

[48] David S. Painter, *From the Nixon Doctrine to the Carter Doctrine: Iran and the Geopolitics of Oil in the 1970s, in* AMERICAN ENERGY POLICY IN THE 1970S 61, 72 (Robert Lifset ed., Okla. Univ. Press 2014).

[49] E.g., Thomas O'Toole & Peter Milius, *Nixon Defers Decision on Gas Rationing*, WASH. POST, Dec. 1973, at A1.

[50] Federal Power Commission, The Potential for Conversion of Oil-Fired and Gas-Fired Electric Generating Units to Use of Coal 3 (1973).

[51] 1973–74 curtailments were estimated to be 1.2 tcf, equivalent to about 0.5 million barrels per day of petroleum if all the curtailed gas was replaced by oil. Office of Technology Assessment, Analysis of Impact of Projected Natural Gas Curtailments for the Winter 1975–76, 1975. p. 3. *See also* Paul W. MacAvoy, *The Natural Gas Policy Act of 1978*, 19 NAT. RES. J. 811, 818 (1979) (discussing varying estimates of mid-1970s natural gas curtailments).

[52] YERGIN, *supra* note 13, at 614; PETER Z. GROSSMAN, U.S. ENERGY POLICY AND THE PURSUIT OF FAILURE 18 (Cambridge Univ. Press 2013). Nixon's November 7, 1973, national address warned of a potential 10 percent shortfall in petroleum supply – possibly increasing to up to 17 percent, a number roughly two weeks later he described as "anticipated." In his analysis of the period, De Marchi posits that the shortfall was only between 2 and 2.5 million barrels a day (originally projected to be between 3 and 3.5 million barrels per day). De Marchi, *supra* note 11, at 456.

[53] CLAYTON, *supra* note 2, at 111–12.

(EPAA),[54] required the president to continue price controls on domestic crude oil and all downstream sales of petroleum products, as well as to administratively prescribe how scarce petroleum products were to be distributed throughout the economy. EPAA set up a pricing regime that controlled production from existing wells and fields at 1972 prices, spread the higher cost of imported crude among all refiners, and then regulated the downstream sale of all refined petroleum products. The regulation also provided for allocation of petroleum products throughout the distribution chain, based on 1972 sales. EPAA turned out to be massively dysfunctional – price controls reduced incentives for conservation and did not provide effective incentives to increase domestic oil production from existing fields, and the allocation system at times made petroleum shortages worse. The price differential between price-controlled crude ("old oil") and uncontrolled crude ("new oil") provided ample opportunity for producers and traders to profit by illegally converting old oil to new oil by various stratagems. According to Meg Jacobs, this approach "wreaked havoc on the market."[55] The government mounted an ambitious but slow-moving enforcement program under EPAA, with litigation continuing even fifteen years after Reagan ended price controls in 1981.[56]

The embargo, though, spawned a plethora of additional congressional and executive actions, reports, and analyses. Nixon announced to the nation, in November (initially on the seventh and again on the twenty-fifth), that the country was confronting an energy crisis. The United States would be short roughly 10 percent of its demand for petroleum. He urged that the country move toward a path of avoiding dependence on foreign oil, or Project Independence. It was, in Meg Jacobs' words, "born from ideological convictions" toward a market-oriented solution.[57] His proposals, such as avoiding having utilities convert coal plants to oil, increasing fossil fuel production, relaxing environmental standards, and even presumably promoting conservation and renewables, received mixed responses, particularly because many energy experts believed such efforts came too late for the upcoming winter season.[58] Shortly thereafter he created an Energy Emergency Planning Group (which ceased functioning within a year), as well as the FEO. In December, Congress also officially concluded that the country was facing "severe energy shortages, especially" for the

---

54   Emergency Petroleum Allocation Act of 1973, S. 1570, P.L. 93–159, 87 Stat. 627, Nov. 27, 1973. Its stated purpose was to grant the executive authority to temporarily "deal with shortages of crude oil, residual fuel oil, and refined petroleum products or dislocations in their national distribution system."
55   JACOBS, *supra* note 32, at 106.
56   A task force report, known as the "Sporkin Report" (after then-SEC enforcement chief and later US District Court Judge Stanley Sporkin), highlighted the agency's "ineffectiveness." JOSEPH P. TOMAIN & SHEILA S HOLLIS, ENERGY DECISION MAKING: THE INTERACTION OF LAW AND POLICY 135 (Lexington Books 1983); *see also ibid.* at 134 ("by 1976, it was clear to most observers that any ostensible enforcement program by FEA was a failure").
57   JACOBS, *supra* note 32, at 136.
58   *See* Tim O'Brien, *Nixon Energy Plan Held Too Late for This Winter*, WASH. POST., Nov. 9, 1973, at A1.

upcoming winter, and changed Daylight Savings Time and implemented highway speed limits.[59]

On January 23, 1974, Nixon delivered another "Special Message to the Congress on the Energy Crisis," replacing his FEO by promoting a Federal Energy Administration (FEA) and recounting his Project Independence effort. He announced that "if successful," Project Independence "would by 1980 take us to a point where we are no longer dependent to any significant extent upon potentially insecure foreign supplies of energy." He emphasized, for example, increased development from the Outer Continental Shelf (OCS) as well as from Alaska, along with stimulating synthetic fuel production – which already enjoyed a long lineage.[60] He further remarked about the need for more R&D, improving urban transportation, and evaluating energy-efficiency products. To promote energy development and conservation, he specifically identified several components:

- He requested that Congress provide "competitive pricing" for newly developed natural gas;
- He encouraged resource development in the Alaska Naval Petroleum Reserve and limited production from Elk Hills Reserve in California;
- He encouraged Congress to pass the Mined Area Protection Act – a precursor to the modern federal reclamation program;
- He encouraged Congress to pass legislation for the licensing of construction and operation of deepwater port facilities;
- He encouraged Congress to pass an investment tax credit incentivizing new oil and gas exploratory drilling;
- He encouraged Congress to consolidate mineral leasing into a single program (combining hard-rock mining under the 1872 Mining Law with the Mineral Leasing Act, something that all Democratic presidents in recent times have supported);
- He encouraged Congress to remove the 22 percent foreign depletion allowance for US companies producing oil overseas;
- He encouraged Congress to pass a windfall profits tax, "preventing major domestic energy producers from making unconscionable profits as a result of the entropy crisis";
- He encouraged Congress to pass efficiency labeling legislation (appliances and automobiles would have labels identifying their energy use and efficiency);
- He encouraged accelerating the licensing of nuclear facilities;

---

[59] Emergency Daylight Saving Time Energy Conservation Act of 1973, Pub. L. 93–182, 87 Stat. 707, Dec. 15, 1973; Emergency Highway Energy Conservation Act, Pub. L. 93–239, 87 Stat. 1046, Jan. 2, 1974, *amended* Federal-Aid Highway Amendments of 1974, Pub. L. 93–643, 88 Stat. 2281, Jan. 4, 1975.

[60] Vietor observes that despite earlier synfuels failures, it "was to be the foundation of a major new initiative by the U.S. government during the 1970s." VIETOR, *supra* note 3, at 189.

- He encouraged Congress to pass legislation governing energy facility siting and coordination, as well as modifying aspects of the Clean Air Act (particularly deadlines); and
- He encouraged Congress to approve his reorganization efforts, including establishment of the FEA.

Experts, though, treated the self-sufficiency goal as unrealistic, and it was later modified to avoiding dependence on oil from unstable regions.

Other initiatives complemented Project Independence. On the international front, Henry Kissinger participated in a February Consumer Energy Conference in Washington, DC, where participants worked toward what would become the International Energy Agency (IEA) and a program for international energy cooperation to counter OPEC.[61] Kissinger, in part, sought an international price floor for petroleum imports, hoping that it would "underwrite investment in conventional *and* alternative" energy sources.[62] At home, Congress in 1974 established the Federal Energy Administration (FEA), a predecessor to the Department of Energy (DOE), as well as the Energy Research and Development Administration (ERDA) – a signature item for Ford, ERDA assumed various R&D tasks from the National Science Foundation, Interior Department, and the Environmental Protection Agency. In the same legislation, Congress further established a short-lived Energy Resources Council charged with advising and coordinating energy policy across the executive branch. It also passed legislation promoting solar energy research, declaring the "urgency of the Nation's critical energy shortages and the need to make clean and renewable energy alternatives commercially viable."[63] And Congress enacted the Energy Supply and Environmental Coordination Act (ESECA), discussed later in the context of coal conversion.[64]

Experts, though, considered these initiatives insufficient for achieving energy independence. Produced under the direction of Eric Zausner, the approximately 800-page Project Independence report released in November 1974 even concluded that the energy-independence goal was infeasible. The report instead laid out a suite of measures for mitigating import dependence. A principal measure was increasing

[61] Ronald Koven, *U.S. Shifts on Sharing Domestic Oil*, WASH. POST, Feb. 16, 1974, at A13. For a discussion of IEA, *see* William F. Martin & Evan M. Harrje, *The International Energy Agency*, in ENERGY AND SECURITY: TOWARD A NEW FOREIGN POLICY STRATEGY 97 (Han H. Kalicki & David L. Goldwyn eds., Johns Hopkins Univ. Press 2005).

[62] De Marchi, *supra* note 11, at 530.

[63] Solar Energy Research, Development, and Demonstration Act of 1974 (S. 3234), Pub. L. No. 93–473, 88 Stat. 1431, Oct. 26, 1974.

[64] Energy Supply and Environmental Coordination Act of 1974, Pub. L. No. 93–319, 88 Stat. 246, June 22, 1974; Federal Energy Administration Act of 1974, Pub. L. No. 93–275, 88 Stat. 96, May 7, 1974 (FEA); P. L. No. 93–438 (ERDA). While Congress also passed a nonnuclear energy research program, Pub. L. 93–577, 88 Stat. 1878, Dec. 31, 1974, the Energy Emergency Act (S. 2589) struggled through the Senate and initially was vetoed by Nixon. For a discussion of the history, *see* Congressional Quarterly, Energy Policy, 24-A to 26-A (Cong. Quarterly, Inc. April 1979).

domestic supply, but the report also looked at what was then called "energy conservation" (now called "energy efficiency"), alternative fuels, and reserve stocks of petroleum.

A second, equally influential report – *Time to Choose*, a study by the Ford Foundation[65] – took a broader approach than the Project Independence report. Written under the direction of S. David Freeman, it laid out three scenarios for energy policy. The first scenario, "Historic Growth," did not constrain energy use but assumed an increase in imported and domestic resources sufficient to keep the economy viable. It predicted a future US energy use of about 200 quads. The second scenario, "Technical Fix," projected that with energy efficiency and with then-nascent renewables we could reduce the growth in energy use very considerably. Finally, the study put forward a "Zero Energy Growth" scenario, which projected that by the 1990s the United States could stop energy growth at about 100 quads per year – about 40 percent above 1975 consumption. This third scenario seemed wildly improbable at the time but was eerily prescient – US energy use has in fact plateaued at about 100 quads.[66] These studies, and others, framed the debate on US energy policy – were we going to increase supply, constrain demand, or use a combination of both? In the jargon of the time, would we take the "hard path" versus the "soft path?" As a conservationist, Freeman, in *Time to Choose*, "documented the case for greater efficiency and renewables," and yet he would later lament how the next thirty years became a "time to snooze."[67]

Debates surrounding embargo-era energy legislation often occurred amid conversations about broader contemporary social and political issues preoccupying the United States. During one particularly colorful late-night session, the House considered Congressman John Dingell's amendment relating to school busing (no petroleum to transport public school students further than the nearest public school),[68] Congresswoman Elizabeth Holtzman's amendment on Vietnam (no petroleum for the war in Vietnam), and a Republican amendment to the Holtzman amendment that would also bar oil for Israel.[69] A near riot ensued. Meanwhile, segments of the public were skeptical that there was, indeed, a crisis. Noted environmentalist Barry Commoner told an audience that the crisis did not occur because of a mistake in matching demand with supply but instead because "of the way oil companies do business for profit."[70] Others, such as Ralph Nader and

---

[65] Energy Policy Project of the Ford Foundation, A Time to Choose: America's Energy Future (Ballinger 1974).

[66] EIA, *Monthly Energy Review, Energy Overview*, Dec. 2015.

[67] S. David Freeman, Winning Our Energy Independence: An Energy Insider Road Show 2 (Gibbs Smith 2007).

[68] 119 Cong. Rec. 41267–69 (Dec. 13, 1973) (amendments to the Emergency Energy Act).

[69] Jacobs, *supra* note 32, at 67.

[70] Tim O'Brien, *Energy Office Set to Shift Gas Supply for Hard-Hit Areas*, Wash. Post, Feb. 18, 1974, at A5.

Jesse Jackson, echoed similar sentiments, blaming the industry for fabricating a false crisis narrative. The industry, after all, had recorded record profits in 1973.

Beginning with the Energy Policy and Conservation Act (EPCA) in 1975, Congress took formidable steps that have since framed the basis for much of our energy policy for the next forty years. It was not what President Ford had hoped for, and it reflected more a compromise than a consensus. Indeed, Ford's misgivings rose almost to the level of a veto (he did veto a decontrol extension bill), but energy expert Frank Zarb (FEA Administrator, 1974–77) cautioned against it because it might affect Ford's 1976 election bid.[71] The first step would be to deal with physical security of supply, which meant, first and foremost, building a strategic petroleum reserve storing crude oil in Gulf Coast salt domes so that when the next supply interruption came along, the United States would be able to ride it through without significant physical supply disruption. Coupled with that would be a series of international agreements, principally the Agreement on an International Energy Programme (IEP), with the signatory countries agreeing that they would all set up petroleum reserves, coordinate the release of those reserves, and coordinate steps to reduce consumption in the event of a supply interruption. In EPCA, Congress established the Strategic Petroleum Reserve (SPR) and provided for implementation of the IEP. This has been described as the first effort to develop an emergency reserve for civilian use and enjoyed wide support. Only tapped a few times and with varying success, though, President Trump has since suggested that it should be eliminated – as a tool for raising revenue rather than as a safety net for oil supply.[72]

A second step would be eliminating price controls. Policymakers debated the merits of allocation schemes, price controls, various mechanisms for incentivizing domestic production and conserving resources, and challenging OPEC, all while trying to address the effects of recession and inflationary trends. But most reports credited inexpensive crude imports for retarding domestic production and unnecessarily encouraging consumption. The Ford administration's principal recommended policy tool for reducing demand for energy was eliminating oil price controls and price controls on natural gas production. Ford warned Congress that he would impose an import fee on crude oil until Congress removed oil price controls. And he warned Americans, in January 1975, that a higher price of oil was necessary for promoting the nation's independence from foreign oil, and he submitted to Congress his Energy Independence Act. Democrats then in Congress balked. Coauthor Robert Nordhaus was a counsel to the House Commerce Committee at the time and later reported to Yanek Mieczkowski how some

[71] Mieczkowski, *supra* note 32, at 19, 29–38; *see also* De Marchi, *supra* note 11, at 475 (discussing energy policy debates during Ford's term). William Simon "pushed most vehemently for a veto." JACOBS, *supra* note 32, at 149.

[72] Energy Policy Conservation Act, Pub. L. No. 94–163, 89 Stat. 871, Dec. 22, 1975 (Part B); Bruce Beaubouef, *The U.S. Strategic Petroleum Reserve and Energy Security Lessons of the 1970s, in* AMERICAN ENERGY POLICY IN THE 1970S 163, 176 (Richard Lifset ed., Okla. Univ. Press 2014).

members became apoplectic. They rejected pricing as a demand-constraint tool. Many feared that removing controls would exacerbate the effects from an already strained inflationary period. They also objected to the president's assertion of executive authority, price controls, to prod congressional action – in the immediate wake of Watergate.[73] Not surprisingly, a "Resources for the Future" analysis observes how "EPCA represented a reversal of the principles originally supported by the Ford administration."[74]

EPCA merely replaced price controls under the EPAA and extended the life of oil price controls for six years, until October 1981, and it avoided natural gas producer price controls. As passed, EPCA "continued the two-tier structure for crude oil, maintained the price of old oil at $5.25 a barrel and placed a cap on the roughly one-third of 'uncontrolled' domestic crude at $11.28 a barrel."[75] Numerous studies, though, explored how price controls affected US refineries' choice between foreign and domestic crude, the amount of refined or unrefined crude being imported, and consumer costs. A seminal study of the price controls concluded that they "extracted inframarginal rents from crude oil producers," distributing the "rents among refiners and consumers," and effectively constituted federal regulatory "monopsonistic price discrimination."[76] Price controls on oil remained in place until January 1981, when ended by Reagan days after taking office.[77] For natural gas, it would take a little over another decade before producer regulation was finally ended with the passage of the Natural Gas Wellhead Decontrol Act of 1989.

The third step was constraining ever-increasing demand for energy, especially oil. A broad range of conservation measures was essential to reducing oil consumption because, at the time, oil use seemingly transcended most sectors of the economy.

---

[73] JACOBS, *supra* note 32, at 135; Mieczkowski, *supra* note 32, at 19, 25.
[74] BOLI & RUSSELL *supra* note 18, at 339. *See also* VIETOR, *supra* note 3, at 249. Certain aspects of EPCA were amended the following year, particularly pricing mechanisms for stripper wells. *Ibid.* at 255.
[75] De Marchi, *supra* note 11, at 504.
[76] JOSEPH P. KALT, THE ECONOMICS AND POLITICS OF OIL PRICE REGULATION: FEDERAL POLICY IN THE POST-EMBARGO ERA 100 (MIT Press 1981). The RAND Corporation years earlier concluded that price controls had not benefited consumers by reducing the price for refined products. RAND Corporation, Petroleum Regulation: The False Dilemma of Decontrol (RAND Corp. 1977). But, as the Energy Department noted in 1979, "other studies conclude[d] that decontrol would cause domestic product prices to increase." Department of Energy, Analysis Memorandum: The Role of Refined Product Imports in the Domestic Fuel Market 3 (DOE April 1979). The Department, instead, acknowledged how "[t]he results of such studies have been muddled because of the inherent difficulty in accounting for the effects of the crude oil embargo, recession, and domestic coal strike" that occurred a few years earlier. *Ibid.* at 4. Looking back on the program, David Vietor suggests that "most analysts have agreed that the benefit to American consumers was far outweighed by the costs." VIETOR, *supra* note 3, at 270.
[77] Executive Order No. 12287. Decontrol of Crude Oil and Refined Petroleum Products, Jan. 28, 1981. Reporting on President Reagan's decision, the *New York Times* noted that the administration believed that decontrol would have occurred under the process started by President Carter and that with decontrol gasoline prices would rise, oil consumption would decrease slightly, oil production would be stimulated, and the US Treasury would raise "additional money" from "higher corporate income and the 'windfall profits' tax." Robert D. Hershey, Jr., *President Abolishes Last Price Controls on U.S.-Produced Oil*, N.Y. TIMES, Jan. 29, 1981.

Unlike today, electric generation was a major consumer of oil, and efficiency standards for electric appliances, for example, could have a significant impact on oil use. EPCA created a program for efficiency standards for appliances, along with programs to enhance energy efficiency in buildings and nascent programs on renewables. It also established the now-well-known Corporate Average Fuel Economy (CAFE) program for light-duty motor vehicles (described in Chapter 9).

The fourth step involved measures for increasing domestic oil and gas production – principally through opening production from naval petroleum reserves, accelerating production from the OCS and of Alaska North Slope crude, and changing federal lands leasing policy. Understandably, though, it would take years before production from major new fields would reach the market. Project Independence under Nixon and Ford sought to boost oil and gas development along the OCS.[78] The 1953 Outer Continental Shelf Lands Act (OCSLA) had established a program for generating oil and gas development from submerged lands in federal waters off the nation's coastline. For the most part, these are waters beyond 3 nautical miles of the coastline of the adjoining state (9 nautical miles for Texas and the Florida Gulf). Yet marginal development had occurred prior to the 1970s, and it would not be until later in the decade, in 1978, that Senator Jackson could confidently claim that offshore development was "America's best hope for finding additional oil and gas resources and reducing [our dependence] on foreign oil."[79] In 1976, for instance, FEA projected that the nation could produce between 12 and 14 million barrels per day by 1985 if it "strong[ly] pursued" OCS development, while deregulating oil and gas prices could simultaneously drop imports to 5.9 million barrels per day.[80]

Beginning in the 1970s, increased offshore production appeared likely, because technological developments made it easier to produce in deeper waters.[81] Following Nixon's 1971 message to Congress proposing expanded offshore leasing, the Interior Department accelerated offshore leasing and published a five-year schedule for awarding new leases. The Department expected that while overall energy demand would increase by 4.5 percent annually over the next fifteen years, demand for oil and natural gas between 1970 and 1985 would "increase at a 3.2 and a 3.8 percent

---

[78] Richard Nixon, Special Message to the Congress on Energy Policy, April 18, 1973 ("domestic production of conventional fuels, sales of oil and gas leases on the Outer Continental Shelf have been increased" and proposing to triple annual leased acreage by 1979). Nixon further tasked the Interior Department with developing a long-term program for all energy resources on offshore and onshore public lands.

[79] 124 Cong. Rec. 13,994 (Aug. 22, 1978).

[80] Frank Zarb, Federal Energy Administration, 1976 National Energy Outlook xxv- xxviii, 25–28 (FEA-N-75/713 1976). With fears of peak oil, FEA expected that declining oil reserves after 1990 would be offset by new technologies.

[81] Tyler Priest, *Diving into Deep Water: Shell Oil and the Reform of Federal Offshore Oil Leasing, in* AMERICAN ENERGY POLICY IN THE 1970S 123, 127, 150, 158 (Robert Lifset ed., Okla. Univ. Press 2014). *See also* TYLER PRIEST, THE OFFSHORE IMPERATIVE: SHELL OIL'S SEARCH FOR PETROLEUM IN POSTWAR AMERICA (Texas A&M Univ. Press 2007).

average annual rate, respectively."[82] For 1975, the Interior Department therefore expected that it could lease 10 million acres, "as much as had been handed out in the entire twenty-year history of OCS leasing."[83] This precipitated a robust debate over the next few years about the role of the states in the leasing process and the adequacy of environmental considerations – with Congress even inducing states with coastal assistance. In 1978, Congress, after years of consideration, amended the OCSLA to promote the orderly leasing of offshore oil and gas resources in federal waters. However, even with accelerated OCS leasing, production from the OCS could not be expected to increase materially for several years. By 1976, accelerated leasing plans projected that roughly half a billion barrels of oil could be produced by 1985 from the OCS (offsetting the need to convert oil power plants to coal), but OCS production would be "insufficient" to replace dwindling natural gas supplies.[84]

New production from Alaska's North Slope presented a similar problem: years would lapse before Alaskan crude could reach the market. Between 1968 and 1970, explorations at Prudhoe Bay off the North Slope of Alaska triggered a massive effort to develop and transport the projected nearly 10 billion barrels of crude oil. But years of permitting and construction intervened before the roughly 790 mile Trans-Alaska Pipeline would be available to carry its crude to the gulf at Valdez.[85] In 1971, Interior Secretary Morton commented how transportation was the "limiting factor" for North Slope oil development.[86] It took an act of Congress, moreover, to remove limitations on the pipeline's right-of-way authority and shield the pipeline from future environmental litigation surrounding its construction.[87] The Senate Conference Report noted that the country's dependence on higher-priced foreign oil from the eastern hemisphere along with the desire for lower-sulfur crude from Alaska purportedly explained why "no witness seriously proposed that it would be in the national interest to postpone the development of Alaska Arctic oil and gas" and

---

[82] Department of the Interior, Final Environmental Statement: Proposed 1972 Outer Continental Shelf Oil and Gas General Lease Sale Offshore Eastern Louisiana, June 16, 1972, at 18.

[83] Priest, *supra* note 81, at 123, 130. "After the nation experienced the disruptive effects of the first 'Arab oil boycott,' the OCS program was 'accelerated' by Presidents Nixon and Ford to offer far more acreage and thereby make a greater contribution to national energy independence." E. Edward Bruce, *The History, Status and Future of OCS Leasing*, 24A ROCKY MTN. MIN. L. INST. 1 (1989). *See also* Sam Kalen *Cruise Control and Speed Bumps: Energy Policy and Limits for Outer Continental Shelf Leasing*, 7 ENVTL. & ENERGY L. & POL'Y J. 155 (2012).

[84] Coal Conversion Program: Final Revised Environmental Impact Statement, May 1977, at viii-16, 74.

[85] For a history of oil development in Alaska, *see* WALTER R. BORNEMAN, ALASKA: SAGA OF A BOLD LAND 441–96 (HarperCollins 2003); PETER A. COATES, THE TRANS-ALASKA PIPELINE CONTROVERSY: TECHNOLOGY, CONSERVATION, AND THE FRONTIER (Univ. of Alaska Press 1993); STEPHEN HAYCOX, FRIGID EMBRACE: POLITICS, ECONOMICS AND ENVIRONMENT IN ALASKA (Oregon State Univ. Press 2002); HARVEY MANNING, CRY CRISIS! REHEARSAL IN ALASKA (Friends of the Earth 1974); JOHN STROHMEYER, EXTREME CONDITIONS: BIG OIL AND THE TRANSFORMATION OF ALASKA (Cascade Press 2nd edn, 2003).

[86] The President's Energy Message, Pursuant to S. Res. 45: A National Fuels Policy Study, Hearing before the Committee on Interior and Insular Affairs, U.S. Senate, 92nd Cong., 1st Sess., Serial No. 92–1, at 15, June 15, 1971 (testimony of Secretary Morton).

[87] Trans-Alaska Pipeline Authorization Act, Pub. L. No. 93–153, 87 Stat. 576 (S. 1081), Nov.16, 1973.

that the country's energy situation "reflects rapidly changing public perceptions of the nation's energy needs."[88] Oil, though, didn't flow until 1977. Eventually, 3 million barrels per day of OCS and North Slope crude would reach the market.[89]

While these four steps produced a suite of energy policies that form much of the statutory foundation of what we have today, Congressman Jim Wright (D.-Tex.) lamented in 1976 how Congress merely played around the edges and did nothing "practical to increase the supply of energy and reduce our dependence upon foreign sources."[90]

CARTER'S NATIONAL ENERGY PLAN

By 1977, a consensus formed that the US energy situation had grown to "crisis" proportions. The United States, after all, had become more dependent on higher-priced foreign oil – particularly from the Middle East. Oil imports rose to almost 50 percent of US oil consumption. Some regions of the country were acutely affected. Petroleum furnished New England with over 80 percent of its energy needs. Combined, New York, New Jersey, and Pennsylvania consumed roughly two-thirds of the country's residual and distillate fuels.[91] As one House committee stated: "The fundamental problem for U.S. Energy Policy is the insecurity of its oil supply ... The United States faces the problem of making the transition from an era of cheap abundant energy to relative scarcity of expensive energy supplies."[92]

On April 20, 1977, two days after delivering his message to the nation that our energy situation presented the "moral equivalent of war (MEOW)," President Carter submitted to Congress his National Energy Plan (NEP), drafted during the preceding eight weeks under the direction of James Schlesinger. As an eminent economist with an illustrious career in various administration positions, Schlesinger was uniquely well suited for the task. And he enlisted the aid of several experienced energy experts, including S. David Freeman (author of Nixon's first environmental message and *Time to Choose*) and Bob Nordhaus, described by James Cochrane as providing "a strong influence in getting the group to think of solving the energy problem through taxation."[93]

[88] Federal Lands Rights-of-Way Act of 1973, Senate Rep. 93–207, 93rd Cong., 1st Sess., at 18, June 12, 1973. Of course, one issue was whether the Alaskan crude could be imported or if was even needed for the western US region.

[89] EIA Statement of Adam Sieminski before Senate Committee on Energy and Natural Resources, July 7, 2014, at 5. One initial problem with Alaskan crude was that it neither could be exported nor easily shipped to the gulf, and the western US enjoyed a surplus. James L. Cochrane, *Carter Energy and the Ninety-Fifth Congress, in* ENERGY POLICY IN PERSPECTIVE: TODAY'S PROBLEMS, YESTERDAY'S SOLUTIONS 547, 593 (Craufurd D. Goodwin et al. eds., 1981).

[90] Congressional Quarterly, Energy Policy, 4-A (1979).

[91] The Impact of the President's Energy Plan on the Northeast, Hearing before the Subcommittee on Energy, Joint Economic Committee, 95th Cong., 1st Sess. 1 (May 1977).

[92] Ad Hoc Comm. on Energy, National Energy Act (1977).

[93] Cochrane, *supra* note 89, at 547, 554.

Once again, addressing constraints on oil supply would capture much of the attention. Any "comprehensive energy policy," after all, would require formulating "oil pricing and taxing provisions."[94] The political right would challenge Carter's plan as effectively a liberal tax plan. Yet, reducing petroleum imports, encouraging domestic production, and promoting conservation were imperative. Schlesinger, who previously questioned market controls, presented Carter with a plan that "induced conservation by raising the price of energy through a combination of government-mandated price increases and higher taxes."[95] The administration also later expressed concern that artificially low US prices were causing an international "embarrassment" and promoting consumption rather than conservation.[96] But Carter delivered his MEOW speech to a public and Congress skeptical that his 113 proposals were necessary, while liberal economists feared how decontrol (and rising prices) would affect consumers and benefit industry – and yet other economists, including William Simon, objected to governmental intrusion into the marketplace.

Congress eventually responded by passing five pieces of legislation, collectively known as the National Energy Act of 1978 (NEA): the Energy Tax Act, the Powerplant and Industrial Fuel Use Act (Fuel Use Act), the National Energy Conservation Policy Act, the Natural Gas Policy Act, and the Public Utility Regulatory Policies Act. Much of the congressional debate surrounding the NEA focused on natural gas pricing and tax issues. Carter also promoted and Congress acquiesced in establishing the Department of Energy (DOE), consolidating energy functions carried out by several existing federal agencies. David Vietor describes one of those prior agencies, the FEA, as having been technically incompetent, bureaucratically inept, criticized by all, and yet within just two years producing 5,000 pages of regulations.[97]

What precise authority the proposed new DOE would possess presented a few challenges, however. At one point, for instance, the draft DOE Act contemplated a shared arrangement between the Interior Department and DOE on issuing regulations for developing OCS resources. This, of course, predated the OCSLA Amendments. How the Federal Power Commission (FPC) would fare, too, remained slightly unclear, because early proposals would have created a board within the new DOE for pricing – such as with natural gas. That changed once

[94] Report to the Congress by the Comptroller General of the United States, An Evaluation of the National Energy Plan, at 4.36 (July 25, 1977).
[95] JACOBS, *supra* note 32, at 172.
[96] W. CARL BIVEN, JIMMY CARTER'S ECONOMY: POLICY IN AN AGE OF LIMITS 153, 158 (Univ. North Carolina Press 2002).
[97] Energy Tax Act of 1978, Pub. L. No. 95–618, 92 Stat. 3174, Nov. 9, 1978; Powerplant and Industrial Fuel Use Act, Pub. L. No. 95–620, 92 Stat. 3289, Nov. 9, 1978; National Energy Conservation Policy Act, Pub. L. No. 95–619, 92 Stat. 3206, Nov. 9, 1978; Natural Gas Policy Act, Pub. L. No. 95–621, 92 Stat. 3351, Nov. 9, 1978; Public Utility Regulatory Policies Act, Pub. L. No. 95–617, 92 Stat. 3117, Nov. 9, 1978; The Department of Energy Organization Act of 1977, Pub. L. No. 95–91, 91 Stat. 565, Aug. 4, 1977. See VIETOR, *supra* note 3, at 256–57.

the FPC became an independent agency, the Federal Energy Regulatory Commission (FERC), and was folded inside the Department. Although as hold-over of that conversation about what entity would have pricing authority, Section 403 of the Act remained and contemplated that the DOE Secretary could recommend regulations to the FPC for pricing – this all before the passage of the NGPA. This seeming anachronism was recently used by Secretary Perry when he sought to influence the Commission on pricing policies favoring coal and nuclear power plants. While some, such as Milton Friedman, ridiculed a new DOE, the measure easily passed Congress, and Schlesinger became its first Secretary.

Carter's NEP embraced six principal objectives it sought to achieve by 1985, including reducing the growth rate for energy consumption to below 2 percent annually, reducing oil imports to less than 6 million barrels per day, reducing by 10 percent gasoline consumption, weatherizing almost all homes and new buildings, and increasing annual coal production as well as solar energy. To these ends, it contained three major components. First, it established an ambitious conservation program for all sectors of energy use to reduce the annual rate of growth of demand. An administration witness testified how "[c]onservation, including increased fuel efficiency, is the cornerstone of the Plan."[98] Second, the NEP promoted measures to induce industries and utilities using oil and natural gas to convert to coal and other more abundant fuels. This was married with pricing and production policies to incent new production.

Third, the NEP pursued a vigorous R&D program and price incentives for renewable energy, "unconventional" natural gas, and other resources. The Plan anticipated reducing industrial oil consumption by about 3 million barrels per day. By 1985, oil imports could be reduced by 4.5 million barrels per day. And it further assumed that after 1985 the country's dependence on petroleum would be replaced by increased coal utilization, which would then "buy time to move to a long-term technology solution of the energy problem based on solar or geothermal means and perhaps fusion."[99] For the most part, Carter's plan was not necessarily novel, drawing on proposals from the prior years. And reports about the plan suggest that it underwent significant revisions and compromises before it was submitted – with erroneous assumptions and not necessarily with Schlesinger's full support.[100]

For oil, the NEP did not propose any statutory change in EPAA, but changes in EPAA regulations would be used to provide price signals to encourage production

---

[98] Statement of John F. O'Leary, Administrator, Federal Energy Administration, Part 1: National Energy Act, Hearings before the Subcommittee on Energy and Power of the Committee on Interstate and Foreign Commerce, House of Representatives, 95th Cong., 1st Sess., on H.R. 6831, et al., at 371, 372 (May 9, 10, 11, and 16, 1977).

[99] Cochrane, *supra* note 89, at 547, 560, 564.

[100] *Ibid.* at 588–89. Meg Jacobs describes the difficulty and compromises necessary for the plan to pass the Senate. JACOBS, *supra* note 32, at 184–90.

from new fields. New taxes would promote conservation by confronting oil and gas users with increased prices while preventing windfall profits to producers. The NEP also called for expanding the Strategic Petroleum Reserve to 1 billion barrels, diversifying sources of oil imports, and accelerating the development of contingency plans to reduce US vulnerability to foreign oil supply interruption. In the energy-efficiency arena, the NEP – building on EPCA – proposed developing mandatory minimum energy efficiency standards for major appliances (under EPCA, appliance standards had been discretionary with FEA). The NEP also proposed tax credits for energy-saving investments (including solar energy equipment) and conservation retrofits of buildings.

The NEP received a rocky reception on Capitol Hill. Nearly all critiques of the NEP were skeptical. And while it quickly cleared the House, not so with the Senate. During the summer of 1978, Carter even threatened to impose an import fee on crude oil if Congress didn't act. After eighteen months of debate, it finally passed – with five principal pieces. Meg Jacobs describes the final package as a "series of half measures, promoting conservation through a combination of weakened regulations and tax incentives" and not what "Carter had wanted." In fact, the natural gas title as the plan's signature component "no one liked."[101] The tax, fuel use, and conservation components are described next, whereas the nontax provisions involving electric power and natural gas are addressed elsewhere.

Oil and Natural Gas Taxes.   Even though the central concern driving the NEP was reducing dependence on imported oil, the NEP proposed retaining the dysfunctional EPAA price-control and allocation regime. Rather, the president's proposal to Congress relied heavily on tax incentives and disincentives to elicit new energy production and discourage inefficient uses of price-controlled oil and gas. Not unpredictably, the tax incentives fared better than the disincentives in the legislative process. In the Energy Tax Act of 1978, Congress adopted most of the incentives. However, with minor exceptions, none of the tax disincentives survived the legislative process.

Incentives.   The NEA, as introduced, provided for residential and business energy conservation tax credits, as well as tax incentives for geothermal production and changes in alternative minimum tax treatment of oil and gas intangible drilling expenses. As enacted, the Energy Tax Act retained the residential and business tax credits to encourage energy conservation investments and added incentives to produce renewable energy, alternative fuels, and certain high-cost natural gas.

Disincentives.   The NEA proposed several different energy taxes. First, a standby gasoline tax at up to 50 cents per gallon was proposed to take effect if national

---

[101]   JACOBS, *supra* note 32, at 190. *See also* BIVEN, *supra* note 96, at 161–63.

targets for reducing gasoline consumption were not achieved. Second, a Crude Oil Equalization Tax (COET) would impose a tax equal to the difference between the ceiling price for price-controlled crude oil and the world price of oil,[102] thus increasing the (after-tax) price of price-controlled crude oil to market levels. A critical component of Carter's plan, COET is described by David Vietor as a "compromise for the Democratic Party, with the objective of "impos[ing] world market prices on consumers, provid[ing] some incentive for producers, and ... captur[ing] for the government the economic rents created by OPEC."[103] It was not, however, decontrol as advocated by many. The administration projected that COET and another tax would reduce imported crude oil by about 2.5 million barrels per day. Third, consumption taxes on industrial and utility uses of petroleum products and natural gas were designed to shift consumption to other fuels. Finally, a "gas-guzzler tax" and rebate program was proposed for low-fuel-efficiency vehicles. The objective was to strengthen EPCA's program by achieving a CAFE of 27.5 miles per gallon by 1985.

Except for the gas-guzzler tax, Congress rejected these tax disincentives. The standby gasoline tax was wildly unpopular with the public and did not survive the House. The industrial oil and gas consumption taxes were not enacted. COET, opposed by the industry and even consumer advocates, fell by the wayside in the Senate. It was uniquely unpopular with the oil industry because the administration had proposed both to retain price controls on the industry and to increase its taxes. But once killed in the Senate, other price-signal measures never surfaced to take its place. The experience with COET was instructive, however. Two years later, the administration reformulated the tax as a windfall profits tax designed, among other things, to tax gains accruing to producers after decontrol of oil prices. This tax, according to University of Texas Professor James Katz, presumably was "the political price the oil industry had to pay to achieve decontrol of domestic crude oil." It was enacted as the Crude Oil Windfall Profits Tax Act of 1980.[104]

Fuel Use. The 1978 Powerplant and Industrial Fuel Use Act (Pub. Law 95–620) was designed to reduce dependence on oil and petroleum products by expanding the use of alternative fuels by electric power plants and major industrial installations, as well as to conserve scarce natural gas and petroleum for uses when no feasible

---

[102]   Executive Office of the President, Energy Policy and Planning, The National Energy Plan, 51 (April 1977).

[103]   VIETOR, *supra* note 3, at 260.

[104]   James Everett Katz, *US Energy Policy: Impact of the Reagan Administration*, ENERGY POLICY, 135, at 138 (1984). This became part of the program for oil decontrol. *See* BIVEN, *supra* note 96, at 171–78 (discussing deliberations on whether decontrol should be contingent on windfall profits tax). David Vietor provides a short summary of the issues and lobbying surrounding the tax. VIETOR, *supra* note 3, at 261–70.

substitutes exist. The Fuel Use Act, discussed in Chapter 7, prohibited new base-load power plants and new industrial facilities from using petroleum or natural gas as a primary energy source for generation of steam or electricity unless an exemption was obtained from the DOE.

Once the shortages in gas and petroleum products eased, opposition to the Act grew. The Fuel Use Act discouraged industrial and large-volume gas use, artificially kept the demand for gas low, and prevented the construction of new power plants that would use gas as the primary fuel source. Most important, it facilitated the construction boom in coal-fired power plants, leaving the United States with a legacy of large, badly controlled generators that the EPA is struggling to control to this day. The statute's repeal in 1987 encountered little opposition.

Energy Conservation.   The theme of conservation was pervasive in the NEP. As President Carter stated to Congress when he submitted his energy proposals in 1977: "the cornerstone of our policy is to reduce demand through conservation. Our emphasis on conservation is a clear difference between this plan and others which merely encouraged crash production efforts. Conservation is the quickest, cheapest, most practical source of energy."[105]

As passed, the 1978 National Energy Conservation Policy Act (NECPA, Pub. Law 95–619) provided three major roles for the government in energy conservation: setting energy-efficiency standards to cut energy consumption by energy-intensive products or uses, disseminating information about energy conservation opportunities, and improving the efficiency of federal buildings (thereby cutting the government's own energy bill). NECPA also included a program for low-income weatherization assistance, grants and loan guarantees for energy conservation in schools and hospitals, and energy-efficiency guidelines for new construction. Initiatives in many of these areas continue today.

By the end of 1978, moreover, regardless of the many faults with the NEP, the administration and Congress perhaps accomplished something else of significance – albeit subtly. To be sure, as James Cochrane notes, energy had become a "minor cottage industry" before the embargo,[106] but with the NEP the nation developed a cadre of new energy experts; by replacing the FPC with the FERC and consolidating some energy-related programs into the new DOE, the country's struggle with integrating aspects of energy policy took a step forward – albeit still disjointed, as the nation would learn with the need to better integrate environmental and energy law and policy. And lastly on that score, law firms with energy expertise also proliferated.

---

[105]   President Carter's Address on the National Energy Plan, 1 Public Papers 657–58 (1977).
[106]   Cochrane, *supra* note 89, at 547, 588.

IRAN AND THE SECOND OIL SHOCK

Carter and Energy Secretary James Schlesinger correctly perceived that one of America's greatest economic vulnerabilities – as well as one of Carter's greatest political risks – was another major oil shock. The NEA was designed to head off that possibility, along with the ability for a coordinated response through the IEA. The NEA, though, turned out to be too little, too late. Within months of the NEA's enactment in November 1978, the Iranian revolution erupted, the Shah fled Iran, and Iranian oil exports stopped altogether. Secretary Schlesinger reported in January 1979 that while Iranian oil curtailment removed over 5 million barrels per day from the world market, other nations increased production, leaving a worldwide shortfall of only about 1.5 to 2.0 million barrels per day. While ostensibly other countries (e.g., Japan, Turkey, Spain, Portugal, Germany, France, Brazil, and India) felt the loss of Iranian oil more than the United States, the international community distributed the reduction – and the United States replaced some lost oil with increased production from Saudi Arabia and elsewhere. But the United States was worried about the shock from increased prices. World oil prices, having tripled in the first oil shock, almost tripled again. OPEC informed the world that it was raising the price of oil by 14.5 percent (and some prices were $4 to $5 a barrel higher than OPEC-posted prices). Gasoline lines reappeared in the United States for the first time since 1974. And energy policy and its relationship to national security, particularly with the Middle East and Russia, once again captured attention.[107]

The NEA might have provided the tools to deflect the Iranian oil crisis, but it had not been in effect long enough to be implemented. In addition, DOE's failure to update the still-applicable petroleum product allocation system under EPAA made gasoline shortages worse. Petroleum products were still being allocated based on 1972 consumption, even though there had been major shifts in population and patterns of use in the intervening seven years. The Rust Belt did fine for the most part with adequate supplies (population was not growing and industrial production was declining), whiler fast-growing Sun Belt states experienced gasoline lines – and levels of desperation among motorists.

The gasoline lines required a political response from Carter. "The administration sought to deal with the loss of Iranian oil by calling for voluntary energy conservation and by working for a concerted approach" through the IEA.[108] In June, while

---

[107] See YERGIN, *supra* note 13, at 681–82, 692 (1991); Memorandum from Secretary of Energy Schlesinger to President Carter, Jan. 4, 1979, Doc. 181, *in* Department of State, Foreign Relations of the United States 1969–1976, Vol. XXXVII: Energy Crisis, 1974–80, at 578.

[108] Joseph A. Yager, *The Energy Battles of 1979*, *in* ENERGY POLICY IN PERSPECTIVE: TODAY'S PROBLEMS, YESTERDAY'S SOLUTIONS 601, 604 (Craufurd D. Goodwin et al. eds., 1981). Jacobs reports that Schlesinger told Carter it was time to remove governmental intervention in energy markets. JACOBS, *supra* note 32, at 199.

policymakers debated deregulating the national trucking industry and truckers began striking in protest of gas shortages, Carter urged a national renewable-energy standard of 20 percent by 2000, with considerable reliance on solar energy – Carter even installed solar panels on the White House. By August 1979, the world's then largest solar demonstration plant became operational at California's Mt. Laguna Air Force Base. The DOE anticipated that within roughly a decade, solar would become cheap enough to compete with coal and nuclear power.[109]

But liberal Democrats attacked Carter, claiming that he was too conciliatory toward the industry. Indeed, Senator Kennedy would later challenge Carter and urge adopting mandatory programs and gas rationing. Many around the president also advocated for retaining price controls.

With few allies, declining poll numbers, and trying to push the Democratic Party toward the center for the upcoming presidential election, Carter reacted by proposing a few major energy initiatives, outlined in his July 15, 1979, speech where he first questioned the nation's moral resolve. The first was a windfall profits tax on increased profits the oil industry would make as price controls were lifted on oil.[110] The second was an ambitious program for producing synthetic fuels from coal or oil shale, through an Energy Security Corporation (ESC). A few days before his speech, reports already indicated that focusing on increased synthetic fuels as a replacement for at least 2 million barrels a day of crude enjoyed sufficient traction.[111] Congress, of course, in the 1940s had previously attempted to promote synthetic fuels. Oil price controls were scheduled to end on September 30, 1981, and Carter ultimately agreed to decouple windfall profits from decontrol and began the latter in a phased approach in June 1979.[112]

Congress enacted both initiatives in 1980, along with directing the filling of the SPR and requiring the preparation of annual energy targets.[113] Carter also

---

[109]   Paul Jacobs, *World's Largest Solar Power Station Serves 141 People at Air Force Base*, WASH. POST, Aug. 21, 1979, A3.

[110]   Jay E. Hakes, *Conflict or Consensus?: The Roots of Jimmy Carter's Energy Policies, in* AMERICAN ENERGY POLICIES IN THE 1970S 47, 52 (Robert Lifset ed., Okla. Univ. Press 2014).

[111]   John M. Berry, *DOE Gives Carter 4 Options for Reducing Imports for Oil*, WASH. POST, July 12, 1979, A1.

[112]   "'Old' oil, which was crude oil discovered before 1973 and under price controls sold for approximately $6, would sell at roughly $13 a barrel. 'New' oil, crude discovered after 1973, would move incrementally from its current price of $13 to world prices. Another third from smaller wells, also known as stripper wells, would sell at the market price, which was round $16. Controls would ease until their expiration on October 1, 1981." JACOBS, *supra* note 32, at 210, 258–59 (windfall profits tax).

[113]   Energy Security Act, Pub. L. 96–294, 94 Stat. 611, June 30, 1980. *See* VIETOR, *supra* note 3, at 44–63 (chapter "'Stepping Right Out' with Synthetic Fuels" for programs during the 1940s and 1950s); Elaine F. Rappaport, *The Synthetic Fuels Corporation and A New Industry's Exemption from NEPA*, 9 B.C. ENVTL. AFF. L. REV. 863 (1981). Other provisions of the over 160-page statute required a National Academy of Sciences study of carbon dioxide, a task force program for acid deposition, and incentives for biomass, alcohol fuels, geothermal, conservation, and generally renewable energy. The ESC triggered opposition from liberals, fiscal conservatives, conservatives favoring limited government, and even westerners fearing that it would invade their space and diminish their water supplies.

requested authority for an Energy Mobilization Board, for facilitating energy project construction and permitting, and he further unsuccessfully sought a gas-rationing plan (Congress instead gave the president the authority to develop and submit to Congress a plan). After Carter lost the election, Secretary of State Muskie and new Energy Secretary Duncan informed Carter that the United States had higher oil inventories than previously, but a "realistic oil import ceiling" might be useful, along with an international allocation system.

Yet roughly thirty days after their memorandum to Carter, President Reagan was sworn into office. And five years later, oil prices returned to pre-Iran levels and shortages disappeared. The synfuels program was quietly dismantled. The windfall profits tax afforded political cover for ending oil price controls while producing some revenue, especially after Reagan ended controls. Congress then repealed the tax in 1988.

1970S' POLICIES IN TODAY'S WORLD

Plummeting world crude oil prices after 1981, a recession, and the absence of a Mideast crisis relegated energy policy to the background until the First Gulf War in 1991. Regulatory programs responding to energy shortages and price spikes were arguably less pressing. Notably, even though Congress favored legislation giving the president additional standby authority to impose controls during another shortage, Reagan refused to accede to having further governmental intrusion and vetoed the bill. As Grossman explains, President Reagan championed free-market rhetoric and accelerated the already initiated decontrol of oil prices, but except for changing the "energy narrative," he arguably accomplished little. He even unsuccessfully sought to dismantle DOE – possibly influencing current Secretary of Energy Rick Perry's initial similar suggestion, before he was tapped as the Secretary and learned more about its functions. Of course, Grossman adds that Reagan's approach to decontrol "virtually guaranteed that the United states would eventually import more oil, not less."[114]

President Reagan nevertheless arguably tilted rather than significantly altered the nation's energy policy path. For instance, he signed the Energy Emergency Preparedness Act of 1982, expressing Congress's continuing policy of preparing for future petroleum shortages by employing strategies to supplement the free market. The Act extended certain EPCA deadlines, required the White House to submit to Congress a legal memorandum on executive authorities for emergency response, directed that the executive prepare a plan for how it might deploy its authorities to

---

The Iranian hostage crisis, however, saved the ESC. JACOBS, *supra* note 32, at 238–43. *See also* GROSSMAN, *supra* note 52, at 262 (Synfuels Corp. under Reagan).

[114] GROSSMAN, *supra* note 52, at 254–59.

respond to emergencies, and further amended the SRP program. When it came to conservation, however, Reagan expressed little sympathy. He cut funding for renewables and even removed Carter's solar panels from the White House. With his Interior Secretary James Watt, he conversely promoted increased coal and onshore and offshore oil and gas development on public lands. And in other areas, both CAFE and the appliance energy-efficiency program went through various travails during his presidency. EPCA had set the 1985 fuel economy standard for cars at 27.5 miles per gallon but permitted DOE administratively to lower the standard to 26 miles per gallon. Standards for light trucks were to be set administratively. The Reagan administration in 1984 lowered the car standard to 26 miles per gallon for model years 1986–88. For light trucks, the standard was lowered briefly for model year 1985. The 27.5 miles per gallon standard was restored for model year 1990.[115]

The NEA, under NECPA, had strengthened the appliance energy-efficiency standards program established under EPCA by requiring energy-efficiency standards for thirteen types of appliances to the extent that such standards were technologically feasible and economically justified. But, in 1982, Reagan's DOE concluded that the energy standards envisioned under NECPA could not be "economically justified." Years of litigation and subsequent congressional action were necessary before appliance energy-efficiency standards would be established.[116] In 1987, Congress adopted the National Appliance Energy Conservation Act (NAECA) specifying energy-efficiency standards and requirements for periodic updating of such standards for a variety of major household and commercial appliances. Congress amended NAECA in 1988, again in 1992, and periodically thereafter.[117] Today efficiency standards have been prescribed for all major categories of consumer products. This standards program is currently regarded as an important policy tool for reducing greenhouse gas emissions, although the Trump administration, when it delayed several energy efficiency standards (for portable air conditioners, uninterruptible power supplies, air compressors, and packaged boilers), seemingly has signaled its disinterest in promoting the program.

The First Gulf War and the corresponding oil price run-up reminded the public and Congress that energy policy could still matter. Congress, for instance, in 1989 already had passed legislation – years in the making – decontrolling the wellhead price for natural gas. And then in response to the events of 1991, Congress enacted the Energy Policy Act of 1992 (EPAct 92), reinforcing some key aspects of the 1970s

[115]   NHTSA, Summary of Fuel Economy Performance (2011). The United States Court of Appeals for the District of Columbia Circuit upheld the light-truck miles per gallon reduction in *Center for Auto Safety* v. *NHTSA*, 793 F.2d 1322 (D.C. Cir. 1986).

[116]   E.g., *NRDC* v. *Herrington*, 768 F.2d 1355 (D.C. Cir. 1985).

[117]   National Appliance Energy Conservation Act, Pub. L. No. 100–12, 101 Stat. 103, March 17, 1987; National Appliance Energy Conservation Amendments of 1988, Pub. L. No. 100–357, 102 Stat. 671, June 28, 1988; The Energy Policy Act of 1992, Public Law No. 102–486, 106 Stat. 2776, Oct. 24, 1992.

policies (e.g., energy-efficiency standards), increasing the size of the SPR, and changing aspects of electric power regulation. Indeed, described by one contemporary as an "unbelievable accomplishment" for "pulling together widely diverse issues," EPAct 92 often is credited with initiating the electric utility's march toward disaggregated competitive markets.[118] When, therefore, Grossman suggests that EPAct 92 "did not have much effect on energy markets. Not then or ever,"[119] he perhaps undervalues too much how foundationally, according to many of us involved in energy debates for decades, it began to spur changes in industries and markets.

The next robust piece of energy legislation occurred when Congress passed the Energy Policy Act of 2005 (EPAct 05), following the oil price surge after the Second Gulf War in 2003, the hurricanes of 2005 (Katrina, Rita, and Wilma), and deepening concerns about US oil supply, oil imports, and vulnerabilities to events in the Middle East. EPAct 05 included many components, including establishing the Renewable Fuel Standard Program (RFS) mandating minimum percentages of renewable fuel, such as ethanol, in gasoline and other motor fuels – labeled by Grossman as "the most pernicious energy panacea ever."[120] One of the nation's most prominent environmental scholars, Arnold Reitze, Jr., adds that not only has the program been "grossly ineffective" but also that "[t]he overall potential contribution of biofuel to reducing petroleum demand is minimal."[121] We examine this program further in Chapter 8. Then, finally, in 2007 Congress resolved some of EPAct 05's unfinished business by passing the Energy Independence and Security Act (EISA). With fifteen substantive titles, EISA reflects the product of a mélange of lobbying efforts, including delegating to the Department of Transportation (DOT) clear authority to strengthen CAFE standards and increasing the stringency of the now-dubious 2005 RFS program.

The post-1970s legislation, including EPAct 92, EPAct 05, and EISA, largely continued and in some cases strengthened the 1970s' policies – ensuring physical security from oil interruptions, strengthening energy-efficiency programs, increasing domestic oil and gas production (to the extent consistent with environmental law), and maintaining the long-term trend of removing price controls when feasible to do so. Yet administrations from George H.W. Bush, Bill Clinton, George W. Bush, and even Barack Obama continued to experience what are perceived of as energy crises – often associated with high oil prices and correspondingly high gasoline prices. Grossman captures the problem succinctly when noting how "[t]he crisis label has

---

[118] Shortly after its passage, it was described as an "unbelievable accomplishment" for "pulling together widely diverse issues." DAN R. WILLIAMS & LARRY GOOD, GUIDE TO THE ENERGY POLICY ACT OF 1992 1 (Fairmont Press 1994).

[119] GROSSMAN, *supra* note 52, at 276.   [120] *Ibid.*, at 289, 304–5.

[121] Arnold W. Reitze, Jr., *Biofuel and Advanced Biofuel*, 33 J. ENVT. L. 309, 364 (2015). *See also* Arnold W. Reitz, Jr., *Biofuels: Snake Oil for the Twenty-First Century*, 87 OR. L. REV. 1183 (2008).

been invoked so often that a concept with little meaning to begin with has become almost completely empty."[122] It nonetheless continues as a justification for promoting a favored energy agenda, whether President Bush's 2001 National Energy Plan, President Obama's "All of the Above" strategy, or more recently, President Trump's initial budget to Congress calling for opening the Alaska National Wildlife Refuge to oil and gas development – repeating the refrain of two earlier Republican presidents and the accompanying mantra echoed by Sarah Palin of "drill baby drill." This time, though, the Republican-controlled 115th Congress obliged by opening the 1002 area of the refuge to leasing. The Bush–Vice President Cheney energy plan, for instance, observes Michael Klare in *Blood and Oil*, contemplated producing more oil from the Persian Gulf to feed the world's increasing appetite for oil and further diversifying America's import partners. This, Klare adds, presumably justifies tying US military activities with preserving free-flowing oil – black gold tarnished by blood. Of course, Klare describes how President Clinton also employed similar reasoning when promoting expanded activities in the Caspian Basin – including a pipeline through several countries, Turkey being the most prominent.

Yet, while present federal energy policies appear tethered to the decisions of the 1970s, through the Nixon, Ford, and Carter administrations, we are now in a much different energy world than we were in the 1970s. First, today's pattern of US oil production and use is vastly different because of significant reductions in oil consumption and corresponding substantial increases in oil production. If history has taught us anything, Blake Clayton reports, it is that we should recognize that the market and technology will continually react when necessary to undermine any lingering naysayers who preach peak oil theories. The United States is now the world's largest oil producer. Oil imports in 2015 had dropped to 40 percent of their 2005 peak.[123] Our situation with imports is thus nowhere near as dire as it looked in the middle of the last decade: oil production is up, and motor gasoline use has been down (but is rising again because of cheap gasoline), and the petroleum content of gasoline is down even farther because of the almost 10 percent ethanol content of the gasoline supply. In 2016, according to the EIA, US petroleum consumption was at approximately 19.6 million barrels a day (71 percent used for transportation), with crude oil production at roughly 8.9 million barrels a day, imports at 7.9 million barrels a day, and dependence on net petroleum imports at only 25 percent – with Canada and OPEC countries vying for an almost even split for most imports. In June 2017, moreover, US refineries averaged a record high. Of course, with that said, some politicians still proclaim the need to "drill baby drill" while environmental advocates promote policies for "leave it in the ground."

Second, the United States no longer has a physical security issue for oil. The SPR, moreover, unless Trump manages to sell it off, stores enough oil at the 2014 level of imports (at about 695 million barrels) to ride through about 140 days of total interruption of imports of oil (which, of course, would not happen because a large

[122] GROSSMAN, *supra* note 52, at 286–87.   [123] *Ibid.*

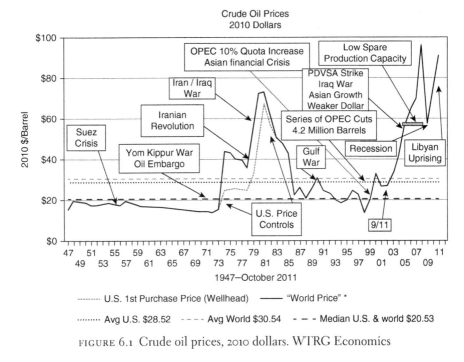

Crude Oil Prices
2010 Dollars

FIGURE 6.1 Crude oil prices, 2010 dollars. WTRG Economics

portion of our imports come from Canada and Mexico).[124] It's highly unlikely that some disturbance in the Middle East is going to cause us to lose the oil supplies necessary to run our economy. What has not changed, of course, is the price impact of oil disruptions – they are likely to still be there. The historical relationship between events in the Middle East and world crude oil prices is illustrated in Figure 6.1.

Third, the US automobile fuel economy program has grown considerably. It now has two legs, both examined further in Chapter 8. One is the CAFE program from 1975, significantly strengthened by EISA in 2007; the other is the greenhouse gas (GHG) emission standards for light-duty motor vehicles, adopted by the EPA in 2010, under the CAA. (One of the principal means to reduce GHG emissions from motor vehicles is to increase fuel economy.) Collectively, they are the principal regulatory measures for reducing US transportation-sector fuel use and GHG emissions. Looking at the history of the fuel economy standards, we see a steep climb in the decade after 1975, a long plateau from 1985 to 2008, and then increases under the current standards. What is on the books now going out to 2025 might represent a major increase in fuel economy and a decrease in oil use and GHGs from the light-

---

[124] EIA, U.S. Net Imports of Crude Oil and Petroleum (1/23/16); U.S. DOE, SPR Quick Facts and FAQs, Current Inventory (1/23/16). The Department of Energy reports that the reserve has been used only sporadically, under the authority granted in the 1975 Energy Policy and Conservation Act. In 2005, Congress directed that DOE to explore expanding the reserve from roughly 727 million barrels to 1 billion barrels, but that effort ceased in 2011.

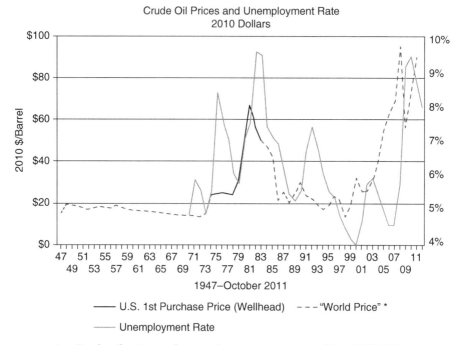

FIGURE 6.2 Crude oil prices and unemployment rate, 2010 dollars. WTRG Economics

duty motor vehicle fleet. To put this in context, the average fuel economy before the embargo was 12 miles per gallon; by contrast, today's goal for new cars and light trucks combined will be 54.5 miles per gallon in 2025 (though current projections indicate that this goal will not be met unless standards are strengthened, and the Trump administration is trying to reverse the Obama administration's effort).[125] We therefore are less skeptical, but only slightly so, than Grossman, who argues that the program "has been limited, much less effective than high gas prices."[126]

As such, today's energy world is much different from when Congress cobbled together the existing statutory framework. In some respects, the different world is better than expected, with security of oil supply, reduction of oil imports, and increased domestic oil production, as well as the increase in natural gas production and GHG emission reductions. Can the United States just declare victory and stop worrying about an energy policy tied to oil? Of course not. More remains.

As we have suggested, the United States is at a point where it enjoys a physical security for oil supply. What it lacks is any way of insulating the domestic economy from the price impacts of a major disruption in oil markets. Figure 6.1 shows the close correlation between the events in the Middle East and spikes in oil prices (the red line is the lower US price during the period of price controls). These events have

[125] 2016 Draft DOE/NHTSA Technical Assessment Report: ES 7–8.
[126] GROSSMAN, *supra* note 52, at 311.

occurred with some regularity. Even more interesting is the relationship between oil price spikes and the US unemployment rate. While Figure 6.2 is not an econometric study, it does match up changes in the unemployment rate with changes in oil prices. And it's quite remarkable that until this decade, every six months to a year after a major oil price run-up there has been a significant increase in the US unemployment rate.

Whether there is a causal connection (or simply a correlation) remains uncertain. Grossman's review suggests that with some caveats, there might be a relationship between "oil shocks" and "recession," but the question is not settled.[127] Unquestionably, though, a political establishment connection exists when increases in oil and correspondingly gasoline prices occur. Depending on political or ideological perspective, it allows those who favor more exploration and development to claim that we are confronting a shortage and encourage more production and for those more concerned with climate change to urge with greater alacrity the nation's switch to renewable resources. Either ignores what history has shown.[128]

Specifically, after the embargo spike in 1974, Congress enacted major legislation in 1975 (EPCA), in 1976 (Energy Conservation and Production Act [ECPA], as well as the Naval Petroleum Reserves Production Act and an electric and hybrid vehicle demonstration program), and in 1978 (the NEA). After the spike in 1979, Congress enacted the synfuels program and the windfall profits tax – both later removed. After the spike in 1991 (following the First Gulf War), Congress passed the Energy Policy Act of 1992. After the price run-up beginning with the Second Gulf War and continuing through Katrina (a climate rather than a geopolitical disruption), it enacted EPAct 05 and EISA. The salient point, though, is that world oil prices affected our economy and, perhaps more significantly, our politics, although oil price volatility today has less of an effect on the economy than in prior years.[129]

One of the abiding problems in energy policy is how to deal with economic effects of events in the Middle East and in the oil market generally. A Middle East conflict could close the Strait of Hormuz, exit point from the Persian Gulf, and possibly double or triple oil prices overnight. This is not something that the US economy can survive totally unscathed. Nor do we possess great tools to deal with disruptions of this magnitude.

Of course, what goes up can also go down. From June 2014 to January 2016, world crude oil prices dropped 75 percent,[130] a boon for consumers but a disaster for many domestic oil producers and a difficult time for alternative energy. Petroleum use for transportation began climbing again, and fuel economy of new automobiles dropped because of changes in product mix: consumers bought pickups and SUVs rather than

---

[127]   *Ibid.*, at 291–95.   [128]   CLAYTON, *supra note 2*, at 35.
[129]   In 1973, petroleum use constituted 5.7 percent of GDP. A $50 increase in oil prices would take almost 6 percent of income out of the pockets of consumers and businesses (other than oil producers). By 2015, because of growth in the economy, that percentage declined to 2.1 percent.
[130]   EIA, Petroleum and Other Liquids, Europe Brent Spot Price FOB, Jan. 23, 2016.

more fuel-efficient cars.[131] Thus, plummeting oil prices – as occurred in 2015 – disrupt both oil markets and other energy markets by making high-cost oil production (such as deep offshore drilling) uneconomical and reducing the cost-effectiveness of energy-efficiency investments. A mechanism for dampening the extreme volatility of world oil markets would both benefit national economies (on the upside) and help carry out energy and climate policy objectiveness (on the downside).

The most pressing other unfinished business for the oil sector is climate. Petroleum currently remains elemental for the functioning of modern economies and appears likely to remain so at least for a few more decades. But how efficiently it is used and whether and how quickly lower-carbon energy sources can be substituted for it are paramount global questions for reducing our carbon footprint. The 1970s' oil policies, by increasing energy efficiency and removing price controls, advanced GHG reduction objectives. Trying to increase domestic oil production may not be, because, while it reduces the need for imports, it also lowers world oil demand and prices. But most important, while current oil policies as a general matter are directionally correct, they nonetheless are insufficient for attaining GHG reductions necessary in the twenty-first century.

OIL POLICY: FOLLIES AND SUCCESSES

Post-embargo oil policy commenced with oil price controls, mandatory petroleum allocation rules, and fuel use restrictions – all ineffective or counterproductive, or both. Many assumptions about domestic production capacity were later dispelled – to such a degree that conversations over the past several decades about energy "independence" have now morphed into a Trump administration dialogue about energy "dominance." Once the country abandoned the 1970s' era petroleum rules and restrictions, US oil policies have been surprisingly effective at meeting their original objectives. The United States addressed the physical security issue through SPR and the IEP. That, of course, is being questioned today, because President Trump believes that we no longer need the SPR. Energy-efficiency measures and unexpected technological developments (horizontal drilling and fracking) have dramatically reduced reliance on imported oil. Transportation-sector petroleum use and GHG emissions have dropped from a decade earlier. But what the current incarnation of our 1970s' policies have not done is to insulate the United States from the economic impacts of oil market disruption (both on the upside and on the downside). Nor have we successfully developed a regulatory mechanism for offsetting the changes in motor vehicle product mix that surface during periods of low crude oil and gasoline prices. And perhaps most critically, conforming policies affecting oil production and use with necessary GHG reduction goals remains our fundamental denouement.

[131] EIA Monthly Energy Review, December 2015, Table 3.7c; UMTRI Monthly Monitoring of Vehicle Fuel Economy and Emissions, Jan. 2016.

7

Carter Crowns Coal King

Coal's War on People

The rhetoric surrounding former President Obama's alleged "war on coal" is striking – and untethered to the industry's history, environmental impacts, or current travails. The claim is that the Obama administration waged a war on coal through new environmental programs targeting air emissions, new rules to protect streams from being contaminated by coal mining, regulations designed to protect fish from being sucked into power plants' cooling water intakes, and efforts to address coal ash as a by-product of coal-fired generation. Murray Energy Company's CEO Robert Murray even charged that President Obama's policies made him "the greatest destroyer that America has ever seen in the White House."[1] The rhetoric, however, overlooks how abundant low-priced shale gas has made coal, in the colorful words of Michael Bloomberg, "a dead man walking."[2] Nor does it mention the public health dangers from coal usage that have impelled much of the current round of regulation or coal's contribution to US carbon dioxide (CO_2) emissions.

Perhaps most strikingly, the war-on-coal rhetoric skips over coal's efforts in the 1970s to reverse its declining market share for electric generation by trying to convince policymakers from Presidents Nixon through Carter that coal was the nation's salvation to the energy crises. And successive administrations embraced a suite of coal-centric policies, even though throughout the policymakers of the 1970s were well aware of the health and environmental threats posed by coal combustion. Indeed, well before current studies portrayed how fine particulates acutely threaten human health, scientists recognized that coal combustion was causing acid rain, that particulate matter and sulfur oxides were causing illnesses and premature deaths, and that CO_2 from coal-fired power plants could contribute to climate change.

Following World War II, coal's market share for energy declined as electric utilities switched from coal to other fossil fuels. But, after the first oil shock, policymakers faced a quandary as the nation's electric generation needs escalated and as

[1] Ben Wolfgang, *Lawsuit to Stop "War on Coal" Could Derail Obama Environmental Agenda*, Wash. Times, Nov. 18, 2015.
[2] Manuel Quinones, *"Coal Is a Dead Man Walking"* – *Bloomberg*, E&E News (Feb. 27, 2013).

constraints emerged for energy sources other than coal. The nation's abundant coal supplies offered a seemingly easy solution – produce and combust more of our virtually inexhaustible coal resources. Presidents Nixon, Ford, and then Carter all accepted that solution. The Carter administration, moreover, assumed – naively in hindsight – that the Clean Air Act (CAA) and new control technologies would minimize health and environmental threats from increased coal usage. This chapter tells that story: how President Carter crowned coal as king despite coal's known health and environmental effects and the Environmental Protection Agency's (EPA's) limited ability to control the industry's emissions under the CAA. It further illustrates what most economists today tout – that markets, cheap natural gas, and a host of other factors will continually diminish coal's contribution to our electricity future.

COAL'S DECLINING PREEMBARGO MARKET SHARE

Coal seemingly enjoys an almost mystical past, obscuring its checkered use for electric generation (steam coal) as opposed to its use for steel production (metallurgical coal). Coal's initial dominance as an energy fuel source occurred during the late 1880s and lasted through the years immediately following World War II.[3] During this period, coal supplied roughly half the nation's energy requirements, and its "input to energy consumption peaked in the first two decades of the twentieth century when it provided over 70 percent of energy needs."[4] But by the time of the energy crisis in the early 1970s, coal's preeminence as a fuel source diminished. In 1977, the Federal Energy Administration (FEA) reported, whether correctly or not, how "[o]ver the last 75 years, the United States has switched from using coal for over 90 percent of its energy needs to depending on oil and gas for 75 percent of its energy."[5] That same report acknowledged coal's abundance, noting though that it only provided "18 percent of the Nation's consumed energy."[6]

Coal's importance to economic growth captured national attention during the early part of the twentieth century. When the 1902 coal strike threatened to

---

[3] SAM H. SCHURR & BRUCE C. NETSCHERT, ENERGY IN THE AMERICAN ECONOMY, 1850–1975: AN ECONOMIC STUDY OF ITS HISTORY AND PROSPECTS 57–83 (Johns Hopkins Univ. Press for Resources for the Future 1975). For a classic account of coal's beginnings, see Alfred D. Chandler, Jr., *Anthracite Coal and the Beginnings of the Industrial Revolution in the United States*, 156 BUS. HIST. REV. 141 (1972).

[4] JOHN G. CLARK, ENERGY AND THE FEDERAL GOVERNMENT: FOSSIL FUEL POLICIES, 1900–1946 xxi (Univ. of Illinois Press 1987). Reed Moyer adds that "[c]oal's golden era occurred in the first two decades of the 20th century when output rose steadily, and coal accounted for 67% of the United States' energy consumption." Reed Moyer, *The Role of Coal: Problems and Policies*, 18 NAT. RES. J. 761 (1978).

[5] Federal Energy Administration, Coal Conversion Program: Final Revised Environmental Impact Statement, Vol. 1 1–1 (May 1977) ("Coal Conversion EIS"). In 1968, however, a FPC economist apparently assumed that coal "supplies most of the fuel at powerplants today," albeit recognizing that its use varied considerably by region. Federal Air Pollution R.&D on Sulfur Oxides Pollution Abatement, 90th Cong., 2nd Sess. 12, 16–18 (Sept. 5, 1968) (Statement of Frederick W. Lawrence).

[6] Coal Conversion EIS, *supra* note 5.

leave homes and businesses without a source of heat over the winter, President Theodore Roosevelt personally intervened and helped facilitate a resolution. With the threat of shortages and coal's availability on federal lands, he also issued an order that withdrew coal from being available for disposal from roughly 66 million acres of public lands. A decade later, as an extreme 1917–18 winter approached and on the heels of soon-to-be more coal strikes, Congress entered the fray and passed the 1917 Lever Food and Fuel Act to assist the war effort by encouraging production and conserving the supply of food and fuel. This was followed by President Wilson's World War I creation of the Fuel Administration (exercising authority over the price, production, and distribution of coal as well as oil) and eventually the federal 1920 Mineral Leasing Act for the leasing of coal and other fuel resources.[7] The country's largest annual increase in the production of coal from 1849 to 1918 occurred between 1906 and 1907, and coal production (combined bituminous and anthracite) climbed from 113,680,427 tons in 1886 to 678,211,904 tons in 1918. A trade advisor, writing in 1920, posited that coal's dominance "seems sure to prevail indefinitely."[8] To be sure, the next several decades witnessed the coal market's growth as the electric grid became more and more dependent on large thermal central generating stations. Coal's abundance made feasible building larger plants and expanding the electric grid's reach. And, indeed, between 1950 and 1970, 727 coal-fired electric plants (the largest number during any twenty-year period) were constructed, for a total combined 113,357 MW of generation capacity.

But coal's dominant market share was threatened by increasing imports of residual fuel oil and by other energy resources, such as natural gas. Oil consumption for electric generation increased from 93 million barrels annually in 1965 to 494 million barrels annually in 1972. Reportedly by 1974 some 400 coal-fired plants had switched away from using coal as a fuel source.[9] It was during this period, according to energy historian Vietor, that "[t]he coal industry stagnated" as the "U.S. economy shifted from its primary dependence on solid fuels to fluid fuels."[10] In 1970, coal furnished only about 20 percent of our total energy supply, while crude oil supplied roughly 43 percent, gas about 33 percent, hydroelectric energy at approximately 4 percent, and nuclear energy at under 1 percent. Looking at the period 1950 through 2013, coal's percentage of total energy consumption reached its lowest ebb in the early 1970s.[11] Coal's annual share of fossil

[7] This rich history is portrayed by John Clark's fascinating book, *Energy and the Federal Government: Fossil Fuels Polices, 1900–1946, supra* note 4.

[8] Walter S. Tower, *The Coal Question*, 2 FOR. AFFAIRS 100, 101 (1923–24).

[9] Clean Air Act Oversight Hearings, 93rd Cong., 2nd Sess., Serial No 93–H42, Part 1, 646, 650 (May 1974); Bureau of Power, Federal Power Commission, Staff Report: The Potential for Conversion of Oil-Fired and Gas-Fired Electric Generating Units to Use of Coal 1 (Sept. 1973).

[10] RICHARD H. K. VIETOR, ENERGY POLICY IN AMERICA SINCE 1945: A STUDY IN BUSINESS-GOVERNMENT RELATIONS 3 (Cambridge Univ. Press 1984).

[11] Coal, for instance, went from supplying 48% of our energy needs in 1948 to 17% in 1972. Dr. Dixy Lee Ray, A Report to Richard M. Nixon, President of the United States, The Nation's Energy Future 39 (Dec. 1, 1973) (coal went from supplying 48% of our energy needs in 1948 to 17% in 1972); A RESOURCES

fuel–fired electric power generation generally declined between the 1950s and the energy crisis of the early 1970s.[12]

Moreover, by 1970, coal combustion had contributed to a series of public health crises. Cities had become shrouded in haze – generated not only from automobiles but also from power plants burning high-sulfur coal and oil. In 1911, reportedly more than a thousand people died in Glasgow, Scotland, from coal combustion emissions.[13] The Public Health Service apparently considered sulfur oxides as precipitating a significant health threat during the infamous 1948 Donora incident in Pennsylvania.[14] Four years later in London, England, upwards of 4,000 deaths were attributed to poor air quality.[15] And in 1966, a four-day inversion in New York City apparently caused eighty deaths, while during the summer of 1969, Tokyo's air quality problems forced the hospitalization of 8,000 people.[16] Coal combustion releases sulfur, which, when combined with air, produces sulfur dioxide. Sulfur dioxide and particulate matter (along with other coal combustion pollutants) were known at the time to at least cause respiratory problems. (Also, when sulfur dioxide mixes with water vapor, it produces sulfuric acid, one of the principal constraints of acid rain.) The years following Donora witnessed an escalating federal interest in addressing air pollution, eventually culminating in the comprehensive clean air legislation of 1970, which only exacerbated coal's early 1970s' anguish.

States, particularly those on the East Coast, sought to mitigate harmful emissions by reducing coal combustion. Utilities in New England and the Mid-Atlantic region shifted toward greater reliance on oil and nuclear power. The coal industry naturally questioned these proactive state environmental efforts, claiming that overly strict and unnecessary state air quality standards, if continued as proposed, might "eliminate the use of coal in the nation's largest metropolitan areas."[17] As J. Clarence Davis III wrote in 1970, "[t]here was no question that the sulfur regulations represented a decision which had major ramifications for the nation's economy."[18] Indeed, as noted earlier, about 400 coal-fired power plants switched away from coal and began using oil to avoid problems with sulfur

FOR THE FUTURE STAFF REPORT, U.S. ENERGY POLICIES: AN AGENDA FOR RESEARCH 5–7 (Johns Hopkins Univ. Press 1968) (coal's share of energy consumption declined to roughly a little over 20% by the mid-1960s). In fact, "[f]rom 1950 to 1975, coal made up a progressively smaller percentage of the nation's total energy requirements." Coal Conversion EIS, *supra* note 5, at 1–2.

[12] EIA, Today in Energy, Competition among Fuels for Power Generation Driven by Changes in Fuel Prices, Annual Share of Fossil-Fired Electric Generation, 1950–2012 (July 13, 2012).

[13] *See* A.E. Martin, *Mortality and Morbidity Statistics and Air Pollution*, 57 PROC. R. SOC. MED. 969–75 (Oct. 1964).

[14] J. CLARENCE DAVIES III, THE POLITICS OF POLLUTION 163 (Pegasus 1970).

[15] *See* CHARLES O. JONES, CLEAN AIR ACT: THE POLICES AND POLITICS OF POLLUTION CONTROL 137–55 (Univ. of Pittsburgh Press 1975).

[16] Gordon Young & James P. Blair, *Pollution, Threat to Man's Only Home*, in OUR ECOLOGICAL CRISIS 738, 747 (National Geographic ed., 1970).

[17] DAVIES, *supra* note 14, at 56.   [18] *Ibid.* at 167.

dioxide.[19] But Richard Vietor possibly captures the industry's frustrations best when he observes how "[t]he coal industry had been down for a very long time, taking second place to government-sponsored nuclear power, government-subsidized petroleum imports, and government-regulated natural gas."[20]

COAL'S POSTEMBARGO RENAISSANCE

However dismal coal's prospects might have seemed in the early 1970s, the oil shortages of the embargo era prompted a major reassessment of coal's role. A central policy animating postembargo energy legislation throughout the Nixon, Ford, and Carter administrations was decreasing oil and gas usage by increasing the use of coal, particularly by electric utilities. There seemed little alternative. The previous decades had witnessed lagging efforts to plan for future energy resources to meet the demands of a growing economy. Electric generator use of oil had to be reduced to an absolute minimum.

The oil crisis described in Chapter 6 was magnified by severe natural gas shortages in many consumer markets, as discussed in Chapter 5. Natural gas's highest percentage of use by the electric energy sector, in any year prior to 1995 (counted in five-year increments), occurred in 1970. From 1950 until roughly around the 1973 energy crisis, the country experienced rising production and consumption of natural gas. Natural gas's overall market grew steadily from 1960 until 1974, though by the early 1970s, Federal Power Commission (FPC) policies chilled incentives toward exploration, production, and interstate transportation and marketing of natural gas destined for interstate markets. And just a few years later, dwindling supplies of natural gas transported through interstate pipelines combined with the extraordinarily cold 1976–77 winter to trigger a severe natural gas shortage precipitating school closings and manufacturing plant shutdowns. Unemployment rose into the millions, and even homes and hospitals were at risk of having no heat. This natural gas emergency reinforced for Carter and his administration the need to move electric generation away from natural gas as rapidly as possible and to husband what then appeared to be limited supplies of gas for other, more valuable uses.

---

[19] Energy and Environmental Standards, 93rd Cong., 1st & 2nd Sess. 280, Sept. & Oct. 1973. When low-sulfur oil became scarce, EPA Administrator Russell E. Train testified that the agency was exploring temporary variances from state implementation plan sulfur (described as the agency's "concern") requirements. *Ibid.* at 450–57. Some states, such as Ohio, according to Train, incorporated into their plans overly aggressive CAA secondary standards for sulfur that could not be achieved absent available low-sulfur fuel. And Train attributed the lack of sufficient low-sulfur oil to the import quota system, rather than insufficient "desulfurizing refining capacity." *Ibid.* at 454.

[20] *See* RICHARD H.K. VIETOR, ENVIRONMENTAL POLITICS AND THE COAL COALITION 51–54, 158–59, 170, 175, 178, 205, 206 (Texas A&M Univ. Press 1980). Industry, though, achieved some success in 1970 when it secured from President Nixon Executive Order No. 11523 establishing the National Industrial Pollution Control Council and affording industry a voice for economic policy during dialogues about environmental threats.

The heyday of growth of hydroelectric power generation, too, was finished. While, in the west, for instance, hydroelectric power generation furnished about 80 percent of the region's generating capacity in 1950, that percentage dropped to roughly 58 percent by 1960 – with natural gas supplying much of the needed increased energy demand.[21] Having tripled its generation capacity between 1920 and 1940, waterpower had lost much of its luster. Proposed federal hydroelectric projects that contemplated damming such iconic areas as the Colorado River and Dinosaur National Park had generated significant environmental opposition. Later, President Carter would even identify a hit list for federal water projects, highlighting the economic costs and environmental consequences of such large-scale projects, including dams.[22]

Consolidated Edison's (Con Ed) ill-fated effort to construct a pumped hydroelectric project at Storm King Mountain in the Hudson River Valley in New York State illustrated these difficulties.[23] When confronted with a perceived pressing need for additional generation capacity for the New York City area, Con Ed would become the poster child for environmental activism when, in the early 1960s, it proposed the Cornwall Project, at the time the largest proposed pumped storage project in the world. That Con Ed pursued development of hydroelectric power generation was unsurprising, after all, New York had experienced the nation's worst sulfur dioxide (SO_2) problems as well as a major blackout in 1965, and it would be years before the utility could add additional nuclear capacity at its Indian Point facility. But Con Ed's proposal threatened the valley's scenic beauty, it threatened to destroy the valley's historic charm, and, it threatened to disrupt the area's ecological resources. The project therefore triggered years of citizen opposition, several decisions by federal and state courts, and eventually a decision by the company to abandon the project – a decision signaling the environmental difficulties confronting any future hydroelectric project.

Of course, policymakers initially idealized that over the long term, power plant fuel usage could shift from oil and gas not only to coal but also to nuclear power. During the Kennedy and Johnson years, nuclear energy became touted as an abundant form of future cheap electricity. Dozens of experimental plants popped up in the early part of the decade. Over fifty contracts for new nuclear plants were executed in just two years (1966 and 1967) of the Johnson administration. When Nixon entered office, "utilities had ordered over sixty-five large nuclear plants (each with capacity exceeding 500 megawatts), thirty of which were already being built."[24]

[21] *See generally* Federal Power Commission, 1964 National Power Survey, Part 1.
[22] Walter Pincus, *Carter Narrows "Hit List," Seeks Halt to 17 Projects,* WASH. POST, April 19, 1977. President Carter arguably rolled out his hit list awkwardly, as noted by various historical accounts. E.g., WILLIAM WYANT, WESTWARD IN EDEN: THE PUBLIC LANDS AND THE CONSERVATION MOVEMENT 359 (Univ. of California Press 1982).
[23] Con Ed's challenge of having sufficient capacity to satisfy an increasing demand is captured by Richard Lifset, *Environmentalism and the Electrical Energy Crisis, in* AMERICAN ENERGY POLICY IN THE 1970S 283 (Robert Lifset ed., Okla. Univ. Press 2014).
[24] James L. Cochrane, *Energy Policy in the Johnson Administration: Logical Order versus Economic Pluralism, in* ENERGY POLICY IN PERSPECTIVE: TODAY'S PROBLEMS, YESTERDAY'S SOLUTIONS 337, at 366 (Craufurd D. Goodwin et al. eds., 1981).

One of the nation's most prominent chemists and Noble Prize recipient, Glenn T. Seaborg, wrote with his colleague in 1971 how "[n]uclear prophets see the *nuclear energy complex* or *Nuplex* concept as an important key to future world development. In this vision, all animals and machines will draw on the atom's energy as if it were a second sun."[25] Seaborg offered how nuclear power potentially could reduce annually by 2016 projected emissions of CO_2 and SO_2 by a little over 4 billion tons and 67.5 million tons, respectively.[26] A few years later, in an April 1973 address to Congress, President Nixon proclaimed how nuclear energy could generate half the nation's power by the end of the century. President Ford followed suit. In his 1975 State of the Union Address, Ford called for the construction of 200 major nuclear power plants by 1985.[27]

The allure of nuclear power, however, largely dissipated as the decade unfolded. The reason, according to Seaborg, is "more complex than most people think." Early proposals for plants may have been at below the actual cost of construction. The technology, moreover, may have been deployed too quickly and without considering all the technological options, or so Seaborg posits when agreeing with Richard Rhodes' assessment in *Nuclear Renewal*. Plants, he adds, were "prematurely escalated in size to proportions that strained the technology and magnified the potential consequence of an accident, no matter how unlikely."[28] The industry experienced financing difficulties, licensing delays, escalating costs, and finally an increasing public concern about the safety and security implications of reliance on nuclear energy. In 1975, an accident at the Brown's Ferry nuclear plant led to the establishment of extensive new licensing requirements, further increasing the cost and complexity of siting and constructing new plants.

The final dagger for this round of nuclear power occurred with the accident at Three Mile Island (TMI) in 1979, when a series of events allowed coolant from reactor number 2 to escape and the core to melt. The fiasco was a product of many "goofs," but as a *Washington Post* reporter would note a year later, "Wall Street [would] decide the fate of nuclear power."[29] The public's reaction made it clear that there would be little support for the massive expansion of nuclear capacity necessary if nuclear power were to displace oil- and gas-fired electric power production. Wall Street then followed suit. In fact, no new nuclear units were ordered after TMI – and while more recently utilities have expressed some renewed interest in new construction, that interest too seems to have become diffused.

---

[25] GLENN T. SEABORG & WILLIAM R. CORLISS, MAN AND ATOM: BUILDING THROUGH NUCLEAR TECHNOLOGY 128 (E.P. Dutton & Co. 1971).

[26] *Ibid.* at 147.

[27] President Gerald R. Ford's Address before a Joint Session of the Congress Reporting on the State of the Union, Jan. 15, 1975.

[28] GLENN T. SEABORG & ERIC SEABORG, ADVENTURES IN THE ATOMIC AGE: FROM WATTS TO WASHINGTON 241–47 (Farrar, Straus and Giroux 2001).

[29] Joanne Omang, *Three Mile Island: Nuclear's Tet, a Year Later*, WASH. POST, March 28, 1980, at A2.

Because of these developments, by the late 1970s, the Carter administration confronted an increasingly narrow set of policy options for the power sector: the interstate natural gas shortage ruled out any increased use of natural gas for base-load power production and argued for the eventual phase-out of its use for that purpose. The need to reduce the country's dependence on imported oil required eliminating power plant use of petroleum products wherever feasible. The 1975 Brown's Ferry incident and later the 1979 TMI near meltdown chilled the promise of increased reliance on nuclear power. The promise for any significant new hydroelectric power generation had long since eroded. And renewables were at too early a stage for quick commercial development. In the administration's view, this left coal as the major new electric supply option.

Some alternative option seemed necessary. On the demand side, the US appetite for energy had become unrelenting. In 1971, *National Geographic* described the nation as having "developed a relentless hunger for enormous amounts of electricity."[30] In 1971, Paul McCracken, Nixon's chairman of the Council of Economic Advisers, described the previous four years as a rapid growth of energy demand "that was unanticipated in most earlier projections."[31] The country's consumption of electricity had doubled each decade between 1940 and 1970, and the FPC predicted that it would double yet again by 1980.[32] Electricity consumption grew during the 1960s at about 7 percent annually.[33] And electricity consumption was becoming a larger share of overall energy consumption.[34]

Amory B. Lovins, in a widely read *Foreign Affairs* article, described the nation's energy options as having two paths. The first path would aggressively promote offshore and Alaskan oil and gas, along with increased coal production and use – with coal coming from both eastern mines and newly developed surface mines in the intermountain west. The second path he posited (what he called the "soft path") "combines a prompt and serious commitment to efficient use of energy, rapid development of renewable energy sources matched in scale and in energy quality to end-use needs, and special transitional fossil-fuel technologies." Cogeneration, for instance, he observed, furnished only about 4 percent of the nation's electric generation, 25 percent less than that of West Germany, and it was "institutional barriers" rather than technology that inhibited its further growth. Quite presciently, he further warned that choosing coal's path could "make [] the doubling of

[30]   Henry Still, *Energy: A Crisis in the Offing*, in As WE LIVE AND BREATHE: THE CHALLENGE OF OUR ENVIRONMENT 78, 79 (National Geographic Society ed., 1971).

[31]   The President's Energy Message, A National Fuels and Energy Policy Study, Pursuant to S. Res. 45, 92nd Cong., 1st Sess., Serial No. 92–1, 4 (June 15, 1971).

[32]   Still, *supra* note 30, at 78, 80.

[33]   Council on Environmental Quality, Energy and the Environment: Electric Power 1 (1973) (3.6%). *See also* FINAL REPORT BY THE ENERGY POLICY PROJECT OF THE FORD FOUNDATION, A TIME TO CHOOSE: AMERICA'S ENERGY FUTURE 19 (Ballinger 1974) (3.4%).

[34]   Ecologists warned about an impending population bomb, threatening to accelerate our appetite for more energy resources; indeed, the US population by 2000 was projected to increase by over 100 million people.

atmospheric carbon dioxide concentration early in the next century virtually una-voidable, with the prospect then or soon thereafter of substantial and perhaps irreversible changes in global climate."[35]

Yet, by the time Lovins published his article, Congress had already embarked on an alternative path. The 1974 Energy Supply and Environmental Coordination Act (ESECA) authorized the FEA to compel existing oil- and natural gas–fired power plants to convert their facilities to burning coal if the plant could burn coal and be consistent with the 1970 CAA. ESECA's basic objective was to require power plants that had converted from coal to oil or gas to convert back to coal. The authority to issue such orders was slated to expire at the end of 1984. Policymakers apparently believed that the FEA would implement the coal conversion policy under ESECA, a vain hope, as we recount below. President Ford's 1975 proposed Energy Independence Act, a comprehensive energy policy proposal, called for enhancing the ESECA program for coal conversions. When explaining this package to the Economic Summit Meeting in November of 1975, Ford lamented the lengthy and slow process before Congress and noted how the United States had "undertaken major programs to expand the use of coal in place of oil and gas in existing power plants and to encourage construction of new power plants for electrical generation that do not depend on imported oil."[36]

Roughly a month later, Congress passed the Energy Policy and Conservation Act of 1975 (Pub. L. 94–163, EPCA). EPCA contained perhaps some of the most successful programs of the 1970s, but it did little to make ESECA more workable.

FEA, throughout its three-year existence, struggled with implementing ESECA. Admittedly, "FEA ordered almost eighty power plants to burn coal rather than other fuels."[37] Flaws, however, permeated the program. Senator Scoop Jackson, for instance, commented on how the program was "too cumbersome and time-consuming."[38] While the FEA purportedly examined a facility's economic feasibil-ity for conversion, by the summer of 1975, a little over thirty targeted plants "firmly opposed" converting their facilities and were willing to go to court to challenge a conversion order. Many of those that acquiesced apparently did so because they already had begun the conversion process prior to any conversion order.[39] The CAA, however, shouldered much of the blame for the program's glacial pace.

[35] Amory B. Lovins, *Energy Strategy: The Road Not Taken?*, 55 FOR. AFF. 65, 67, 74, 79 (1976–77).
[36] Department of State Papers: Foreign Relations of the United States 1966–76, Vol. XXXVII, *Energy Crisis, 1974–80*, at 298–9. Mieczkowski explains how "the Ford administration decontrolled 50 per-cent of the finished products from a barrel of crude oil," and Ford similarly sought to decontrol natural gas – an effort quickly abandoned by President Carter. Yanek Mieczkowski, *"The Toughest Thing": Gerald Ford's Struggle with Congress over Energy Policy*, in AMERICAN ENERGY POLICY IN THE 1970s 39–40 (Robert Lifset ed., Okla. Univ. Press 2014).
[37] Mieczkowski, *supra* note 36, at 40.
[38] Senator Henry M. Jackson, *The Role for Greater Coal Utilization for the United States' National Energy Policy*, 29 U. KAN. L. REV. 303, 303–7 (1981).
[39] Oversight Hearings: Coal Combustion R.&D. For Utility-Power Plants and Industrial Uses, 94th Cong., 1st Sess., No. 44, Vol. II, 2 (July 1975).

It appears that the FEA may have difficulty in winning the necessary EPA backing for many of the conversions without forcing the utilities to spend large amounts of money on environmental protection. Sixteen of the plants had formerly converted away from coal, or have been prevented from changing back to coal, because to do so would violate Federal or State standards, and, in one case, local environmental standards. Thirteen of the utilities said that to implement the FEA orders would cost them over $1 million apiece in reequipping their plants to handle coal ... Furthermore, the Government's program to encourage industry to switch to coal fuel boilers on a voluntary basis has not been successful. Figures compiled by the American Boiler Manufacturer's Association for 1974 show that the new orders were 39 percent for gas-fired boilers with oil conversion possibility, 35 percent for oil, and only 6 percent for coal. The main reason for this disappointing result seems to be just one thing: The high cost of environmental controls.[40]

By roughly around early 1977, the FEA had issued prohibition orders to only thirty-two plants – for seventy-four generating units, while it was considering another 229 plants.[41] Most of those orders were in the Northeast, where oil had become a dominant energy source.[42]

The FEA projected that by 1985 the "national coal demand could increase up to 119.5 million tons annually [for just existing, not new power plants]" and that through conversions the United States could "save 303 million barrels of oil and 969 billion cubic feet of gas annually by 1985."[43] This proved fanciful. The FEA initially targeted eighty-four existing plants for conversion back to coal, plants that were constructed within the prior twenty-three years and larger than 25 MW.[44] A 1977 report of the House Ad Hoc Committee on Energy to accompany legislation that would enact the Carter National Energy Plan (H.R. 8444) was highly critical of FEA's optimism and the ESECA program itself:

The FEA's 3-year old program for ordering oil- and gas-fired electric powerplants and major fuel-burning installation to switch their boiler fuel from oil and gas to

[40] *Ibid.*
[41] Progress in the Prevention and Control of Air Pollution in 1976, Annual Report of the Administrator of the Environmental Protection Agency to the Congress of the U.S., 95th Cong., 1st Sess., Doc. No. 95–75, 58 (Nov. 1977).
[42] *See* The Impact of the President's Energy Plan on the Northeast, Hearing before the Subcommittee on Energy, Joint Economic Committee, 95th Cong., 1st Sess. 1 (May 1977) (hereinafter Impact of the President's Energy Plan on the Northeast).
[43] Coal Conversion EIS, *supra* note 5, at IV-91. The base case assumed that seventy-two conversions would occur in 1977, although the EIS oddly added that "[i]f the existing power plants are required to meet primary ambient air quality standards in order to convert in 1977, fewer power plants will be able to convert than in the base case." *Ibid.* at iv-94. The EIS did not necessarily anticipate that coal would be mined from low-sulfur western deposits because western coal reportedly had a lower heat value and, as such, made it "difficult [for some] to burn," and it produced more coal ash. *Ibid.* at IV-170. Notably, FEA promoted conservation and solar power's (and possibly nuclear's) potential as an eventual alternative to coal, "although major uncertainties exist as to the speed which these goals will be achieved." *Ibid.* at VIII-6.
[44] *Ibid.* at A-13, table A-4.

coal has been a failure. Three years after enactment of [ESECA] in June 1974, the Nation has yet to save a single drop of oil or cubic foot of natural gas through this program.[45]

The Committee described the intricate bureaucratic structure of ESECA, with its multiple required findings and certifications by FEA and EPA, which resulted in bureaucratic infighting and delays.[46] Similar themes surfaced during industry's comments on the environmental impact statement (EIS) for FEA's program implementation.[47]

That EIS also accepted some strikingly dubious assumptions about the difference in SO_2 emissions between coal- and oil-fired generation and unquestionably sought to justify increased coal usage.[48] The EIS assumed that coal conversions would comply with the CAA primary air quality standards and accompanying state implementation requirements.[49] Even so, the EIS projected that coal conversions by 1980 could produce an additional half million tons per year of SO_2 emissions, a number that could double by 1985. Texas's Air Control Board, moreover, warned that coal conversions in Houston might become "unacceptable from an air quality viewpoint" – impeding that community's compliance with air quality standards for particular matter.[50] The FEA also assumed that utilities could burn low-sulfur coal and that those lacking access to low-sulfur coal could, by 1980, install flue gas desulfurization (FGD) pollution-control equipment.[51]

These were questionable assumptions. Baltimore Gas & Electric, for example, had received a June 1975 prohibition order and explained how the assumption that it could burn low-sulfur coal and employ FGD technology within thirty-nine months of the order was neither reasonable nor economical.[52] Conversely, Virginia Electric & Power Co. (VEPCO) commented how ten of its plants had received prohibition orders and that, while two facilities easily converted (they already had installed electrostatic precipitators), it might be too costly to convert the other eight. VEPCO added that the FEA had to "fully confront . . . [the fact] that [abundant coal] must be

---

[45]   Report of the Ad Hoc Subcommittee on Energy and Power, U.S. House of Representatives, on H.R. 8444, Report No. 95-543, Vol. II: Appendix, 95th Cong., 1st Sess. 475 (July 27, 1977) (hereinafter Ad Hoc Committee Report on NEP). One member described how this ad hoc committee was unique, the first of its kind "to reconcile the recommendations of the standing committees and fashion a comprehensive legislative package." Report of Proceedings, Transcript, Hearing held before the Committee on Rules, H.R. 8444, 253 (July 28, 1977).

[46]   Ad Hoc Committee Report on NEP, *supra* note 45, at 475–77. An earlier May 1977 staff memorandum to the chair of the House Committee on Energy and Power leveled similar observations. Memorandum from Subcommittee Staff to Chairman John D. Dingell, Coal Conversion Program, May 25, 1977, *reprinted in* National Energy Act, Part 4, Hearings before the Subcommittee on Energy and Power, Committee on Interstate and Foreign Commerce, U.S. House, Serial No. 95-25, 846 (May 1977).

[47]   Coal Conversion EIS, *supra* note 5.   [48]   *Ibid.* at IV-5, 29–30, 44, 57–59, 62–64.

[49]   *Ibid.* at IV-77. The analysis is misleading in some respects, because FEA assumes "no air emission limitation on conversion candidates" under the base case. *Ibid.* at IV-109.

[50]   *Ibid.* at IX-28.   [51]   *Ibid.* at IV-81–82, 86.   [52]   *Ibid.* at IX-30–35.

mined, processed and transported to locations where it will be utilized. And it must be of a type and quality that will permit such use, given existing air pollution regulations."[53] But perhaps even more telling, the New England Power Company explained how its history illustrated why the program made little sense. Until the late 1960s, the company had burned coal; then it switched to burning oil to reduce its sulfur emissions. Massachusetts' Clean Air Act imposed stringent requirements that could be satisfied with (apparently low-sulfur) oil much more easily than with (likely high-sulfur) coal. When the company switched to coal in 1974 following the embargo, it could no longer satisfy the CAA requirements without a variance and suspension of the air quality program. Once its ability to rely on variances and suspensions expired, the company reverted to burning oil once again. And now the coal conversion program was threatening to order the company to retreat to coal, at considerable cost to its customers and without a clear path toward compliance with Massachusetts' air quality program. The company agreed that it would voluntarily switch some of its units back to coal, but it would oppose any coercive conversion order.[54]

CARTER'S COAL PROGRAM

Against this mosaic, President Carter entered the White House four years after the embargo and at the height of the 1976–77 natural gas emergency. Carter became convinced that national security and the domestic economy required prompt and effective action to address energy shortages. FEA Administrator John O'Leary exhibited the administration's perspective when he testified how low energy prices had increased consumption, resulting in a shift toward "oil imports as domestic production of oil and natural gas peaked. The crux of our energy problem," he added, "is clear: Economic and national security considerations make future reliance on unrestrained growth of oil imports unwise."[55] Carter's 1977 National Energy Plan (NEP) therefore unveiled a comprehensive suite of programs for addressing energy security.

One of the administration's ten fundamental tenets accepted the path set by prior administrations and called for boosting coal usage in new plants and maximizing coal's usage in existing plants, consistent (it hoped) with public health needs.

> [W]e must conserve the fuels that are scarcest and make the most of those that are plentiful. We can't continue to use oil and gas for 75 percent of our consumption, as we do now, when they only make up 7 percent of our domestic reserves. We need to

---

[53]   *Ibid.* at IX-41.
[54]   New England Power Company Letter to Congressman Dingell, May 19, 1977, *reprinted in* National Energy Act, Part 4, Hearings before the Subcommittee on Energy and Power, Committee on Interstate and Foreign Commerce, U.S. House, Serial No. 95–25, 906 (May 1977).
[55]   Impact of the President's Energy Plan on the Northeast, *supra* note 42, at 6.

shift to plentiful coal, while taking care to protect the environment, and to apply stricter safety standards to nuclear energy.[56]

During his April 18, 1977, "moral equivalent of war" (MEOW) address, Carter would describe coal as the nation's best weapon in the battle for energy independence and energy security. The country's "plentiful" coal supply already had begun flooding the market, with coal production increasing dramatically between 1965 and 1975, particularly following western coal's first significant contribution to production occurring from 1973 on.[57]

The NEP promoted an extensive array of policy prescriptions related to coal usage. It contemplated at the outset that coal production would almost double between 1975 and 1985.[58] Under the plan, conversion by industry and utilities to coal and other fuels would be encouraged by taxes on the use of oil and natural gas. A University of California, Berkeley, business administration professor commented in 1978 on how Carter's program sought "to encourage coal consumption by taxing oil and natural gas use by utilities and industrial firms, and by banning these alternative fuels in new electric utility plants and new large industrial installations." And he added how tax credits were available to entice installation of "new coal equipment."[59]

Coal therefore became an energy-shortage savior for Carter's NEP, and that translated into strengthening the program initiated with the 1974 ESECA. Senator Jackson explained in 1981 that Congress responded by removing some of the barriers embedded in the 1974 act and promoting "the substitution of indigenous coal for oil and natural gas."[60] Carter's proposed coal program under the NEP would prohibit all new utility and industrial boilers from burning oil or natural gas, except under specified conditions. Of course, many utilities already had abandoned plans for any new oil- or gas-fired units.[61] Conversely, existing facilities would not be allowed to burn oil or gas if they had coal-burning capability. This reflected one of the practical limitations of the coal conversion policy, namely that coal conversion was economically feasible only for power plants that had originally been designed to burn coal and had thereafter switched to oil or gas.

---

[56] Coal Conversion EIS, *supra* note 5, at 4.
[57] *See* U.S. Energy Information Administration, Annual Energy Review 2011, at 200 (Sept. 2012). For production off federal lands, *see* THOMAS S. KLEPPE & WILLIAM L. FISHER, ENERGY PERSPECTIVES 2 111–23 (Dept. of Interior 1976). In their report on energy policy, Secretary of Commerce Eliot L. Richardson and FEA Administrator Frank Zarb observed in 1976 how coal production had "only recently exceeded levels reached in the 1920's and its percentage of total energy demand has fallen dramatically." Elliot L. Richardson & Frank G. Zarb, Perspectives on Energy Policy 1 (Dec. 16, 1976).
[58] Moyer, *supra* note 4, at 762. For a thoughtful history of coal, particularly federal coal, *see* A. Dan Tarlock, *Western Coal in Context*, 53 U. COLO. L. REV. 315 (1981).
[59] Moyer, *supra* note 4, at 762.   [60] Jackson, *supra* note 38, at 308.
[61] *See* Donald P. Irwin & K. Dennis Sisk, *The Fuel Use Act and DOE's Regulations: A Utility Industry Perspective*, 29 U. KAN. L. REV. 319, 322 (1981).

In the 1978 Power Plant and Industrial Fuel Use Act (Fuel Use Act), Congress enacted the bulk of Carter's coal use proposals. Subject to several exceptions (including one for power plants that could not comply with the Fuel Use Act without violating the CAA), this legislation, described by a prominent energy expert as a "bold experiment,"[62] had two primary objectives. First, it prohibited new electric power plants from burning natural gas or oil and prohibited using natural gas as a primary energy source in existing electric power plants beginning in 1990. Second, the legislation authorized the Department of Energy (DOE) to prohibit the use of oil or natural gas in any existing power plant if it was economically and technically feasible to burn an alternative fuel.

In 1979, a DOE report to the president on accelerating coal production and use concluded that "coal must play the major role in meeting the nation's incremental energy needs." This report, moreover, expressly endorsed coal's bright prospects, observing how

> [g]iven the meager prospects for improvement in world oil supply and the long lead times for the introduction of other alternatives, the United States will require much greater use of coal to grapple effectively with the energy problems of the 1980's and 1990's.[63]

Unfortunately, though, the Fuel Use Act was not, in the administration's view, achieving enough conversions.[64] In a March 1980 letter to Congress, Carter advocated removing the "financial and institutional barriers" to conversion, including funding to help offset some of the capital costs associated with a conversion. But, notwithstanding the various complaints about the Fuel Use Act, by the time of the Act's repeal in 1987, coal's share of electric generation had risen during the intervening ten years from 44.2 percent to almost 57 percent.

---

[62] Richard J. Pierce, Jr., *Introduction: Symposium on the Powerplant and Industrial Fuel Use Act of 1978*, 29 U. KAN. L. REV. 297 (1981). *See also* Erik Dryburgh, *Coal Conversion and the Powerplant and Industrial Fuel Use Act of 1978*, 8 ECOLOGY L. Q. 774 (1980); Richard L. Gordon, *The Powerplant and Industrial Fuel Use Act of 1978: An Economic Analysis*, 19 NAT. RES. J. 871 (1979); Richard B. Herzog, *The Coverage of the Fuel Use Act: How to Avoid Unpleasant Surprises*, 13 NAT. RES. LAW. 553–69 (1981); Edward L. Lublin & Marvin G. Pickholz, *Introduction to the Powerplant and Industrial Fuel Use Act of 1978: Securing Exemptions for Utilities and Major Industrial Users*, 29 AM. U. L. REV. 485 (1980).

[63] Report on Increasing Coal Production and Use, by the Secretary of Energy James R. Schlesinger, as Requested by the President on April 5, 1979 (June 4, 1979), *reprinted in* Clean Air Act and Increased Coal Use: Environmental Protection Agency Oversight, Hearings before a Subcommittee on Government Operations, U.S. House of Representatives, 96th Cong., 1st Sess. 203 (Sept. 11 and 18, 1979). *See also* Staff Report to the President's Commission on Coal, The Acceptable Replacement of Imported Oil with Coal (March 1980).

[64] Jackson, *supra* note 38, at 313. President Carter, in Executive Order No. 12217, Federal Compliance with Fuel Use Prohibitions, June 18, 1980, had ordered that federal facilities also consult with the Secretary of Energy about converting any federal oil and natural gas plants to coal.

ENVIRONMENTAL PROTECTION AND COAL POLICY

Administration officials shielded themselves by asserting how the NEP was developed assuming changes in the CAA such that "significant coal conversions would not occur – and should not be allowed – in some areas due to environmental constraints."[65] Constraints already had secured cleaner air in places like New York City, where decreases in particulates between the 1950s and early 1970s were "attributed primarily to the gradual elimination of coal for power generation and heating and its replacement by fuel oil and natural gas."[66] After all, almost 400 power plants nationwide had switched from coal to lower-sulfur oil.[67] For New York alone, the move away from coal for space heating and power generation had dramatically positive effects on both SO_2 and particulates, and unless Con Ed's additional nuclear generation satisfied its increasing demand, "the trend from coal burning will reverse because of the increasing scarcity of natural gas and decreasing availability of domestic petroleum."[68]

The Carter administration gamely attempted to reconcile its energy and environmental objectives as it considered the environmental impacts of its program for increasing coal usage. In June 1977, the EPA's deputy administrator briefed Congress on the NEP and explained how the plan had been developed from the outset with environmental considerations at the forefront – a fundamental difference, she added, from prior proposals. She explained how coal usage, then at about 600 million tons per year, would increase without the NEP to about 1 billion tons annually by 1985 and that the plan would only add an additional 200 million tons by 1985 to that 1 billion ton projection. Emission increases associated with that additional 200 million tons would be offset, she testified, by conservation measures and CAA changes. For the most part, she indicated that increases would occur from new coal-fired power plants that would be required to install the best available control technology.[69] As the FEA and DOE struggled with promoting coal utilization

[65] Testimony of Douglas M. Costle, Administrator, Environmental Protection Agency, Subcommittee on Energy and Power, Committee on Interstate and Foreign Commerce, Environmental Implications of Coal Conversion, Hearing before the Subcommittee on Environmental Pollution of the Committee on Environmental and Public Works, U.S. Senate, Serial No. 95–H26, 95th Cong., 1st Sess., 74 (May 24, 1977).

[66] Merril Eisenbud, Sc.D., *Levels of Exposure to Sulfur Oxides and Particulates in New York City and Their Sources*, 54: 991–1011, at 997, Dec. 1978.

[67] *See supra* note 9 (Federal Power Commission Staff Report, 1 [Sept. 1973]).

[68] Merril Eisenbud, Sc.D., *Levels of Exposure to Sulfur Oxides and Particulates in New York City and Their Sources*, 54: 991–1011, at 1010, Dec. 1978.

[69] Statement of Ms Barbara Blum, Briefing on the National Energy Act, Ad Hoc Committee on Energy, U.S. House, 95th Cong., 1st Sess. 2–3 (June 22, 1977). She assumed that all new facilities (effectively plants built after 1980, because of the agency's interpretation of the CAA) would install scrubbers by 1985, existing facilities would install systems to comply with CAA standards by 1985 (noting that this would require a level of compliance not yet seen), pollution control equipment would be maintained and operated efficiently, and the coal conversion program would be implemented to protect public health. A good portion of the questioning focused on the use of scrubbers versus washing coal to remove the sulfur.

policies, the EPA proceeded along a parallel path for implementing the 1970 CAA and the 1977 Clean Air Act Amendments, as we describe in Chapter 8. While the 1970 CAA and the EPA's rules permitted utilities to use low-sulfur coal for purposes of compliance with SO_2 standards, that changed in 1977 when Congress required a technological rather than a fuel-choice solution. The *New York Times* reported how the Carter administration's aggressive reliance on coal was coupled with its request to Congress that new coal plants be required to employ the "best available pollution control technology" and, in lieu of simply using low-sulfur coal, "a requirement that new coal-burning boilers be fitted with pollution-filtering, flue gas scrubbers."[70] Congress responded in the 1977 CAA Amendments, requiring new source performance standards for new coal-fired power plants. And the EPA implemented this provision by requiring scrubbers to remove 90 percent of the SO_2 emissions.[71]

In 1977, though, the General Accounting Office warned how effective implementation of the CAA might impede the administration's coal policies.[72] Two years later, a DOE official testified that the "[n]ation's energy situation" necessitated that "the mechanisms used to implement the Clean Air Act [would] need to be examined."[73] During hearings on the NEP energy legislation, the administration published a study on expected air quality impacts of its coal policies.[74] The study predicted that almost all power plants coming on line were slated to use coal. As a result, the administration projected that coal usage by power plants and industrial facilities would increase from about half a billion tons per year in 1975 to roughly 1.2 billion tons per year in 1985 with the NEP, compared with a 1985 reference case (i.e., without the NEP) increase of about 0.9 billion tons per year.[75] The administration

[70] Ben A. Franklin, *Use of Scrubbers with Coal Boilers Pushed by Carter*, N.Y. TIMES, May 31, 1977, at p. 15. Franklin's article also notes how the Sierra Club questioned the existing requirement that facilities remove with scrubbers only 70 to 75 percent of the SO_2 "unless the coal being burned is of such low sulfur content – less than seven-tenths of 1 percent – that sulfur oxide emissions are curtailed without flue gas treatment down to the E.P.A.'s emission standard." *Ibid.*

[71] For critical questions on this policy, *see* BRUCE A. ACKERMAN & WILLIAM T. HASSLER, CLEAN COAL/ DIRTY AIR: OR HOW THE CLEAN *Air* ACT BECAME A MULTIBILLION-DOLLAR BAIL-OUT FOR HIGH-SULFUR COAL PRODUCERS AND WHAT SHOULD BE DONE ABOUT IT (Yale Univ. Press 1981).

[72] General Accounting Office, An Evaluation of the National Energy Plan 520 (US GPO 1977).

[73] Clean Air Act and Increased Coal Use: Environmental Protection Agency Oversight, Hearings before a Subcommittee of the Committee on Governmental Operations, 96th Cong., 1st Sess., 195 (Sept. 1979). The agency identified a December 1978 report prepared for DOE (An Assessment of National Consequence of Increased Coal Utilization) that concluded that air quality issues posed the most significant constrain on coal's increased usage. *Ibid.* at 196.

[74] Executive Office of the President, Energy Policy and Planning and Environmental Protection Agency, Air Pollution Impacts of the Oil and Gas Replacement Program in the Utility and Industrial Sectors (June 20, 1977); *see also* Executive Office of the President, Energy Policy and Planning, Replacing Oil and Gas with Coal and Other Fuels in the Industrial and Utility Sectors, June 2, 1977, *reprinted in* Coal Conversion Legislation, Hearings before the Subcommittee on Energy Production and Supply of the Committee on Energy and Natural Resources, U.S. Senate, on S. 272, Pub. No. 95-46, Part 2, 1691 (April and June 1977).

[75] *See also* Office of Technology Assessment, Analysis of the Proposed National Energy Plan 45 (Aug. 1977). The General Accounting Office expressed skepticism that, absent the NEP, the

projected that even with this 33 percent increase in coal usage under the NEP as compared with the reference case, emissions of NO_x and SO_2 would drop by 9 percent because of conservation measures recommended in the NEP (many of which were, however, never enacted into law). In addition, administration officials projected that of the power plants affected by coal utilization policies, 90 percent would be new plants and only 10 percent would be existing plants.[76] Yet the EPA at the time projected that up to half the existing coal-fired plants might not have been achieving air quality standards and that coal consumption by utilities would increase another 60 percent (according to the FPC) by 1980 – a little over 20 percent coming from new facilities.[77]

The administration's objective posed a dilemma, as aptly captured by American Electric Power's (AEP's) earlier 1974 testimony. AEP's vice president and general counsel testified that under the 1970 CAA, the "safest" and possibly "only method of ensuring that the lights will continue to burn in our service area" is to burn low-sulfur coal. In short, he opined how

[t]hus, at a time when the technology has not yet arrived, when oil and natural gas are in critically short supply – at such time man-made SO_2 limitations have ruled out the use of most of our eastern coal and a moratorium has been imposed by our own government on the development of most of our western coal – coal, the only fuel that exists in abundance to meet our Nation's energy requirements. Coal is the only answer today and for many years into the future. We must dig it and put it to work just as quickly, cleanly and efficiently as possible. In order to do that, we must make the necessary modifications in the Clean Air Act so that our Midwestern coals can be burned.[78]

For those 90 percent of new coal-fired power plants, Congress responded in the 1977 CAA Amendments by placing its faith in the availability of scrubbers, as we

United States would see coal production increase to 1 billion tons by 1985. Elmer B. Staats, GAO, Report to Congress: An Evaluation of the National Energy Plan, EMB-77–48, 5.30 (July 25, 1977).

[76] "One thing I would point is that the President's energy plan really relies only on 10 percent of this to come from conversion of oil plants, and essentially 90 percent on new." Testimony of Douglas M. Costle, Administrator, Environmental Protection Agency, National Energy Act, Part 4, Hearings before the Subcommittee on Energy and Power of the Committee on Interstate and Foreign Commerce, U.S. House, Serial No. 95–25, 788 (May 1977). A memorandum to the Secretary of Health, Education, and Welfare reported that the NEP's increased reliance on coal tentatively was "safe ... through 1985, if strong environmental and safety polices are followed. Report of the Committee on Health and Environmental Effects of Increased Coal Utilization, Dec. 23, 1977, *reprinted in* Environmental Implications of the New Energy Plan, Hearings before the Subcommittee on Environment and the Atmosphere, Committee on Science and Technology, U.S. House, 95th Cong., 1st Sess., No. 45, 813 (June, July, Sept. 1977).

[77] Control of Sulfur Oxides, Report of the Administrator of the Environmental Protection Agency to the Congress of the United States in Compliance with Section 119(k) of Public Law 93–319, The Energy Supply and Environmental Coordination Act of 1974, 94th Cong., 1st Sess. 1–3, 11, 14 (Feb. 1975). In 1973, coal-fired generation (most of it using high-sulfur coal) accounted for about 48 percent of all fossil fuel generation, while low-sulfur oil was at about 17 percent. Coal-fired generation, therefore, produced roughly 60 percent of total sulfur emissions. *Ibid.* at 7.

[78] Clean Air Act Oversight Hearings, 93rd Cong., 2nd Sess., Serial No 93–H42, Part 1, 34 (May 1974).

discuss in Chapter 8.[79] Years of congressional hearings, after all, had generated reams of testimony on the barriers to using low-sulfur coal by the Eastern and Midwestern utilities – utilities that presumably could convert from using natural gas or oil to coal.[80]

The numbers would change over the next two years with the worsening situation for oil imports. In his summer of 1979 report to Carter, Secretary Schlesinger warned that earlier projections of the amount of available imported oil were too high. The options were limited. Domestic production was not predicted to increase sufficiently; after TMI, nuclear energy was unlikely; and not until the next century would commercial quantities of renewable energy be available. This, of course, left coal: "[t]he only conclusion that can be drawn," he told the president, "is that coal must play the major role in meeting the nation's incremental energy needs for the rest of this country [*sic*: century]. The alternative is no longer imported oil because it will not be available. The only other alternative is a permanent slowdown of the economy."[81] Yet, in the same year as he made this pronouncement, the White House Council on Environmental Quality (CEQ) touted the ability for conservation and low growth in energy demand – albeit primarily for transportation, industrial (including through greater use of cogeneration), and residential heating and cooling. If, however, the nation experienced a high energy-growth future, it might require three times more coal production than at 1979 consumption levels, and assuming that electric generation is responsible for 70 percent of coal's consumption, then the country would need almost 300 new coal plants by 2000, or one plant per month for the remainder of the century.[82]

---

[79] *See* Bruce Ackerman & William T. Hassler, Clean Coal, Dirty Air: Or How the Clean Air Act Became a Multi-Billion-Dollar Bail-Out for High-Sulfur Coal Producers and What Should be Done About It (Yale Univ. Press 1981).

[80] *See* Air Quality and Stationary Source Emission Control, A Report by the Commission on Natural Resources, National Academy of Sciences, National Academy of Engineering, National Research Council, Prepared for the Committee on Public Works, U.S. Senate, Pursuant to S. Res. 135, 94th Cong., 1st Sess., Serial No. 94–4, 363–80 (March 1975) (noting, conservatively, a potential deficit of 150,000 million tons of low-sulfur coal for 1975). This report concluded that if scrubbing technology was not available to achieve air quality standards, some low-sulfur eastern coal was available, but that coal was high quality and slated for use by sources other than power generation. *Ibid.* at 366. By contrast, low-sulfur western coal was far from necessary markets, might take between three and ten years to be developed, and "located in areas where the construction of large new mines would have a major impact on the socio-economic conditions of the region." *Ibid.* at 367. One prominent industry executive testified that "it is really almost a national tragedy that we are trying to move western coals into eastern United States when we are blessed in eastern United States with higher quality, certainly higher Btu content coal that can be brought to market without taxing our transportation systems and our entire economy by virtue of this diversion." Clean Air Act Oversight Hearings, 93rd Cong., 2nd Sess., Serial No 93–H42, Part 1, 657 (May 1974) (Testimony of C. Howard Hardesty, Jr.). Factors affecting the dynamic between low- and high-sulfur coal arguably changed during the 1980s. *See* Congressional Budget Office, Staff Working Paper, Achieving Sulfur Dioxide Reduction through Coal-Switching (April 1987).

[81] Clean Air Act and Increased Coal Use: Environmental Protection Agency Oversight, Hearings before a Subcommittee of the Committee on Governmental Operations, 96th Cong., 1st Sess. 204 (Report on Increasing Coal Production and Use) (Sept. 1979).

[82] Council on Environmental Quality, The Good News about Energy 22–25 (1979).

To be sure, some in Congress pressed administration officials for an assessment of how Carter's coal policies would affect CAA implementation. Congressman Moffett, for instance, asked DOE's Assistant Secretary for the Environment if she had sent any memos directly to Secretary Schlesinger on "the question of increased use of coal and the impact on the Clean Air Act of the increased use of coal." The congressman's conversation with the Assistant Secretary even became testy when she indicated that it would be inappropriate for her to testify about anything in Secretary Schlesinger's 1979 memo to the president – a memo that already had been introduced into the record! Later, Congressman Moffett asked her to comment on Schlesinger's statement that the CAA affected coal's demand, to which she refused to respond directly and simply stated that the act "may possibly affect the use of coal," to which the congressman curtly replied that everyone on the street could say "may affect" and as a senior environmental person at DOE "for heaven's sake" she should be able to be more definitive. As a follow-up, the Assistant Secretary even received a subsequent letter from the Committee chairman questioning whether she had complied with her obligation to provide forthright testimony. And the existence of such memos to the Secretary was apparent, nonetheless, by the 1979 report's recommendations suggesting relaxing certain aspects of the CAA without comprising air quality standards. It also was apparent that the administration and Congress had been active at many levels in studying the intersection of its favored coal policy with the CAA. In 1978, the Office of Technology Assessment had released a "broad study" on coal, including its "analysis of the environmental and public health effects of increased coal use."[83] Subsequent congressional hearings even specifically targeted the effects of increased coal utilization, with Senator Muskie commenting in 1980 how "[b]urning coal without precautionary measures can result in increased amounts of sulfur dioxide, nitrogen dioxide, carbon dioxide, visibility problems, and acid precipitation."[84]

Yet, by the decade's end, coal had achieved significant success, notwithstanding its health and environmental effects and the hurdles under the CAA. Western coal production roughly tripled just between 1970 and 1977, and it was predicted to more than triple once again between 1975 and 1985.[85] To facilitate western production, however, new policies would be warranted to address how federally owned coal on public lands and leased to private interests could be encouraged. Historically, western coal had been used primarily by the railroads, and by 1970, the Interior Department had leased a considerable amount of coal lands, yet as Dan Tarlock explains, "91.5 percent of the total leased acreage was unproductive."[86] The Carter

[83] Clean Air Act and Increased Coal Use: Environmental Protection Agency Oversight, Hearings before a Subcommittee of the Committee on Governmental Operations, 96th Cong., 1st Sess. 201, 205, 207–8, 221, 289, 320 (Sept. 1979).

[84] Environmental Effects of the Increased Use of Coal, Serial No. 96–H45, Hearings before the Subcommittee on Environmental Pollution, of the Committee on Environment and Public Works, U.S. Senate, 96th Cong., 2nd Sess. 1 (March 19, April 21, 24, 1980).

[85] Moyer, *supra* note 4, at 766–67. [86] Tarlock, *supra* note 58, at 334.

administration's focus on planning extended to coal production, and it "initiated a system of central planning" mirroring the newly established DOE's broader mission; the Department, for instance, would calculate "individual production goals" for specifically identified coal regions throughout the country.[87] What ensued, however, was a several-year fight to craft a workable federal coal program, one that also addressed the environmental effects of strip mining. When, in fact, Congress had earlier sent to President Ford legislation that addressed strip mining, Ford vetoed the measure, fearing that it might hamper coal production. The federal coal program, though, would remain in a "stalemate" between 1971 and January 1981, with coal production growing "during this period only because," according to Robert Nelson – the noted economist who helped craft federal coal polices – "many new federal coal leases had been sold by the federal government to coal mining companies in the 1960s."[88]

Many in Congress, though, seemed intent on ensuring that sufficient coal supplies would become available. Once the moratorium on the federal coal program was lifted, first in 1981 and then again following the lifting of another moratorium in 1987, Congress passed amendments to address federal coal leasing – including adding requirements that federal leases be developed diligently (rather held speculatively) – and western coal production climbed. And with it the ability to consume ever-increasing amounts of coal became assured. In a 1979 House hearing, Republican Congressman Steve Symms from Idaho noted that "[f]or every ton of coal we burn to generate electricity we free up 4 barrels of oil to run our cars and heat our homes" and that as the largest single source of domestically "available fossil fuel," it had to "be developed [and] used."[89] He quoted a memo that Energy Secretary James Schlesinger wrote to the White House, and it quite simply stated that "[w]ithout greatly expanded use of coal, this country just may not make it."[90]

In the years following passage of the 1970 CAA, utilities increased their coal-fired generation but until 1974 continued to convert some plants to oil. Coal's overall use rose by 3.6 percent annually between 1972 and 1977, but the growth in electric generation occurred mostly *after* 1974.[91] Coal's consumption in the energy sector rose to 75,000 short tons between 1960 and 1970 and increased only slightly by 86,000 short tons the following five years. It was, instead, between 1975 and 1980, with explicit policies favoring coal, that the number jumped to roughly 163,000 short tons. While 727 coal-

---

[87] ROBERT H. NELSON, PUBLIC LANDS AND PRIVATE RIGHTS: THE FAILURE OF SCIENTIFIC MANAGEMENT 290 (Rowman & Littlefield 1995).

[88] *Ibid*. at 287.

[89] Federal Coal Management Program: Oversight Hearings before the Subcommittee on Mines and Mining, of the Committee on Interior and Insular Affairs, 96th Cong., 1st Sess., Serial No. 96–15 Part 1, 1 (June & Sept. 1979).

[90] *Ibid*. at 2.

[91] Clean Air Act and Increased Coal Use: Environmental Protection Agency Oversight, Hearings before a Subcommittee of the Committee on Governmental Operations, 96th Cong., 1st Sess. 127 (Sept. 1979).

fired plants were built between 1950 and 1970 compared with 262 coal-fired plants built between 1970 and 1980, the megawatt capacity of the facilities built in the 1970s surpassed the entire capacity constructed during the previous two decades.

COAL'S WAR ON PEOPLE

The health and environmental effects posed by such increased coal usage are dramatic – and appreciated at the time. Coal combustion produces fine particulates, mercury, sulfur oxides, and precursors of ozone (smog), all of which threaten pulmonary, neurologic, or cardiovascular damage – to a degree that for some population segments they can contribute to premature death. It is difficult to correlate precisely increased coal usage with premature deaths because of too many variables, including technological changes to facilities, changes in our economy and demographics, and how much and what type of fuel was used at particular times. Premature deaths might also be a product of prolonged exposure to a host of shifting pollutants. But the presence of a statistically significant nexus is unassailable. After all, a classic study on the impact of particulates observed how "[a]n association between human health and air pollution has been proposed for more than 50 years."[92] And by 1990, epidemiologic "[r]esearch [confirmed] a correlation between air pollution and not only respiratory diseases but also heart disease, cancer and a weakened immune system."[93] The EPA's study of fine particulates, for instance, links that pollutant with increased mortality.[94] Indeed, one study of fine particulates went so far as to posit that coal-fired generation can produce more deaths than from homicides.[95] For instance, in 2011 (after a decade of increasingly stringent emission controls on power plants), the EPA projected that its new standards for mercury being emitted from electric generating units (EGUs) could prevent up to 11,000 annual premature deaths and "more than 100,000 heart and asthma attacks each year."[96]

---

[92] Douglas Dockery & Arden Pope, *Epidemiology of Acute Health Effects: Summary of Time-Series Studies, in* PARTICLES IN OUR AIR: CONCENTRATIONS AND HEALTH EFFECTS 123 (Richard Wilson & John Spengler eds., Harvard Univ. Press 1996).

[93] Alice Bredin, *On Ill Health and Air Pollution,* N.Y. TIMES MAG., 7 Oct. 1990. Biography in Context, Web, 1 June 2016 (referencing, in part, one study suggesting up to 100,000 annual premature deaths from sulfur dioxide).

[94] Dockery & Pope, *supra* note 92, at 126–29, 143–44. Dockery and Pope suggest that while it is difficult to draw conclusions because of numerous variables, evidence suggests "that respirable particulate air pollution, at levels common to many urban and industrial areas in the United States, contributes to human morbidity and mortality." *Ibid.* at 166. An early 1980s law review article similarly observed how even then, "[d]espite the potential problems that exist with [earlier] ... studies, replication of the general results through analysis of different data sets using different methods suggests that a relationship does indeed exist between air pollution, measured in annual averages, and mortality." Robert C. Anderson & Bart Ostro, *Benefits Analysis and Air Quality Standards,* 23 NAT. RES. J. 565, 571 (1983).

[95] Michael J. Lynch & Kimberly L. Barrett, *Death Matters: Victimization by Particulate Matter from Coal Fired Power Plants in the U.S., a Green Criminological View,* 23 CRIT. CRIM. 219–34 (2015).

[96] EPA Fact Sheet: Mercury and Air Toxic Standards: Benefits and Costs of Cleaning Up Air Toxic Air Pollution from Power Plants (2011).

In his thoughtful summary of available research, Alan Lockwood's book, *The Silent Epidemic*, explores existing information on how coal combustion contributes to adverse health effects. His "Bottom Line" is that studies demonstrate "significant correlations between exposure to various air pollutants produced by burning coal and general measures of morbidity and mortality."[97] He acknowledges the difficulty with linking health effects to particular pollutants, from particular sources, but nonetheless explains how evolving research can link, for instance, sulfides, particulate matter, and hazardous air pollutants to increasing health risks – including mortality.[98] Of particular note are health effects from fine particulate matter – with electric utilities contributing the second-largest amount.[99] Lockwood's analysis was confirmed in a 2013 MIT study that linked emissions from power generation (albeit not just coal) to approximately 52,000 annual premature deaths.[100] This was roughly the same number that some epidemiologists had used for air pollution emissions in the latter 1990s.[101] A subsequent 2015 Harvard School of Public Health report found a similar correlation between fine particulate air emissions and premature deaths.[102] And two principal studies calculate the costs of these health effects (one based on 2007 dollars) at somewhere in the range of $62 billion annually to several hundred billion dollars.[103]

The more damning observation is that policymakers in the 1970s were aware of the potential health and environmental impacts of increased coal usage and went forward anyway. By the early 1970s, many in the scientific community recognized the pernicious health effects from burning fossil fuels, particularly from emissions of sulfur oxides and particulate matter. To be sure, the signs that air emissions posed an intolerable threat surfaced sporadically along with the dialogues about killer fogs. Yet, as of 1961, a *Scientific American* article reported how "as yet no solid evidence" existed that air pollution poses "a serious threat to the 'healthy' as opposed to otherwise sensitive populations, such as older individuals or those who already suffered with some form of bronchopulmonary disease."[104] But, a decade later,

---

[97]   ALAN H. LOCKWOOD, THE SILENT EPIDEMIC: COAL AND THE HIDDEN THREAT TO HEALTH 109 (MIT Press 2012). Two noteworthy studies are EPA, Study of Hazardous Air Pollutant Emissions from Electric Utility Steam Generating Units: Final Report to Congress, EPA pub. 453/R-98-004a (EPA 1998); National Research Council, Hidden Costs of Energy: Unpriced Consequences of Energy Production and Use (National Academy of Sciences 2009).

[98]   LOCKWOOD, *supra* note 97, at 7, 23.   [99]   *Ibid.* at 36.

[100] Jennifer Chu, *Study: Air Pollution Causes 200,000 Early Deaths Each Year in the U.S.*, MIT NEWS, Aug. 29, 2013.

[101] *Clearing the Air: Air Quality Special Report*, CONSUMER REPORTS, Aug. 1997, at 62 (50,000 deaths attributed to air pollution).

[102] Alissa Greenberg, *Air Pollution Linked to Increased Mortality even below EPA Limits Study*, TIME, June 5, 2015 ("The results indicate that exposure to air pollution on both the short- and long-term was significantly associated with higher death rates even in zip codes where measurements fell below EPA s standards, a trend suggesting that, as with toxins such as lead, there may be no safe level of exposure.").

[103] LOCKWOOD, *supra* note 97, at 200–3.

[104] Walsh McDermott, *Air Pollution and Public Health*, SCIENTIFIC AMERICA, 205: 49–57, at 49, Oct. 1961.

a group led by Ralph Nader published its scathing diatribe, *Vanishing Air*, where the authors referenced a 1969 scientific study of New York that suggested that an additional 1,100 to 2,200 people might die every year in the city as a result of elevated levels of sulfur dioxide.[105] One witness suggested in testimony in the late 1970s that sulfide emissions might have been responsible for between 150,000 and 186,000 premature deaths annually.[106]

Professor William Rodgers, a leading environmental law scholar, testified in 1972 how the EPA's 1972 Community Health and Environmental Surveillance System (CHESS) report on the suspended sulfate problem "left little doubt that even complying with the existing air quality standards was not sufficient to protect significant numbers of our citizens."[107] He quoted EPA's Carl Shy, who from 1967 to 1973 was EPA's director of the Human Studies Laboratory in Research Triangle Park, that "[w]e now have scientifically defensible evidence that definite increases in deaths occur at exposures below existing significant harm levels for sulfur oxides and particulate matter."[108] And Shy would later inform Congress that while emissions had decreased by the mid-1970s, two "reasons for concern" had surfaced: first, sufficient supplies of natural gas and low-sulfur coal were not easily available for the eastern United States, and second, energy growth seemed assured, and that growth was tied to burning more fossil fuels. EPA Administrator Russell E. Train, too, touted the CHESS analysis and echoed these same thoughts when he testified how sulfur dioxide might even pose health hazards at low levels.[109] This mirrored an almost identical conclusion from a 1970 National Research Council report.[110] But to Shy this result threatened further health risks, particularly in the East and Midwest, where studies already suggested that "concentrations are above the threshold level associated with adverse effects on health."[111] Shy therefore concluded that fossil fuel power generation presented too great a risk and that the nation should turn to nuclear power.

To be fair, not all agreed respecting sulfates. Tennessee Valley Authority's (TVA's) chairman of the board of directors, for instance, testified that any "connection

---

[105] JOHN C. ESPOSITO, VANISHING AIR: RALPH NADER'S STUDY GROUP REPORT ON AIR POLLUTION 8–9 (Grossman 1970).

[106] Clean Air Act and Increased Coal Use: Environmental Protection Agency Oversight, Hearings before a Subcommittee of the Committee on Governmental Operations, 96th Cong., 1st Sess. 4 (Sept. 1979). For sulfides, witnesses since the late 1960s had noted that coal's use for electric generation accounted for the highest amount of sulfates in the atmosphere. *See, e.g.*, Federal Air Pollution R.&D on Sulfur Oxides Pollution Abatement, 90th Cong., 2nd Sess., Sept. 5, 1968, at 12; Maria H. Grimes, Cong. Res. Serv., The Sulfur Oxide Tax, Feb. 10, 1972, at 6.

[107] Energy and Environmental Standards, 93rd Cong., 1st & 2nd Sess., No. 45, 40 (Sept. & Oct. 1973).

[108] *Ibid.*   [109] *Ibid.* at 452–53.

[110] National Research Council, Abatement of Sulfur Oxide Emissions from Stationary Combustion Sources (1970); *see also* National Research Council, Abatement of Particulate Emissions from Stationary Sources (1970); National Research Council, Abatement of Nitrogen Oxides from Stationary Sources (1970).

[111] Research and Development Related to Sulfates in the Atmosphere, 94th Cong., 1st Sess. No. 99, 388 (July 8, 9, 14, 1975).

between sulfur dioxide emissions and adverse health effects caused by suspended sulfates remains theoretical."[112] A federal entity, TVA operated twelve coal-fired power plants, with most of the plants likely requiring the installation of scrubbers and perhaps a few plants deploying low-sulfur coal and other strategies.[113] Even the Deputy Administrator of the Federal Energy Administration similarly testified in 1975 that fears about sulfates were "unjustified" and that the EPA's analysis was merely "tentative" and did not warrant aggressive reduction strategies.[114]

Others were more nuanced. When, in 1979, the EPA discussed the adverse effects of the coal conversion program, it acknowledged increased health risks while simultaneously suggesting that gross analysis of effects was too imprecise – that only a plant-by-plant inquiry would yield accurate results.[115] When testifying about his office's 1979 report "Direct Use of Coal," Office of Technology Assessment Project Director Alan T. Crane underscored how the science was "far from final" in linking emissions from fossil fuels to particular risks and mortality rates.[116] Crane added that coal burning's increased CO_2 emissions threatened to contribute to global warming "of a magnitude that is difficult to comprehend."[117] A Ph.D. study by Frederick Lipfert, at the time at Brookhaven National Laboratory, entitled "Sulfur Oxides, Particulates, and Human Mortality," confirmed a correlation between particulates and mortality but found little to support a conclusive correlation with sulfur oxides.[118]

The scientific dispute surrounding health effects naturally surfaced because, in the early 1970s, the tools for modeling and quantifying adverse effects were still quite unsophisticated. These tools improved over time. For instance, in 1970, Lave and

[112]   Clean Air Act Oversight Hearings, 93rd Cong., 2nd Sess., Serial No 93–H42, Part 1, at 8 (May 1974) (Statement of Aubrey J. Wagner, Chairman, Board of Directors, Tennessee Valley Authority).

[113]   Ibid. at 8–10.

[114]   Research and Development Related to Sulfates in the Atmosphere, 94th Cong., 1st Sess. No. 99, 639 (July 8, 9, 14, 1975) (Statement of John Hill). FEA provided Congress with a preliminary report, A Critical Evaluation of Current Research Regarding Health Criteria for Sulfur Oxides: A Technical Report, prepared for the Federal Energy Administration, by Tabersha/Cooper Associates, Inc., April 11, 1975. Ibid. at 647.

[115]   Clean Air Act and Increased Coal Use: Environmental Protection Agency Oversight, Hearings before a Subcommittee of the Committee on Government Operations, U.S. House, 96th Cong., 1st Sess. 169, 184 (Sept. 11, 13, 1979).

[116]   Ibid. at 300.

[117]   Ibid. at 301. GAO's 1977 report similarly observed that the long-term effects of greenhouse gas emissions ought to be examined before "irreversible effects are experienced." General Accounting Office, An Evaluation of the National Energy Plan, EMD-77–48, 5.22–23 (July 25, 1977).

[118]   Frederick W. Lipfert, Sulfur Oxides, Particulates, and Human Mortality: Synopsis of Statistical Correlations, 30(4) J. AIR POLL'N CONTROL ASSOC., 30:4, 366–71 (April 1980). Although their methodology seems coarse and fails to account for other contributing factors leading to premature deaths, R. Mendelsohn and G. Orcutt posited upwards of 140,000 to 190,000 premature deaths, with sulfur oxides the principal culprit. See R. Mendelsohn, & G. Orcutt, An Empirical Analysis of Air Pollution Dose-Response Curves, 6(2) J. ENVT'L ECON. AND MGMT. 85–106 (1979). For Lipfert's description of the Mendelsohn and Orcutt study, see FREDERICK W. LIPFERT, AIR POLLUTION AND COMMUNITY HEALTH: A CRITICAL REVIEW AND DATA SOURCEBOOK 290 (Van Nostrand Reinhold 1994).

Seskin analyzed the external costs associated with disease attributable to burning fossil fuels. They concluded that "a 50 percent reduction in urban air pollution would account for 25–50 percent of the excess urban mortality and morbidity from bronchitis, 25 percent of lung cancers, 25 percent of respiratory disease, 10 percent of cardiovascular morbidity and mortality, and 15 percent of cancer in general" – with a savings of around $2 billion in health costs.[119] Lave, by 1981, would testify that fuel switching and economic reasons helped to spur air quality improvement during the 1970s, but he feared that the environment might worsen as the country uses "much more coal than we ever used in the past" and as the economy gets better.[120]

In 1975, the National Academy of Sciences reported that "[i]nformation concerning neither the magnitude of the deleterious effects of sulfur oxide emissions, nor the atmospheric chemistry of sulfur oxides, nor the control of emissions has been found to be sufficiently reliable and extensive to permit resolution of the attendant controversies with a high degree of confidence."[121] Assessing actual human effects was complicated because controlled experiments purportedly yielded skewed results, because the effects of sulfur oxides became magnified when people were exposed to other harmful pollutants that combined with the sulfur oxides. The effects, moreover, would be different for power plants in rural than in urban areas, and measuring those effects became even more complicated when utilities deployed tall stacks to throw off their emissions further downwind. And while the National Academy of Sciences projected increasing SO_x emissions (possibly almost doubling within the decade, after having decreased substantially during the 1960s), it believed those emissions would either occur outside metropolitan areas or be dispersed through tall stacks, or both.[122] With that said, the Academy found it reasonable to predict increased mortality if sulfur dioxide levels increased and strongly recommended abatement measures – including possibly revisiting President Nixon's suggested sulfur charge.

By 1977, even more studies emerged warning us about health effects from burning fossil fuels, particularly coal. Discussing a prominent study by scientists at Brookhaven National Laboratory and Carnegie-Mellon University, a 1977 *Washington Post* reporter began his article by alerting readers that "[a]s many as 21,000 people die prematurely east of the Mississippi River every year because of pollutants exhausted into the air by power plants burning coal and oil." The article went further and cautioned that if the nation used more coal and employed

[119] Air Quality and Stationary Source Control, S Res 135, Serial No. 94–4, 140 (March 1975) (discussing L.B. Lave & E.P. Seskin, *Air Pollution and Human Health: The Quantitative Effect, with an Estimate of the Dollar Benefit of Pollution Abatement Is Considered*, 169 SCIENCE 723–33 [1970]). A subsequent report by other researchers upped the amount to $4.3 billion, with others raising the number even further. *Ibid.* at 141.

[120] Health Standards for Air Pollutants, 97th Cong., 1st Sess., Serial No. 97–97, 84 (Oct. 1981).

[121] Air Quality and Stationary Source Control, S. Res. 135, Serial No. 94–4, xvii (March 1975). By assigning certain costs to identified health effects, the study posited a total cost to society of $53.1 million annually, with, in particular, electric generation responsible for most NO_x emissions and coal being the highest contributor. *Ibid.* at 630, 646, 718.

[122] Air Quality and Stationary Source Control, S. Res. 135, Serial No. 94–4, 264 (March 1975).

scrubbers that would remove only 80 percent of the sulfur, it could still "expect as many as 35,000 premature deaths by the year 2010 instead of the estimated 21,000 taking place right now."[123] By 1981, a Bowdoin economics professor testified how his review of available studies illustrated the difficulty with drawing precise conclusions, and yet various researchers had demonstrated "a significant association between the levels of sulfur compounds . . . and total suspended particulates and mortality."[124]

CONCLUSION

The Carter administration's coal policies reflected two objectives: first, to increase coal usage for electric generation and, second, to do so without increasing emissions of key pollutants or endangering public health and the environment. The administration was eminently successful in carrying out the first objective but failed in the second. The administration assumed that emission loadings of key pollutants would not increase and rather likely might decline because of other administration policies. Of these other policies, administration officials strongly emphasized the mitigating effect of the NEP's proposed conservation and efficiency measures. While coal conversions would tend to increase emissions, the administration's Energy Plan would also encourage energy conservation. The energy conservation measures included peak-load pricing, mandatory insulation standards for new buildings, mandatory standards for new appliances, financial incentives for energy conservation in existing buildings, and oil and gas pricing policies. Unfortunately, many of these policies fell by the wayside and were not enacted in the 1978 National Energy Act.

Next, the Carter administration anticipated that the 1977 CAA Amendments would shield the environment from the effects of increased coal utilization. These amendments and accompanying rulemakings, they hoped, would reduce SO_2 emissions from both new and existing coal-fired power plants. Both new and existing plants, under different programs, would likely install new technological emission controls. In a congressional hearing, the acting Assistant Administrator for Air and Waste Management explained these "critical assumptions" underlying the administration's projection of air quality impacts of the program.

> First, as stated, best available control technology must be required on all new facilities. Second, existing facilities must install equipment needed to meet current emission limitations. Third, the pollution control equipment must be operated and

[123]   Thomas O'Toole, *Premature Deaths Linked to Coal and Oil Burning*, WASH. POST, July 34, 1977. The newspaper reported that, in 1973, power plants produced 17 million tons of sulfur, with 75 percent of that from coal-fired generation, and it described the implications of greater coal utilization as "grim."

[124]   Health Standards for Air Pollutants, 97th Cong., 1st Sess., Serial No. 97–97, 186 (Statement of A. Myrick Freeman III) (Oct. 1981). In urban areas, he calculated that a 20 percent air quality change correlated with approximately 13,900 deaths. *Ibid.* at 187.

maintained properly. Basically, in order to avoid aggravating existing pollution problems through increased coal use, it is necessary to take measures to assure that stringent controls are installed and operated properly wherever possible.[125]

Responding to congressional queries about the costs and complexity of installing new technology, Administration officials took pains to emphasize how increased costs would fall mostly on new plants. Steven Gage, EPA's Deputy Assistant Administrator for Energy, Minerals, and Industry, elaborated on the EPA's position during a congressional hearing.

> The pattern which has been laid out in the Clean Air Act is to set targets for new plants. We are not talking about trying to backfit all of the capital equipment in this country. We are talking about laying out a schedule whereby the designers of new powerplants can aim for targets for emission control. In other words, those plants which are already in existence meet a given set of requirements. Those plants which were built between 1971 and 1975 meet a more stringent level … [T]he current Clean Air Act Amendments would apply to yet a new set of powerplants, which would be built after the effective date of the amendments.[126]

And, notably, an EPA official a few years later testified how the agency assumed that a considerable portion of increased coal usage, regardless of whether from low- or high-sulfur coal, would come from new plants subject to stringent limitations for sulfur.[127]

Taken together, as EPA Administrator Costle testified to Congress, these measures would result in increased coal usage without an increase in harmful emissions. Senator Patrick Moynihan from New York expressed similar optimism when in questioning Costle he posited that "we should carry out the president's coal conversion program, but I think we should do it in a way that – to the maximum degree feasible – avoids exacerbating the acid rain problem. I think Mr. Costle has made clear that we can do this."[128] That did not prove to be the case, either for acid rain or for health-related pollutants such as SO_2. The CAA and its implementing rules were simply not up to the task, as we explain in Chapter 8. Based on recent epidemiology

[125] Statement of Edward F. Tuerk, Acting Administrator for Air and Waste Management, Environmental Protection Agency, National Energy Act, Part 4, Hearings before Subcommittee on Energy and Power, Committee on Interstate and Foreign Commerce, U.S. House, 95th Cong., 1st Sess., Serial No. 95–25, 408, 412 (May 26, 1977).

[126] Testimony of Steven Gage, Deputy Assistant Administrator for Energy, Minerals, and Industry, Office of Research and Development, Environmental Protection Agency, Ad Hoc Committee on Energy, U.S. House (June 22, 1977).

[127] Clean Air Act and Increased Coal Use: Environmental Protection Agency Oversight, Hearings before a Subcommittee of the Committee on Governmental Operations, 96th Cong., 1st Sess., 124–6 (Sept. 1979).

[128] Environmental Effects of the Increased Use of Coal, Hearings before the Subcommittee on Environmental Pollution, of the Committee on Environment and Public Works, U.S. Senate, 96th Cong., 2nd Sess., Serial No. 96–H45, 20 (March 19, April 21, 24, 1980).

studies, hindsight now poignantly illustrates just how misguided were the coal policies of the 1970s.

Today we confront the fruits of choosing policies designed to aggressively increase coal utilization without having the regulatory tools in place for mitigating its public health and environmental impacts. Though we cannot precisely quantify the death toll, a fair inference suggests that these policies resulted in hundreds of thousands of premature deaths over a thirty-year period. Another result was an increasingly destructive acid rain problem for the Northeast states and eastern Canada. Coal-fired power plants therefore generally are considered, aside from their greenhouse gas (GHG) emissions, one of the most environmentally costly industries – producing annual damage of anywhere between $50 billion to a quarter of a trillion dollars.[129] Some of this might have been avoided, as we chronicle in Chapter 8, if the CAA had been aggressively implemented and not chilled by the fear of energy shortages.

A third, yet even more destructive result was a substantial increase in CO_2 emissions from US coal-fired power plants. By 2005, their emissions accounted for almost 10 percent of global CO_2 emissions. The Obama administration valiantly sought to address these emissions when it crafted detailed CAA regulations for both existing and new coal-fired power plants. Within the first six months of the Trump administration, however, it became abundantly clear that the new administration would never let those regulations become effective.

---

[129] National Academy of Sciences, Hidden Costs of Energy: Unpriced Consequences of Energy Production and Use (2010); Nicholas Z. Muller, Robert Mendelsohn, & William Nordhaus, *Environmental Accounting for Pollution in the United Sates Economy*, 101 AM. ECON. REV. 1649, 1664 (2011); Paul R. Epstein et al., *Full Cost Accounting for the Life Cycle of Coal*, 1219 ANN. N.Y. ACAD. SCI. 73 (2011).

8

Energy Eclipsing Air

The year 1970 became a watershed for environmental protection, albeit one that would soon be eclipsed by the nation's hunger for energy resources – producing a result that took almost fifty years before the coal industry would claim that it was confronting an ostensible war. The convergence of energy and environmental policy surfaced simultaneously as the energy crisis of the 1970s confronted the 1970 environmental decade – blossoming from 1969 as the "Year of Ecology" so dubbed by *Time*. On January 1, President Nixon signed what has since been described as the "nation's environmental Magna Charta," the National Environmental Policy Act (NEPA). Congress in December of that year passed the first comprehensive environmental pollution-control statute, the Clean Air Act (CAA), which Congress revised in 1977 and 1990. The CAA has since become the quintessential environmental law milestone, serving as a model for many subsequent pollution-control programs. Two years later, Congress passed the Federal Water Pollution Control Act (FWPCA) as well as the Coastal Zone Management Act (CZMA). Today we accept how these and other programs ushered in a new paradigm for federal environmental protection.

But this push for a healthier and sustainable environment occasionally softened under the clamor for increased energy development. The CZMA, for instance, included a specific provision accepting energy development's importance. The congressional debates surrounding the FWPCA focused considerable attention on effects from energy development – and potentially avoiding unnecessarily costly technological requirements. NEPA early on, for example, confronted whether and how to apply the Act to the development of nuclear power, as well as buckling under Congress's decision to insulate the trans-Alaska pipeline from any further NEPA challenges.

The CAA, though, presented an acute challenge for the electric utility industry. The Act provided clear requirements for development and implementation of federal ambient air quality standards, new source performance standards, hazardous air pollutant regulation, and tailpipe standards for mobile sources. Senator Muskie, the Act's architect and sponsor, noted in September 1970 how "[t]he bill we consider today ... faces the environmental crisis with greater urgency and frankness than any previous legislation," and it "states that all Americans in all parts of the Nation should have clean air to breathe, air that will have no adverse effects on their health. And this bill is aimed at putting in motion the steps necessary to achieve that level of air quality within the next five years."[1] The fact that the electric utilities today still produce about 35 percent of our total greenhouse gas (GHG) emissions and, based on 2015 and 2016 data, about 44 percent of SO_2 emissions, 10 percent of NO_x emissions, and 48 percent of mercury emissions counsels that any attempt to reduce public health dangers or environmental damage for those pollutants unescapably requires regulation of energy production and use. The CAA, therefore, naturally became a de facto component of the US energy regulatory regime.

Unquestionably, the CAA as amended has reduced emissions and enhanced air quality. Indeed, through the Act's first decade, SO_2 emissions reportedly decreased by 40 percent.[2] And overall since 1970 those emissions decreased dramatically. Just between 1990 and 2014, one report suggests the electric utility sector decreased its SO_2 emissions from 15.73 million tons to 2.62 million tons.[3] But sulfur emissions from coal-fired utilities, particularly in the Midwest, remain high, and sulfur oxides along with nitrogen oxides and particulates continue to threaten human health and our environment.

The CAA (in its original form and somewhat through subsequent amendments) has been encumbered by several fundamental assumptions and design flaws, limiting its effectiveness, unnecessarily increasing compliance costs, spawning political controversy and seemingly endless litigation, and arguably retarding rather than advancing deployment of efficient, low-emission technologies. The original Act's weaknesses surfaced almost immediately when the newly created Environmental Protection Agency (EPA) confronted the nation's energy crisis. These design issues include the "grandfathering" policies embedded in the 1970 Act and subsequent amendments, extensive reliance on state implementation plans to carry out much of the regulatory system, the Act's cumbersome interstate transport provisions, and the

---

[1] Committee Print, A Legislative History of the Clean Air Amendments of 1970 Together with a Section-By-Section Index: Prepared by the Environmental Policy Division of the Congressional Research Service for the Committee on Public Works U.S. Senate, Serial No. 93–18, 93rd Cong., 2nd Sess. Vol. 1, at 224 (Jan. 1974) (hereinafter Serial No. 93–18).

[2] Sandra Sugawara, *Clean Air Act Rewrite Targeted in Thicket of Conflicting Interests*, WASH. POST, Aug. 2, 1982, A6. *See* NAT'L RESEARCH COUNCIL, AIR QUALITY MANAGEMENT IN THE UNITED STATES 37–39 (Nat'l Acad. Science Press 2004). Most reductions likely occurred from fuel switching or the flattening economy, because SO_2 emissions only decreased by 20 percent annually between 1973 and 1978. NATIONAL COMMISSION ON AIR QUALITY, TO BREATHE CLEAN AIR 1 (1981). The principal early decrease occurred between 1970 and 1973, before the CAA had much of an impact. Annual Report of the Administrator of the Environmental Protection Agency to the Congress of the United States, Progress in the Prevention and Control of Air Pollution in 1976, Serial No. 95–75, 95th Cong., 1st Sess. 1 (Sept. 1977).

[3] AAPCA, THE GREATEST STORY SELDOM TOLD: PROFILES AND SUCCESS STORIES IN AIR POLLUTION CONTROL (April 2017). For downward emission trends in New York, *see* Shannon M. Buckley & Myron J. Mitchell, *Improvements in Urban Air Quality: Case Studies from New York State, USA*, SPRINGER: WATER AIR SOIL POLLUT., April 16, 2010.

"layering" of multiple (and sometimes redundant) regulatory requirements on the same source.

EMERGENCE OF MODERN AIR REGULATION

For centuries, societies have confronted the pernicious effects from burning fossil fuels. England, as early as 1273, employed a smoke-abatement measure for addressing smoke from fuel combustion, succeeded by commissions exploring smoke abatement in 1285, 1288, and shortly thereafter during the early 1300s – with even a 1307 Royal Proclamation. Writing in the 1930s, Henry Obermeyer describes how "[b]y the year 1812, London and the large manufacturing centers in the North were faced with a serious situation resulting from the unrestricted combustion of smoke-producing fuel."[4] An 1847 Town Improvement Clauses Act responded by attempting to mitigate factory smoke, followed shortly thereafter by the 1863 Alkali Acts addressing sulfuric acid and then Parliament's more elaborate 1875 Public Health Act. Harold Platt, though, credits an English smoke-abatement exposition during 1881–82 as marking "a propitious moment in urban environmental reform" – where urban health merged with scientific inquiry to explore opportunities for arresting environmental health threats. And thirty years later, Dr. H. A. Des Voeux founded the British National Smoke Abatement Society and reportedly coined the term "smog" to capture industrialization's air quality problem.[5]

The United States mirrored aspects of England's nascent efforts for arresting soot and smoke when American communities began passing smoke-abatement ordinances – Chicago being one of the earliest in 1881. Professor David Stradling quite aptly portrays in *Smokestacks and Progressives* how "progressives" between 1881 and 1951 developed state and local programs for abating the threat of smoke and corresponding air emissions.[6] Some communities, for instance, banned locomotives from

---

[4] HENRY OBERMEYER, STOPE THAT SMOKE! 5 (Harper & Brothers 1933).

[5] For smoke abatement history in England, *see* ERIC ASHBY & MARY ANDERSON, THE POLITICS OF CLEAN AIR (Clarendon Press 1981); PETER BRIMBLECOMBE, THE BIG SMOKE: A HISTORY OF AIR POLLUTION IN LONDON SINCE MEDIEVAL TIMES (Methuen 1987); SMOKE AND MIRRORS: THE POLITICS AND CULTURE OF AIR POLLUTION (E. Melanie DuPuis ed., N.Y. Univ. Press 2004) (two chapters, Peter Brimblecombe, Perceptions and Effects of Late Victorian Air Pollution, 15; and Harold L. Platt, "The Invisible Evil": Noxious Vapor and Public Health in Manchester During the Age of Industry, 27, 29); ALAN GILPIN, AIR POLLUTION (Univ. of Queensland Press 1971); A.C. STERN, AIR POLLUTION: A COMPREHENSIVE TREATISE (1968).

[6] DAVID STRADLING, SMOKESTACKS AND PROGRESSIVES: ENVIRONMENTALISTS, ENGINEERS, AND AIR QUALITY IN AMERICA, 1881–1951 (Johns Hopkins Univ. Press 1999). Shortly after the turn of the century, the federal government also began researching technologies for diminishing smoke. *Ibid.* at 97. Another useful history of this period is SCOTT HAMILTON DEWEY, DON'T BREATHE THE AIR: AIR POLLUTION AND U.S. ENVIRONMENTAL POLITICS, 1945–1970 (Texas A&M Univ. Press 2000). *See also* JOEL A. TARR, THE SEARCH FOR THE ULTIMATE SINK: URBAN POLLUTION IN HISTORICAL PERSPECTIVE (Univ of Akron Press 1996); CHARLES O. JONES, CLEAN AIR: THE POLICIES AND POLITICS OF POLLUTION CONTROL (Univ. of Pittsburgh Press 1975); DONALD MACMILLAN, SMOKE WARS: ANACONDA COPPER, MONTANA AIR POLLUTION, AND THE COURTS 1890–1920 (Montana Hist. Soc'y Press 2000).

burning bituminous coal when traveling through their streets, while Pittsburgh attempted to limit new beehive coke ovens within its urban confines. The Ringelmann Chart, created by Parisian Professor Maximillian Ringelmann in 1888 and published here in the United States in the late 1890s, allowed inspectors to measure whether a source emitted too much smoke. For example, in their classic study of pollution in Los Angeles, James Krier and Edmund Ursin observe that

> [l]egislative action regarding the pollution problem in the Los Angeles area began as early as 1905, with a city ordinance aimed at emissions of dense smoke from flues, chimneys, and smokestacks . . . [a 1907] ordinance, adopted after a six-month fight, established the city's first position of smoke inspector and regulated discharges of smoke from industrial structures and appliances. Smoke and fumes were the subject of further local legislation in 1908, 1911, 1912, 1930, 1937, and 1945; objectionable odors, in 1930; and oil burning orchard heaters, in 1931 and 1937.[7]

"By 1912," Scott Dewey recounts, "twenty-three of the twenty-eight American cities of more than 200,000 inhabitants had smoke abatement bureaus, while thirty-one smaller cities also had smoke ordinances or inspectors."[8] One example is that by the early 1930s, Salt Lake City's ordinance limited emitting smoke for no more than six minutes in any one-hour period.[9] According to Arthur Stern, president of the Air Pollution Control Association during part of the 1970s, "municipal ordinances reached their zenith in the period from 1945 to 1950."[10] We should be cautious, though, before heralding these early efforts too much, as Noga Morag-Levine reminds us. Enforcement either by local officials or by the courts was less than robust, and smoke inspectors apparently received insufficient funding.[11]

To be sure, soot and sulfur dioxide captured most of the interest in America as well as in Great Britain, and while many of these programs focused narrowly on smoke abatement, some addressed air pollution more generally. By the late 1960s, the air quality in large metropolitan areas could classified – albeit crudely – according to the levels of suspended particulates, sulfur dioxide, and photochemical smog. Of salience, some later ordinances, moreover, required installing certain technologies or even switching fuels.[12] Indeed, California's 1960 Motor Vehicle Pollution

---

[7] JAMES E. KRIER & EDMUND URSIN, POLLUTION AND POLICY: A CASE STUDY ON CALIFORNIA AND FEDERAL EXPERIENCE WITH MOTOR VEHICLE AIR POLLUTION 1940–1975 46 (Univ. of California. Press 1977); DEWEY, *supra* note 6, at 38–110.

[8] DEWEY, *supra* note 6, at 24.

[9] OBERMEYER, *supra* note 4, at 150. An excellent account of Pittsburgh's efforts is in Joel Tarr's *The Search for the Ultimate Sink*, *supra* note 6, at 221–67, while Mathew Crenson offers a detailed account of efforts in East Chicago and Gary, Indiana. MATHEW A. CRENSON, THE UN-POLITICS OF AIR POLLUTION: A STUDY OF NON-DECISIONMAKING IN THE CITIES (Johns Hopkins Univ. Press 1971).

[10] STERN, *supra* note 5, at 46–47.

[11] NOGA MORAG-LEVINE, CHASING THE WIND: REGULATING AIR POLLUTION IN THE COMMON LAW STATE 112–22 (Princeton Univ. Press 2003).

[12] *See, e.g.*, William L. Andreen, *Of Fables and Federalism: A Re-Examination of the Historical Rationale for Federal Environmental Regulation*, 42 ENVTL. L. 627, 670, 670 n.396 (2012) (Pittsburgh and St. Louis); *cf. ibid.* at 633–34 (noting the industry's fight against efforts to curtail burning coals). *See*

Control Act required that, within a set period, all new automobiles sold into the California market be equipped with exhaust-control devices.

Recognition that federal intervention might be warranted surfaced at least as early as 1950. Following the six-day 1948 Denora, Pennsylvania, smog and a subsequent event in London, President Truman directed the Interior Department to explore the nation's air pollution problems. Denora was a small industrial community in the western part of Pennsylvania, and about half of its roughly 28,000 residents became ill, with twenty dying.[13] And, of course, London's 1952 "killer smog" reportedly was responsible for an additional 1,000 or more deaths that year (and 340 deaths presumably occurred during a subsequent event in December 1963).[14] As early as 1955, Congress began crafting legislative programs for avoiding "endangerment" to the "public health and welfare" caused by air emissions.[15] Although it never advanced, a 1957 proposal bill would have prohibited the sale in interstate commerce of any motor vehicle whose emissions were deemed harmful to human health. In April 1963, the US Senate established its first subcommittee to address air and water pollution (under the Senate Committee on Public Works). Over 50 percent of the population then living in urban areas faced some form of air pollution problem.[16] The subcommittee's first staff report unsurprisingly championed establishing "air quality standards in terms of known and suspected effects on what is necessary for the protection of human health and welfare, agriculture, and property."[17] The report suggested that annually burning even only 2 percent sulfur content coal could produce enough sulfur dioxide to damage vegetation over a 46,000-square-mile area.[18] The British government already had passed its Clean Air Act following the London fog, and that act addressed coal-burning practices for reducing particulates.

A 1963 version of the CAA authorized federal "advisory" criteria for states and local governments and empowered the Secretary of Health, Education, and Welfare (HEW) to pursue abatement actions against private actors when the activity endangered public health or welfare.[19] This occurred, however, within an admittedly

also MORAG-LEVINE, *supra* note 11, at 112 ("The first smoke ordinances (in St. Louis and Pittsburgh) were in essence technology standards restricting the use of bituminous coal and requiring tall stacks.").

[13] Serial No. 93–185, *supra* note 1, at 246. 1963 staff report only said that one-third became ill. Committee Print, A Study of Pollution-Air: A Staff Report to the Committee on Public Works, U.S. Senate, 88th Cong., 1st Sess. 13 (Sept. 1963) (hereinafter 1963 Staff Report).

[14] *Ibid.* The 1963 report suggested upwards of 4,000 deaths from the 1952 killer smog. *See* Peter Thorsheim, *Interpreting the London Fog Disaster of 1952, in* SMOKE AND MIRRORS: THE POLITICS AND CULTURE OF AIR POLLUTION 154 (E. Melanie DuPuis ed., N.Y. Univ. Press 2004). High air pollution levels may also have been responsible for 200 excess deaths in New York City in 1953. A Report of the Surgeon General to the U.S. Congress in Compliance with Pub. L. 86–493, Motor Vehicles, Air Pollution, and Health 21, House Doc. No. 489, 87th Cong., 2nd Sess. 41 (June 1962) (hereinafter Surgeon General 1962).

[15] Christopher D. Ahlers, *Origins of the Clean Air Act: A New Interpretation*, 45 ENVTL. L. 75, 80 (2015).

[16] Randall B. Ripley, *Congress and Clean Air: The Issue of Enforcement, 1963, in* CONGRESS AND URBAN PROBLEMS 224 (Frederic N. Cleaveland ed., Brookings Institution 1969).

[17] 1963 Staff Report, *supra* note 13, at viii.   [18] *Ibid.* at 5.

[19] *Ibid.* at 90. Clean Air Act, Pub. L. No. 88–206, § 5, 69 Stat. 322, 396 (1963).

powerful political constraint: the need to avoid usurping the traditional or "primary" role of the states.[20] "The philosophy of the Clean Air Act of 1963," wrote Senator Muskie, "was to encourage state, regional and local programs to control and abate pollution, while spelling out the authority of the national government to step into interstate situations with effective enforcement authority."[21] California, after all, had become a leader in responding to acute air issues confronting that state – particularly from automobile emissions. But other state and local governments did not similarly "respond [] adequately to this challenge," prompting Muskie to assert that "[i]t is clear that enforcement must be toughened if we are to meet the national deadlines. More tools are needed, and the Federal presence and backup authority must be increased."[22] After all, while before 1963 only eleven states had passed general air pollution legislation, all states adopted programs in the years before what would become the 1970 CAA.[23]

Yet, between 1963 and 1970, Senator Muskie became convinced of the need for a prescriptive program. Technological and economic feasibility for emission controls needed supplementing with a stronger implementation regime. Congress had become enamored of the prospect of promoting technologically based pollution-control standards. Indeed, judges in private common-law cases already had paved the way for exploring the relative economic and environmental merits of forcing emitters to install pollution-control technologies.[24] And Muskie listed several examples of when industry developed technology swiftly in response to governmental directives.[25] As a key Senate staffer engaged during the 1960s observed, "because [the 1963 Act] did not affirmatively press technology, the law, in a perverse turn, actually

---

[20] Ahlers, *supra* note 15, at 81, 84.

[21] Edmund S. Muskie, *The Role of the Federal Government in Air Pollution Control*, 10 ARIZ. L. REV. 17, 18 (1968). Although Muskie eventually accepted national ambient air quality standards, he initially favored affording states the primary responsibility for adopting emission standards (outside the context of automobile emissions standards). *See* Sidney Edelman, *Air Pollution Abatement Procedures under the Clean Air Act*, 10 ARIZ. L. REV. 30, 31(1968). Another attorney at the EPA noted how "federal *enforcement*" under the 1967 Act "was limited to *interstate* air pollution, except when federal action was requested by the governor of the state involved." Terry A. Trumbull, *Federal Control of Stationary Source Air Pollution*, 2 ECOLOGY L.Q. 283, 288 (1972).

[22] Serial No. 93–18, *supra* note 1, at 226.

[23] *See* Arthur C. Stern, *History of Air Pollution Legislation in the United States*, 32 J. AIR POLLUTION CONTROL ASS'N 44, 47–48 (1982). *See also* ARNOLD W. REITZ, JR., AIR POLLUTION CONTROL LAW: COMPLIANCE AND ENFORCEMENT 9–16 (Envt'l Law Inst. 2001).

[24] *See generally* DUNCAN MAYSILLES, DUCKTOWN SMOKE: THE FIGHT OVER ONE OF THE SOUTH'S GREATEST ENVIRONMENTAL DISASTERS (2011). For other examples involving the judiciary, *see* Dutton v. Rocky Mountain Phosphate, Inc., 450 P.2d 672, 674–76 (Mont. 1969); United States v. Luce, 141 F. 385, 422–23 (D. Del. 1905). Even if a defendant installed pollution-abatement equipment, the failure to establish that it "did everything reasonably possible to eliminate or minimize the damage" might justify not only compensatory damages but also punitive damages. McElwain v. Ga.-Pac. Corp., 421 P.2d 957, 959–60 (Or. 1966). In cases involving emissions allegedly violating a nuisance ordinance, the same considerations often applied. E.g., Koseris v. J.R. Simplot Co., 352 P.2d 235, 239 (Idaho 1960); State v. Lloyd A. Fry Roofing Co., 158 N.W.2d 851, 852–53 (Minn. 1968); State v. Mundet Cork Corp., 86 A.2d 1, 8 (N.J. 1952).

[25] Serial No. 93–18, *supra* note 1, at 227.

authorized restraint."[26] The 1965 legislation sought to reverse this by incentivizing new technology, focusing primarily on establishing standards for motor vehicles – albeit requiring that the agency first consider technical and economic feasibility.[27] But the need for broader legislation quickly became clear. Several events in 1966 underscored the urgency, including congressional hearings, a prominent national air pollution conference, and a 1966 thanksgiving air pollution episode in New York City.[28] And on January 30, 1967, President Johnson delivered his message, "Protecting Our National Heritage," where he not only touted the need for a better coordinated energy policy but also addressed at length the need to establish national emission levels. Some policymakers, though, feared that HEW already was considering sulfur oxide standards that threatened utilities' operations in some cities.[29]

Congress responded cautiously by passing the 1967 Air Quality Act, although shortly thereafter modifying it significantly.[30] In the first report mandated by that Act, the HEW explained the Act's charge.

> Under the act, [HEW] must first delineate broad atmospheric areas of the Nation ... Next, the Department must designate air quality control regions based on meteorological and other technical factors, as well as social and political factors. Concurrently, the Department must develop and publish air quality criteria indicating the extent to which air pollution is harmful to health and damaging to property, as well as detailed information on techniques for preventing and controlling air pollution ... States are then expected to develop ambient air quality standards and plans for implementing these standards in air quality control regions. The Department will review and evaluate these standards and plans, and once they are approved, the States will be expected to take action to control pollution sources in the manner outlined in their plans. If a State's efforts prove inadequate, the Secretary is empowered to initiate abatement action."[31]

In addition, utilities burning high-sulfur fuels secured a marginal victory when Congress required that the agency "reconsider its criteria for sulfur oxides."[32] This reconsideration generated considerable controversy, particularly among the coal industry; the agency nevertheless recommended a stringent 0.1 parts per million

[26] Thomas Jorling, *The Federal Law of Air Pollution*, in FEDERAL ENVIRONMENTAL LAW 1058, 1061 (Erica L. Dolgin & Thomas G.P. Guilbert eds., West 1974).

[27] 79 Stat. 992, Oct. 20, 1965. The 1963 Act was set to expire in 1966, and Congress extended it with Pub. L. No. 89–675, 80 Stat. 954, Oct. 15, 1966.

[28] STERN, *supra* note 5.

[29] J. CLARENCE DAVIES III, THE POLITICS OF POLLUTION 56, 156, 160–61 (Pegasus 1970) (in New York City, a 0.02 ppm of sulfur dioxide warranting a reduction of current emissions by 83 percent and a standard of 0.34 lb/MMBtu).

[30] Pub. Law No. 90–148, 91 Stat. 485, Nov. 21, 1967.

[31] First Report of the Secretary of Health, Education and Welfare to the United States Congress Pursuant to Pub. L. 90–148, The Air Quality Act of 1967, Progress in the Prevention and Control of Air Pollution, Doc. No. 92, 90th Cong., 2nd Sess. 2 (June 28, 1968) (hereinafter 1968 Report).

[32] DAVIES, *supra* note 29, at 57.

(ppm) over a 24-hour period, discussed later in this chapter.[33] California's 1967 standard for "adverse" consequences was 1 ppm for 1 hour or 0.3 ppm for 8 hours. By the second report, the Department recommended additional legislation favoring the "adoption of national applicable ambient air quality standards and national emission standards for major new stationary sources. In addition it added with respect to stationary source pollutants that may be extremely hazardous to health," it recommended "the application of national emission standards to existing, as well as new, sources."[34]

Yet, as consumer advocate Ralph Nader's classic 1970 study on air pollution chronicled, a dire need surfaced to address our "vanishing air."[35] When, therefore, these earlier efforts proved ineffective, Congress responded in December 1970 by passing Senator Muskie's Clean Air Act (CAA).

The CAA contained a suite of programs, many of which had the potential to affect the power sector. Nixon's reorganization plan created the EPA in December 1970, and the CAA delegated to the EPA robust authority for controlling air pollution emissions. The CAA's most comprehensive authority resides in its regulation of "criteria pollutants" under Title I of the CAA. Section 108 of the CAA directs the EPA to publish a list of air pollutants whose emissions will, in the EPA's judgment, "cause or contribute to air pollution which may reasonably be anticipated to endanger public health or welfare." Under this regime, the EPA issues criteria for those pollutants, identifying threshold levels for the pollutants' effects on public health and welfare (thus the term "criteria pollutants"). For each criteria pollutant, the EPA establishes both a primary (health-based) and a secondary (public welfare) national ambient air quality standard (NAAQS). These standards specify the maximum permissible level of an air pollutant in the ambient air, usually in parts per million measured hourly, daily, monthly, or annually. Based on the criteria, NAAQS are set at a level requisite to protect public health and public welfare, "allowing an adequate margin of safety." While establishing a NAAQS can have substantial legal and economic consequences, cost of compliance is not a congressionally permissible consideration when establishing a NAAQS. And the CAA requires a periodic (five-year) review of each NAAQS.

Once the EPA establishes a NAAQS, Section 110 requires that each state adopt and submit for EPA approval a plan for attaining and maintaining the ambient standard within the state (state implementation plan [SIP]). The SIP is the Act's principal regulatory mechanism: states must develop SIPs sufficient to attain public health and welfare–based ambient standards in each area of the state. A SIP's

---

[33] *Ibid.* at 161–69.

[34] Report of the Secretary of Health, Education, and Welfare, in Compliance with Pub. Law No. 90–148, Air Quality Act of 1967, National Emission Standards Study, Doc. 91–63, 91st Cong., 2nd Sess. iii (March 1970).

[35] JOHN C. ESPOSITO, VANISHING AIR: THE RALPH NADER STUDY GROUP REPORT ON AIR POLLUTION 81–83 (Grossman 1970).

essential function is to translate a limit on concentration of a pollutant in the ambient air into enforceable emission limitations (potentially applicable to thousands of individual sources) that are sufficient to satisfy the standard. Often this is a challenging task: a state must first determine what sources emit the pollutant in question (or its precursors) and in what amount (the "emission inventory"). Next, it must determine the emission reductions necessary to meet the standard and then determine the sources from which emission reductions will be required – in short, which industries will bear the economic brunt of reductions.

An EPA-approvable SIP must meet numerous statutory requirements for controlling criteria pollutant emissions (certain criteria pollutants, like ozone, are formed from chemical reactions of precursor pollutants emitted by mobile or stationary sources, in which SIPS also control emissions of the precursors from sources within the state), as well as monitoring, enforcement, and related requirements. A state must demonstrate through an emission inventory and modeling that its SIP's measures will attain and maintain compliance with the NAAQS. If a state fails to submit a compliant SIP, EPA must then promulgate a federal implementation plan (FIP) sufficient to bring the state into compliance. States, moreover, may employ standards that are more stringent than the federal standards.

Areas within a state that fail to meet a NAAQS are designated as "non-attainment areas." For these areas, a state must impose emission limitations and other measures on existing and new sources necessary to bring the area into attainment with the standard, within the Act's specified timeframes, including emission control and offset requirements for new and modified sources of the pollutant. "Attainment areas" (areas of the state in compliance with a specific NAAQS) must maintain compliance with the NAAQS. In addition, states must adopt emission limitations and other measures (principally applicable to new and modified stationary sources) to prevent significant deterioration of air quality ("PSD measures"). The Act further requires that SIPs include new source review (NSR) provisions, requiring preconstruction review and imposing technology-based standards on new or modified sources.

In addition to providing for EPA and state regulation of criteria pollutants through the NAAQS/SIP process, the CAA provides the EPA with authority to prescribe performance standards for large stationary sources, such as electric power plants. Section 111(b) directs that EPA designate categories of stationary sources that cause, or contribute significantly to, air pollution that may reasonably be anticipated to endanger public health or welfare and to prescribe standards of performance for new and modified sources within each such category. These new source performance standards (NSPS) must reflect the degree of emission limitation achievable under the best system of emission reduction EPA determines has been adequately demonstrated, considering, among other factors, the cost of achieving such reduction. Performance standards under Section 111 are typically expressed in terms of emissions per unit of input or output (e.g., pounds per million British thermal units [lb/MMBtu]) rather than emissions per period (e.g., tons per year).

As a corollary to Section 111(b), EPA may require, under Section 111(d), that states submit plans (like Section 110 SIPs) to control emissions of certain pollutants from existing, unmodified stationary sources in those categories designated under Section 111(b). Such pollutants can only be noncriteria pollutants and those not otherwise regulated under Section 112 as hazardous pollutants (and some also argue not emitted by source categories regulated under Section 112). Section 111(d) was the cornerstone of the now defunct Obama administration's Clean Power Plan and the goal of reducing GHG emissions from existing power plants.

Section 112, revised in the 1990 CAA Amendments, establishes a detailed and fairly prescriptive system for regulating stationary-source emissions of hazardous air pollutants (HAPs), including provisions for National Emission Standards for Hazardous Air Pollutants (NESHAPs) that implement Section 112's maximum available control technology (MACT) requirements. In 2012, for instance, after many years in development, EPA finalized its mercury and air toxics (MATS) rule, applicable to mercury and other HAP emissions from electric generating units.[36] The MATS rule has been mired in litigation, going all the way to the Supreme Court, and now back before the DC Circuit, only to be put on hold (as of this writing) as the Trump administration explores options for removing what has since become a significant driver for coal-fired power plant retirements.

A modern SIP also must contain "regional transport" or "good neighbor" provisions designed to prevent source emissions in one state from contributing significantly to a violation of a NAAQS in any other state.[37] This presents unique challenges. At the outset, establishing a causal connection between emissions in an upwind state and a NAAQS violation in a downwind state is difficult. The Supreme Court aptly opined how "pollutants do not emerge from the smokestacks of an upwind State and uniformly migrate downwind."[38] Next, EPA must demonstrate that its remedial action appropriately mitigates an upwind state's contributions to a downwind state's nonattainment of the NAAQS and that the mitigation burdens are apportioned correctly among states. These showings are cumbersome and fraught with legal and methodological pitfalls, often exploited by litigants. The EPA, for instance, has attempted in a series of formidable rulemakings to control transport of ozone and fine particulate matter in the

[36] Final Rulemaking, National Emission Standards for Hazardous Air Pollutants from Coal and Oil-Fired Electric Utility Steam Generating Units and Standards of Performance for Fossil-Fuel-Fired Electric Utility, Industrial-Commercial-Institutional, and Small Industrial-Commercial-Institutional Steam Generating Units, 77 Fed. Reg. 9,304 (Feb. 16, 2012).

[37] CAA, §§ 110(a)(2)(D), 126, 42 U.S.C. §§ 7410(a)(2)(D), 7426. The Act also establishes interstate transport commissions and gives the EPA direct authority to order individual stationary sources to reduce emissions if they significantly contribute to nonattainment in another state. CAA § 176A, 42 U.S.C. § 7506a.

[38] EPA v. EME Homer City Generation, 134 S. Ct. 1584 (2014).

eastern United States. Its two principal efforts entangled the agency in years of rulemakings and litigation.[39]

Also, not all harmful interstate transport results in a violation of an ambient air quality standard. The best example is acid deposition. SO_2 and NO_x emissions from coal-fired power plants and other sources in upwind states produce acid rain and other acid deposition in downwind states, even though there may be no violations of any ambient air quality standard in the downwind state. The pre-1990 CAA lacked a ready mechanism for addressing this type of pollution problem directly. The solution required a departure from the Act's general approach. Rather than requiring that EPA demonstrate that individual sources or sources in specific states contributed to acid deposition in downwind states, Congress in a newly crafted 1990 Title IV responded to the long-identified problem with acid deposition by enacting a national cap-and-trade program for all coal-fired power plants, as well as NO_x emission limitations.[40]

Finally, modern SIPs must also contain a host of other requirements. These include, for instance, provisions designed to mitigate visibility impairment and regional haze from stationary sources, including best available retrofit technology (BART) requirements, a 1990 Title V national operating permit program for major stationary sources designed to incorporate all emissions limitations applicable to the source, and various provisions in Title II governing emission standards for new motor vehicles and other mobile sources, as well as motor vehicle fuel standards.

The CAA, though, enjoys some characteristics of Scripture – Congress adds but does not delete chapters. The statute consequently has grown by accretion since its original enactment, as Congress enacted new regulatory requirements to remedy flaws or gaps in the original scheme. The 1977 CAA Amendments, for instance, added the prevention of significant deterioration (PSD) program to codify a judicial decision requiring that EPA protect air quality in attainment areas from deteriorating to the point of nonattainment.[41] The 1990 CAA Amendments expanded on the 1977 provisions by adding a suite of additional programs, such as the acid rain title discussed earlier, amendments to Section 112 establishing today's prescriptive hazardous air pollutant program (including requirements for MACT), and a national operating permit program for major stationary sources. Also, the 1990 CAA Amendments strengthened the visibility and regional haze programs and the interstate transport provisions.

[39] Cross-State Air Pollution Rule (CSAPR), 76 Fed. Reg. 48,208 (Aug. 8, 2011); EPA v. EME Homer City Generation, 134 S. Ct. 1584 (2014); EME Homer City Generation v. EPA, 795 F.3d 118 (D.C. Cir. 2015); North Carolina v. EPA, 550 F.3d 1176 (D.C. Cir. 2008); North Carolina v. EPA, 531 F.3d 896 (D.C. Cir. 2008); Rule to Reduce Interstate Transport of Fine Particulate Matter and Ozone (Clean Air Interstate Rule or CAIR), 70 Fed. Reg. 25,162 (May 12, 2005); Finding of Significant Contribution and Rulemaking for Certain States in Ozone Transport Assessment Group Region for Purposes of Reducing Regional Transport of Ozone, 63 Fed. Reg. 57,356 (Oct. 27, 1998).
[40] *Market-Based Solutions, Acid Rain and the Clean Air Act Amendments of 1990, in* JUDITH A. LAYZER, TRANSLATING VALUES INTO POLICY 414 (3rd edn, CQ Press 2012).
[41] Sierra Club v. Ruckelshaus, 344 F. Supp. 253, 256 (D.D.C. 1972), *aff'd*, Civ. No. 72–1528 (D.C. Cir. 1972), *aff'd by an equally divided Court sub nom.* Fri v. Sierra Club, 412 U.S. 541 (1973). For a historical explanation, *see* Jorling, *supra* note 26, at 1077–81.

Perhaps remarkable is that while Congress added these layers of new requirements, it left in place the existing regulatory substructure. As such, a large stationary
source, a power plant, for instance, is subject to the following limits:

- **From the 1970 Act:**New source performance standards (both for original
  construction and for modifications), limitations on emissions of noncriteria pollutants under Section 111(d), and state regulation of criteria
  pollutants under a SIP[42];
- **Added by the 1977 Amendments:**PSD limits, NSR requirements
  (including BACT or LAER), and visibility and regional haze requirements (including BART requirements)[43]; and
- **Added by the 1990 Amendments:**Allowance surrender requirements for
  SO_2 emissions and NO_x emission limitations under the acid rain program, regulation of SO_2 and NO_x emissions under regional transport
  programs, NESHAP and MACT requirements under Section 112 (if the
  EPA makes an "appropriate and necessary" finding), and enhanced
  requirements under the regional haze program.[44]

Arguably some of these later layers make earlier layers potentially redundant: for
example, BACT/LAER, in application, generally are more stringent than NSPS, yet
both standards – with different measures of compliance – must be satisfied. And
current interstate transport requirements applicable to SO_2 are more stringent than
the acid rain program's limits, rendering the acid rain program less of a constraint on
SO_2 emissions, even though sources subject to the program must continue to
surrender acid rain program allowances to cover their emissions. Sources subject
to the stringent SO_2 and NO_x limitations under the interstate transport rules may
also be subject to even more stringent emission limitations under the regional haze
program's BART requirements, and MACT requirements for HAPs under
Section 112 may require control technologies in addition to those required earlier.[45]

SIGNIFICANCE FOR THE ENERGY SECTOR

When in 1970 and thereafter coal dominated most conversations about energy
policy, as explained in Chapter 7, federal policymakers were well aware of the
CAA and assumed that the Act and its accent on promoting technology would either

---

[42] CAA §§ 110, 111, 42 U.S.C. §§ 7410, 7411.

[43] CAA §§ 160–69, 169A-B, 171-79B, 42 U.S.C. §§ 7470–79, 7491–92, 7501–9a.

[44] CAA §§ 112, 401–16, 169B, 42 U.S.C. §§ 7412, 7651–510, 7491–92. Under CAA § 112(n)(1), added by the
     1990 Amendments, EPA would regulate EGU HAPs if such regulation was "appropriate and neces-
     sary." 42 U.S.C. § 7412(n)(1). EPA so concluded in 2000 and reinforced in the 2012 MATS rule.
     Regulatory Finding on the Emissions of Hazardous Air Pollutants from Electric Utility Steam
     Generating Units, 65 Fed. Reg. 79,825 (Dec. 20, 2000).

[45] For a further elaboration on this point, *see* Robert R. Nordhaus, *Modernizing the Clean Air Act:
     Is There Life after 40?*, 33 ENERGY L. J. 365 (2012).

avert or mitigate any further environmental harm from increased coal usage. After all, when Congress passed the 1963 CAA, the two principal aspects of the "national air pollution problem" were "motor vehicle pollution and sulfur oxides pollution arising from the burning of coal and fuel oil."[46] Again as noted in Chapter 7, sulfur oxides were considered acutely harmful to human health and the environment and presented the most visible challenge for the energy industry, which at the time was almost doubling "its output every 10 years."[47]

Sulfur oxides, along with particulate matter and nitrogen oxides, garnered the most attention. When Congress passed the CAA, for instance, studies suggested that adverse health risks occurred when annual mean concentration levels of sulfur dioxide exceeded 0.04 parts per million (ppm). Chicago's level in 1968 was 0.12 ppm, whereas Philadelphia was at 0.08 ppm.[48] Many cities responded by restricting or limiting the burning of high-sulfur fuel. In Pittsburgh by 1950, residential customers already had reduced by half the amount of bituminous coal used for heating, shifting from coal to natural gas (from outside the state). This, of course, occurred before the infamous *Phillips* case discussed in Chapter 5 and a shrinking interstate market for natural gas.

A similar scenario unfolded in other major cities, whether before or after 1950.[49] During the late 1960s, New York City adopted a program for limiting the maximum sulfur content for fuels – albeit somewhat hampered by diminishing supplies of low-sulfur fuel. Even so, Consolidated Edison increased how much natural gas or low-sulfur oil it was burning, and in 1968, the city had lowered sulfur oxide emissions "by at least 250,000 tons a year, or 28 percent of the total, and the amount of particulates by about 9,000 tons, or 10 percent of the total," expecting considerable further reductions the following year.[50] Between 1964 and 1970, consequently, New York already had reduced by half its SO_2 concentrations.[51]

It would seem, therefore, that commensurate with the CAA's passage, restrictions on emissions of sulfur oxides and particulate matter from the energy sector would be unassailable – particularly considering annual growth in energy consumption and potential risk to human health and the environment. When in April 1971 EPA released the NAAQS for sulfur oxides and particulate matter, Administrator William Ruckelshaus called them "tough." The criteria document from 1969 formed the basis for EPA's sulfur standard (sulfur dioxide served as the measure for the sulfur oxide standard), which for a 24-hour period the agency set at 365 micrograms per cubic meter (0.14 ppm) not to be exceeded more than once a year. It established a corresponding secondary standard at 0.1 ppm. The comparable

[46] 1968 Report, *supra* note 31, at 1.   [47] Serial No. 93–18, *supra* note 1, at 252   [48] *Ibid.* at 247.
[49] TARR, *supra* note 6, at 228–29.
[50] LEONARD B. DWORSKY, CONSERVATION IN THE UNITED STATES: A DOCUMENTARY HISTORY: POLLUTION 759 (Chelsea House 1971).
[51] INDUR GOKLANY, CLEARING THE AIR: THE REAL STORY OF THE WAR ON AIR POLLUTION 31 (Cato Institute 1999).

primary particulate matter standard was 260 micrograms per cubic meter, and the secondary standard was 150 micrograms per cubic meter. EPA in October added that significant health effects would likely occur for SO_2 at 1.0 ppm per 24-hour average for particulate matter at 1,000 micrograms per cubic meter per 24-hour average.

While identifying seven metropolitan areas that might struggle to meet these standards, Ruckelshaus indicated that most regions could satisfy the standards by switching to low-sulfur fuels or employing, for particulate matter, existing technology for controlling emissions. Signaling out New York City, he added that it would need a 300 percent increase in natural gas use to comply with the particulate matter standard. Six other metropolitan areas would need a roughly 7.5 percent increase in natural gas usage. This seemed consistent with the national trend between 1965 and 1972 toward significant increases in the use of natural gas and oil by electric utilities.

And Nixon's June 1971 Special Message to Congress on Energy Resources only underscored the need either for fuel switching or for arduously working on new technology for reducing emissions. Nixon observed how a clean energy program required reducing sulfur emissions from coal and oil-fired facilities and that the nation needed a "new technology which will make it possible to remove the sulfur." He reiterated his message from the previous year, while Congress debated the CAA, that we should consider a sulfur oxide emissions charge. Most utilities generating coal-fired electricity were burning high-sulfur coal produced in the eastern United States.[52] Such a dramatic, albeit unsuccessful, proposal reflected the urgency of addressing sulfur oxide emissions. Many CAA state implementation plans called for achieving both primary (health-based) and secondary (protecting public welfare) standards by 1975, a milestone that even the EPA by 1972 believed – absent a tax on sulfur – was not likely "attainable" – for lack of enough desulfurization facilities, sufficient low-sulfur coal or oil, or available natural gas supplies.[53]

The EPA soon began relaxing states' obligation to control their sources of pollutants such as SO_x from existing power plants. The 1970 Act required that SIPs provide for attaining primary standards within three years of EPA approval of a SIP. The EPA could extend that date by another two years on a governor's request. This became a meddlesome and often litigated issue during the Nixon administration. HEW Secretary Elliot Richardson warned Congress in November 1970 that the Senate CAA Amendments only allowed for a judicially permitted one-year extension on a governor's request. He found this unworkable and suggested instead that the EPA be allowed to extend the deadline if "adequate control technology is not

[52] By 1980, EPA would testify that total sulfur emissions in the United States would rise from 22 million tons in 1940 to about 30 million tons in 1980, with the principal difference "that electric utilities in 1940 accounted for only 3 million of that 22 million tons," while in 1980 "they account for 19½ million tons." Environmental Effects of the Increased Use of Coal, Hearings before the Subcommittee on Environmental Pollution, of the Committee on Environment and Public Works, U.S. Senate, Serial No. 96–H45, 96th Cong., 2nd Sess., 17 (March 19, April 21, 24, 1980).

[53] EPA, Approval and Promulgation of Implementation Plans, 37 Fed. Reg. 1–942, 10843–44 (May 31, 1972).

available and not likely to be available." Within months of the CAA's enactment, EPA issued standards for SO_2, particulate matter, and NO_x, all affecting the power sector. States had until roughly January 1972 to submit plans identifying measures that would ensure attainment – again from sources such as power plants. The EPA then developed regulations outlining the state submission process.[54] One EPA staffer would later write in 1972 that "[i]t is doubtful that state implementation plans can provide all the components required by the 1970 Amendments."[55]

Secondary standards for SO_2 suffered from the outset. Those standards only had to be achieved within a "reasonable" time, and states could request an additional eighteen-month extension for submitting a SIP for secondary standards. But they are still quite important. Standards for SO_2 served as a surrogate for controlling sulfates. Sulfates are not only the prime ingredient for acid rain, but as reported in 1973, "many environmental health specialists have known of their potential for trouble for years."[56] In the words of one of the principal congressional staffers involved in creating the CAA, Thomas Jorling, secondary standards are critical for protecting the "basic integrity of the biosphere," and yet by 1973 EPA bowed to states and the electric industry in what it would accept. The agency altered how it would measure compliance, allowing the use of tall stacks and intermittent control systems (ICSs). This, according to Jorling, "'pack[ed]' the biosphere with SO_2 and exacerbat-[ed] the acid rain effect," all as a nod toward the energy crisis and the need to allow burning high-sulfur fuel.[57]

The EPA, in short, exhibited a willingness to provide states with sufficient flexibility to adopt the most suitable control strategy for their region(s), even if states could not submit timely compliant SIPs. In 1972, EPA Administrator Ruckelshaus testified how states could require that sources switch fuels, use low-sulfur fuels, or install technology such as wet scrubbers for removing sulfur oxides from the emission stream.[58] The agency, moreover, would consider extending compliance when a control strategy was not possible "because the necessary

[54] 36 Fed. Reg. 6,680 (April 7, 1971); 36 Fed. Reg. 15,486 (Aug. 14, 1971). This late release date, only months before SIPs were due, left states in a quandary and reportedly occurred because of intervening OMB review. *See* CHARLES O. JONES, CLEAN AIR ACT: THE POLICES AND POLITICS OF POLLUTION CONTROL 230–47 (Univ. of Pittsburgh Press 1975).

[55] Terry A. Trumbull, *Federal Control of Stationary Source Air Pollution*, 2 ECOL. L. Q. 283, 310 (1972).

[56] John F. Burby, *Environmental Report/Sulfates Present Major New Problem in Growing Debate over Clean Air Act*, NAT'L. J., Sept. 22, 1973, 1412, at 1414.

[57] Jorling, *supra* note 26, at 1085, 1092 ("Both the ICS and tall stack techniques are based on the premise that dilution is the solution to pollution, which out-of-sight, out-of-mind mentality apparently is now considered by EPA to be an acceptable control strategy").

[58] *See generally* Implementation of the Clean Air Act Amendments of 1970, Part 1 (Title I), Hearings before the Subcommittee on Air and Water Pollution, Committee on Public Works, U.S. Senate, Serial No. 92–H31, 92nd Cong., 2nd Sess. 223–56 (Feb. 1972). The following year Russell Train described the administration's 1972 Clean Fuel Policy as urging state relaxation of secondary CAA standards while encouraging coal production and accompanying techniques such as gasification, liquefaction, and flue gas technologies. Low-sulfur western coal was considered "quite a ways off." Clean Air Oversight, Part 1, Hearings before the Subcommittee on Public Health and the

technology or alternatives will not be available soon enough to permit such compliance."[59]

Yet, by August 1971, the EPA already had determined that not enough low-sulfur fuels were available for the power sector. That, after all, had been the conclusion of the 1970 report from the National Research Council. The Council added, therefore, that "the reduction of SO_2 emissions from stationary combustion sources, in the next 5 to 20 years, will depend very largely on the development, demonstration, and application of a combination of technologies designed to prevent the sulfur in coal and petroleum products from reaching the atmosphere through the combustion processes."[60]

This unfortunately left states in a quandary when developing SIPs capable of complying with the new sulfur and particulate matter NAAQ standards. Some states with more stringent SO_2 regulations responded by revising their plans (the Act allows for more stringent state standards). Several states concerned about existing power plants worked assiduously with their utilities to develop a schedule for installing technologies for reducing sulfur and particulate matter emissions. Compliance with the NAAQS, though, often was pushed off. In New Mexico, for instance, the Four Corners power plant delayed for at least eight years having to install equipment to control sulfur oxides and particulate matter.[61] Almost immediately, Congress examined the Nixon administration's CAA implementation (e.g., OMB review and tinkering) by convening hearings on EPA's approach for ensuring compliant SIPs. The EPA's principal expert at the time, John Quarles, describes these events vividly in *Cleaning Up America*. He notes, for instance, how the Natural Resources Defense Council's air expert, Dick Ayers, claimed that the EPA's approach to SIPs has "mostly become little more than weak-kneed apologies for each state's present

Environment, Committee on Interstate and Foreign Commerce, U.S. House, Serial No. 93–62, 93rd Cong., 1st Sess. 7 (Sept. 1973). EPA, by 1973, testified how it previously concluded that adequate supplies of low-sulfur coal were not available. *Ibid.* 13, 16 (Acting Administrator John A. Quarles). *See also* The Fuel Shortage and the Clean Air Act, Hearing before the Subcommittee on Air and Water Pollution, Committee on Public Works, U.S. Senate, Serial No. 93–H26, 93rd Cong., 1st Sess. (Nov. 1973). Relationship of Energy and Fuel Shortages to the Nation's Internal Development, Hearings before the Subcommittee on Flood Control and Internal Development, Committee on Public Works, U.S. House, Serial No. 92–47, 92nd Cong., 2nd Sess. 329 (Aug. 1972).

59   36 Fed. Reg. 15,485, 15493 (Aug. 14, 1971). A state could request a one-year extension on the application of any control strategy to a stationary source.

60   Ad Hoc Panel on Control of Sulfur Dioxide from Stationary Combustion Sources, National Research Council, Abatement of Sulfur Oxide Emissions from Stationary Sources 2 (1970). Interior Secretary Morton in 1972 similarly cautioned that "most of the coal found east of the Mississippi and near the major markets is too high in sulfur content to meet the new environmental standards, while the low-sulfur western coal entails high transportation costs." Fuel and Energy Resources, 1972, Part 1, Hearings before the Committee on Interior and Insular Affairs, on Fuel and Energy Resources, Serial No. 92–42, U.S. House, 92nd Cong., 2nd Sess. 10, 57, 66 (April 1972).

61   *See* Winston Harrington, THE REGULATORY APPROACH TO AIR QUALITY MANAGEMENT: A CASE STUDY OF NEW MEXICO 36–41, 50, 102 (Resources for the Future 1981).

program."[62] Testifying later in the week with reporters and cameras all trained on him, Administrator Ruckelshaus on his first day of testimony denied OMB's involvement, indicating instead that he, reading and implicitly parroting a letter written by Senator Muskie, decided that states should have flexibility to frame their control strategies based on local conditions and issues.[63] His testimony was well received and most assuredly delivered in earnest, but on reflection, EPA's initial approach to SIPs, including not requiring that states with regions in attainment still protect air quality, became an early hindrance to offsetting the adverse effects of the nation's shift toward more coal-fired electric generation.

Absent economically available low-sulfur fuel, the principal other strategy for states would be requiring that utilities install control technology. Removing sulfur from coal or oil requires desulfurizing either the fuel or the flue gas and breaking down the element's compound molecular structure. How much sulfur must be removed, though, may depend on how much sulfur is in the fuel to begin with. For instance, coal's sulfur content can range roughly between 0.2 percent and upward of 10 percent by weight. Writing in 1971, Alan Gilpin opined how sulfur dioxide removal from flue gases "has concerned power stations authorities in all countries over many decades."[64] As of the CAA's passage, a host of scrubbing processes had been tested for removing sulfur from the flue gas, and while some had been applied on a commercial scale, technological limitations remained.[65] Most available processes employed "wet" scrubbing, or using a limestone slurry mixture to remove the sulfur, and produced a sulfur-bearing sludge as a by-product. Later a "dry" scrubbing process would emerge, in which a reagent (lime or sodium carbonate, for instance) could be injected into the flue gas for bonding with the sulfur dioxide. The EPA informed states that scrubbing could feasibly clean stack gas with about 70 percent removal, allowing bituminous coal to produce about 0.7 percent sulfur.[66]

When issuing its August 1971 regulations governing SIP submittals, EPA observed how different regions and circumstances would likely dictate the type of control strategy, such as the use of low-sulfur fuels. For areas where such fuels might not be easily available, it acknowledged the possible need for planning and a phase-in compliance period. Imported residual oil, for instance, capable of being desulfurized to 0.3 percent sulfur, might only be available along the coasts – and its cost was rising. And the Agency's own estimates suggested that only limited tonnages of

---

[62] JOHN QUARLES, CLEANING UP AMERICA: AN INSIDER'S VIEW OF THE ENVIRONMENTAL PROTECTION AGENCY 82 (Houghton Mifflin 1976).

[63] *Ibid.* at 87. [64] GILPIN, *supra* note 5, at 38.

[65] AIR POLLUTION CONTROL: PART 1 125 (Werner Strauss ed., John Wiley & Sons 1971). *See also AIR POLLUTION AND CLEAN ENERGY* (Charanjit Rai and Lloyd A. Spielman, eds. American Institute of Chemical Engineers 1976). In 1970, the National Resources Council reported "that industrially proven technology for the control of sulfur oxides resulting from fossil fuel combustion does not now exist. Only one of the several processes under development has been installed in 100-MW or larger boilers, and it has operated only intermittently." Ad Hoc Panel, *supra* note 60, at 42.

[66] 36 Fed. Reg. at 15,496.

0.7 percent or less sulfur coal was then being mined, mostly in the west and not easily or cheaply transported to eastern markets. By May 1972, the EPA concluded that satisfying the standards by 1975 would require sufficiently available supplies of clean (low-sulfur) fuels, and yet, "these naturally clean fuels are not likely to be available in quantities necessary to meet the projected demand." Indeed, it warned that "[g]iven the limits on the supply of naturally clean fuels in the short run, the well publicized shortage of natural gas in this country, and the physically disruptive task of substituting the use of huge amounts of clean fuels by energy producers and users at the time when traditional fuels, such as natural gas, are in short supply, it is apparent that the Nation faces a difficult task."[67] The Agency added that absent Congress passing a then-pending sulfur tax, it seemed unlikely that the standards could be achieved within the Act's timeframe. To this end, the EPA encouraged Congress to develop energy policies promoting available supplies of clean fuels.

EPA, moreover, attempted to soften aspects of the Act. Most states hit the Act's deadline for SIP submittals, but some states received various extensions, and their SIPs allowed for control strategies promoting interstate transport. Georgia's SIP, for instance, allowed power plants to control emissions of sulfur dioxide and particulate matter by using tall stacks, or throwing the emissions higher into the air and allowing the pollutants to be dispersed less locally. When the Natural Resources Defense Council challenged EPA's resolution of Georgia's SIP, the Fifth Circuit opined that Congress did "not contemplate control of pollution from new sources or of hazardous pollutants by dispersion techniques, or by any other techniques besides emission limitation."[68] A blanket reliance on tall stacks would, according to the court, flout the nondegradation policy the judiciary forced EPA to adopt. When the EPA and Georgia then revisited the state's SIP and reliance on tall stacks, some stacks already were under construction. Some of those stacks then justified the state and EPA's conclusion that the SIP would attain compliance with NAAQS. This time around the court again condemned tall stacks but declined to preclude their use – reasoning that it would not apply its earlier ruling retroactively.[69] This fight over

---

[67] 37 Fed. Reg. 10,843, 10,843–44 (May 31, 1972).

[68] The court did not preclude a tall stack strategy but required that it satisfy conditions. Natural Resources Defense Council, Inc. v. EPA, 489 F.2d 390, 407 (5th Cir. 1974), *vacated in part by* NRDC v. EPA, 516 F.2d 488 (5th Cir. 1975). In Train v. NRDC, 421 U.S. 60 (1975), the Court affirmed EPA's policy allowing state variances for sources unable to comply with the SIP's emission standards.

[69] Natural Resources Defense Council v. EPA, 529 F.2d 755 (5th Cir. 1976). By this time, the administration, among other things, had proposed a ten-year interim intermittent control systems strategy that would support using tall stacks – a move that the environmental community claimed would "undermine the program to install sulfur oxide control equipment" and "reduce the cost of the energy development of the West." Clean Air Act Amendments, 1975, Part 2, Hearings before the Subcommittee on Health and the Environment, of the Committee on Interstate and Foreign Commerce, U.S. House, on Titles V and VI of H.R. 2633 & H.R. 2650, 94th Cong., 1st Sess., Serial No. 94–26, at 709 (March 1975). Opening remarks at the hearing suggested that of the 394 existing coal-fired power plants, 194 were in compliance but that by 1980 only "222 out of a possible 625 plants would be in compliance." *Ibid.* Part 1, at 2.

Georgia's SIP mirrored other SIP challenges involving power plants and reached the Supreme Court, when the Court, in 1976, addressed whether the EPA could consider economic and technological infeasibility when approving or rejecting a SIP.[70]

Second, EPA's approach to establishing a technology standard for electric power plants devolved into debates about commercially available technologies and cost. The NSPS program authorized the EPA to establish a standard based on "the degree of emission limitation achievable through the application of the best system of emission reduction [considering cost] the Administrator determines has been adequately demonstrated." What could be "adequately demonstrated" and considering "cost" would prove problematic. The EPA skirted the issue in December 1971 when it set the first NSPS for fossil fuel utilities at 1.2 lb/MMBtu, but did not further identify any standard for compliance – such as scrubbing. And while the 1971 NSPS applied to plant modifications, existing plants that switched fuels could avoid the NSPS under EPA's definition of modification, which excluded facilities that used an "alternative fuel" if it had been "designed to accommodate such alternative use."[71] This approach mirrored what was already happening with the trend toward low-sulfur fuels and favored low-sulfur coal where available – such as in Wyoming, Montana, and North Dakota.

By April 1973, Nixon recounted how fuel competition and environmental concerns hampered coal's consumption.

> Production of coal has been limited not only by competition from natural gas – a competition which has been artificially induced by Federal price regulation – but also by emerging environmental concerns and mine health and safety requirements. In order to meet environmental standards, utilities have shifted to natural gas and imported low-Sulphur fuel oil. The problem is compounded by the fact that some low-Sulphur coal resources are not being developed because of uncertainty about Federal and State mining regulations.[72]

But Nixon continued by warning how an unnecessarily stringent implementation of the 1970 CAA would potentially "prevent the use of up to 155 million tons of coal per year."[73]

Nixon singled out the CAA secondary air quality standards for sulfur, which he said should be implemented judiciously rather than by otherwise requiring strict compliance by 1975. (Under the CAA, primary health-based standards had to be implemented on a fixed schedule, but states and the EPA enjoyed greater flexibility for secondary standards.) Here he cited his EPA Administrator's message to states

---

[70] *See* Duquesne Light Co. v. EPA, 522 F.2d 1186 (3d Cir. 1975), *vacated by* Environmental Protection Agency v. Duquesne Light Co., 427 U.S. 902 (1976) (remanded considering Union Electric Co. v. EPA, 427 U.S. 246 (1976)). The *Union Electric* Court upheld EPA's judgment that it lacked authority to consider economic or technological infeasibility.

[71] Standards of Performance for New Stationary Sources, 36 Fed. Reg. 24,877 (Dec. 23, 1971).

[72] Richard Nixon, Special Message to the Congress on Energy Policy, April 18, 1973.   [73] *Ibid.*

that they should avoid forcing utilities to use low-sulfur fuel during periods of shortage, unless necessary to achieve primary rather than secondary air quality standards.

Controlling potential future sulfur oxide emissions from power plants became even more challenging after the 1973 oil embargo and passage of the Energy Supply and Environmental Coordination Act of 1974, discussed in previous chapters. While acknowledging the need to protect public health, Congress barred some power plants from burning natural gas or oil as their primary fuel source. It coupled this with authorizing the issuance of compliance date extensions and suspensions of compliance with secondary standards. The 1975 Energy Policy and Conservation Act furthered those goals by incentivizing underground low-sulfur coal mining – if EPA certified that the coal could be used in compliance with the CAA.

Consequently, the likelihood of increased coal usage, coupled with the desire not to retard it, sharpened attention on emission controls. The news media ran full-page advertisements debating "the virtues and deficiencies of systems of control" and the "problems of energy supply and demand."[74] A March 1975 report by the National Academy of Science's Commission on National Resources promoted the use of scrubbers but favored additional flexibility, including considering the circumstances of each power plant. In July 1975, Federal Energy Administration (FEA) Deputy Administrator John Hill testified how increased reliance "on coal in the future may prevent substantial reductions nationwide in sulfur dioxide emissions from power plants." But tempering these remarks, he intimated how perhaps the country's concern over sulfates was "not great" nationally and further added how the cost for compliance might top $11 billion in expenditures for a pollutant that itself may not be as problematic. He warned Congress that "premature implementation of a sulfate control strategy could interfere with energy independence and cost the American people billions of dollars over the next decade with questionable health and environmental benefits."[75]

As the nation's production and consumption of energy fuels in the utility industry veered away from oil and natural gas between 1970 and 1977, Congress entertained hearings confronting questions about the NSPS program for electric utilities, eventually culminating in the 1977 CAA Amendments. It had been the trend toward increased natural gas usage that EPA attributed to declining SO_2 levels, and the shift

---

[74] A Report by the Commission on Natural Resources, National Academy of Sciences, National Academy of Engineering, National Research Council, Prepared for the Committee on Public Works, U.S. Senate, Pursuant to S. Res. 135, Air Quality and Stationary Source Emission Control, Serial No. 94-4, 94th Cong., 1st Sess. xvii (March 1975).

[75] Research and Development Related to Sulfates in the Atmosphere, Hearings before the Subcommittee on the Environment. and the Atmosphere, Committee on Science and Technology, U.S. House, Serial No. 39, 94th Cong., 1st Sess. 638–39 (July 1975). For FEA's involvement in the effects of sulfur oxides, *see ibid.* at 640 (Electrical Utilities, the Clean Air Act Amendments, and Sulfates); *ibid.* at 647 (Tabershaw/Cooper Associates, Inc., Preliminary Report: A Critical Evaluation of Current Research Regarding Health Criteria for Sulfur Oxides: A Technical Report Prepared for the Federal Energy Administrator [April 1975]).

back to high-sulfur fuel and having states relax their SO_2 regulations posed potential threats several years out. The Carter administration's energy plan discussed in previous chapters focused in large measure on increasing coal usage – and convincing Congress and perhaps themselves that technology would avert any adverse environmental threats. Coal by 1976 accounted for roughly 38 percent of the country's total generating capacity and about 46.3 percent of total electrical energy production.[76] EPA Administrator Douglas Costle testified how the nation's increased use of coal had to be offset by effective environmental measures.[77] Ensuring technological controls, therefore, became critical with natural gas shortages and passage of the Power Plants and Industrial Fuel Use Act of 1978 – designed to shift utilities away from burning oil and gas. And the 1977 CAA Amendments required that EPA revise the SO_2 NSPS within a year.[78]

In their path-breaking study *Clean Coal Dirty Air*, Bruce Ackerman and William Hassler show how special interests combined with bureaucratic malaise and environmental interests to hamper the NSPS program.[79] They detail how Secretary Schlesinger initially justified Carter's energy plan by relying on universal scrubbing to avoid environmental and health threats (the Department of Energy [DOE] later questioned universal scrubbing). Environmentalists favored universal scrubbing as a mechanism for protecting clean areas of the country; eastern coal interests, often associated with high-sulfur coal, similarly favored universal scrubbing as a market equalizer against low-sulfur western coal. Anything lower than a proposed alternative standard of 0.55 lb/MMBtu and 85 percent scrubbing efficiency, for instance, would likely require using western low-sulfur coal.

Consequently, establishing a sulfur standard and assessing the merits of scrubbing presented the administration with an economic, environmental, and political decision of some magnitude. A White House regulatory review group, established by a 1978 Carter executive order and under the leadership of Council on Economic Advisors member William Nordhaus, suggested that a lower standard and perhaps partial scrubbing might be more effective and economic. While the EPA Administrator initially favored universal scrubbing at a 90 percent level, intense lobbying described in contemporary news accounts witnessed him change toward

---

[76]   Sierra Club v. Costle, 657 F.2d 298, 313 n.9 (D.C. Cir. 1981).

[77]   National Energy Act: Hearings on H.R. 6831, H.R. 687, H.R. 1562, H.R. 2088, H.R. 2818, H.R. 3317, H.R. 3664, and H.R. 6600 before the Subcommittee on Energy and Power, U.S. House Committee on Interstate and Foreign Commerce, Part 3, 95th Cong., 1st Sess. 109, 111–15 (1977).

[78]   Sierra Club sued when EPA was going to miss that date, and an agreement eventually required that the standard be finalized by the summer of 1979.

[79]   Bruce A. Ackerman & William T. Hassler, Clean Coal Dirty Air: Or How the Clean Air Act Became a Multibillion-Dollar Bail-Out for High-Sulfur Coal Producers and What Should be Done About It (Yale Univ. Press 1981). Another excellent account is William C. Banks, *EPA Bends to Industry Pressure on Coal NSPS – and Breaks*, 9 Ecology L. Q. 67 (1980). *See also* Richard E. Ayers & David D. Doniger, *New Source Standard for Power Plants II: Consider the Law*, 3 Harv. Envtl. L. Rev. 63 (1979); Daniel B. Badger, Jr., *New Source Standard for Power Plants I: Consider the Costs*, 3 Harv. Envtl. L. Rev. 48 (1979).

favoring retaining the 1.2 lb/MMBtu standard and a flexible approach of sulfur removal of between 70 and 90 percent based on the coal's sulfur content.[80] Secretary Schlesinger, too, favored relaxing the standard and avoiding mandatory scrubbing – allowing instead intermittent control strategies such as tall stacks.[81] The EPA, after all, had informed Congress in 1977 that SO_2 was no longer a serious issue confronting metropolitan areas.[82]

Even Congress in September 1979 responded to the open dialogue between the DOE and the EPA by conducting hearings.[83] A Sierra Club witness testified how the "principal threat to the environment" would "come primarily from new power-plants," rendering EPA's NSPS for SO_2 of critical importance. For existing power plants, the witness warned that EPA's modeling showed that pre-1970 plants would become a primary SO_2 contributor by the turn of the century. And the resulting sulfates and interstate transport in the East and Midwest would become dramatic – a threat EPA recognized.

EPA enjoyed enough leeway, however, because allegedly sufficient uncertainty surrounded the health effects of sulfur dioxides, EPA's original SO_2 criteria, as well as the state of technology. The agency's last-minute solution was twofold. It would accept a new, cheaper form of scrubbing – dry scrubbing with only 70 percent efficiency – and a new 0.6 lb/MMBtu standard and alternatively requiring 90 percent scrubbing at the higher 1.2 lb/MMBtu standard. Reportedly, "seventy-five percent of the Nation's coal reserves will not have to meet the 90 percent standard."[84] While the DC Circuit subsequently upheld EPA's decision, it criticized the Agency and its lack of supporting data.[85] Congress, too, had compromised in the 1977 CAA Amendments by including Section 125, which afforded some flexibility on the use of locally mined coal when "necessary to prevent or minimize significant local or

---

[80] *See* Margot Hornblower, *EPA Will Relax Pollution Rules for Coal Power*, WASH. POST, May 5, 1979, at A1. For GAO's critique of EPA's approach, *see* GENERAL ACCOUNTING OFFICE, AIR QUALITY: DO WE REALLY KNOW WHAT IT IS? (May 31, 1979). The previous year, in the context of SIP development for PSD compliance, a similar issue surfaced when Carter administration economists feared that new PSD regulations would impose too high a cost on industry. *See* Bill Richards and Helen Dewar, *EPA Is Pressed to Relax Clean Air Rules in Fight on Inflation*, WASH. POST, June 1, 1978, at A2. Congressional hearings mined much of the issues. E.g., Oversight: Effect of the Clean Air Act Amendment on New Energy Technologies and Resources, Hearings before the Subcommittee on Fossil and Nuclear Energy Research, Development, Committee on Science and Technology, U.S. House, Serial No. 70, 95th Cong., 2nd Sess. (April 1978).

[81] Margot Hornblower, *Key EPA Aid Raps Schlesinger on Coal Burning*, WASH. POST, June 22, 1979, at A12.

[82] Progress in the Prevention and Control of Air Pollution in 1976, Annual Report of the Administrator of the Environmental Protection Agency to the Congress of the United States, Serial No. 95–75, 95th Cong., 1st Sess. 2, 14 (Sept. 1977).

[83] Clean Air Act and Increased Coal Use: Environmental Protection Agency Oversight, Hearings before a Subcommittee of the Committee on Government Operations, U.S. House, 96th Cong., 1st Sess. (Sept. 1979).

[84] Sierra Club v. Costle, 657 F.2d 298, 313 (D.C. Cir. 1981).

[85] 44 Fed. Reg. 33,580 (June 11, 1979); Sierra Club v. Costle, 657 F.2d 298, 354 (D.C. Cir. 1981).

regional economic disruption or unemployment."[86] Indeed, Murray Energy invoked this section when challenging the Obama administration's Clean Power Plan.[87] With Congress's nod toward eastern coal and EPA's relaxed standard, the coal industry called the NSPS result a "big victory" for America.[88]

The indirect beneficiaries of universal 70 percent scrubbing and a somewhat lower NSPS standard were older, high-sulfur-content coal-burning power plants. The NSPS program only applied to new or modified sources, and Congress withdrew the authority to issue a NSPS for SO_2 or particulate matter from existing power plants. The 1970 Congress contemplated that pre-1970 power plants would be subject to SIP-based controls for ensuring NAAQs compliance. But such SIP implementation lagged, particularly with continual challenges to the standards. And, for air quality control regions in compliance with the NAAQs, it took litigation and eventually amendments in 1977 to codify the PSD program for these areas. By 1980, reportedly only forty existing power plants had installed scrubbers.[89] The result, explain Ackerman and Hassler, was to induce utilities to continue operating their older plants rather than invest in costly scrubbing – a result they suggest may not have occurred if the EPA had more thoroughly explored larger regional rather than local (air quality control region) compliance, the actual health effects of sulfates, or the various tradeoffs and cost/benefit analyses of allowing coal washing or just using low-sulfur coal.

Next, the 1970 CAA "grandfathering" policy – carried forward in subsequent amendments – is today frequently cited as one the Acts' principal design flaws. Congress's 1970 approach focused attention on federal technology-based performance standards for new or *modified* facilities, on the theory that advanced pollution-control equipment could be most economically installed when a facility is constructed or is otherwise undergoing major changes. For this reason, the 1970 new source performance standards applied only to *new* and *modified* stationary sources. Modification was defined as a *physical or operational change that results in an increase in emissions.* Existing, unmodified sources were not subject to NSPS. Their emissions of criteria pollutants were to be regulated – if at all – under SIPs, and their emissions of noncriteria, non-HAP pollutants were to be regulated by the states under the rarely used "SIP-like" process prescribed in Section 111(d). The presumption was that these facilities, when retired at the end of their useful life, would be replaced by new facilities fully subject to NSPS.

---

[86] Pub. L. 95–95, 91 Stat. 685, 723 (Aug. 7, 1977). The following year Congress tempered the provision. National Energy Conservation Policy Act of 1978, Pub. L. 96–619, 661, 92 Stat. 3206 (1978).

[87] Murray Energy Corp. v. EPA, 861 F.3d 529 (4th Cir. 2017). Congressional hearings investigated the availability of low-sulfur coal along the East Coast. Low-sulfur eastern coal existed – often in deeper, costlier-to-mine deposits and possibly more profitable for use in steel production.

[88] Margot Hornblower, *EPA Issues Rules on Power Plant Coal Emissions*, WASH. POST, May 26, 1979, at A1.

[89] Philip Shabecoff, *Efforts to Soften Rules for Coal Seems Likely*, N. Y. TIMES, Nov. 18, 1980, at D1.

The 1977 CAA Amendments carried the distinction between *new* (or *modified*) sources and unmodified existing sources forward into the newly established PSD program. That program, together with the more stringent parallel program for new or modified sources in nonattainment areas, is today commonly known as the New Source Review (NSR) program. The NSR program imposes preconstruction permit requirements on new or modified major stationary sources. And it requires that sources in PSD areas employ the best available control technology (BACT), while sources in nonattainment areas must satisfy, along with other requirements, the lowest achievable emission rate (LAER) standard. Importantly, existing sources could escape the bulk of this regulation if their owners could successfully argue that no modification had occurred at the source.

And the story goes that many did. Quite cogently, Richard Revesz and his colleague portray, in their book, *Struggling for Air*, how this grandfathering policy created a considerable loophole and helped shield bad actors in their quest to avoid NSR compliance.[90] To begin with, existing high-sulfur-content coal-burning utilities could avoid installing new, costly technology. The assumption seemed to be that those facilities would either be retired or, if not, then new technology standards (and accompanying emission-control equipment) would be installed when those facilities underwent a modification. What happened, instead, is that many utilities favored operating an old plant beyond its useful life rather than retiring it, and they did whatever they could to circumvent having any physical changes at a plant that might be treated as modification possibly triggering NSPS or NSR review.

Focusing on new coal-fired generation and grandfathering existing plants presented several problems: first and most obviously, under the CAA, power plants that commenced construction before an NSPS was proposed were excluded. This exempted about 220 GW of coal-fired capacity from the 1977 CAA Amendments' scrubber requirement.[91] Second, even if a plant was subject to NSPS when first constructed, it was exempt from any future, more stringent NSPS rules that reflected changes in control technology or pressing public health needs. Third, savvy plant operators early on figured out how to quickly "commence construction" of a facility before the proposed NSPS rule came out and then to bide their time in actually building the plant, which when completed would be grandfathered. The problem associated with grandfathering old coal-fired facilities, as Revesz and Lienke explain,

---

90   RICHARD L. REVESZ & JACK LIENKE, STRUGGLING FOR AIR: POWER PLANTS AND THE "WAR ON COAL" (Oxford Univ. Press 2016). *See also* Jonathan R. Nash & Richard L. Revesz, *Grandfathering and Environmental Regulation: The Law and Economics of New Source Review*, 101 Nw. U. L. REV. 1677 (2007).

91   EIA found that 73 percent of the 313 GW of coal generation operating in 2010 was more than thirty years old and had been in operation in 1980. EIA, Today in Energy, Most Coal-Fired Capacity Was Built Before 1980, June 28, 2011. The scrubber requirement applied only to plants when construction commenced after September 28, 1978. It is unlikely that any plant operating in 1980 started construction after that 1978 date because coal plant construction typically requires more than twenty-seven months.

became accentuated once utilities made physical or operational changes to these plants – whether illegally or not – and extended the life of these grandfathered plants well beyond their assumed retirement dates, all the while attempting to avoid installing modern emission controls.

EPA, for its part, embarked on a tortious effort to define activities triggering a modification. Early in the Act's implementation, it became apparent that the original definition of modification raised practical implementation difficulties. A small physical change or change in method of operation could, as the EPA acknowledged, "encompass the most mundane activities at an industrial facility (even the repair or replacement of a single leaky pipe or a change [in] the way the pipe is utilized)."[92] As a result, EPA crafted exclusions for routine maintenance, repair, and replacement; increases in production rate or hours of operation; and use of alternative fuels, among other activities.[93] Revesz and Lienke explain how former Congressman Henry Waxman described one of these exclusions as a product of the electric industry's "fingerprints."[94] The emission increase part of the "modification" definition has been equally troublesome. The Agency has struggled with capturing what constitutes an emissions increase, the "potential to emit," measuring baseline (pre-modification) emissions, estimating future (post-modification) emissions, and whether to use hourly or annual emission rates. The Reagan administration almost immediately offered the utility industry a carrot for modernization when it allowed a source to conceptually draw a bubble over a plant and examine whether a net increase in emissions had occurred. Presidential candidate Ronald Reagan, after all, had criticized the EPA for not caring enough about coal – asserting how Mt. St. Helens produces more SO_2 than other emission sources.[95]

Because of elemental conceptual difficulties surrounding the definition of "modification," decades of litigation ensued involving what activities constituted "routine" maintenance, repair, and replacement.[96] "By the mid-1980s," Revesz and Lienke report, it became "public knowledge that the power sector was undertaking heroic efforts to extend the life of grandfathered generators."[97] Eventually, the Clinton administration responded by waging an aggressive NSR enforcement initiative targeting sources allegedly impermissibly circumventing NSR review.[98] Today, after twenty years of NSR litigation, producing a mélange of EPA wins and losses and

92 Final Rulemaking, Requirements for Preparation, Adoption and Submittal of Implementation Plans; Approval and Promulgation of Implementation Plans; Standards of Performance for New Stationary Sources, 57 Fed. Reg. 32,314, 32,316 (July 21, 1992).

93 40 C.F.R. § 60.14(e)(1)–(4). The DC Circuit largely rebuffed EPA's 2002 attempts to liberalize these exclusions. New York v. EPA, 413 F.3d 3 (D.C. Cir. 2005).

94 REVESZ & LIENKE, *supra* note 90, at 71.

95 Joanne Omang, *Reagan Criticizes Clean Air Laws and EPA as Obstacles to Growth*, WASH. POST., Oct. 9, 1980, at A2.

96 *E.g.*, Wisconsin Elec. Power Co., v. Reilly (WEPCO), 893 F.2d 901 (7th Cir. 1990).

97 REVESZ & LIENKE, *supra* note 90, at 66.

98 U.S. EPA, Guidance on the Appropriate Injunctive Relief for Violations of Major New Source Review Requirements (Nov. 17, 1998).

a number of company-specific settlements, there still appears to be no clear, generally applicable standard for what constitutes routine maintenance, repair, and replacement.[99] What has become clear, though, according to the National Academy of Sciences, is that the CAA's regulatory construct of modification remains problematic.[100]

Grandfathered plants were not entirely shielded from installing new controls. They were still subject to state implementation plans. But state implementation plans in that era were principally designed to control in-state emissions to the extent necessary to bring the state into compliance with the applicable national ambient air quality standards. Both the 1970 and 1977 Clean Air Acts had "good neighbor" provisions designed to ensure that emissions in the upwind states would not impede compliance with ambient standards in downwind states. These provisions were, however, ineffective and prior to the 1990s almost never enforced. The result was that if a power plant could ensure that its emission would not push its home state into nonattainment, it would generally be free from SIP requirements to upgrade controls. Utilities employed a few strategies for avoiding further controls. One strategy that *Struggling for Air* describes is the use of tall stacks, or high smoke stacks capable of dispersing emissions further up into the atmosphere so that the emission plume did not reach ground level until it was out of state – making the resulting deterioration of air quality the neighboring state's problem. Indeed, according to Revesz and Lienke, only a few stacks were over 500 feet tall in 1970, and yet utilities had installed 172 such stacks by 1980. This, of course, contributed to widespread acid rain.

It would be almost fifteen years, though, before Congress would amend the CAA to address acid rain, to strengthen the "good neighbor" policy, and to give the EPA specific authority to require controls necessary to prevent downwind nonattainment. Meanwhile, emissions from increased coal-fired generation produced acid rain and CO_2.

More important, the Act effectively produced a perverse disincentive for technological improvements at grandfathered facilities.[101] The routine maintenance exclusion allowed the operator to maintain the facility as it was originally designed (though there are questions even as to this interpretation). Upgrading a facility's original design clearly falls outside the ambit of routine maintenance, and requires the operator to show that no increase in emissions will result from the improvement. Plant operators, concerned how design upgrades might trigger having to install costly BACT measures, occasionally opted to forgo plant modernization; and, because new facilities (which must comply with NSPS and BACT/LAER) have

---

[99] *See generally* Bernard F. Hawkins, Jr. & Mary Ellen Ternes, *The New Source Review Program, in* THE CLEAN AIR ACT HANDBOOK 137 (Julie R. Domike & Alec C. Zacaroli eds., 4th edn 2016).

[100] NAT'L ACAD. OF PUB. ADMIN., A BREATH OF FRESH AIR: REVIVING THE NEW SOURCE REVIEW PROGRAM (2003).

[101] *See, e.g.,* Nash & Revesz, *supra* note 90, at 1707–18; Howard K. Gruenspecht & Robert N. Stavins, New Source Review under the Clean Air Act: Ripe for Reform, RESOURCES, Spring 2002, at 19, 21.

higher capital costs than the facilities they might replace, strong incentives push operators toward keeping existing facilities running as long as possible.[102] The effect of the Act's grandfathering policies is quite evident in the electric power sector. To begin with, such policies have failed to effectively control many coal-fired power plants. By 2012, almost a third of the US coal fleet still operated without modern pollution controls.[103] Second, grandfathering, moreover, might have contributed to retarding technological improvement in the industry and possibly locked in thermally inefficient 1960s coal combustion technology.[104] Richard Hirsch describes how, by the 1960s, utility managers determined that increased thermal efficiency was neither worth the additional costs nor the risk to a plant's reliability.[105] But even more significantly, the average thermal efficiency of US coal-fired power plants decreased from 33.2 percent in 1970 to 32.7 percent in 2009,[106] even though modern coal plants can attain thermal efficiencies approaching 40 percent. A state-of-the-art West Virginia Longview supercritical coal-fired plant reportedly averages about 8,850 Btu/kWh, or roughly 20 percent better than other older plants. And Japan's coal-fired units, for instance, apparently average a little over 40 percent in their efficiency, with China not far behind.

Carter championed his energy plan in April 1977 as one guided by the need to protect the nation's environment. As the nation turned to coal, he implored, "we must be sure that we will not fall short of the goals we have established to protect human health and the environment." As the 1970s ended, Carter's DOE Assistant Secretary for Environment testified before Congress how we must balance our desire for energy with our need for a healthy environment. To do this, she suggested that the CAA and our energy plan needed to work together better than they had under the CAA. She explained how a National Coal Utilization Assessment Report suggested that the CAA had hindered Carter's coal utilization goals. It had raised the cost for

---

[102] Howard K. Gruenspecht & Robert Stavins, *New Source Review Under the Clean Air Act: Ripe for Reform*, 147 RESOURCES 19 (Spring 2002); John A. List, Daniel L. Millimet, & Warren McHone, *Unintended Disincentive in the Clean Air Act*, 4 ADVANCES IN ECON. ANALYSIS AND POL'Y 1, 14 (2004). *See also* ART FRAAS, MIKE NEUNER, & PETER VAIL, EPA'S NEW SOURCE REVIEW PROGRAM: EVIDENCE ON PROCESSING TIME, 2002–2014 (Resources for the Future Feb. 2015).

[103] Bernstein Research, U.S. Utilities: Coal-Fired Generation Is Squeezed in the Vice of EPA Regulation; Who Wins and Who Loses? 7–8 (Oct. 2010). *See also*, U.S. Gov't Accountability Office, GAO-12-545R, Air Emissions and Electricity Generation at U.S. Power Plants 3 (Apr. 18, 2012). GAO found that older, less controlled units were responsible for a disproportionate share of SO_2, NO_x, and CO_2 emissions.

[104] It is worth noting that, because of major technological advances in natural gas generation, natural gas generating capacity almost doubled between 2000–2012 (mostly highly efficient natural gas combined cycle units); however, this new gas generation did not significantly displace existing coal-fired generation until the dramatic decline in natural gas prices in 2009. U.S. Energy Information Administration, Electric Power Monthly, 13 table 1.1 (June 2012); U.S. Energy Information Administration, Annual Energy Review 2010, 205 table 6.7 (Oct. 2011).

[105] RICHARD F. HIRSCH, POWER LOSS: THE ORIGINS OF DEREGULATION AND RESTRUCTURING IN THE AMERICAN ELECTRIC UTILITY SYSTEM 56–57 (MIT Press 1999).

[106] U.S. Energy Information Administration, Annual Energy Review 2009, 229 table 8.2b, 240 table 8.4b (2010).

new coal-fired power plants and potentially chilled efforts to convert existing oil- and gas-fired plants to coal. Toward the close of her remarks, she acknowledged how coal usage might raise atmospheric CO_2 concentrations and potentially "significantly alter the global environment" – but added how more research was necessary.[107] Of course, now, almost forty years later, we are left with the lingering challenges confronting coal-fired power plants.

[107] Statement of Ruth C. Clusen, Assistant Secretary for Environment, U.S. Department of Energy, Before the Environment, Energy, and Natural Resources Subcommittee of the House Committee on Government Relations, Sept. 13, 1979.

9

Oil, Cars, and Climate

The transportation sector contributes roughly one-third of US greenhouse gas (GHG) emissions and worldwide has been one of the fastest-growing sources of air emissions. When Congress passed the 1970 Clean Air Act (CAA), the transportation sector (cars primarily) was "the greatest source of air pollution," contributing roughly "42 percent of all pollutants by weight."[1] After all, Christopher Well's fascinating book, *Car Country*, chronicles how following World War II and through the 1960s the automobile profoundly reshaped our natural landscape, national demography, and economy.[2] But transportation generally and the automobile more specifically also drove air emissions and the corresponding need for federal air pollution legislation. California Congressman Anderson lamented in 1970 how "automobile emissions account for 87.7 percent of the air pollution in the Los Angeles Basin."[3] Indeed, University of Chicago Law Professor David Currie wrote in 1970 that "[a]utomobiles have single-handedly ruined the atmosphere of Los Angeles."[4] Another congressman opined that "[a]utomobile pollution is the most serious source of contaminants in our Nation's – and the world's – air."[5] Of course, early-twentieth-century reports in Germany already alerted lawmakers that carbon monoxide and lead from automobiles were poisonous.[6] And the Council of Environmental Quality (CEQ) that same year added how "[a]ir pollution alters climate and may produce global changes in temperature."[7]

---

[1] Committee Print, A Legislative History of the Clean Air Amendments of 1970 Together with a Section-by-Section Index: Prepared by the Environmental Policy Division of the Congressional Research Service for the Committee on Public Works, U.S. Senate, Serial No. 93–18, 93rd Cong., 2nd Sess. Vol. 1, at 244 (Jan. 1974) (hereinafter Serial No. 93–18).

[2] CHRISTOPHER W. WELLS, CAR COUNTRY: AN ENVIRONMENTAL HISTORY (Univ. of Washington Press 2012).

[3] Serial No. 93–18, *supra* note 1, Vol. 1 at 118 (Dec. 1970 House Consideration of Conference Report).

[4] David P. Currie, *Motor Vehicle Air Pollution: State Authority and Federal Pre-Emption*, 68 MICH. L. REV. 1083, 1084 (1970).

[5] Serial No. 93–18, *supra* note 1, Vol. 1 at 120 (Dec. 1970 House Consideration of Conference. Report).

[6] Frank Uekoetter, *The Merits of the Precautionary Principle: Controlling Automobile Exhausts in Germany and the United States Before 1945, in* SMOKE AND MIRRORS: THE POLITICS AND CULTURE OF AIR POLLUTION (E. Melanie DuPuis ed., N.Y. Univ. Press 2004).

[7] Council on Environmental Quality, Environmental Quality: The First Annual Report 71 (Aug. 1970).

Total annual emissions from vehicles are a function of three factors: fuel economy of vehicles, vehicle miles traveled (VMT), and the carbon content of fuel. The transportation sector accounts for roughly 71 percent of US petroleum use. And about two-thirds of transportation use of petroleum occurs with cars and light trucks. Policies aimed at fuel economy and VMT therefore can reduce both oil use and pollutants, as well as GHG emissions. This means that the efficacy of any fuel standard depends on how the standard is designed. A low-carbon standard, for instance, would advance both the GHG and the oil objectives. An alternative fuel standard (which, for example, permitted use of natural gas) or liquids from coal might reduce petroleum use but would not necessarily be effective at achieving significant GHG reductions. The federal government reports that the nation's highway vehicles produce about 1.7 billion tons of GHGs. Compared with petroleum, for instance, natural gas as a transportation fuel would reduce emissions by about 25 percent; coal liquids would increase them by at least 35 percent depending on the grade of coal and how it is liquefied.

This chapter explores the US transportation sector, including its GHG emissions and petroleum use, the 1975 Corporate Average Fuel Economy (CAFE) program under the Energy Policy and Conservation Act (EPCA) and its revision in 2007, the Environmental Protection Agency's (EPA's) authority under the CAA to control GHG emissions from motor vehicles, the Obama administration's combined CAA/CAFE program, as well as the renewable fuel standard and other alternative fuels strategies.

AUTOMOBILES DRIVING AIR QUALITY

In February 1970, President Nixon's environmental message addressed how the nation needed more stringent vehicle emission standards by the 1975 model year. Earlier CAA legislation already authorized regulating new motor vehicles, and the first national standards were established for 1968 model year automobiles, followed by stricter standards for 1970 and 1971 (e.g., in 1970, 23 grams per mile of CO). Indeed, earlier federal efforts to control air emissions emphasized automobile emissions and the resulting photochemical smog created by the industry in cities such as Los Angeles.[8] Those efforts, noted in a 1963 congressional report, included a recognition that "the amount of carbon dioxide in the atmosphere is increasing as a consequence of human activities. This increase is raising the temperature of the

---

[8] *See* Committee Print, A Study of Pollution-Air: A Staff Report to the Committee on Public Works, U.S. Senate, 88th Cong., 1st Sess. (Sept. 1963) (hereinafter 1963 Staff Report). The report echoed a study that suggested that "for every 1,000 gallons of gasoline used by cars, there are discharged 3,000 pounds of carbon monoxide, 200 to 400 pounds of hydrocarbons, and 50 to 150 pounds of nitrogen oxides," as well as other pollutants. *Ibid.* at 5. In 1970, Clarence Davies noted how "[s]ince the 1951 discovery that automobiles were the major source of Los Angeles smog, it had been clear that auto exhausts were a prime contributor to air pollution." J. CLARENCE DAVIES, THE POLITICS OF POLLUTION 53 (Pegasus 1970).

Earth's atmosphere by intercepting infrared heat waves going out from the Earth into space."[9]

But that legislation was limited and, other than for California, preempted states' ability to establish more stringent emission standards.[10] While Congress acceded to the automobile manufacturers' plea for uniformity, fearing varying state programs would be too problematic, it carved an exception for California: only California could convince Congress that its state's "peculiar local conditions" warranted separate treatment.[11] California, after all, as a pioneer had passed its own Motor Vehicle Pollution Control Act in 1960.[12]

Senator Boggs explained how Nixon purportedly favored "new procedures" for inspecting cars "on the assembly line to assure that they meet the low-pollution standard," a concept incorporated into Title II of the 1970 CAA.[13] The bulk of Congress's time debating the 1970 CAA legislation focused on Title II of the Act and automobiles. Congress pointedly sought to encourage, through grants and research and development (R&D), the development of zero- or low-emission vehicles – something that the surgeon general had noted was a fertile avenue for R&D back in 1962 (electric vehicles, for instance, only had a range then of seventy-five miles).[14]

Title II provided the EPA with authority to establish emission standards for new motor vehicles. Title II, explained Senator Muskie, reflected a comprise between the Senate and the House, with the Senate not securing all it had hoped for but in other respects producing a stronger bill than either chamber initially passed. "The key decision, the one which the committee focused most over the past few months," Muskie informed the Senate in December 1970, "was the deadline for the

[9] 1963 Staff Report, *supra* note 1, at 22.
[10] Currie, *supra* note 4, at 1090. In 1960, Congress passed the Schenck Act, commissioning a study of the health effects from automobiles. JAMES E. KRIER & EDMUND URSIN, POLLUTION AND POLICY: A CASE ESSAY ON CALIFORNIA AND FEDERAL EXPERIENCE WITH MOTOR VEHICLE AIR POLLUTION 1940–1975 169 (Univ. of California Press 1977). That study reported how gasoline-powered vehicles in Los Angeles "pollute the air daily with 1,180 tons of hydrocarbons, 330 tons of nitrogen oxides and 8,950 tons of carbon monoxide." A Report of the Surgeon General to the U.S. Congress in Compliance with Pub. L. 86–493, Motor Vehicles, Air Pollution, and Health 21, House Doc. No. 489, 87th Cong., 2nd Sess. (June 1962) (hereinafter Surgeon General 1962). Two years later, Congress "directed the surgeon general to continue permanently the motor vehicle exhaust studies that had been initiated under the Schenck Act." KRIER & URSIN, *supra* at 170.
[11] Currie, *supra* note 4, at 1090.
[12] Harold W. Kennedy & Martin E. Weeks, *Control of Automobile Emissions: California Experience and the Federal Legislation*, 33 LAW & CONTEMP. PROBLEMS, 297 (Spring 1968). California's first standards limited exhaust emissions to 275 ppm of hydrocarbons and 1.5 percent by volume of CO. There were no standards for NO_2. Even before requiring that they do so, automobile manufacturers began installing crankcase control technology in 1961. Surgeon General 1962, *supra* note 10, at 28, 37. In 1962, the surgeon general reported how, although taking longer than expected, "[a] great many manufacturers, both large and small, throughout the country are vigorously engaged in efforts to produce exhaust control devices which will meet the requirements of the California Motor Vehicle Pollution Control Board." *Ibid.* at 31.
[13] Serial No. 93–18, *supra* note 1, Vol. 1 at 242.   [14] Surgeon General 1962, *supra* note 10, at 29.

cleanup of the internal combustion engine in the passenger automobile."[15]
Section 202(a) required standards for any vehicle emissions that "contribute to air
pollution which may reasonably be anticipated to endanger public health or welfare." Standards apply to new motor vehicles only, and they generally apply on
a vehicle-by-vehicle basis, and explicit authority for fleet-wide averaging is limited
(EPA over the years, however, has found a legal basis for an averaging policy).

While EPA could grant a one-year extension, Congress established
a January 1, 1975, deadline for achieving a 90 percent reduction in tailpipe
emissions of carbon monoxide (CO) and hydrocarbon (HC) gas and a January 1,
1976, date for achieving a 90 percent reduction in nitrous oxides (NO_x).
The 1970 Congress assumed that extant technology did not exist to achieve
those standards, and its insistence on such high reductions has become the
classic example of a technology-forcing program: it required industry to develop
technology capable of achieving the identified standards. An extension request
seemed almost certain, and the EPA's decision on an extension would be
informed by a National Academy of Sciences report on the status of catalytic
converter technology. Even if the standards could not be achieved, the EPA had
to establish strict interim standards, and Congress would have to address any
further relaxation.[16]

Next, Congress expressly precluded states from prescribing new motor vehicle emissions standards, with a caveat. Section 209(b) of the Act effectively
recognized California's unique role in regulating emissions and it allowed the
state to request a waiver from EPA that would allow the state to implement its
own standards. If California determines that its standards "will be, in the
aggregate, at least as protective of public health and welfare as applicable
Federal standards," the EPA must approve the standards unless it concludes
that California acted arbitrarily and capriciously, that the state's standards are
not necessary to satisfy compelling and extraordinary conditions, or that they
might endanger human health or welfare. Then, under Section 177 of the
CAA, other states may then opt into California standards if the EPA grants
a waiver – provided those standards are not imposed on any model year for at
least two years.

Finally, Title II included a fuels program. Congress authorized the EPA to
"control or prohibit manufacture or sale of any motor vehicle fuel or fuel additive
if any emissions therefrom will endanger the public health or welfare, or if
emission products of such fuel or additive will impair to a significant degree
the performance of any emission control device or system which is or will be in
general use." And, in 1990, and then again in 2005 and 2007, Congress strengthened this program.

---

[15] Serial No. 93–18, *supra* note 1, Vol. 1 at 128.
[16] *See* International Harvester Co. v. Ruckelshaus, 478 F.2d 615 (D.C. Cir. 1973).

FUEL ECONOMY STANDARDS UNDER THE 1975 CAFE PROGRAM

The program for controlling automobile emissions seemingly languished almost from the outset. The automobile industry lamented how technology for reducing emissions under the CAA was not ready. The "big three" manufacturers eventually received a one-year suspension of the 1977 standards, for instance, when they convinced the EPA that their catalytic converters would reduce HC and CO gas emissions but increase the level of sulfates.[17] Section 5 of the 1974 Energy Supply and Environmental Coordination Act (ESECA) tinkered with the program by directing specific interim standards and applying the 1975 interim standards to the 1976 model year.[18] Yet marginal gains in miles per gallon (MPG) occurred, with the average fuel economy of all cars increasing from 13.9 MPG in 1974 to 17.6 MPG in 1976.[19]

Then, in the 1975 EPCA, Congress established today's CAFE standards program. Congress conceived of the program as a measure for reducing the nation's crude oil consumption. Industry naturally was reluctant, yet President Ford favored a mandatory fuel efficiency program. The energy crisis, with its gasoline lines, rationing, and even its nationwide 55 miles per hour speed limit, helped forge a consensus for its passage. The energy crisis, however, did something else as well. Japanese imports increased dramatically, illustrating a consumer willingness (during energy-crisis times) to purchase more fuel-efficient vehicles. This prodded US manufacturers. The same year as the EPCA, General Motors introduced the Chevrolet Chevette, described by the *Chicago Tribune* as "a minicar that probably is one of the most important automobiles out of Detroit since Ford's Model T." Perhaps naively optimistic and discounting the power of the country's car culture, the *Tribune* boldly claimed that General Motors's car reflected "the realization that the once-basic American automobile – the gas-guzzling 20-footer – is going to disappear."[20]

This now-familiar CAFE program establishes annual average fuel economy standards (in MPG) for automobile manufacturers' new vehicles. It applies to three separate "fleets." Each manufacturer must comply separately with applicable CAFE standards and associated labeling requirements for

[17] Annual Report of the Administrator of the Environmental Protection Agency to the Congress of the U.S.in Compliance with Sections 202, 306e, and 133 of Pub. L. 91–604, The Clean Air Act, As Amended, Progress in the Prevention and Control of Air Pollution in 1976, Serial No. 95–75, 95th Cong., 1st Sess. 81 (Nov. 1977) (hereinafter Serial No. 95–75).

[18] Energy Supply and Environmental Coordination Act of 1974, Pub. L. No. 93–319, 88 Stat. 246, 258, June 24, 1974. The statute further authorized requesting a suspension from the 1977 light-duty vehicle and engine emission standards.

[19] Serial No. 95–75, *supra* note 17, at 86. Fuel economy, however, "decreased gradually" between 1968 and 1974. *Ibid.* at 93.

[20] *Chevette Called Dawn of Auto Era*, CHICAGO. TRIB., Sept. 15, 1975, at C8. *See also* Brian Black, *The Consumer's Hand Made Visible: Consumer Culture in American Petroleum Consumption of the 1970s, in* AMERICAN ENERGY POLICY IN THE 1970S 257 (Robert Lifset ed., Okla. Univ. Press 2014).

- Domestic passenger automobiles (cars),
- Imported passenger automobiles, and
- Non-passenger automobiles (light trucks and SUVs), whether imported or domestic

The statute provides for substantially different standards for cars and light trucks/ SUVs. Congress initially established car standards, increasing from 18 MPG in 1978 to 27.5 MPG by 1985. Standards for light trucks/SUVs must be administratively set by the National Highway and Traffic Safety Administration (NHTSA), an agency within the Department of Transportation (DOT). Congress, moreover, delegated to NHTSA the authority to establish passenger-car standards after the 1985 model year. When setting the standards, the agency must consider what is maximally feasible – i.e., technologically and economically feasible, which can include consumer choice, safety, and economic hardship to the industry. It also now includes monetizing the benefits of GHG emission reductions.[21] States were preempted from having their own fuel economy standards, as well as any standard "related to" fuel economy.[22]

Congress built significant flexibility into the EPCA. CAFE's fundamental requirement, that each manufacturer meet an average fuel economy standard (in contrast to a requirement that each vehicle meet a specific standard), represented a significant departure from the then-prevalent regulatory architecture (in contrast to Title II of the CAA and the National Traffic and Motor Vehicle Safety Act). Manufacturers who overcomply in one year may carry forward or back, permitting compliance on a multiyear basis. Another notable feature is that CAFE is enforced by civil penalties only (with no provision for injunctive relief or criminal enforcements typical in most regulatory statutes). This allows manufacturers willing to pay the civil penalty free to violate the standard – but at a price. The statutory penalty is $55 (since adjusted for inflation to roughly $140 for 2019 model year and beyond, although now being reconsidered by the Trump administration) for each mile per gallon a manufacturer falls short of its average fuel economy for a specific model year multiplied by the number of vehicles in the affected fleet. Some companies accept the penalty rather than adjust their fleets. Jaguar Land Rover, Daimler, Porsche, and Fiat each have paid millions in fines.

The statute, though, contains several idiosyncratic features that increase its complexity while decreasing its effectiveness. Trucks and SUVs enjoy far less stringent standards than cars. Compliance with the standard is determined separately for vehicles manufactured in the United States, Canada, or Mexico and vehicles

---

[21] Center for Biological Diversity v. National Highway Traffic Safety Admin., 538 F.3d 1172 (9th Cir. 2008). In 2006, the NTHSA modified the program for light trucks in MY2008 through MY2010, with the CAFE rising to 23.7 MPG. Average Fuel Economy Standards for Light Trucks Model Years 2008–2011, 71 Fed. Reg. 17,566 (Apr. 6, 2006) (hereinafter Light Truck Standards).

[22] Pub. L. 94–163, 89 Stat. 871 (1975); Congress subsequently re-codified the statute. Pub. L. No. 103–272, 108 Stat. 745 (1994).

manufactured elsewhere but used in the United States. And electric and alternative fuel–capable vehicles enjoy some special credit.

The 1975 CAFE program, with its roughly 28 MPG standard since the 1985 model year, remained essentially unchanged until 2007. That year Congress passed the Energy Independence and Security Act of 2007 (EISA), restructuring the program and phasing in substantial increases in stringency of average fuel economy standards, beginning in model year (MY) 2011. Congress had earlier considered legislation designed to boost fuel efficiency, but with little success.[23] EISA required NHTSA to set standards that resulted in industry-wide new automobile (cars plus trucks) average fuel economy meeting a minimum of 35 MPG in MY2020. Separate standards must be established for cars and trucks, which standards are "attribute based" or based on vehicle attributes related to fuel economy, such as size. Under prior law, manufacturers exceeding an applicable average fuel economy standard may earn credits usable in future model years. EISA made these credits tradable among manufacturers.

TITLE II OF THE CLEAN AIR ACT

Frustrated by the Bush administration's abject failure to regulate carbon dioxide (CO_2), the California legislature in 2002 responded to the vacuum. For decades, Congress had been passing legislation hinting about the need to address GHG emissions. Early congressional discussions about the increased use of coal throughout the 1970s are riddled with statements about the potential effects on climate change. When Congress passed the 1972 Coastal Zone Management Act, it included a specific provision on rising sea levels – from climate change. Finally, in 1978, Congress established the National Climate Program, designed to collect, assess, and disseminate information. The 1980 Energy Security Act directed the National Academy of Sciences to examine energy's contribution to CO_2 emissions and its accompanying effect on climate. By 1987, Congress through the Global Climate Protection Act formally recognized how anthropocentric activities might be altering the Earth's temperature. That Act required the EPA to develop and propose to Congress a "coordinated national policy on global climate change."

By this time the worldwide scientific community exhibited its consensus that climate change was occurring because of increased GHG emissions from anthropocentric forces. This consensus became evident in the Intergovernmental Panel on Climate Change (IPPC) 1990 report, and Congress again in 1990 (bolstered two years later) adopted the Global Change Research Act fostering a greater understanding of global climate change. Amending the CAA in 1990, Congress required that the EPA examine the "global warming potential" for various substances, and it

---

[23] *See* OFFICE OF TECHNOLOGY ASSESSMENT, IMPROVING AUTOMOBILE FUEL ECONOMY: NEW STANDARDS, NEW APPROACHES (OTA-E-504) (Washington, DC: US Govt. Printing Office, Oct. 1991).

required a regulatory regime for monitoring and reporting GHG emissions. Then in 1992 the United States signed, and Congress ratified, the United Nations Framework Convention on Climate Change (UNFCCC). Although a significant event, it was only a nonbinding agreement of 154 nations that they would reduce their atmospheric concentrations of GHGs. But the parties to the UNFCCC subsequently negotiated the Kyoto Protocol, containing mandatory GHG reductions. While the United States signed the Kyoto Protocol, President Clinton, knowing that it would not be ratified, never submitted it to Congress – a point underscored later when Congress expressed quite clearly that it would not ratify the Protocol.

Against this background, the California state legislature passed AB 1493 in 2002. The legislation directed the state's air board, the California Air Resources Board (CARB) to develop regulations for reducing, considering cost and feasibility, GHG emissions from automobiles. CARB then employed a study by the Northeast States Center for a Clean Air Future to assess various technologies and options for lowering automobile emissions. Because most carbon exhaust from cars is CO_2 emissions, with the average vehicle emitting annually about 4.7 metric tons of CO_2 (each gallon of gasoline produces roughly 20 lb of GHGs), the principal mechanism for reducing emissions is from increasing miles per gallon, or fuel efficiency. By 2004, CARB issued the AB 1493 implementing regulations. The program was stringent and established how many grams per mile of CO_2 could be emitted for passenger cars, light-duty trucks, and medium-duty passenger vehicles – translated to miles per gallon, it required a 42.1 MPG fleet average by 2016 for passenger cars (almost 10 MPG higher than the 2005 car fleet average). CARB considered that the benefits far outweigh the costs, with increased costs to consumers of roughly $1,000 from MY2009 through MY2016 and thereafter less than $400. This effectively meant more hybrids in the California market – the largest market in the United States. The "big three" car manufacturers claimed that they could not feasibly produce enough hybrids at a reasonable cost and suggested that the Japanese manufacturers were selling their hybrids into the United States at below cost – illegally. Under Section 177 of the CAA, states other than California could follow either the EPA or California (states that adopt the California standards are referred to as "Section 177 States"). And they did. Thirteen states adopted or took steps to adopt the AB 1493 standards.

Car manufacturers feared that Section 177 states' adoption of the California standard would become cumbersome by requiring state-by-state compliance, and it responded by waging multiple legal challenges. Plaintiffs in preemption cases in California, Vermont, and Rhode Island argued that EPCA expressly preempted California standards because those standards related to fuel, and the CAA preempted CARB's rules unless and until the EPA granted a waiver under Section 209 of the CAA, which it had not. The Bush administration agreed; NHTSA advanced its conclusion that EPCA preempted state CO_2 requirements because the only effective way to control CO_2 would be by regulating the amount of fuel consumption.[24] The CAA included language barring any state from adopting or attempting to "enforce any standard relating to the control of emissions from new motor vehicles or new motor vehicle engines." EPCA commensurately prohibited any state from adopting or enforcing "a law or regulation related to fuel economy standards or average fuel economy standards for automobiles."

Courts uniformly rebuffed industry's challenges. Plaintiffs in California federal court principally claimed that the CAA and EPCA preempted CARB's rules but further asserted that the rules were preempted by the Constitution's assigning to the federal government exclusive jurisdiction over foreign policy (GHGs are an international matter and therefore involve foreign policy), that they violated the antitrust laws, and that they were preempted by the Constitution's dormant Commerce Clause – assigning to Congress the authority to regulate interstate commerce and implicitly removing that authority from the states unless otherwise authorized by Congress. The District Court initially stayed the California challenge pending the Supreme Court's consideration of whether the EPA impermissibly refused to regulate GHG emissions from automobiles.

That occurred in 2007, when the Supreme Court decided what has since become one of the Court's most prominent and historic environmental cases, *Massachusetts v. EPA*. The case started when Massachusetts and other plaintiffs petitioned the EPA to impose GHG standards under Title II of the CAA. Title II imposes on the EPA the obligation to establish standards when any pollutant might endanger human health or the environment – referred to as an "endangerment finding." In 2003, the Bush EPA denied the petition, in part reasoning that GHGs were not pollutants under the Act and that, regardless, it enjoyed discretion to decide whether to regulate. The Court reversed, making it clear that the EPA has authority under the CAA to regulate GHG emissions, that CO_2 is indeed any "pollutant," and that if the EPA makes an "endangerment" determination in Section 202(a), then it must issue regulations under Title II of the Act. In response, the Bush administration merely issued a lengthy Advanced Notice of Proposed Rulemaking but took no further action.

When Judge Ishii finally considered the merits of industry's claims against CARB, he assumed that the EPA would grant California's CAA Section 209 waiver and that, if that occurred, the state's program was not preempted by either the EPCA or the CAA. He accepted that the EPCA charged the NHTSA with balancing several factors when establishing CAFE standards, and one of those factors was fuel efficiency – an area into which California's program intruded. Having two separate programs effectively sending different signals for industry posed, according to the NHTSA, potentially difficult economic consequences. But he equally appreciated California's argument that Congress was aware of California's efforts when it passed the EPCA, and Congress intended to preserve California's options – through

---

[24] Light Truck Standards, *supra* note 21, at 17654.

specific language in the EPCA and Section 209 of the CAA. Initially, Judge Ishii seemed inclined to accept that the EPCA may have prevented California's program. When, however, he next revisited the issue after the Supreme Court's decision in *Massachusetts* v. *EPA* and after the court in Vermont issued its decision on the same standards, he observed how the legal landscape had changed.

In the fall of 2005, Vermont had followed California and established California's GHG standards for new automobiles. The industry challenge presented a potpourri of claims, and the state likewise responded with an array of procedural ploys. Notably, industry sought to exclude the bulk of the testimony from Dr. James Hansen, such as on whether the Earth was approaching a tipping point and on potential ice sheet disintegration. Dr. Hansen is perhaps one of the most widely respected and credited champions for the threat posed by climate change, occasionally described as the "father of climate change awareness."[25] His testimony was informative, pointed, and quite reliable according to the court – and as such allowed in court over industry's protestations. In the Vermont lawsuit, *Green Mountain Chrysler* v. *Crombie*, Judge Sessions ruled that the CARB rules were not "related to" fuel economy under the EPCA.[26] And the court averted the CAA claim by assuming that the EPA would grant California's CAA Section 209 waiver.

Judge Sessions' opinion, when combined with the Supreme Court's strong language in *Massachusetts* v. *EPA*, convinced Judge Ishii that the EPCA did not preempt California's program – if or when the EPA were to subsequently grant the state a waiver under the CAA. The EPA and California, he reasoned, "are equally empowered through the Clean Air Act to promulgate regulations that limit the emission of greenhouse gasses, principally carbon dioxide, from motor vehicles." Even though the NHTSA sets maximum feasible average mileage standards, he concluded that affording California the ability to limit GHG emissions does not necessarily interfere with the NHTSA's charge, and if any inconsistency occurs, NHTSA can address that inconsistency by changing CAFE standards. Judge Ishii also found unconvincing industry's additional arguments, such as that California's program impeded the White House's ability to conduct foreign affairs.[27]

The state was less successful, though, in other litigation against the automobile industry. California augmented CARB's program by seeking to wrest damages from

---

[25] Annie Sneed, *Legendary Climate Scientist Likes a GOP Proposal on Global Warming*, Sci. Am., April 10, 2017.

[26] Green Mountain Chrysler Plymouth Dodge Jeep v. Crombie, 508 F. Supp.2d 295 (D. Vt. 2007). Conversely, when Boston attempted to mandate all hybrid taxis in the city, a district court held that the EPCA preempted its effort. Ophir v. City of Boston, 647 F. Supp.2d 86 (D. Mass. 2009). *See also* Metropolitan Taxicab Bd. of Trade v. New York, 615 F.3d 152 (2d Cir. 2010). Voluntary programs are unobjectionable. Green Alliance Taxi Cab Ass'n v. King County, 2010 WL 2643369 (W.D. Wash. June 29, 2010). *See generally* Drew Sander, *Note, Hailing Progress: Regulatory Difficulties in Promulgating Hybrid Taxi Laws*, 14 Conn. Pub. Int. L. J. 243 (2015).

[27] *See* Central Valley Chrysler-Jeep v. Witherspoon, 456 F. Supp.2d 1160 (E.D. Calif. 2006); Central Valley Chrysler-Jeep v. Goldstone, 529 F. Supp.2d 1151 (E.D. Calif. 2008); Central Valley Chrysler-Jeep v. Goldstone, 563 F. Supp.2d 1158 (E.D. Calif. 2008).

the industry for manufacturing and selling cars producing GHG emissions and contributing to global warming. The state claimed that the industry's product constitutes a public nuisance under both federal common law and state law and that the state had been harmed. The industry shot back that the CAA and EPCA preempted any such claims, even if they were legitimate torts. The judiciary, to begin with, exhibited reluctance toward endorsing a federal common-law public nuisance tort for GHG emissions. Lower courts struggled with federal public nuisance claims against stationary sources, such as utilities, and the Supreme Court eventually held that the CAA displaced those federally based claims.[28] In September 2007, a US District Court in California dismissed California's claims. It rejected allowing any federal common-law nuisance claim to proceed, and any lingering state-law claim would need to be fielded in state not federal court.[29]

Once the Court decided *Massachusetts* v. *EPA*, the EPA was forced to decide California's waiver application. The state had submitted many waiver requests over the years, and the presumption and burden were on the EPA to explain why any request should not be granted. California had submitted its waiver request in December 2005. After the Court issued *Massachusetts* v. *EPA* and forced the administration's hand, President Bush's EPA Administrator, Stephen Johnson, on March 6, 2008, denied the waiver.

Almost immediately charges were leveled against the administration that its decision was politically motivated and flouted the CAA. Congress entered the fray, even submitting a subpoena request to the EPA for documents. This occurred along with a House Oversight and Government Reform Committee hearing on the EPA's denial. The Committee concluded by finding that career EPA employees and even the Administrator initially favored granting the waiver – at least in part – but that the administrator ultimately reversed his position because of White House influence. In a May 2008 memorandum, the Committee indicated that its record "suggests that the White House played a pivotal role in the decision to reject the California petition."[30] *Washington Post* reporter Juliet Eilperin described how, during a hearing in the other chamber before the Senate Environment and Public Works Committee, former EPA Deputy Associate Administrator Jason K. Burnett testified that "President Bush and his deputies have influenced the agency's decisions on climate policy ... and ordered him to reverse the decision."[31] Conversely, a December 2008 report by the EPA's inspector general, charged with investigating any impropriety, countered the Committee's suggestion by concluding that Administrator Johnson's decision was based on the permissible conclusion that

---

[28] *See* American Elec. Power Co. v. Connecticut, 564 U.S. 410 (2011); Native Village of Kivalina v. ExxonMobil Corp., 696 F.3d 849 (9th Cir. 2012); Comer v. Murphy Oil, 585 F.3d 855 (5th Cir. 2009).

[29] California v. General Motors, 2007 WL 2726871 (N.D. Cal. Sept. 17, 2007).

[30] Memorandum from Majority Staff, Committee on Oversight and Government Reform, to Committee Members, re EPA's Denial of the California Waiver (May 19, 2008).

[31] Juliet Eilperin, *Ex-EPA Official Says White House Pulled Rank*, WASH. POST, July 23, 2008.

California had not established a need to meet compelling and extraordinary air quality conditions unique to California.[32]

California, along with sixteen other states and several environmental organizations, challenged the waiver decision in the United States Court of Appeals for the DC Circuit. That lawsuit proved unnecessary, however.

Within a week of entering office, President Obama issued a Presidential Memorandum directing the EPA to reconsider the waiver denial. He noted how such waivers had been granted for decades and that the EPA had to assess the merits of California's application under the CAA. On reconsideration, the EPA formally granted California's waiver request in June of 2009. In so doing, the new administrator expressly rejected Administrator Johnson's departure from prior practice and interpretation of the CAA. "Applying EPA's traditional interpretation," he concluded in an extensive analysis, left the agency with little choice but to conclude that California was entitled to the waiver because the EPA could not support a finding that any of three criteria for denying the waiver applied. And earlier in March, the administration already had issued its determination that GHG emissions were indeed endangering human health and the environment – the "endangerment finding."

The automobile industry was now in a quandary. If adopted in other states, the California standards would require state-by-state compliance with the California GHG standards, so the industry went forward with a court challenge to EPA's grant of the waiver. But even before the waiver was granted, the industry – worried that the litigation strategy might fail – entered negotiations (brokered by the White House) with the EPA, the NHTSA, and California. The Obama EPA, however, proposed an endangerment determination in March 2009 and followed with a final GHG standards and fuel economy rule in 2010.

THE COMPROMISE EPA/NHTSA/CA PROGRAM

An unusual confluence of events – the GM and Chrysler bankruptcies, concern about state-by-state application of the California standards, and California's willingness to agree to joint federal and state standards – led to a landmark agreement among the automobile industry, the EPA, the NHTSA, the White House, and California to implement a common set of standards. The basic terms of phase I for the program were as follows:

- The EPA and NHTSA would issue a joint rule requiring the automobile industry in MY2016 to achieve a fleet average of 35.5 MPG (assuming a 60/40 car/truck product mix) and equivalent GHG emission reductions.

[32] US EPA Office of Inspector General, *EPA's California Waiver Decision on Greenhouse Gas Automobile Emissions Met Statutory Procedural Requirements* (Dec. 9, 2008).

- The EPA would grant a waiver to California that would allow it to enforce AB 1493 for MY2009–11, with key regulatory changes. For MY2012–16, California would accept compliance with the EPA program as "deemed" compliant with AB 1493.

The agreement became finalized in May 2010. That month the federal agencies issued a final regulation for GHG emissions and CAFE standards for passenger and light-duty vehicles. For CO_2 emissions, the EPA required that MY2016 light-duty vehicles achieve an "estimated combined average emissions level of 250 grams/mile of CO_2."[33] NHTSA's CAFE standard for passenger and light-duty vehicles became 34.1 MPG, although combined with the EPA's requirement this translated into 35.5 MPG. As part of the agreement with the automobile industry, all EPCA preemption litigation challenging AB 1493 was dismissed, and the automobile manufacturers agreed not to challenge the program through MY2016. Industries outside of automobile manufacturing, however, mounted judicial challenges to the combined program rules. Because of the impact regulation of GHGs under Title II of the CAA had on Title I (GHGs had become a "regulated pollutant"), many industry groups and states challenged EPA's GHG rules – including the combined program. The automobile industry, California, and Section 177 states supported the combined program, which the federal appellate court in DC upheld in July 2012. The Supreme Court granted certiorari on the relationship between Titles I & II but not for the basic motor vehicle program, which went forward as agreed.

As EPA and NHTSA finalized phase I in 2010, the parties reached a historic compromise for phase II. They coalesced around a process for phase II of the original compromise – setting GHG/CAFE limits for passenger and light-duty vehicle MY2017–25. The federal agencies announced their final rule reflecting that agreement in August of 2012, with the White House announcing that the administration had "finalized groundbreaking standards" that would "nearly double the fuel efficiency" and "save consumers more than $1.7 trillion at the gas pump and reduce U.S. oil consumption by 12 billion barrels." The EPA projected an oil import reduction of 2 million barrels per day in 2025 from the phase I and phase II rules. The EPA described the rule as "the most significant federal action ever taken to reduce GHG emissions and improve fuel economy."[34] On its website, the White House posted the sticker shown in Figure 9.1.

Phase II provides for 44.7 MPG in MY2021 and 54.5 MPG (or 163 grams/mile of CO_2) in MY2025 for passenger cars, light-duty trucks, and medium-duty passenger

---

[33] Light-Duty Vehicle Greenhouse Gas Emission Standards and Corporate Average Fuel Economy Standards, 75 Fed. Reg. 25,324, 25,329 (May 7, 2010).

[34] EPA Office of Transportation and Air Quality, EPA-420-F-12-51, EPA and NHTSA Set Standards to Reduce Greenhouse Gases and Improve Fuel Economy for Model Years 2017–2025 Cars and Light Trucks 2 (Aug. 2012).

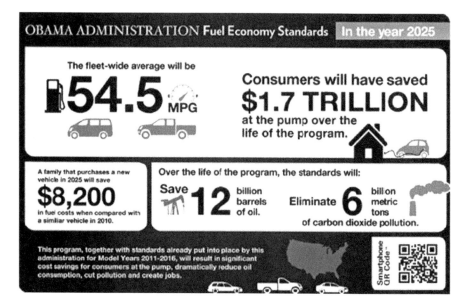

FIGURE 9.1 White House sticker on fuel economy standards

vehicles.[35] The industry championed a lower standard, while some in the environmental community pushed for 60.0 MPG; at least one manufacturer suggested that
the new standard would cost consumers $6,000, while the government countered with
a cost figure of only $2,375.[36] California agreed that compliance with federal GHG
standards would be compliance with its standard. The agencies engaged in a similar
process developing rules for reducing GHG emissions from medium- and heavy-duty
vehicles, finalizing new phase II standards shortly before Obama left office.[37]

As part of a 2012 arrangement, both EPA and NHTSA agreed to assess at a midpoint
between 2012 and 2025 the reasonableness of the 54.4 MPG standard. As it was leaving
office, the Obama EPA issued what otherwise would have been an April 2018 evaluation –
within weeks of President Trump's inauguration – concluding that the standards should
remain. This caught some by surprise, and the administration defended its decision to
engage in the early review by explaining how "[t]here has been years' worth of work to get
us to this point, and it is the administrator's view that this record was sufficient and
compelling enough for her to indicate in this process that there isn't a reason at this point

---

[35] 2017 and Later Model Year Light-Duty Vehicle Greenhouse Gas Emissions and Corporate Average
      Fuel Economy Standards, 77 Fed. Reg. 62,624 (Oct. 15, 2012).
[36] Juliet Eilperin, *New Vehicle Rules to Curb Greenhouse Gas Emissions Spark Debate*, WASH. POST,
      July 3, 2011.
[37] *See* Greenhouse Gas Emissions and Fuel Efficiency Standards for Medium-and-Heavy-Duty Engines
      and Vehicles: Phase 2, 81 Fed. Reg. 73,478 (Oct. 25, 2016); National Research Council, Reducing Fuel
      Consumption and Greenhouse Gas Emissions of Medium – and Heavy-Duty Vehicles, Phase Two:
      First Report (2014).

to consider changing the standards."[38] While not immediately attacking the standards, the trade associations for the automobile industry requested that the Trump administration withdraw EPA's decision. This, of course, may not sit well with California, which soon thereafter decided that it would strengthen its standards and potentially set up a "face-off" with the new president.[39] It is too early to predict the outcome, but in August 2017, Administrator Pruitt announced that his agency was soliciting comments on whether to reconsider the 2022–25 standards. The EPA also is reconsidering its joint MY2016 NTHSA phase II rules for fuel efficiency from heavy-duty vehicles, tractor-trailers, and school buses. The NTHSA reportedly caught literally everyone by surprise," reported Dave Cooke for the Union of Concerned Scientists, when it decided to review model years beginning in 2021 and not just 2022.[40] What both NHTSA and EPA eventually will decide, respectively, for MY2021–25 and MY2022–25, remains unknown. The dilemma, nevertheless, has by spring 2018 prodded industry to seek a negotiated resolution among the industry, California, and the Trump administration.

The CAFE program undoubtedly moderated US fuel use during its nascent years, but its benefit since has been less dramatic for a few reasons. To begin with, Congress froze the standards for many years. And during that time, the program overlooked the increasing proportions of truck, SUV, and minivan sales. In fact, in 1985, the ending of when the first set of standards had been solidified, oil prices declined, industry developed more gas guzzlers, and minivan, truck, and SUV sales began capturing an ever-increasing market share – with SUVs going from 1.8 percent of the market in 1975 to 6.3 percent in 1987 and then to 25 percent by 2002. Starting in 2001, when Congress lifted its freeze on changing CAFE standards, light-duty trucks accounted for over 50 percent of vehicles sold[41] – all outside the CAFE program. In his study of petroleum consumption in the transportation sector and critique of the CAFE program, Christopher Knittel reported that between 1979 and 2011, as average fuel economy increased, "fleet fuel economy fell as consumers shifted away from cars and into trucks."[42] Consequently, Congress's decision to freeze the

[38] Camille von Kaenel, *EPA Shocks Carmakers and GOP by Springing Surprise Decision*, E&E News, Dec. 1, 2016.
[39] Hiroko Tabuchi, *California Upholds Auto Emissions Standards, Setting Up Face-Off with Trump*, N.Y. Times, March 24, 2017; Ryan Beene & John Lippert, *Auto Mileage Rules Could Change Earlier than Planned*, BNA Daily Envt., Aug. 11, 2017. In July 2017, the NHTSA announced that it was preparing an environmental analysis for 2022–25 model year CAFE standards. Notice of Intent to Prepare an Environmental Impact Statement for Model Year 2022–2025 Corporate Average Fuel Economy Standards, 82 Fed. Reg. 34,740 (July 26, 2017).
[40] Camille von Kaenel, *In Surprise Move, NHTSA to Consider 2021 Standards*, E&E News, July 25, 2017.
[41] Michelle Maynard, *Bracing for Soft Sales, Carmakers Seek Out Higher Ground*, N. Y. Times, Jan. 11, 2002, at F1; Dept. of Transportation and Related Agencies Act of 2001 for FY 2002, Pub. L. No. 107–87, 115 Stat. 833 (2001); Meg Jacobs, Panic at the Pump: The Energy Crisis and the Transformation of American Politics in the 1970s 310 (Hill & Wang 2016).
[42] Christopher R. Knittel, *Reducing Petroleum Consumption from Transportation*, 26(1) J. Econ. Perspect. 93–118, at 97 (Winter 2012).

standards throughout most of the 1990s, combined with the change in product mix, effectively decreased the ability of the program to moderate fuel use.

Second, real gasoline prices have declined, encouraging more driving and dampening incentives for drivers to demand more efficient vehicles. Accordingly, even though fuel economy for cars has improved markedly since CAFE's enactment, overall fuel use – and, therefore, GHG emissions – has risen steadily.

Of course, policymakers did not design CAFE as a domestic GHG regulatory program. It instead was a mechanism for reducing domestic oil consumption. For the legislation to have functioned effectively in reducing GHG emissions, Congress could have removed the freeze on more stringent standards, or it could have promoted faster development of the electric or alternative vehicles, or it could have translated miles per gallon into pounds of CO_2 to account for the carbon content of the fuel.

RENEWABLE FUEL STANDARD

Congress established the modern federal renewable fuels program (RFS) in 2005 with the Energy Policy Act of 2005 and expanded it two years later in the Energy Independence and Security Act of 2007 (EISA). An earlier reformulated gas (RFG) component of the 1990 CAA focused primarily on reducing ozone concentrations and the sulfur content in diesel fuels. Congress designed the RFS program, by contrast, to replace petroleum-based transportation fuels by phasing in greater amounts of renewable fuels over time, principally biomass-based diesel, advanced biofuel, and cellulosic biofuel. Intense lobbying accompanied Congress's formation of the program as industries vied for market share, whether increased corn-based ethanol or emerging technologies for producing cellulosic ethanol. And originally Congress accompanied the program with the now-expired Volumetric Ethanol Excise Tax Credit, benefiting the ethanol industry. As illustrated in the EPA's chart (Figure 9.2), Congress expected that the transportation sector would consume a minimum of 36 billion gallons of renewable fuels by 2022. And until then, the EPA must annually set an RFS target following incremental statutory targets – which the EPA can adjust annually under certain conditions. Congress further capped corn-based ethanol at 15 billion gallons. The Act's volumetric limits could be waived if EPA concludes that implementing the requirement would "severely harm the economy or environment of a State, a region, or the United States" or when "there is an inadequate domestic supply."

Building on a laxer standard from 2005 (primarily focused on corn-based ethanol), Congress chose in the EISA to mandate that EPA use a lifecycle GHG reduction threshold for qualifying renewable fuels. The EPA describes a lifecycle analysis as "including each stage of [the fuel's] production and use," along with "significant indirect emissions." This ostensibly accounts for the entire GHG impact of the fuel, from its inputs to production, land use, the production itself, transportation and

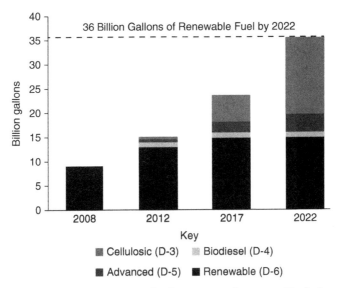

FIGURE 9.2 Congressional volume target for renewable fuels
Environmental Protection Agency

distribution, and eventual use of the fuel. California similarly employs a lifecycle analysis in its own low-carbon fuel standard (LCFS), allowing fuel providers to satisfy the LCFS by blending, using low- or zero-carbon fuels, or purchasing credits from other suppliers of low-carbon fuels. Although somewhat adjustable by the EPA, any new renewable fuel must reduce its GHG lifecycle emissions by 20 percent from an average 2005 petroleum-based fuel, any biomass-based diesel or advanced biofuel must achieve a corresponding 50 percent reduction, while cellulosic biofuel goes even higher at a 60 percent reduction.[43]

Compliance is achieved by targeting what are called "obligated parties," effectively today only refiners or importers of gasoline or diesel fuel. These parties must either blend their transportation fuel, by volume, with a renewable fuel or acquire a renewable identification number (RIN) sufficient to satisfy an annually established EPA-specified renewable volume obligation (RVO). The RVO is set annually by EPA's calculation of a percentage that obligated parties must meet based on a review of the CAA requirements and projections of gasoline and diesel production. A RIN represents one gallon of renewable fuel, and RINs may be traded, purchased, or even

---

[43] For a treatment of the lifecycle analysis, *see* Alexandra B. Klass & Andrew Heiring, *Life Cycle Analysis and Transportation Energy*, 82 BROOK. L. REV. 485 (2017). California first established a LEV and clean fuels program in 1990; AB 1493 then required that CARB develop automobile GHG standards for MY2009 and beyond, more recently modified after the California governor's 2007 executive order. Once CARB developed its post-2007 rules, implementing a low-carbon fuel standard and assigning a poor lifecycle carbon value to out-of-state corn-based ethanol fuel, the standard was immediately challenged. *See* Rocky Mountain Farmers Union v. Corey, 730 F.3d 1070 (9th Cir. 2013).

carried over for compliance into the next year. Because renewable fuels are not all created equal, the RIN program allows for nesting – that is, a fuel with a higher GHG reduction threshold can satisfy compliance for any lower GHG reduction threshold fuel. And obligated parties may obtain a cellulosic waiver credit (CWC), separate from the Act's general waiver provision, by purchasing CWCs along with an advanced RIN – thus avoiding having to blend cellulosic biofuel or obtain a corresponding RIN.

The implementation of the RFS program, though, has fallen short of its ideals. Perhaps too complicated understates the RFS program. It has become encumbered by fraud among greedy actors, allegations of impropriety by possibly innocent parties, political calculations by the EPA, and decisions by the agency that seemingly skirt some of Congress's directives. Generating over $60 million in fraudulent credits, two individuals associated with an Indiana producer were sentenced to over two years in jail. Other obligated parties become culpable even though they may honestly sell their product and lack any ability to influence what happens with it next. A former EPA investigator said fraud, upwards of $1 billion, was "absolutely" happening and in part because those responsible "have essentially little or no influence on how renewable fuel is blended and overseen" – a "fundamental problem in the market" that opens the door for "fraud and exploitation."[44] The EPA, moreover, has found aspects of the program challenging to implement. For instance, Congress allowed the Agency to grant small refiners an exemption if participation would cause them "disproportionate economic hardship," a result the DOE concluded in 2011 would apply to thirteen refiners. When the EPA denied an exemption to one of those, Sinclair Refinery in Wyoming, the company successfully argued that EPA acted contrary to the meaning and purpose of the statute.[45]

In February 2016, Agriculture Secretary Tom Vilsack predicted that the program would generate "constant litigation" driven by agricultural and petroleum interests.[46] That year, ethanol production hovered around 15 billion gallons, with consumption running in the range of about 14 billion gallons.[47] The American Petroleum Institute challenged EPA's failure to achieve the 2014 and 2017 targets while simultaneously claiming that the agency required too much cellulosic ethanol in 2016. Conversely, DuPont, with investments in cellulosic ethanol, participated by trying to maintain its market viability.[48]

---

[44] OnPoint, *Former EPA Investigator Parker Says RIN Fraud Ongoing, Becoming More Sophisticated*, E&ETV, Oct. 5, 2016; Doug Parker, E&W Strategies, White Paper Addressing Fraud in the Renewable Fuels Market and Regulatory Approaches to Reducing this Risk in the Future (Sept. 4, 2016).

[45] Sinclair Wyoming Refining Co. v. EPA, No. 16–9532 (10th Cir. 2017).

[46] Mario Parker, *Ethanol Mandate Triggers Litigation*, BNA DAILY ENVT., Feb. 2, 2016.

[47] Marc Heller, *Record U.S. Production Could Go Higher if Corn Prices Rise*, GREENWIRE, Feb. 9, 2016.

[48] Ams. For Clean Energy v. EPA, No. 16–1005, 2017 WL 3202630 (D.C. Cir. July 28, 2017); *see also* Monroe Energy v. EPA, No. 16–1032 (D.C. Cir.); Monroe Energy, LLC v. EPA, 750 F.3d 909 (D.C. Cir. 2014). In the first case, Americans for Clean Energy successfully argued that the EPA impermissibly considered the volume of renewable fuel available to consumers (e.g., demand) rather than what

Along with litigation, increased production of renewables does not uniformly affect society equally. More corn-based ethanol may indirectly affect the price of corn available for tortillas. More palm oil may affect harvesting in sensitive ecosystems in Africa. And while, according to Nadia Ahmad, today's second-generation biofuels, such as those "derived from algae, seaweed, and waste biomass," seemingly can be produced sustainably and possibly "have enormous growth potential," it is not altogether clear that these second-generation biofuels are what Congress anticipated in 2007.[49]

The merits of a RFS program also seems inevitably and inextricably linked with politics. President George W. Bush's 2007 State of the Union Address favoring ethanol (35 billion gallons by 2017) no doubt was an attempt to assist Archer Daniels Midland and the market for ethanol. In a June 2017 speech in Iowa, President Trump proclaimed how "we're saving your ethanol industries in the State of Iowa just like I promised I would do in my campaign."[50] Of course, when running for president and campaigning successfully in Iowa, Senator Cruz challenged Iowans by questioning the program and a ready market for corn-based ethanol.[51] And in spring 2018, Iowa's Senator Chuck Grassley questioned the Trump administration's decision to grant a financial hardship waiver (for the RFS program) to CVR Energy's refinery owned by Car Icahn, a wealthy businessman who early in the administration advised President Trump.

CAA expert Professor Arnold Reitze perhaps most aptly summarizes the program's failure. While joining others in recognizing how second-generation biofuels produce fewer adverse environmental externalities, he cautions how the program has been both "ineffective and costly." For him, the "relatively insignificant" contribution made by these fuels to our "nation's fuel supply . . . should lead to caution when considering the desirability of costly federal subsidies, mandated purchase, and other incentives that distort the free market."[52] While a free market may not be the solution, neither it seems is Congress picking winners and losers.

BACK TO THE FUTURE

Our policies for reducing GHG emissions from automobiles are less than stellar. They indirectly began by focusing principally on miles per gallon as a surrogate for reducing petroleum consumption following the energy crisis of the 1970s.

was available to obligated parties. The issue arose because after several years of the program "the supply of ethanol was much greater than the demand in the market."

[49]   Nadia B. Ahmad, *Blood Biofuels*, 27 DUKE ENVTL. L. & POL'Y F. 265 (2017).

[50]   Mario Parker & Jennifer A Dlouhy, *Trump Pledges Support for Ethanol Even as Administration Stokes Uncertainty*, BLOOMBERG POLITICS, June 22, 2017.

[51]   Jennifer A. Dlouhy, *Cruz Win Hits Corn's Clout, Emboldens Senate Ethanol Foes*, BNA DAILY ENVT., Feb. 3, 2016; Amanda Reilly, *Did Cruz Win Debunk "Third Rail" Theory of Iowa Politics?*, E&E NEWS, Feb. 3, 2016.

[52]   Arnold W. Reitze, Jr., *Biofuel and Advanced Biofuel*, 33 U.C.L.A. J. ENVT. L. & POL'Y 309, 365 (2015).

The mantra then was simply "energy independence." Of course, many contemporaries even championed abandoning the internal combustion engine in favor of electric vehicles. If we use miles per gallon as a surrogate for emissions reduction, the average fuel economy for passenger and light-duty vehicles remained somewhat stable for several years. To be sure, average fuel economy increased. But then so did annual vehicle miles traveled. One person traveling 100 miles in a car achieving 25.0 MPG produces 78 lb of CO_2 emissions, whereas two people each traveling 100 miles in cars achieving 30.0 MPG produce 129 lb of CO_2. Annual vehicle miles increased, except for four years, every year between 1957 and 2007. If we take, for instance, just the month of January, the Federal Highway Administration estimates that in January 2015, Americans traveled 237.4 billion vehicle miles, in 2016 an estimated 240.7 billion vehicle miles, and in 2017 an estimated 242.3 billion vehicle miles. Urban planning, longer commutes, and reduced emphasis on mass transportation all contributed to even more vehicles on the road. The number of vehicles registered in the United States went from roughly 193 million in 1990 to almost 264 million in 2015. And a record of approximately 17 million cars and trucks were sold in the United States in 2016. One report suggests that worldwide the number of cars by 2040 could double.[53] The top US vehicle was the Ford F series pickup, with its various models achieving at best a combined average fuel economy in the low 20 MPGs. Even California's standards couldn't offset the state's increase in emissions between 2014 and 2015 from the transportation sector, with light-duty vehicles producing 69 percent of the sector's emissions.[54] Of course, the EIA's latest (2017) report predicts that unless oil prices rise dramatically again, gasoline prices will remain stable with possibly a slight upward trend toward 2040, and gasoline consumption due to increased fuel efficiency will decline considerably over that period – this despite Christopher Knittel's apt jab that the program "focuses on the wrong thing – fuel economy instead of total fuel consumption."[55] With all that, the CAFE program has proved both politically palatable and economically beneficial, along with its attendant environmental attributes.[56]

Undoubtedly new vehicle technologies have the capacity to reduce emissions. Today, along with hybrid and electric vehicles, we also have compressed natural gas vehicles, more cars with continuously variable transmissions, cylinder deactivation devices at traffic stops, direct injection fuel systems, variable valve timing, and new and more diesel engines. For 2015, the EIA reports that over 250,000 hybrid vehicles were sold that year and roughly 118 electric vehicles (EVs). By then, about 173,000 zero-emission vehicles were registered in California alone. The following year, according to the Sierra Club, represented the largest sales ever, with a 37 percent

[53] World Economic Forum, The Number of Cars Worldwide Is Set to Double by 2040, April 22, 2016.
[54] NEXT 10 & NOEL PERRY, CALIFORNIA GREEN INNOVATION INDEX (9th edn, Aug. 2017).
[55] Knittel, *supra* note 42, at 112.
[56] *See* Arnold W. Reitze, Jr., *Controlling Greenhouse Gases from Highway Vehicles*, 31 UTAH ENVT. L. REV. 309 (2011).

jump from 2016. By the end of 2016, there reportedly were over 540,000 electric vehicles sold in the United States. Chevy's Bolt and Volt both received accolades, along with the more popular and trend-setting Tesla Model S.

The trend toward increased electric vehicles (EVs) now seems almost certain. In 2006, President Bush informed the nation how "[w]e must also change how we power our automobiles. We will increase our research in better batteries for hybrid and electric cars, and in pollution-free cars that run on hydrogen." States, local communities, and even federal fleet requirements all assisted in initially pushing away from traditional gasoline-powered engines. But today, Tesla's experience demonstrates how, with more recently emerging battery technology, EVs will garner continued consumer attention and market share. The company targets selling 430,000 cars by the end of 2018. Many programs also may prod an increase, whether through rebates, guzzler taxes, special state electricity rates for charging EVs, the ability to park in special places, or even allowing EV owners to use HOV lanes.[57] The National Academies of Science's 2017 *Advancing Automated and Connected Vehicles: Policy and Planning Strategies for State and Local Transportation Agencies* presents some of these strategies. To be sure, considerable work remains for installing additional infrastructure along with an architecture and rate structure supporting vehicle to electric grid connections, which will not only provide correct price signals for charging but also allow the electric grid to benefit from the hookups. Some may recall that Milton Friedman wrote about this in *The World Is Flat* back in 2005.

Some in the automobile industry already seem willing to entertain producing only alternative vehicles, regardless. Joining Tesla, Volvo, during the summer of 2017, announced that it will only sell EVs after MY2019. Hyundai followed suit by shifting away from its prior focus on fuel cell technology and, as the fifth-largest automobile manufacturer, indicated that it would make EVs the loci of its future strategy. August 2017 reports suggested that the European Commission would establish a quota system – although possibly avoiding promoting one technology over another. France presently remains committed to removing fossil fuel–fired vehicles by 2040, and Paris may commit to do so by 2030. Norway's EV sales, between 1999 and 2016, reportedly averaged more than a 90 percent annual rate of growth, with EVs now 5 percent of the country's cars.[58] And China, too, has embarked on what could turn into a robust EV campaign.

[57] *See generally* Sanya Carley, Natalie Messer Betts, & John D. Graham, *Innovation in the Auto Industry: The Role of the U.S. Environmental Protection Agency*, 21 DUKE ENVTL. L. & POL'Y F. 367 (2011); Mark Detsky & Gabriella Stockmayer, *Electric Vehicles Rolling over Barriers and Merging with Regulation*, 40 WM. & MARY ENVTL. L. & POL'Y REV. 477 (2016); Bryan Lamble, *Of Nesting Dolls and Trojan Horses: A Survey of Legal and Policy Issues Attendant to Vehicle-to-Grid Battery Electric Vehicles*, 86 CHI.-KENT L. REV. 193 (2011); John C.K. Pappas, *A New Prescription for Electric Cars*, 35 ENERGY L. J. 151 (2014).

[58] *See* Robert Rapier, *Norway's Oil Consumption Rises Despite Surging Electric Vehicle Sales*, FORBES, July 12, 2017.

But what does all this say about Congress's CAA and EPCA programs and the agencies' implementation of them? After all, debating whether we should retain a 54.5 MPG standard for 2025 may be less consequential if by 2025 most new car purchases will be electric. Also, while Obama Energy Secretary Moniz rejected the notion that we could see hydrogen fuel cells anytime soon, that same form of pessimism previously surrounded the push for EVs. Historically as well, Americans generally purchase more fuel-efficient vehicles when gasoline prices rise, suggesting that price, along with comfort and perhaps handling, affect what types of vehicles can be sold rather than any specific governmental program. Consequently, once the infrastructure and market mechanisms mature, the switch to other than gasoline-powered vehicles seems inevitable. But the reason likely will be because of the convergence of a host of factors, including technological innovations, vehicle price, fuel costs, and market signals to the manufacturing industry, along with federal, state, and local polices and worldwide trends. A futuristic urban transportation network and national highway system capable of accommodating autonomous EVs eventually may be as transformative as the original 1950s' highway system. The Center for American Progress cautions that before that happens, we should first assess whether autonomous vehicles will produce a net environmental benefit.[59] As originally designed, the EPCA and the CAA's fuels program played only a contributing role in shaping this future and may prove ill suited for addressing new challenges.

Those challenges correspond with the country's changing electric grid, discussed in previous chapters. Will our electric grids be upgraded quickly enough to allow integrated vehicle-to-grid technology? Will these upgraded grids remain as they are today or be more decentralized; if not decentralized, how will regional organizations such as RTOs and reliability organizations assess the proper integration questions? Will vehicle electrification lead to increased electric consumption and an expanded electric grid, and if that consumption is natural gas, will the increased use of natural gas offset the gains from reducing coal-fired generation? Or, in lieu of natural gas, will an integrated vehicle-to-grid system depend more heavily on renewables? And will urban, suburban, and rural communities rebuild their landscapes and adjust to a different transportation paradigm?

These questions seem unlikely to be resolved through the current EPCA and CAA programs, nor by any political ideology. President Trump's selection of Scott Pruitt as EPA administrator seems unlikely to reverse the last few decades of progress. Granted, Pruitt's open questioning of climate change science undoubtedly suggests that the remaining years of the Trump administration will not witness much federal interest in reducing GHG emissions from the transportation sector. Early in the administration the Competitive Enterprise Institute and others sought to persuade

---

[59] Myriam Alexander-Kearns, Mirada Peterson, & Alison Cassady, The Impact of Vehicle Automation on Carbon Emissions: Where Uncertainty Lies (Center for American Progress, Nov. 18, 2016).

the EPA that the Obama administration's endangerment finding under the CAA ought to be reconsidered. These gestures seem somewhat hollow, however. After twenty-five years of tinkering around the edges, we have learned that technology, markets, price, and worldwide trends toward reducing GHG emissions will define the future transportation system – surely not science denial, and equally not political ideology.

10

Embedded Judgments and Energy-Resilient Transitions

The challenges we confront today are acutely different from those during the first 100 years of our nation's evolution of national energy policy. From the passage of the 1920 Federal Water Power Act through the 1980s, Congress, courts, and the executive branch each confronted issues focused principally on adequate and cheap supplies of energy – whether for electric power, heating, or transportation fuel. This same period witnessed energy serving as a surrogate for national defense and economic policy – from President Wilson's Muscle Shoals, the development of the Tennessee Valley Administration, the Boulder Canyon Project, and even to the post–World War II atoms for peace program. And then, of course, baby boomers grew up listening to the executive office mantra proclaiming the urgency of energy independence – only now to wake to President Trump's refrain about energy dominance – while the world confronts the realities of climate change.

Four lessons imbue our country's history with tinkering with energy resource markets and industries. First, the march of time is marred by myopic responses to perceived crises often exacerbated by ill-conceived choices. Congress passed the 1920 Federal Water Power Act out of a concern for losing the nation's waterpower resources – only to realize much later that hydroelectric power would not become as dominant as those in the 1910s projected. And the legislation would have devastating ecological effects necessitating further program changes. The Pacific Northwest today must continually wrestle with the unique challenges of protecting salmon species threatened by the hydrologic changes wrought by the region's many dams. Our interstate electric transmission and wholesale markets were shaped by the Supreme Court's 1927 *Attleboro* decision, a crabbed and soon-to-be discarded approach to allocating regulatory power between states and the federal government. And when Congress then stepped in, it solidified through the 1935 Federal Power Act (FPA) a regulatory program that today cannot easily adapt to the subsequent expansion of the electric grid, modern technology, and the need for greater flexibility in deploying low- or zero-carbon energy resources. The nation's expansion of its interstate natural gas system was unnecessarily hampered as well by the Supreme Court's 1954 *Phillips* decision. That case enjoys the dubious distinction of facilitating a dual natural gas market and keeping an ever-growing demand for natural gas from reaching the interstate market.

The result, by the 1970s, was that if energy demand would grow continuously, as people expected, the nation would have to welcome nuclear energy, produce or import more oil and natural gas, or tap the nation's vast coal resources. The nation's policies toward imported oil, particularly residual fuel oil, when coupled with the country's car culture and early efforts by utilities to shift to burning oil rather than high-sulfur coal, contributed to oil's dominance for driving energy policy – a challenge once that dominance and our reliance on increasing oil imports became problematic. Or, of course, we could, in the words of Amory Lovins, have focused primarily on a "soft path" – energy conservation, efficiency, and wind, solar, and geothermal energy. While President Carter's National Energy Plan did, indeed, tout conservation, efficiency, and renewables, and those around his administration felt strongly about promoting efficiency and conservation, the perceived oil and natural shortages during the 1970s joined with the geopolitical realities of too much dependence on potentially unstable world oil markets to force the inevitable – coal. Policymakers, however, took solace in the hope that technology and the Clean Air Act (CAA) would intervene and avert coal's known dangers (although not for carbon dioxide).

They were too naive, perhaps. The importance of energy eclipsed a sufficiently robust implementation of the CAA. The CAA, moreover, contained both in its original form and as amended enough flaws to allow the nation's dependence on coal to intensify. More large coal-fired power plants were installed in the years after the CAA, and older plants were grandfathered and avoided, whether legally or not, installing technology to control emissions. We today are now left with the consequences: greenhouse gas (GHG) emissions from those – mostly aging – plants. The Obama administration tackled the problem through the ill-fated Clean Power Plan, an elaborate program for addressing GHG emissions from existing fossil fuel–fired power plants. That plan, along with its partner program for new fossil fuel facilities, would have dramatically reduced GHG emissions from the utility sector and corrected years of neglect. The Trump administration sealed the plan's fate, however. And even if the Trump administration chooses to promote coal, the market for natural gas and renewables effectively will dictate's coal's eventual demise.

While more coal-fed electric utility boilers were built during the 1970s and 1980s, policies aimed at reducing our appetite for oil limped along. Of course, the economy and more oil mitigated any continuing alarm. So, by today, the loci of conversations is not on whether the nation will have enough oil or natural gas; the development of unconventional fossil fuel extraction techniques has muted such past refrains. Fuel efficiency in automobiles, therefore, is no longer about preserving oil. Instead, it is about reducing GHG emissions. And our modern programs built from past presumed crises may not be sufficiently focused on this present rather than the challenge of the 1970s.

A second lesson is that energy policy all too often seems infected by the ideologies and politics of the incumbent president and Congress. President Reagan's inauguration signaled an ever-increasing emphasis on market forces rather than regulation – a dialogue animating those during the Nixon, Ford, and Carter administrations as well. But now the White House would pursue such policies with vigor. This meant having an Environmental Protection Agency (EPA) that was weak on regulating the energy industry; it meant an Interior Department focused on exploring how best to transfer public lands out of federal ownership and promote more resource development on public lands and from the Outer Continental Shelf. Exploitation of resources along the Continental Shelf, for instance, was touted as a "significant national energy program." Acknowledging "energy-environmental conflicts," the administration elevated the role of cost/benefit analysis when resolving energy policy choices.[1]

Reagan's successor, George Herbert Walker Bush, pushed along the same policies, perhaps with less rhetoric. No longer, though, would the administration believe that energy independence was either achievable or desirable.[2] Also, President Bush's 1991 Energy Plan, for example, sought to better integrate energy and environmental policy.[3] But, for the most part, that never occurred because the administration championed resource development.

That approach shifted once the country elected President Clinton. The Clinton administration appreciated the necessity of integrating energy and environmental policy, and with many in the administration focused on protecting and conserving the nation's resources, the natural tilt would be toward conservation. As such, the Clinton administration implemented policies favoring sustainable development and managing resources from an ecosystem-based approach rather than being singularly minded on a specific media or parcel of land. This augured in a philosophy of considering energy resource development within a larger picture. Its 1998 energy plan observed:

> In the past 5 years, the Administration has pursued an energy policy that has provided substantial economic, environmental, and national security benefits for the American public. This policy, however, has been based on a legislative and regulatory framework last revised in the early 1990s. It is not time to take stock of our Nation's energy progress, identify the most substantial challenge that remain, celebrate energy policy goals to the new century, and propose long-term solutions.[4]

---

[1] *See* Department of Energy (DOE), The National Energy Policy Plan (1981); DOE, The National Energy Policy Plan (1983).

[2] MEG JACOBS, PANIC AT THE PUMP: THE ENERGY CRISIS AND THE TRANSFORMATION OF AMERICAN POLITICS IN THE 1970S 294, 300 (Hill & Wang 2016).

[3] *See generally* Symposium, *National Energy Strategy: Energy Check?*, 6 NAT. RES. & ENVT. 3–39, 50–68 (1991).

[4] DOE, Comprehensive National Energy Strategy: National Energy Policy Plan Pursuant to Section 801 of the Department of Energy Organization Act 10 (Apr. 1998).

This meant focusing on the effects of increased fossil fuel generation, whether aggressively pursuing utilities that evaded CAA requirements or exploring opportunities for reducing GHG emissions. But Clinton, too, suggests Vaclav Smil, continued working with "'friendly' OPEC nations to boost their oil output" while leaving effectively unaddressed the rising use of oil by larger sales of SUVs – producing what he describes as an "absence of any rational policymaking."[5]

A flip then occurred with the next transition. In 2001, President George W. Bush talked about the nation's energy weaknesses, suggesting that we must open the Alaska National Wildlife Refuge to oil and gas development, that we should increase domestic production on other public lands, and that we must strive toward energy independence, all the while, according to Michael Klare, his proposals seemed geared toward more foreign oil dependence – possibly influencing our military intervention in the Middle East.[6] And soon after taking office, the president established the National Energy Policy Development Group, designed to revisit the tenets of our national energy policy. Although the history and outcome of this group received widespread public attention, less noticeable was that the administration released two executive orders designed to facilitate quicker consideration of proposed energy projects.[7]

And then energy policy snapped back once President Obama began focusing on GHG emissions. His administration promoted tapping the potential for increasing renewable-energy generation on the public lands, along with increasing requirements for federal agencies to reduce fossil fuel consumption. While initially he nodded toward the past by touting an "all of the above" energy strategy, that changed as his administration wore on. In the wake of the *BP Horizon* oil spill, he restructured a part of the Interior Department and elicited industry's ire when he restricted parts of the Alaska Outer Continental Shelf (OCS) from development. Policies for reducing GHG emissions eventually took center stage: the administration struck its historic deal with the automobile industry to increase Corporate Average Fuel Economy (CAFE) standards; it developed a CAA plan for reducing emissions from both existing and new electric utility fossil fuel–burning resources, while separately regulating the industry's environmental effects on both general air and water quality; it sought to reduce methane emissions from the oil and gas industry; it imposed a moratorium on coal leasing, while, in part, it examined how to address emissions from eventually burning that federally mined coal; and, of course, it signed onto the Paris Agreement for country nonbinding commitments to reduce GHG emissions.

---

[5]   Vaclav Smil, *The Energy Question Again*, 99 CURRENT HISTORY 408, at 412 (Dec. 2000).

[6]   MICHAEL T. KLARE, BLOOD AND OIL: THE DANGERS AND CONSEQUENCES OF AMERICA'S GROWING DEPENDENCY ON IMPORTED PETROLEUM 203–04 (Henry Holt & Co. 2004).

[7]   Exec. Order No. 13,211, 66 Fed. Reg. 28,357 (May 22, 2001); Exec. Order No. 13,337, 69 Fed. Reg. 25,299 (Apr. 30, 2004). *See generally* Gary C. Bryner, *The National Energy Policy: Assessing Energy Policy Choices*, 73 U. COLO. L. REV. 341 (2002).

This all contributed to some coal industry advocates charging that the president was waging a "war against coal."

That rhetoric even swayed newly elected President Trump to once again shift energy policy in a strikingly new direction. As this book is being written, it is too early to assess precisely what the administration will do, but some early initiatives are telling and portray the infusion of politics into energy policy. To begin with, President Trump early in his administration rejected the Paris Agreement and the advice of many of his advisers, at one point questioning the science about the anthropogenic causes of climate change. He has begun examining whether to revisit the CAFE standards from the Obama administration, and the same with the CAA policies and efforts to address methane emissions. He has championed coal mining, while the electric utility industry has nevertheless moved beyond coal. He has initiated an early review of Obama's plan for OCS development and removed the coal leasing moratorium. He successfully worked with Congress to secure the opening of part of the Alaska National Wildlife Refuge – something no other Republican president since before Jimmy Carter could secure. All this presumably is designed to supplant the energy independence rhetoric of the 1970 with energy dominance as a new paradigm.

It seems fair to say, consequently, that energy policy and environmental policy serve as political balls for parrying back and forth as the nation's politics place different people in office. Neil De Marchi summarizes the 1969–74 period as "compris[ing] a series of messages and initiatives whose specific elements reflected current crises or presidential opportunism," sort of like a "match" with one volley being bested by a different return and then afterward turning to an unyielding faith in technology as subsequent administrations came to power.[8] Little arguably has changed as the political match continues, regardless of surrounding circumstances.

Third, the follies portrayed in the earlier chapters demonstrate our hubris. Emanating from the Progressive era, all too often some economists assumed that we could play effectively with energy markets – often addressing a resource, such as oil or coal, in isolation. When assessing fuel policies between 1900 and 1946, John Clark suggests that federal intervention had little impact on energy transitions during this period; indeed, he posits that even without federal intervention, it is likely that the utility, coal, oil, and gas industries "would have arrived at about the same position at the conclusion of World War II." "Thus," he adds, "fuel policies from 1900 to 1946 broadly reflected the interests of the dominant segments of each fuel industry." Each industry, in effect, engaged in rent-seeking, employing "ideology" as a "convenient mask."[9] Paul Joskow perhaps says it best when observing how,

[8] Neil De Marchi, *The Ford Administration: Energy as a Political Good, in* ENERGY POLICY IN PERSPECTIVE: TODAY'S PROBLEMS, YESTERDAY'S SOLUTIONS 475, 543–45 (Craufurd D. Goodwin et al. eds., Brookings Institution 1981).
[9] JOHN G. CLARK, ENERGY AND THE FEDERAL GOVERNMENT: FOSSIL FUEL POLICIES, 1900–1946 382–384 (Univ. of Illinois Press 1987).

prior to the 1970s, "federal energy policy consisted primarily of uncoordinated industry-specific support policies."[10]

Much of the early involvement by the federal government was, as William Barber explains when commenting on the approach during the 1950s, "dampening cyclical disturbances and ... correcting market failures."[11] And so, during the Eisenhower administration, many believed that "[t]he task of government was to provide a healthy climate for private investment; it was distinctly not the government's function to direct the allocation of the economy's resources."[12] But, of course, this is precisely what happened with the oil import program. It occurred from equally disruptive choices made by Congress when passing the 1920 Federal Water Power Act, from the Court's opening salvo in *Attleboro* and Congress's return volley, and from the Court's parlay in *Phillip* and the FPC's subsequent struggles. The restrictions on utility ownership of the Public Utility Holding Company Act of 1935 (PUHCA) led to separate natural gas and electric markets, with today's grid managers wrestling with how to marry the two industries as the grid becomes more dependent on natural gas.

Later, when policymakers responded to perceived fossil fuel shortages in the 1970s, they once again tinkered with markets and industries, with less than stellar results. Peter Grossman's *U.S. Energy Policy and the Pursuit of Failure* presents a compelling case that federal intervention often failed. Robert Zubrin concurs, perhaps even too broadly, when he suggests that promoting coal was the only effective Carter energy program.[13] And the fugue continues, with Meg Jacobs adding in some sense how "we are living with the failures of the 1970s to craft public policies to induce conservation and promote alternative energies." As such, she concludes her analysis of the energy policy of the 1970s with the observation that the policies failed to solve a perceived problem; they failed because they aligned with consumers and holding costs down rather than effectively promoting new technologies or conservation; they failed because of special interests favoring entrenched markets rather than committing "resources to new kinds of technology"; and further, she adds – although perhaps too broadly – they failed from a lack of sufficient governmental involvement.[14]

Tinkering with markets, though, often presumes too much knowledge. Grossman perhaps best sums this up by suggesting that "in making forecasts and policies with respect to them, officials need to admit that they really do not know. The best guess

[10] Paul L. Joskow, *United States Energy Policy during the 1990s*, CURRENT HIST., 101, 653; PAIS International 105, 109, March 2002.
[11] William J. Barber, *The Eisenhower Energy Policy: Reluctant Intervention, in* ENERGY POLICY IN PERSPECTIVE: TODAY'S PROBLEMS, YESTERDAY'S SOLUTIONS 205, 209 (Craufurd D. Goodwin et al. eds., Brookings Institution 1981).
[12] *Ibid.* at 212.
[13] ROBERT ZUBRIN, ENERGY VICTORY: WINNING THE WAR ON TERROR BY BREAKING FREE OF OIL 81 (Prometheus Books 2009).
[14] JACOBS, *supra* note 2, at 311–12.

about the future is only that."[15] Prior to the Energy Information Administration (EIA), the government often relied on reserve estimates collected by the industry, which "were rarely checked, if ever," although that began to change by May 1973.[16] The EIA today, Blake Clayton aptly observes, "does an excellent job" and serves as a "role model" around the globe.[17] But the EIA's excellence, debated by some others, only goes so far. And the public often is reticent to accept government assessments, which the public may consider skewed by ideology or special interests. Many liberals during the energy crisis of the 1970s, for example, believed that gas rationing was a concerted ploy by industry to secure deregulation and greater profits.

Predictions, moreover, about oil and its future are constantly in flux, diminishing their utility for long-term planning. What we see, according to Clayton, is a "sweeping pattern of history – of large price increases leading to widespread new era shortage fears that eventually dissipate when oil production eventually rises and prices moderate."[18] This is now labeled the "boom and bust cycle." Indeed, Clayton notes how numerous books echo some aspect of a peak oil scenario, where the world's oil supply appears inadequate. But, in fascinating detail, Clayton walks us through how oil supply is invariably clouded by economic conditions driving markets and prices, in turn driving optics affecting the public, and finally then driving technological innovation, markets, and even policies. It is the lag between initial markets and prices and the resulting effects that occasionally allows for misguided assumptions. "Those who bet against the forward march of technological innovation," he observes, "have been on the wrong side of history, time and again. Today's unconventional sources of oil have always become tomorrow's conventional ones." Prophecies, therefore, invariably discount human behavior and operative market mechanisms and are often typically wrong. And they can prod developments that later engender further problems, such as, according to Clayton, pushing the US petroleum industry in the early part of the twentieth century and then later in the 1940s to explore foreign resources.[19]

A similar cycle of prophecies occurs elsewhere as well. Beginning at least with early-eighteenth-century economists such as Thomas Malthus, economists and scientists have warned that our ever-increasing population and use of resources threatens to exhaust the Earth's riches, whether its land, air, water, wildlife, minerals, or other ecological resources. To be sure, a little over a hundred years later neoclassical economists rejected the notion that resource constraints might impede economic growth. Of course, that optimism waned as the environmental movement in the 1960s and 1970s talked about "Spaceship Earth," the population bomb, and

---

[15]   Peter Z. Grossman, U.S. Energy Policy and the Pursuit of Failure 352 (Cambridge Univ. Press 2013).
[16]   De Marchi, *supra* note 8, at 514–15.
[17]   Blake C. Clayton, Market Madness: A Century of Oil Panics, Crises, and Crashes 175 (Oxford Univ. Press 2015).
[18]   *Ibid.* at xviii.   [19]   Clayton, *supra* note 17, at 170, 174.

the 1972 Club of Rome and Limits to Growth, all suggesting restraint. After all, it took the "green revolution" and changing agricultural practices (and technology) to increase what otherwise would have been further constraints on worldwide food supply – a phenomenon occurring today because of climate change. Although the theory may have precipitated a debate among economists, President Carter undoubtedly was influenced by its message. Carl Biven explains that while the population at the time may have considered growth as inevitable and oil shocks merely "temporary aberrations," the administration conversely "recognized – and was the first do deal with – the concept of limited resources."[20]

Our final lesson ought to be that energy policy choices seemingly succeed when they either level the playing field and afford equal opportunities for new market entrants, such as through incentives such as tax credits or rate programs, or boost research and development (R&D) funding for those entrants. Luckily, explains Paul Joskow, since at least the Clinton administration, "a bipartisan rejection of the aggressive energy market-intervention policies of the 1970s and early 1980s" prevails, and instead the focus has shifted to supporting policies geared toward "allowing energy markets to work, breaking down regulatory barriers restricting markets from functioning efficiently, and reflecting environmental and national externalities in energy policies through financial incentives and market-based mechanisms."[21] Incentives may be essential for securing sufficient capital willing to invest in new technologies. The Public Utility Regulatory Policies Act (PURPA) leveled the playing field by allowing new renewable energy and cogenerators to enter the electric capacity markets by ensuring a guaranteed purchase obligation at avoided cost rates. A vice president for Louisville Gas & Electric, in the early 1990s, observed how "QFs commercialized new technologies such as circulating, fluidized beds and many environmental control devices."[22] One early company, Luz International, Ltd., demonstrated how, with projects in California, solar technology could become more competitive by greatly reducing the cost per kilowatt hour – although Luz itself went bankrupt in 1991 (subsequently resurfacing as Luz II, Ltd., and later Brightsource Industries, Ltd.).

Today solar energy, first energized by President Carter and incentivized by PURPA, has flourished. The industry installed roughly 14.7 GW of new solar photovoltaic capacity in 2016 and, according to some studies, is on a path to triple its output within the next several years.[23] The same occurred with wind power in California during the late 1980s. State renewable portfolio standards are now building on that record – requiring that utilities either purchase a set percentage of

[20]   W. CARL BIVEN, JIMMY CARTER'S ECONOMY: POLICY IN AN AGE OF LIMITS 258–59 (Univ. of North Carolins Press 2002).
[21]   Joskow, *supra* note 10, at 105, 117.
[22]   B. JEANINE HULL, The Shape of Things to Come: A Competitive Market in the Electric Industry, in THE ELECTRIC INDUSTRY IN TRANSITION 51, 55 (P.U. Reps. 1994).
[23]   National Renewable Electric Laboratory, US Solar Photovoltaic System Cost Benchmark: Q1 2017, Technical Report NREL/TP-6A20-68925 (Sept. 2017).

renewable generation, with a few states now nearing goals of 100 percent renewable energy. And in the first quarter of 2017, we already witnessed more installed wind capacity than in any year since 2009. The latest 2017 report from the EIA suggests that renewable generation will increase the most from a percentage basis (natural gas from a flat perspective will grow more) because of lower costs and state and federal policies – such as net metering, feed-in tariffs, and renewable portfolio standards. Solar energy, both distributed and utility scale, are projected to grow from roughly less than, individually, 50 billion kWh to over 175 billion kilowatt hours by 2040.[24] Conversations today therefore focus less on those early PURPA dialogues about the technology and cost and instead on whether and how we can reach a full or possibly only an 80 percent decarbonization of the grid quickly.[25] Of course, PURPA's continuing relevance to today's electric markets is increasingly being questioned by some.

Governmental engagement in promoting energy R&D, whether directly or through university research grants, enjoys a rich history. During both World War II and the Carter administration, for instance, policymakers pushed for research into testing synthetic fuels development. President Nixon's 1971 energy message was accompanied by a commitment of $10 million federal dollars to a pilot coal gasification project.[26] Some in the Carter administration relished the prospect of having a publicly chartered company test how coal might be converted to a liquid or gas. Others, including an editorial in the *Washington Post*, thought that spending governmental dollars was "absurd" because the resulting gas would cost roughly two-thirds more per thousand cubic feet – unnecessary as more gas discoveries in the United States and elsewhere were appearing.[27] Needless to say, today the Dakota Gasification Company gasifies about 6 million tons of coal annually and has been doing so (originally under Department of Energy ownership) since 1984.

More noticeably, following the development of nuclear weaponry, the United States actively explored its potential for peaceful uses: Project Plowshares, for instance, tested whether technology could unleash trapped oil and natural gas – with two noted experimental explosions, Project Gasbuggy in New Mexico and Project Rulison in Colorado. Thankfully, a third test slated for 1973, Project Wagon Wheel in Wyoming, became delayed and ultimately was abandoned. Yet the program also led to ill-conceived efforts in Alaska, chronicled in *Firecracker Boys*.

[24] ENERGY INFORMATION ADMINISTRATION, ANNUAL ENERGY OUTLOOK (2017).
[25] E.g., Christopher T.M. Clack et al., *Evaluation of a Proposal for Reliable Low-Cost Grid Power with 100% Wind, Water, and Solar*, P.N.A.S. (Feb. 24, 2017).
[26] The President's Energy Message, Hearings before the Committee on Interior and Insular Affairs, U.S. Senate, 92nd Cong., 1st Sess., Pursuant to S. Res. 45, A National Fuels and Energy Policy Study, Serial No. 92–1, at 40 (June 15, 1971) (Testimony of Dr. Pecora). Dr. Pecora further added that he expected that fossil fuel generation would drop from its 83 percent share of electric power to roughly 33 percent by 2000. *Ibid.* at 69.
[27] *Coal, Technology and Consumers*, WASH. POST, Nov. 19, 1978, at C6.

In the 1960s, at President Kennedy's direction, a federally organized energy study group issued a detailed report about technological advancements, the importance of R&D, and where private industry and the United States had collaborated. It noted how the US Geological Service reportedly was spending about $50,000 annually to explore Colorado for high-grade oil shale, splitting with industry $17 million annually for fuel cell technology, and spending overall roughly $300 million annually on civilian energy.[28] And, more recently, a 2012 report by the Breakthrough Institute, for instance, revealed how governmental involvement back in those earlier years helped natural gas pioneer Georg Mitchell develop the modern technology for unleashing unconventional gas and oil production.[29] Many thousands of wells during the 1950s and 1960s had been exploited with emerging fracking technology.[30] That active governmental/private-sector partnership extends across time and technologies, adds the Institute.[31]

Modern-day conversations consequently would be remiss if they discount too much how past dialogues parallel today's challenges. In 1964, the Energy Study Group commented how "[i]f the electric car has future potential, it depends mainly on a continuation of the present trend toward cheaper and more widely used electrical energy and on availability of cheaper and lighter electrical components." That same study continued by suggesting how "research aimed at defining [climate change from CO_2] is needed together with watchful measurement of world temperatures and atmospheric CO_2 concentrations."[32] This suggests why the Trump administration's toying with dramatically reducing the Energy Department's R&D program ought to be thoroughly vetted.[33]

The difference, though, between successful and ill-fated policies often is when governmental policies outline either performance standards or objectives. While picking losers can be part of a sound policy, such as disincentivizing any fossil fuel

---

[28] ENERGY STUDY GROUP & ALI BULENT CAMBEL, ENERGY R&D AND NATIONAL PROGRESS: PREPARED FOR THE INTERDEPARTMENTAL ENERGY STUDY xxvi, 183 (GPO 1964).

[29] MICHAEL SHELLENBERGER, TED NORDHAUS, ALEX TREMBATH, & JESSE JENKINS, WHERE THE SAHEL GAS REVOLUTION CAME FROM: GOVERNMENT'S ROLE IN THE DEVELOPMENT OF HYDRAULIC FRACTURING IN SHALE (Breakthrough Institute May 2012); LOREN KING, TED NORDHAUS, & MICHAEL SHELLENBERGER, LESSONS FROM THE SHALE REVOLUTION: A REPORT ON THE CONFERENCE PROCEEDINGS (Breakthrough Institute Apr. 2015); *see also* John M. Golden & Hannah J. Wiseman, *The Fracking Revolution: Shall Gas as a Case Study in Innovation*, 64 EMORY L. J. 955 (2015); ZHONGMIN WANG & ALAN KRUPNICK, A RETROSPECTIVE REVIEW OF SHALE GAS DEVELOPMENT IN THE UNITED STATES: WHAT LED TO THE BOOM? (Resources for the Future Apr. 2013). The Office of Technology Assessment's (OTA's) 1977 examination of enhanced oil recovery opportunities suggested the need for aggressive R&D, along with removing price controls and amending regulations affecting emissions, injection, and unified field operations. OTA, Enhanced Recovery of Oil and Devonian Gas (Draft June 1997).

[30] NATIONAL PETROLEUM COUNCIL, IMPACT OF NEW TECHNOLOGY ON THE U.S. PETROLEUM INDUSTRY, 1946–65 114–16 (1967).

[31] THE BREAKTHROUGH INSTITUTE, WHERE GOOD TECHNOLOGIES COME FROM: CASE STUDIES IN AMERICAN INNOVATION (Breakthrough Institute Dec. 2010).

[32] CAMBEL, *supra* note 28, at 342, 369 (1964).

[33] David Ferris, *Should DOE Get Out of the Research Business?*, E&E NEWS, March 17, 2017.

generation, it is quite another thing to pick winners. Your chances generally of getting it right enough times are low. It is much easier, therefore, to establish targets and let the marketplace operate, with the least-cost capable technology emerging as victor. That, after all, is the theory behind technology-forcing standards. And it occurred most noticeably with the CAFE standards – although for far too long SUV sales rose without any CAFE constraints, but it also happened less visibly with energy-efficiency programs (both from the 1970s and more recent ones, such as the National Appliance Energy Conservation Act of 1987), whether for new refrigerators, light bulbs, toasters, and the assortment of other every-day consumer products.[34] Today, consequently, we undoubtedly are witnessing the positive effects from these 1970s' energy-efficiency programs. In 2015, the Department of Energy reported that "changes in economic structure and conditions and policies to promote energy efficiency" allowed "U.S. electricity consumption" to remain stable between 2005 and 2014 as "total energy use declined by 1.9 percent."[35]

Building from past successes, much remains. Energy policy today has become enveloped by perhaps our singularly most existential threat to our future from an environmental, cultural, and economic perspective: averting further potential extreme disruptions from the effects of GHG emissions. The paradigmatic early-nineteenth-century utility model is ill suited for twenty-first-century challenges, preferences, and technologies. Our energy grid must become modern and "greener." It must reduce its dependence on fossil fuels. It already has taken formidable steps toward reducing its dependence on coal, but emerging voices warn that we must equally shy away from building out a grid driven primarily by natural gas. This may mean focusing instead on renewables. If so, does this mean slowing the pace of constructing new natural gas pipelines to augment the aging system now in place? Or does it mean removing barriers to infrastructure development, such as additional long-distance transmission lines?[36] But it also might mean not reproducing the central station model with renewables in lieu of fossil fuels but instead shifting toward a distributed, smart grid that delivers renewable energy to customers – possibly such a grid coupled with the likely penetration of utility-scale battery storage.

Traditional rate design, for instance, potentially chills new technologies. Before the late 1980s' restructuring of the electric utility industry, Peter Navarro wrote how cost-of-service rates confronted inflation and rising capital costs and contributed to what is called "rate suppression" – keeping consumer rates too low to support new

---

[34] DAVID B. GOLDSTEIN, SAVING ENERGY, GROWING JOBS AND INVISIBLE ENERGY (Berkeley Labs 2007).

[35] Quadrennial Energy Review, Energy Transmission, Storage, and Distribution Infrastructure S-1 (DOE Apr. 2015).

[36] Quadrennial Energy Review, Energy Transmission, Storage, and Distribution Infrastructure (DOE Apr. 2015); AN INTERDISCIPLINARY MIT STUDY: THE FUTURE OF THE ELECTRIC GRID (MIT Press 2011); JOSEPH H. ETO, BUILDING ELECTRIC TRANSMISSION LINES: A REVIEW OF RECENT TRANSMISSION PROJECTS (Berkeley Labs Sept. 2016).

investments.[37] Similarly, today, large investments, such as in grid modernization, might demand upfront judgments that predetermine the ability of the transmission provider to pass along costs, securing enough certainty to warrant potentially billions in investment.[38] Cost-of-service rates may not be sufficient to incentivize those investments and shoulder the risk of investing capital. Dynamic pricing, such as time-of-use-based rates, may be necessary as well to promote efficient customer use of resources. States and eventually the Federal Energy Regulatory Commission (FERC) will likely incorporate the social cost of carbon into rate policies, whether through a carbon adder or otherwise.[39] Eventually, the relationship between generation (electricity) providers and their customers will need fundamental alteration.

Yet our ability to establish workable structures capable of accommodating an ever-changing economy and technology has proven remarkably poor. The Supreme Court and Congress developed legal structures by glancing in the rear-view mirror, addressing crises that either had or would soon pass, with little appreciation for how quickly or in what manner changes might occur along the road ahead. It seems foolhardy to believe that our legal institutions have the capacity to canvass existing R&D programs and calculate which ones will succeed and those whose fate is sealed. Our past confirms it.

Nor should we rush to deploy lower CO_2 technologies, regardless of how or by whom. The chorus of commentary urging greater state flexibility when establishing energy policy may seem reassuring and necessary because neither the present Congress nor the administration appears willing to engage meaningfully with polices for arresting GHG emissions. State experimentation, including with rate-making, may fill that void: because there is no uniform national system of electric regulation, "the production of a diverse set of regulatory experiments" affords an opportunity to test what works and what doesn't.[40] But state policies may trigger discrepancies with overlapping jurisdictions. They also may adversely affect the objectives of other regulators, or they may be so different from state to state that we retard potentially beneficial policies from taking hold.

We ought to be wary, therefore. Today's encouragements inadvertently may allow future problems to become entrenched. Strengthening a regional structure for organizing energy markets, as many advocate, or expanding the nation's natural gas pipeline infrastructure and additional combined-cycle natural gas plants may be unnecessary if battery technology can marry with renewable energy and afford the

---

[37] Peter Navarro, The Dimming of America: The Real Costs of Electric Utility Regulatory Failure (Ballinger 1985).

[38] Illinois Commerce Commission v. FERC, 756 F.3d 556 (7th Cir. 2014); Illinois Commerce Commission v. FERC, 721 F.3d 764 (7th Cir. 2013); Illinois Commerce Commission v. FERC, 576 F.3d 470 (7th Cir. 2009).

[39] Christopher J. Bateman & James T.B. Tripp, *Toward Greener FERC Regulation of the Power Industry*, 38 Harv. Envtl. L. Rev. 275 (2014).

[40] William Boyd & Ann E. Carlson, *Accidents of Federalism: Ratemaking and Policy Innovation in Public Utility Law*, 63 U.C.L.A. L. Rev. 810, 816 (2016).

opportunity to develop a new type of electric grid. But once investments are made, facilities are built, and markets and people depend on those as integral to a stable economy, altering course is cumbersome at best and insurmountable at worst.

Consequently, two points seem elemental. First, "energy policy" ought to be treated as a misnomer. Society's goal is to ensure the economy functions efficiently and effectively, producing, for instance, a means for moving goods and people, along with electrifying, heating, and cooling buildings. How this is accomplished is governed not by an illusion of some master energy policy but by other choices. Do we want to create a market for coal for economic reasons, or do we want to avoid nuclear power because of fears involving Browns Ferry, Three Mile Island, Chernobyl, and Fukushima? To be sure, at any given point in time the economy might only run effectively on a specific resource, but then it is not that energy policy dictates expanding that resource, it is instead that we must avoid the economic shock of not having that resource – immediately.

A second elemental point is that today's choice must address the need to decarbonize our economy, including the energy sector, as quickly as possible. The challenge, though, is that resilience must imbue how we do so. Doing so may require reordering the relationship between state and federal or regional policies. It may require changing how energy is priced, how the electric grid is operated, and whether or how to move toward distributed renewable generation with battery storage. Or it may require dictating or incentivizing what new capacity is constructed. It might even require reexamining policies promoting natural gas or retarding nuclear power development. Yet, predicting with precision what will be necessary is too tenuous for constructing what can be called a "resilient legal architecture," a framework that is flexible enough to bend toward new technologies, markets, concepts, and challenges.

A resilient legal architecture allows energy transitions to occur commensurate with changes in technologies, markets, and concepts and as necessary for confronting emerging challenges. As we both witnessed over our careers, the legal structure under the PUHCA and the FPA, for instance, limited the ability of the industry to evolve. Change occurred because of the FERC's willingness to explore the breadth of its authority under the FPA to promote an unbundled, market-driven, now mostly regionalized market for wholesale electric generation. And the FERC similarly has been trying to promote long-distance transmission lines capable of transmitting renewable generation. It was, after all, the FERC that unbundled the natural gas industry as well, even before its efforts under the FPA. As a former FERC Commissioner observed, "[p]erhaps the most interesting manner of changing energy law, at least from the vantage of the head of a regulatory body, is through agency reinterpretation of existing law."[41] Agencies may engage in such

---

[41] Hon. Joseph T. Kelliher & Maria Farniella, *The Changing Landscape of Federal Energy Law*, 61 ADMIN. L. REV. 611, 634 (2009).

reinterpretations and receive deference when they do so if Congress's language giving the agency the authority to act in the first place is ambiguous and the agency's interpretation is reasonable.

This type of flexibility is essential because our society and technologies change rapidly. Congress cannot predict what is likely to happen just inside a decade, and we cannot depend on Congress to revisit, possibly even annually or at least every few years, legislation responding to changes in technologies and markets. Either states or some other regulatory body, whether FERC, regional transmission organizations (RTOs), or some other entity, must be afforded that ability to engage timely with changes. This means establishing broad rather than prescriptive contours allowing regulatory bodies to function effectively.

In particular, regulatory agencies must be afforded the ability to address how to balance the need and pace of change with how to slow potentially unnecessary infrastructure development or avoid or account for stranded investments. This arguably is the most challenging aspect of energy transitions. Investments and financial commitments support new pipelines, transmission lines, alternative vehicles, and fossil fuel or renewable generation. Guaranteed rates and the need for the service historically secured those investments. That made them safe. A resilient legal architecture upends all this, however. Rapid changes risk undermining investments, possibly rendering them obsolete. When this occurs, what sector of the economy ought to pick up that cost? The company itself that is constructing and owning or operating the now obsolete facility? That would shift the cost to the workers, to the owners – possibly shareholders or perhaps in some cases arguably even the insurance industry. If in bankruptcy, costs might shift to creditors. And if we allow all this to happen, it likely will chill future investment. Alternatively, new investments can be supported or protected by governmental policies – all at a cost to American taxpayers when those technologies prove obsolete. What sector of the economy should shoulder the economic risk? A resilient legal architecture might provide a forum for allowing those decisions to be made. The key will be to make sure that they are sound, not foolish or myopic, decisions.

When looking at how capitalism fueled the fossil fuel economy, Andreas Malm writes that "[i]f the fossil economy is a train that never stops but always accelerates, even when approaching the precipice, the task is to pull the brakes (or maybe jump off) in time, and if there is a driver who seeks to keep this from happening, she has probably been seated in the locomotive for some time."[42] Perhaps the more serious problem is that many players have been sitting in that seat, and there are too many trains converging on paths not seen by the other conductors. The result? Follies that elide easy explanation and may or may not produce corrections in time or further follies. Either way, the nation suffers.

---

[42] ANDREAS MALM, FOSSIL CAPITAL: THE RISE OF STEAM POWER AND THE ROOTS OF GLOBAL WARMING 15 (Verso 2016).

Bibliographic Note

Energy Follies, along with its references to primary sources, relies on several types of secondary sources, many of which are commended for readers exploring various topics in more depth. At the outset, the reader should appreciate that the book incorporates the analyses, themes, and ideas previously developed and published by the authors. Robert Nordhaus, *The Hazy "Bright Line": Defining Federal and State Regulation of Today's Electric Grid*, 66 ENERGY L. J. 203 (2015); Robert Nordhaus, *Modernizing the Clean Air Act: Is There Life after 40?*, 33 ENERGY L. J. 365 (2012); Robert Nordhaus, *Carbon Dioxide Pipeline Regulation*, 30 ENERGY L. J. 85 (2009); Robert Nordhaus, *New Wine into Old Bottles: The Feasibility of Greenhouse Gas Regulation Under the Clean Air Act*, 15 N.Y. U. ENVT. L. REV. 53 (2007); Robert Nordhaus, *Assessing the Options for a Mandatory U.S. Greenhouse Gas Reduction Program*, 32 BOSTON COLL. ENVT'L AFF. L. REV. 97 (2005); Robert Nordhaus, *Historical Perspectives on §111(d) of the Clean Air Act*, 44 ELR 11095 (2014); Robert Nordhaus, *Energy Policy, 40 Years Later: Meting Challenges – Both Old and New*, 41 HIS ENERGY DAILY 1 (2013); Robert Nordhaus, *Nuclear Power at the Crossroads*, 30 THE ENVT'L FORUM 34 (2013); Sam Kalen, *Historical Flow of Hydroelectric Regulation: A Brief History*, 53 IDAHO L. REV. 1 (2017); Sam Kalen, *Muddling through Modern Energy Policy: The Dormant Commerce Clause and Unmasking the Illusion of an Attleboro Line*, 24 N.Y. U. ENVT. L. REV. 283 (2016); Sam Kalen, *Embedded Choices: A Resilient Energy Legal Architecture*, 52 IDAHO L. REV. 2016 (2015); Sam Kalen, *Thirst for Oil and the Keystone XL Pipeline*, 46 CREIGHTON L. REV. 1 (2012); Sam Kalen, *Coal's Plateau and Energy Horizon?*, 34 PUB. L. & RES. L. REV. 145 (2013); Sam Kalen, *Replacing a National Energy Policy With a National Resource Policy*, 19 NAT. RES. & ENVT. 9 (2005); Sam Kalen, *Cruise Control and Speed Bumps: Energy Policy and Limits for Outer Continental Shelf Leasing*, 7 ENVTL. L. & ENERGY L. & POL'Y 155 (2012); Sam Kalen, *Where Do We Go from Here?: The Federal Coal Leasing Amendments Act – Past, Present, and Future*, 98 WEST. VA. L. REV. 1023 (1996); Sam Kalen, *The BP Macondo Well Exploration Plan: Wither the Coastal Zone Management Act?*, 40 ELR 11079 (2010). Second, the book builds on existing studies of energy law or policy that canvass time periods or singular aspects of either energy law or policy. Numerous sources, for instance, address the rise of our modern energy systems. ROBERT L. BRADLEY, JR.,

EDISON TO ENRON: ENERGY MARKETS AND POLITICAL STRATEGIES (Wiley 2011); ERNEST FREEBURG, THE AGE OF EDISON: ELECTRIC LIGHT AND THE INVENTION OF MODERN AMERICA (Penguin 2013); RICHARD F. HIRSH, POWER LOSS: THE ORIGINS OF DEREGULATION AND RESTRUCTURING IN THE AMERICAN ELECTRIC UTILITY SYSTEM (MIT Press 1999); THOMAS P. HUGHES, NETWORKS OF POWER: ELECTRIFICATION IN WESTERN SOCIETY, 1890–1930 (John Hopkins Univ. Press 1983); CHRISTOPHER F. JONES, ROUTES OF POWER: ENERGY AND MODERN AMERICA (Harvard Univ. Press 2014); JILL JONES, EMPIRES OF LIGHT: EDISON, TESLA, WESTINGHOUSE, AND THE RACE TO ELECTRIFY THE WORLD (Random House 2003); MAURY KLEIN, THE POWER MAKERS: STEAM, ELECTRICITY, AND THE MEN WHO INVENTED MODERN AMERICA (Bloomsbury 2008); RONALD R. KLINE, CONSUMERS IN THE COUNTRY: TECHNOLOGY AND SOCIAL CHANGE IN RURAL AMERICA (John Hopkins Univ. Press 2000); FOREST MCDONALD, INSULL (Univ. of Chicago Press 1962); DAVID E. NYE, ELECTRIFYING AMERICA: SOCIAL MEANINGS OF A NEW TECHNOLOGY (MIT Press 1990); DAVID E. NYE, CONSUMING POWER: A SOCIAL HISTORY OF AMERICAN ENERGIES (MIT Press 1998); HAROLD L. PLATT, THE ELECTRIC CITY: ENERGY AND THE GROWTH OF THE CHICAGO ERA, 1880–1930 (Univ. of Chicago Press 1991); PHILIP F. SCHEWE, THE GRID: A JOURNEY THROUGH THE HEART OF OUR ELECTRIFIED WORLD (J. Henry 2007); VITA A. STAGLIANO, A POLICY OF DISCONTENT: THE MAKING OF A NATIONAL ENERGY STRATEGY (Penwell 2001); JOSEPH C. SWINDLER – POWER AND THE PUBLIC INTEREST: THE MEMOIRS OF JOSEPH C. SWINDLER (Univ. of Tennesse Press 2002); JOHN F. WASIK, THE MERCHANT OF POWER: SAM INSULL, THOMAS EDISON, AND THE CREATION OF THE MODERN METROPOLIS (Palgrave 2006). An excellent source on changing technology and energy markets is RICHARD HIRSCH, TECHNOLOGY AND TRANSFORMATION IN THE AMERICAN ELECTRIC UTILITY INDUSTRY (Cambridge Univ. Press 1989). CHRISTOPHER JONES' book, ROUTES OF POWER, referenced earlier, is another detailed portrayal of how technology and markets operated, particularly with the advent of long-distance oil pipelines. Perhaps one of the most entertaining books on the rise of electrical energy and the dynamic between George Westinghouse, with Nicholas Tesla and his preference toward AC current, and his rival, Thomas Edison, intent on proving the merits of DC current, is the novel GRAHAM MOORE, THE LAST DAYS OF NIGHT: A NOVEL (Penguin/Random House 2016).

Some manuscripts direct their readers to certain periods, portraying the role, influence, or factors affecting electric energy development during those periods. Some excellent sources are GRETCHEN BAKKE, THE GRID: THE FRAYING WIRES BETWEEN AMERICANS AND OUR ENERGY FUTURE (Bloomsbury 2016); ROBERT LIFSET, ed., AMERICAN ENERGY IN THE 1970S (Okla. Univ. Press 2014);PHILIP J. FUNIGELLO, TOWARD A NATIONAL POWER POLICY: THE NEW DEAL AND THE ELECTRIC UTILITY INDUSTRY, 1933–1941 (Univ. of Pittsburgh Press 1973); CRAUFURD D. GOODWIN, ed., ENERGY POLICY IN PERSPECTIVE: TODAY'S PROBLEM'S, YESTERDAY'S SOLUTIONS (Brookings Institution 1981); RICHARD H. K. VIETOR, ENERGY POLICY IN AMERICA SINCE 1945: A STUDY OF BUSINESS-GOVERNMENT RELATIONS (Cambridge Univ. Press 1984); PETER Z. GROSSMAN, U.S. ENERGY POLICY AND THE PURSUIT OF FAILURE (Cambridge Univ. Press 2013); WALTER A. ROSENBAUM, AMERICAN ENERGY:

THE POLITICS OF 21ST CENTURY POLICY (Sage 2015); JAMES L. SWEENEY, THE CALIFORNIA ELECTRICITY CRISIS (Hoover Inst. Press 2002). For readers interested in the development of federal power, some sources are invaluable: MILTON CONOVER, THE FEDERAL POWER COMMISSION: ITS HISTORY, ACTIVITIES AND ORGANIZATION (John Hopkins Univ. Press 1923); LOUIS C. HUNTER, A HISTORY OF INDUSTRIAL POWER IN THE UNITED STATES, 1780–1930, vol. 1: WATERPOWER IN THE CENTURY OF THE STEAM ENGINE (Univ. of Virginia Press 197); JEROME G. KERWIN, FEDERAL WATER-POWER LEGISLATION (Columbia Univ. Press 1926). A host of law review articles similarly address specific issues – whether specific energy policies, technologies, or issues. Many articles, for instance, examine the role of transmission planning, transmission siting, the smart grid, distributed generation, the changing face of the "utility," individual renewable technologies, integrating renewables into the electric grid, strategies for inducing specific technologies or goals or appropriate governmental structures.

Of course, the literature is rife with histories surrounding oil policy and the desire to transition away from an economy dependent on oil. DANIEL YERGIN's now-classic books on oil, THE PRIZE: THE EPIC QUEST FOR OIL, MONEY, AND POWER (1991) and THE QUEST: ENERGY, SECURITY, AND THE REMAKING OF THE MODERN WORLD (Penguin 2011), are quite remarkable and explore the political and geopolitical dynamic affecting decisions involving petroleum policy. Two of the last energy books that my colleague, Robert R. Nordhaus, read before he passed away were PETER GROSSMAN's U.S. ENERGY POLICY AND THE PURSUIT OF FAILURE (Cambridge Univ. Press 2013) and MEG JACOB's account of the 1970s energy crisis in PANIC AT THE PUMP: THE ENERGY CRISIS AND THE TRANSFORMATION OF AMERICAN POLITICS IN THE 1970S (Hill & Wang 2016). Both books are essential for mining the events of the 1970s, but Jacob's portrayal of the crisis places the events aptly within their context. Several other studies are worth exploring as well, such as ANTONIA JUHASZ, THE TYRANNY OF OIL: THE WORLD'S MOST POWERFUL INDUSTRY – AND WHAT WE MUST DO TO STOP IT (William Morrow 2008).

And then, of course, among the all too voluminous array of books urging that we divorce our economy from its dependence on oil and reduce our greenhouse gas emissions, there are KENNETH S. DEFFEYES, BEYOND OIL: THE VIEW FROM HERBERT'S PEAK (Hill & Wang 2005); S. DAVID FREEMAN, WINNING OUR INDEPENDENCE: AN ENERGY INSIDER SHOW'S HOW (Gibbs Smith 2007); MICHAEL T. KLARE, BLOOD AND OIL: THE DANGERS AND CONSEQUENCES OF AMERICA'S GROWING DEPENDENCY ON IMPORTED PETROLEUM (Henry Holt 2004); MICHAEL LEVI, THE POWER SURGE: ENERGY, OPPORTUNITY, AND THE BATTLE FOR AMERICA'S FUTURE (Oxford Univ. Press 2013); PAUL ROBERTS, THE END OF OIL: ON THE EDGE OF A PERILOUS WORLD (Mariner 2004); DAVID SANDALOW, FREEDOM FROM OIL: HOW THE NEXT PRESIDENT CAN END THE UNITED STATES' OIL ADDICTION (McGraw-Hill 2008); *Oil: And the Future of Energy*, SCI. AM. (2007); ROBERT ZUBRIN, ENERGY VICTORY: WINNING THE WAR ON TERROR BY BREAKING FREE OF OIL 81 (Prometheus Books 2009). Another book that examines policies more globally is BRIAN C. BLACK, CRUDE REALITY: PETROLEUM IN WORLD HISTORY (Rowman & Littlefield 2012).

A similar array of sources canvasses our use of natural gas and other fossil fuel resources, such as in JULIAN DARLEY, HIGH NOON FOR NATURAL GAS: THE NEW ENERGY CRISIS (Chelsea Green 2004); JEFF GOODELL, BIG COAL: THE DIRTY SECRET BEHIND AMERICAN'S ENERGY FUTURE (Mariner 2007); and JEREMY RIFKIN, THE HYDROGEN ECONOMY (Penguin 2002). Another excellent book is by a former administrator of the Energy Information Administration, JAY HAKES, A DECLARATION OF ENERGY INDEPENDENCE: HOW FREEDOM FROM OIL CAN IMPROVE NATIONAL SECURITY, OUR ECONOMY, AND THE ENVIRONMENT (Wiley 2008).

Other books are considerably more detailed in their treatment of fossil fuel policies, often emphasizing a specific event or period. JOHN G. CLARK's ENERGY AND THE FEDERAL GOVERNMENT: FOSSIL FUEL POLICES, 1900–1946 (Univ. of Illinois Press 1987) is an excellent example. Clark's book furnishes a detailed and informative account of the political history of fossil fuels during the 1900–46 period. That degree of detail exists in FUNIGIELLO's TOWARD A NATIONAL POWER POLICY, but unfortunately, his book is limited to an eight-year period (1933–41). EUGENE V. ROSTOW also wrote a searching account of oil law and policy but limited to the 1930s and 1940s (A NATIONAL POLICY FOR THE OIL INDUSTRY [Yale Univ. Press 1948]). A broader period is covered by GERALD D. NASH, UNITED STATES OIL POLICY, 1890–1964: BUSINESS AND GOVERNMENT IN TWENTIETH CENTURY AMERICA (Univ. of Pittsburgh Press 1968). One book examines just oil imports and, though somewhat dated, primarily furnishes only an economic and political analysis: DOUGLAS R. BOHI & MILTON RUSSELL, LIMITING OIL IMPORTS: AN ECONOMIC HISTORY AND ANALYSIS (John Hopkins Univ. Press 1978). Similarly, J. STANLEY CLARK provides an insightful political history of oil during its first century here in the United States in THE OIL CENTURY: FROM THE DRAKE WELL TO THE CONSERVATION ERA (Okla. Univ. Press 1958). Such detail also is presented by GOODWIN's ENERGY POLICY IN PERSPECTIVE, which chronicles in considerable detail the political and economic history of energy regulation from the Truman through the Carter administrations. And, of course, numerous legal, political, and environmental accounts describe our nation's program for developing offshore oil and gas resources: BOB CAVNAR, DISASTER ON THE HORIZON: HIGH STAKES, HIGH RISKS, AND THE STORY BEHIND THE DEEPWATER WELL BLOWOUT (Chelsea Green 2010); ROBERT GRAMLING, OIL ON THE EDGE: OFFSHORE DEVELOPMENT, CONFLICT, GRIDLOCK (SUNY 1996); WILLIAM R. FREUDENBURG & ROBERT GRAMLING, OIL IN TROUBLED WATERS: PERCEPTIONS, POLITICS, AND THE BATTLE OVER OFFSHORE DRILLING (SUNY Press 1994); WILLIAM R. FREUDENBURG & ROBERT GRAMLING, BLOWOUT IN THE GULF: THE BP OIL SPILL DISASTER AND THE FUTURE OF ENERGY IN AMERICA (MIT Press 2011); NICK HUNTER, HOT TOPICS: OFFSHORE DRILLING (Heinemann 2012); LOREN C. STEFFY, DROWNING IN OIL: BP AND THE RECKLESS PURSUIT OF PROFIT (McGraw-Hill 2011).

Finally, many sources address unique legal developments or technologies or serve as useful casebooks for instruction. Some of those sources include LINCOLN L. DAVIES, ALEXANDRA B. KLASS, HARI M. OSOFSKY, JOSEPH P. TOMAIN & ELIZABETH J. WILSON, ENERGY LAW AND POLICY (West Academic 2015); K.K. DUVIVIER, THE RENEWABLE ENERGY READER (Carolina Academic Press 2011); JOEL EISEN, EMILY HAMMOND, JIM ROSSI, ET AL., ENERGY, ECONOMICS AND THE ENVIRONMENT: CASES AND

MATERIALS (Foundation Press 4th edn 2015); JOSHUA P. FERSHEE, ENERGY LAW: A CONTEXT AND PRACTICE BOOK (Carolina Academic Press 2014); MICHAEL B. GERRARD, ed., THE LAW OF CLEAN ENERGY: EFFICIENCY AND RENEWABLES (ABA 2011); LAURA NADER, THE ENERGY READER (Wiley Blackwell 2010); JOSEPH P. TOMAIN & JAMES H. HICKEY, JR., SHEILA HOLLIS, ENERGY LAW AND POLICY (Anderson Pub. 1989); *see also* TRAVIS BRADFORD, SOLAR REVOLUTION: THE ECONOMIC TRANSFORMATION OF THE GLOBAL ENERGY INDUSTRY (MIT Press 2006); JOEY LEE MIRANDA, ed., CAPTURING THE POWER OF ELECTRIC RESTRUCTURING (ABA 2009); ARLON R. TUSSING & BOB TIPPEE, THE NATURAL GAS INDUSTRY: EVOLUTION, STRUCTURE, AND ECONOMICS (Pennwell Books 1995). Three books provide highly readable summaries of energy law: K.K. DUVIVIER, ENERGY LAW BASICS (Carolina Academic Press 2017); ALEXANDRA B. KLASS & HANNAH J. WISEMAN, ENERGY LAW (Foundation Press 2017); LINCOLN L. DAVIES & JOSEPH P. TOMAIN, ENERGY LAW IN THE UNITED STATES OF AMERICA (Wolters Kluwer 2015).

Index